KT-519-892

London: Routledge

0415168082

GC 093271   GRIMSBY COLLEGE

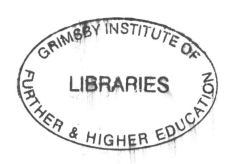

GRIMSBY INSTITUTE OF
LIBRARIES
FURTHER & HIGHER EDUCATION

Sport and Exercise Psychology

Sport and Exercise Psychology

A Critical Introduction

Aidan P. Moran

Routledge
Taylor & Francis Group

LONDON AND NEW YORK

LOCATION HE TDAY
CLASS No. 796.015
ACC No. 093271
WITHDRAWN

First published 2004
by Routledge
27 Church Road, Hove, East Sussex BN3 2FA
Simultaneously published in the USA and
Canada
by Routledge
29 West 35th Street, New York, NY 10001

*Routledge is an imprint of the Taylor & Francis
Group*

© 2004 Aidan Moran

Typeset in Century Old Style by Keystroke,
Jacaranda Lodge, Wolverhampton
Printed and bound in Great Britain by
TJ International Ltd, Padstow, Cornwall
Cover design by Anú Design

All rights reserved. No part of this book may
be reprinted or reproduced or utilised in any
form or by any electronic, mechanical, or other
means, now known or hereafter invented,
including photocopying and recording, or in
any information storage or retrieval system,
without permission in writing from the
publishers.

This publication has been produced with paper
manufactured to strict environmental
standards and with pulp derived from
sustainable forests.

British Library Cataloguing in Publication Data
A catalogue record for this book is available
from the British Library

*Library of Congress Cataloging in Publication
Data*
Moran, Aidan P.
    Sport and exercise psychology : a critical
    introduction / Aidan P. Moran.
    p. cm.
    Includes bibliographical references.
    ISBN 0–415–16808–2 (hard) —
    ISBN 0–415–16809–0 (pbk.)
    1. Sports—Psychological aspects.
    2. Exercise—Psychological aspects.
    I. Title.
    GV706.4.M67 2004
    796′.01—dc22   2003017078

ISBN 0–415–16809–0 (pbk)
ISBN 0–415–16808–2 (hbk)

To three special people in my life: My mother, Nora Moran, my girlfriend, Angela, and my late nephew, Tristan Moran, who died for his love of sport. Ar dheis Dé go raibh a anam dílis.

Contents

CONTENTS

Foreword

With increasing interest in and even a fascination with sport psychology and health psychology in academic environments, to the sports world and exercise settings, it is not surprising to note the variety of books being published on such themes at a rapid rate in recent years. Contents range from the very superficial or highly practical to the exceptionally scholarly and scientific, depending on the purpose and possible audience of the publication. The challenge for the author of a textbook, especially intended for undergraduate students, is to somehow present the research literature in an interesting, informative, useful, understandable, and organized manner. Ideally, the reader would be enthusiastic about learning the subject matter.

Professor Moran succeeds admirably. This is not just another sport psychology textbook. Perhaps what primarily sets it apart from others is the integration of scientific substance with real-sport examples of and reference to many famous athletes and coaches. As a highly respected scholar and practitioner, his passion for sport as well as sport and exercise psychology is obvious throughout the pages of the book. Consequently, the reader becomes absorbed in the contents. Even though I am quite familiar with the areas of sport psychology addressed by Professor Moran, my attention was captured and my motivation sustained as I reviewed the various topics. They include a blend of summaries of investigations and theories, issues needing to be resolved, and anecdotes and references to sports, athletes, and coaches.

What I particularly admired was the recency of the scholarly literature and sport figure references. Professor Moran is evidently very familiar with the latest happenings in the field. His writing style is reader-friendly, and the contents are presented in an interesting and intellectually stimulating way. Helpful are exercise boxes sprinkled throughout the chapters, with questions to challenge the reader. These are intended to spark reflection on issues of debate, as well as to generate possible small-scale research projects. The subject matter throughout the book is organized very well, and evidence supportive of conclusions is indicated as is inconclusive evidence. Thus, the reader can appreciate the difference between scientifically based knowledge vs. intuition and beliefs based on personal experiences and hearsay.

Professor Moran does not attempt to include every conceivable topic or theme associated with sport and exercise psychology in his book. This is a wise decision. The body of knowledge and areas of interest have exploded in contemporary times, making it impossible to do justice to all these topics in one textbook. Professor Moran has included major relevant topics, those that can be addressed with sufficiency in a one-semester class. Mostly considered are what is involved in being a highly skilled athlete and what an athlete can do to improve the possibility of attaining a degree of excellence. Also explored are psychological perspectives about exercise, health, and coping with injury.

The quotes and examples of superstars in their sports relevant to the points made in each section of the book are fascinating and help to blend the scientific with the practical; the laboratory with the athlete's competitive world. The meaningfulness of research and the necessity of it becomes apparent to the reader. Myths about sport psychology topics are recognized or dispelled. Frequently used terms, such as anxiety, arousal, fear, and stress are clarified with implications for understanding relationships to successful or unsuccessful performance. Because psychology is associated with so many terms and expressions about behavior, much confusion exists in the minds of students (as well as researchers!) as to meanings. Professor Moran patiently explains, differentiates, and interprets subject matter in settings that are easy to relate to, and therefore conducive to learning.

This is one of those rare academic textbooks that more than fulfills the intentions of the author, expressed in the Preface. As I said at the beginning, this is not merely another textbook in sport and exercise psychology. Professor Moran has produced a book with attention to substance, communication style, organization and structure, and reader interest. Who says that academic reading cannot be enlightening as well as enjoyable?

Robert N. Singer
Department of Exercise and Sport Sciences
University of Florida
Gainesville, FL USA

Preface

Recent years have witnessed an upsurge of popular and scientific interest in the psychological factors that are associated with athletic success. Against this background, the discipline of sport and exercise psychology has emerged as an exciting new field with intellectual roots in both psychology and sport science. Increasingly, the theories, methods and research findings of this discipline are being taught to students of psychology and sport science at undergraduate and postgraduate levels around the world. In spite of this impressive development, there is a need for an introductory textbook that fills three apparent gaps in the teaching of sport and exercise psychology at present. First, students need to be encouraged to think critically about important conceptual, methodological and semantic issues in this field. For example, to what extent does contemporary sport psychology have agreed objectives, a coherent professional identity, clear academic pathways and an established role within the sporting community? Unfortunately, many of these questions have not been addressed adequately by textbook writers to date. Therefore, I have included a number of boxes labelled "Thinking critically about . . ." in each of the chapters of this book. Second, there is a need for a book which tries to augment its coverage of theoretical ideas with practical insights obtained from the everyday experiences of athletes in various sports. For this reason, I have used illustrative quotations from athletes, coaches and researchers at the beginning of every chapter. Finally, I have learned that students like to receive practical suggestions concerning possible research projects in sport and exercise psychology. In response to this need, I have indicated a number of empirical project ideas at the end of each chapter.

The book is divided into four parts. Part one introduces the field of sport and exercise psychology as both an academic discipline and as a profession. In Part two, I investigate the various psychological processes that affect individual athletes in their pursuit of excellence. Included here are chapters on motivation, anxiety, concentration, mental imagery and expertise. Part three addresses the role of team cohesion in athletic performance. Finally, in Part four, I explore exercise psychology and the psychology of physical injury. In conclusion, I hope that this book manages to convey the theory and practice of contemporary sport and exercise psychology in an accurate and accessible manner.

Acknowledgements

This book would not have been possible without the help that I received from a large number of friends and colleagues. To begin with, I would like to acknowledge the wonderful editorial support and encouragement that I received from Lucy Farr and Ruben Hale of Routledge and Psychology Press. Next, I wish to thank Pádraig Harrington for his kindness over the years as well as for his generous endorsement of my work. I also wish to thank my post-graduate research students – especially, Mark Campbell for his meticulous research assistance and proofreading skills and Tadhg MacIntyre and Olivia Hurley for their enthusiasm, insights and valuable references. Other current and former students who have helped me greatly during the writing of this book are Alison Byrne, Derek Dorris, Nicola McGlade, Sarah Sinnamon and Arlene Egan. I also acknowledge the excellent technical assistance of Mark Beatty (UCD Audio-Visual Centre) and Deirdre Moloney (UCD Sports Centre), Donal Farmer and Norman McCloskey (both from Inpho Photography), John Conboy and Andrew Flood (for their computing expertise), Mark McDermott (Irish Rugby Football Union) and John McClean (UCD Sports Centre) for their rugby knowledge, Sean O'Domhnaill (UCD Audio-Visual Centre for the excellent cartoons), Linton Walsh (Golfing Magazine) and the practical advice on word-processing received from Mary Boyle and Diana Caffrey. Copyright clearance for certain figures in the book was obtained with the help of Retesha Thadison (Human Kinetics Publishers, USA) and Diane Evans (Human Kinetics Publishers, UK). Next, I wish to express my gratitude to a number of academic colleagues who influenced the content and format of this book. In particular, I am extremely grateful to John Kremer (The Queen's University of Belfast) for his friendship, encouragement and generous help at all times. I also wish to thank him and the following scholars for providing many constructive comments and suggestions on earlier drafts of this manuscript: Denise Baden (University of Southampton), Dave Shaw (University of Central Lancashire), Richard Thelwell (University of Portsmouth) and Catherine Woods (Dublin City University). Other academic colleagues in sport psychology who helped me with this book are Albert Carron (University of Western Ontario), Pat Duffy (University of Limerick), Simon Gandevia (University of New South Wales), Iain Greenlees (University College, Chichester), Heather Hausenblas (University of Florida), Chris Janelle (University of Florida), Richard Keeffe (Duke University), David Lavallee (University of Strathclyde), Deirdre Lyons (University of Limerick), Bill Morgan (University of Wisconsin, Madison), Peter Mudrack (Kansas State University), Shane Murphy (Western Connecticut University), Noel McCaffrey (Dublin City University), Alan Ringland (Institute of Technology, Tralee), P. J. Smyth (University of Limerick) and Mark Williams (Liverpool John Moores University). I am also deeply indebted to my mentor and friend, Bob Singer (University of Florida), for agreeing to write the foreword to this book – as well as for his wonderful hospitality, stimulating ideas and tennis matches in the University of Florida! Within University College, Dublin, special gratitude is extended to my colleagues and friends in the Department of Psychology, especially, Ciaran Benson, Nuala Brady, Alan Carr, Betty Cody, Mary Flaherty, Suzanne Guerin, Eilis Hennessy, Mary Ivers, Geraldine Moane, Mick O'Connell, Mark O'Reilly and Chris Simms. I would like to thank Ursula Byrne (Library), Philip Harvey (Campus Bookshop) and Brian Mullins and his staff (UCD Sports Centre) for their friendship and support and also the Dean of the Faculty of Human Sciences, Pat Clancy, for his constant encouragement of my work. Special gratitude is also extended to Ms Julitta Clancy for her painstaking work in compiling the indexes for this book. Finally, I wish to acknowledge the love and support that I have received from my mother, Nora, my girlfriend Angela, my brothers, Ciaran and Dermot, my sister, Patricia, and her husband, Tom, my friends, especially, Brendan Burgess, Neil Hogan, Dermot O'Halloran, Brendan O'Neill, and all my tennis partners in Lansdowne Lawn Tennis Club.

Figures

FIGURES

INTRODUCING SPORT AND EXERCISE PSYCHOLOGY

Overview

Many prominent athletes and coaches believe that although sport is played with the body, it is won in the mind. If so, then sport offers psychologists an exciting opportunity to develop academic theories (e.g., about how expert athletes differ from novices in a variety of mental skills) and practical strategies (e.g., teaching athletes how to cope with pressure situations) about mental aspects of skilled performance. In Part one of this book, I introduce sport and exercise psychology as both an academic discipline and as a profession.

Chapter 1

Introducing sport and exercise psychology: discipline and profession

I think a lot of the game is how you feel upstairs and that's confidence. It generates your persona, your aura, your whole body language. And that comes out on the table. If you're giving off signs, it shakes the other person. (Ken Doherty, 1997 world snooker champion and runner-up in 2003, cited in Watterson, 1997, p. 8)

Eighty per cent of this game is about confidence. It's in the mind. (Glenn Hoddle, manager of Tottenham Hotspur football team and former manager of England, cited in Lacey, 1998, p. 24)

The key to my game in recent times has been my attitude. (Darren Clarke, Ryder Cup player, cited in C. Smith, 1998, p. 1)

Darts is in the mind and you need to be under pressure to throw your best. (Phil "The Power" Taylor, ten-times world champion darts player, cited in Kervin, 2001, p. S6)

The myth has to be dispelled that you are mad to go to a psychologist. You have to get the best out of your mind to get the best out of your body. (David James, West Ham and England goalkeeper, cited in Winter, 2002a, p. S3)

Introduction

As the above quotations show, many prominent athletes and coaches believe that although sport is played with the body, it is won in the mind (see Figure 1.1). If this belief is correct, then psychologists should be able to help sports competitors to enhance their athletic performance by providing them with practical advice on how to do their best when it matters most. Influenced by the potential benefits of such advice, increasing numbers of athletes and teams are turning to sport psychologists in an effort to gain a winning edge over their rivals. Although this trend is apparent in virtually all competitive games, it is especially evident in mentally demanding individual sports such as golf. Not surprisingly, therefore, world-class golfers such as Ernie Els (Davies, 2002), Pádraig Harrington (Gilleece, 2002), Retief Goosen (Hannigan, 2001a), Phil Mickelson (Browne, 2000), Alison Nicholas (St John, 1997) and Colin Montgomerie (Fleming, 2003) have acknowledged the contribution of sport psychologists to their success in recent years. Indeed, according to D. Davies (2003), Davis Love III, who won the 2003 Players' Championship at Sawgrass, consults not one but *three* sport psychologists on a regular basis! It would be wrong, however, to assume that athlete–psychologist consultations are always about performance enhancement. Thus Keefe (2003) suggested that one reason why so many professional golfers hire psychologists is simply that they "need to tell their story to someone" (p. 73) who has little direct involvement in their lives. Unfortunately, this idea that athletes have narrative needs has not been investigated empirically as yet.

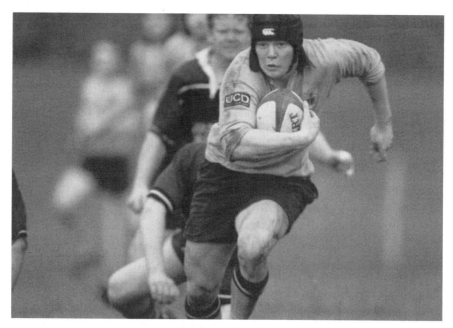

Figure 1.1 Sport is played with the body but won in the mind
Source: courtesy of Sportsfile and UCD Department of Sport

Regardless of whether its origins are pragmatic or therapeutic, athletes' interest in consulting psychologists is particularly noticeable at the elite grade of sport performance because at this level there are minimal differences between competitors in technical ability and/or physical fitness (G. Jones, Hanton and Connaughton, 2002). This observation is endorsed by the English tennis player Tim Henman who proposed that "the mental side is the difference between the top guys and the rest" (cited in Pitt, 1998b, p. 13). Echoing this opinion, Sven-Göran Eriksson, the manager of the England football team, proclaimed that "in the end, it's that psychological difference that decides whether you win or lose" (cited in Winter, 2002a, p. S3). Although anecdotal, these insights into the importance of psychological factors in sport are supported by scientific evidence. For example, reviews of research on the "peak performance" experiences of athletes (J. M. Williams and Krane, 2001; see also Chapter 4) as well as in-depth interviews with Olympic champions (Gould, Dieffenbach and Moffett, 2002) indicate that "mental toughness" and the ability to concentrate effectively are among the factors which distinguish top athletes from less successful counterparts. But apart from having some vague awareness of its importance to athletic success, what do we really know about the "mental side" of sport? More generally, how did the discipline of sport and exercise psychology originate? What type of work do sport psychologists engage in with their clients and how can one qualify as a professional in this field? The purpose of this chapter is to provide some answers to these and other relevant questions, thereby introducing you to sport and exercise psychology both as a scientific discipline and as a profession. Please note, however, that the emphasis in this book is primarily on the *sport* rather than the exercise components of this field (although the latter is considered in Chapters 8 and 9).

The present chapter is organised as follows. To begin with, I shall explore such topics as the mental dimension of sport, mental toughness in athletes and the question of what determines the mental demands of athletic activities. Then, I shall provide a brief sketch of the nature and history of, and research methods used in, the discipline of sport psychology. The third part of the chapter will focus on professional aspects of this field. Included here will be a discussion of four key questions: What type of work do sport psychologists actually do? What is the best way to deliver sport psychology services to athletes and coaches? How can one qualify professionally as a sport psychologist? Where can one learn more about this field? In the fourth section, I shall provide a brief evaluation of the current status of sport and exercise psychology. This section will consider not only the scientific standing of this discipline but also people's views of it. Finally, I shall suggest an idea for a possible research project on the mental side of sport.

At the outset, however, some words of caution are necessary. From the initial paragraphs, you may have assumed that sport and exercise psychology has a single objective (namely, performance enhancement), a coherent identity (i.e., as a sub-discipline of psychology), clearly agreed academic pathways to professional qualifications, and an established role within the sporting community. Unfortunately, each of these four assumptions is questionable. First, as we indicated earlier, performance enhancement in athletes is not the only goal of sport and exercise psychology. To illustrate, over the past decade this discipline has been concerned increasingly with the promotion of health and exercise among people of all ages – whether they are athletic or not (see Chapter 8). Also, sport and exercise psychologists have begun to teach interpersonal skills (such as team building and effective decision making) in an effort to cultivate personal excellence in non-athletic settings (P. S. Miller and Kerr, 2002). Second, the assumption that sport and exercise psychology is an applied field within the discipline of psychology is only partly true – simply because not all sport psychologists are professional psychologists. Thus although some psychologists belong to Division 47 (sport and exercise psychology) of the American Psychological Association (APA) and/or to the sport and exercise psychology section of the British Psychological Society (BPS), others have an academic background in sport science and are members of such interdisciplinary organisations as the North American Society for Psychology of Sport and Physical Activity (NASPSPA) and/or the British Association of Sport and Exercise Sciences (BASES) (see summary of these organisations in Box 1.3). Third, in view of this "twin-track" identity of sport psychologists, there are two ways of qualifying professionally in this field. On the one hand, one can become a sport psychologist through specialist post-graduate training in psychology. Alternatively, one could pursue sport psychology through post-graduate training in sport science (Cockerill, 2002). I shall return to this issue later in the chapter. Finally, and perhaps most controversially, it is important to point out that sport psychology has not always been welcomed or appreciated by athletes and scholars. In this regard, several examples spring to mind. First, performers such as the tennis player Jelena Dokic have expressed scepticism about the value of this discipline. For example, she claimed that she had "never had any help on the mental side. I don't like that sort of thing – you have to figure it out for yourself" (cited in Jago, 2002, p. 18). Similarly, consider the lukewarm views about sport psychology offered by Ronnie "The Rocket" O'Sullivan who won the world snooker championship in 2001 and who is arguably the most gifted ball-potter in the game (e.g., he holds the record for the fastest maximum score in snooker – 147 – achieved in five minutes and twenty seconds). Specifically, he said "I tried a sports [*sic*] psychologist once and I never really got much out of it . . . if you're on, you're on; if you're off, you're off and there's not a lot you can do about it" (cited in White, 2002c, p. 10). Hopefully, this book will convince you that O'Sullivan is wrong to hold a fatalistic view about athletic performance. There is plenty that one can do to increase one's chance of success in sport. A third example of the rejection of sport psychology comes from Ireland's Margaret Johnston, a seven-times world bowling champion. Apparently, she refused to play for her country in the women's home international series in Belfast in 2003 because she did not see the point of engaging in psychology-based relaxation activities during training sessions. At the time, she joked that "if I am going to lie on my back for an hour, I expect to be enjoying myself" (*The Psychologist*, 2003, p. 117). Taken together, these quotations suggest that some athletes are indifferent to, if not openly sceptical of, sport psychology. But are these views shared by researchers? In this regard, Hoberman (1992) compared the discipline of sport psychology to the "human potential" movement of the 1960s because it appeared to propagate "romantic theories of untapped energy and mind-body unity (that) recall the naïve psychophysiology of the *fin de siècle* and its speculations about human limits" (p. 187). Overall, his critique led him to conclude that sport psychology was not an established discipline but merely "an eclectic group of theories and therapies in search of scientific respectability" (pp. 187–188). Although this latter criticism is invalid logically because sport psychology *is* now regarded as an established field of psychology (see Box 1.3), Hoberman's criticism challenges us to adopt an evidence-based approach in evaluating any claims made about sport psychology. For this reason, Hoberman's (1992) critique of sport psychology should be welcomed – not dismissed. I shall return to this issue of scepticism towards sport psychology in the fourth section of this chapter. To summarise, having examined four mistaken assumptions about sport and exercise psychology, let us return from our preamble to explore the first topic in the chapter – namely, an analysis of the mental side of sport.

The mental side of sport

Many sport scientists (e.g., Sellars, 1996) distinguish between four hypothetical aspects of athletic performance: physical, technical, tactical and psychological (see Figure 1.2). Within this quadrant, physical aspects of sport performance refer to phenomena such as fitness, strength and stamina which can be measured objectively. Next, technical aspects of performance refer mainly to the proficiency with which athletes can execute fundamental skills required by their specialist sport. For example, a competitive swimmer in freestyle events must be able to perform a "turn". This skill involves approaching the wall, dropping one's leading arm, lowering one's chin to one's chest, tucking in one's knees and then flipping over one's feet when they hit the wall. The tactical part of the quadrant in Figure 1.2 concerns

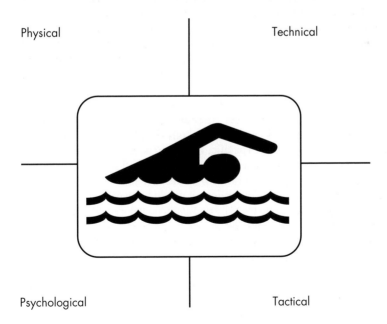

Figure 1.2 Four aspects of athletic performance

strategic aspects of athletic performance. Included here are such skills as planning and decision making. For example, a shrewd tactical performer can devise and adhere to a specific game plan in competitive situations. Finally, we come to the familiar yet mysterious domain called the "psychological" (or "mental") side of performance in sport. At this stage, you should note the paradox of psychology in sport. How can something be familiar yet mysterious? To explain, this domain is *familiar* because, almost every week, we hear about or see athletes who make uncharacteristic mistakes (e.g., missing a penalty-kick in football or a short putt in golf) due to the temporary influence of psychological factors like anxiety (see also Chapter 3). In a sense, therefore, lapses in performance allow us to catch a glimpse of the psychological side of athletes' minds. Unfortunately, despite their ubiquity, mental influences on athletic performance are not well understood in mainstream psychology. This regrettable situation owes its origins to an historical reluctance by psychologists to regard sport as a suitable domain in which to explore how the mind works (Moran, 1996). Given such reluctance to investigate the sporting mind, how do we go about exploring the mental side of athletes' competitive experiences?

Perhaps the most obvious way to investigate the mental side of sport is to ask athletes what they have learned from their personal experience about the mental factors that seem to affect their performance. Using this strategy, we can gain useful insights into the psychological challenges of team and individual sports. For example, an interview with Jonathan Davies, the former Welsh rugby union player, revealed that for him "avoiding over-confidence and keeping your concentration at a high level during a long season is probably the hardest aspect of professionalism to get used to but success is impossible without it" (J. Davies, 1998, p. 12). More recently, Nick Faldo, who has won six major tournaments, highlighted the importance of maintaining momentum and concentration when he observed that "golf is unusual in that you have to pick up where you left off the day before. Four days of mental intensity take it out of you" (cited in Nicholas, 2002, p. S6). Unfortunately, despite its superficial plausibility, the practice of asking athletes about mental aspects of sport performance has at least three major limitations as a research strategy. First, it is difficult to avoid asking "leading" questions or putting words in their mouths when interviewing athletes. Second, it is hard to be unbiased when editing or analysing interview data. After all, most people (including scientists) tend to see what they believe – rather than believe what they see! Third, as athletes' insights are invariably sport-specific, they are rather limited in their generality of application. For example, the world of sailing is full of unknown variables (e.g., variability of wind speed and direction) whereas that of snooker is very predictable. Given these environmental constraints, it would be naïve to expect identical mental preparation strategies to be used by competitive sailors and snooker players.

In view of the preceding difficulties, a more standardised research strategy is required to explore mental aspects of athletic performance. An obvious technique in this regard is the research questionnaire. Using a specially designed survey instrument, Scully and Hume (1995) elicited the views of a sample of elite athletes and coaches about mental aspects of sport. In particular, they asked these participants what the term "sport psychology" meant to them and also inquired about the psychological attributes that they believed to be most influential in determining athletic success. Results revealed that sport psychology was defined mainly in terms of mental preparation for competition (a point to which we shall return later in the chapter). In addition, these researchers found that mental toughness was perceived to be the most important determinant of success in sport. It is interesting to note that this construct was also identified by the golfer Nick Faldo (Nicholas, 2002) and by a sample of Olympic gold medallists as a crucial prerequisite of athletic success (Gould, Dieffenbach and Moffett, 2002). But what exactly is "mental toughness" and how can it be measured?

What is mental toughness? Meaning and measurement

Despite its frequent usage in popular sporting discourse as a synonym for determination or resilience, the term "mental toughness" is seldom found in academic psychology. Fortunately, two recent studies (Clough, Earle and Sewell, 2002; G. Jones *et al.*, 2002) have explored the meaning and measurement of this construct. Before we consider these studies, however, let us examine some athletes' views on mental toughness.

According to the tennis star Tim Henman, mental toughness can be defined simply as the ability "to perform under pressure" (cited in *Coaching Excellence*, 1996, p. 3). This opinion was echoed by Selvey (1998) who described the former England cricketer Mike Atherton as "the most mentally tough batsman of his generation" (p. 2) because of his extraordinary ability to raise his game under pressure. Another perspective on "mental toughness" was offered by Henman's British team-mate, Greg Rusedski, who defined it as "having complete control over your emotions . . . and controlling all situations that you can control" (cited in *Coaching Excellence*, 1996, p. 3). But as we explained previously, athletes' insights into psychological constructs should be treated with caution. Therefore, a more rigorous conceptual analysis of mental toughness is required.

A review of applied psychological research on mental toughness reveals that this term has been used in a variety of ways. Specifically, G. Jones *et al.* (2002) showed that it referred to such different psychological processes as the ability to cope with pressure, the ability to rebound from failure, a determination to persist in the face of adversity, and a form of mental resilience. Given this variability in terminology, what is required in this field is a theoretical rather than an intuitive model of this construct. In this regard, two recent studies of mental toughness are helpful. The first of these studies used a questionnaire-based methodology whereas the second one was based on qualitative techniques (interviews and "focus groups" – see also Box 1.4).

First, Clough *et al.* (2002) attempted to define and measure this construct using a theoretical model developed by Kobasa (1979). Briefly, this latter researcher discovered that some people have a "hardy" personality in the sense that they possess coping skills that enable them to thrive under adverse circumstances. Influenced by this idea, Clough *et al.* (2002) postulated four key components of mental toughness in their "4Cs model" of this construct. The first of these four components is "control" or the capacity to feel and act as if one could exert an influence in the situation in question (a view which is similar to that of Greg Rusedski's concept of mental toughness). The second component of the construct is "commitment" or a tendency to take an active role in events. Third, "challenge" refers to the perception of change as an opportunity to grow and develop rather than as a threat. Finally, "confidence" is a component of mental toughness that designates a strong sense of self-belief. Combining these four elements, Clough *et al*. (2002) defined mentally tough athletes as people who have "a high sense of self-belief and an unshakeable faith that they can control their own destiny" (p. 38) and who can "remain relatively unaffected by competition or adversity" (*ibid*.). In addition, these researchers devised an 18-item measure called the "Mental Toughness Questionnaire" which requires respondents to use a five-point Likert scale to indicate their level of agreement with such items as "Even when under considerable pressure, I usually remain calm" (item 1) or "I generally feel in control" (item 10) or "I usually find it difficult to make a mental effort when I am tired" (item 17). These authors reported a reliability coefficient for this scale of $r = 0.90$ and construct validity data based on predicted relationships with such constructs as self-efficacy or a belief on one's ability to achieve certain outcomes regardless of the situation ($r = 0.56$, $p < .05$). Although such psychometric data are encouraging, a great deal of additional validation evidence is required before this scale can be accepted as a worthwhile tool for the measurement of the rather nebulous construct of mental toughness.

A second study of this construct was carried out recently by G. Jones *et al*. (2002) using qualitative research methodology. More precisely, these researchers used a combination of a "focus group" (i.e., a data collection technique based on group discussion that is led by a trained facilitator) and individual interviews with a sample ($n = 10$) of international sport performers to elicit the meaning of "mental toughness" as well as the characteristics associated with it. Results showed that mental toughness was perceived to comprise both general and specific components. The general component of this construct was a perception of having a "natural or developed psychological edge" that enables an athlete to cope better than his or her opponents with competitive lifestyle and training demands. The specific components of mental toughness were perceived to be the capacity to remain more determined, focused, confident and in control than one's athletic rivals. Curiously, the researchers did not probe this relativistic view of the construct – the perception that it can be understood only in comparative terms. What about the personal characteristics believed to be prerequisites of mental toughness? Twelve attributes were elicited by this question. G. Jones *et al*. (2002) classified these attributes into such categories as motivation, "focus" (or concentration), the ability to deal with pressure and anxiety, and the ability to cope with physical and emotional pain. Unfortunately, the results of this study must be interpreted cautiously due to the small sample size (e.g., the focus group comprised only three participants) and the restricted range of sports represented by the participants.

In summary, we have learned in this section that athletes and researchers regard mental toughness as a key characteristic of successful athletes. But are you really convinced about the validity of this construct? As Box 1.1 shows, there are several unresolved conceptual issues arising from research on mental toughness.

As you can see from Box 1.1, the term mental toughness is far from clear. In passing, a satirical account of the quest for this elusive construct was offered by the fictional footballer Darren Tackle in his weekly column in *The Guardian* newspaper

Box 1.1 Thinking critically about ... mental toughness in sport

Many athletes and coaches regard mental toughness as a crucial prerequisite of success in sport. Furthermore, this construct has been described as "the very essence of sport psychologists' work" (G. Jones *et al.*, 2002, p. 213) with elite performers. But what have we really learned about mental toughness from research in this field? Here are some questions to think about.

Critical thinking questions
First, do you think that it is valid to define mental toughness without reference to any aspect of behaviour other than winning? Recall that the athletes interviewed by G. Jones *et al.* (2002) claimed that this construct gives performers a "psychological edge" over their rivals. But how is this edge evident? Is it present only if an athlete defeats someone else? Could mental toughness not also influence an athlete to perform better than s/he has done previously – regardless of the presence of others? Can you think of a way of defining mental toughness in a more objective manner? Is there a danger of circularity defining this construct because of the lack of an independent index of mental toughness? Second, is there a danger that mental toughness involves so many different psychological characteristics (e.g., G. Jones *et al.*, 2002, identified twelve attributes associated with this construct) that it is effectively meaningless as a scientific term? Third, one way of exploring people's understanding of a term is to ask them to identify the opposite of it. What is the opposite of mental toughness? Finally, is mental toughness learned or innate? Whereas most psychologists regard it as a mental skill that can be trained (see R. E. Smith and Smoll, 1996), the athletes in G. Jones *et al.* (2002) indicated that it could be inherited or "natural". Which view do you favour and why?

(Tackle, 1998). In particular, when one of Tackle's fictional team-mates was asked to visualise a victory, he reported the image of a Big Mac meal with extra fries and a milkshake! Clearly, the theory that mental toughness can be developed through the use of techniques like mental imagery (see Chapter 5) has been lampooned by certain journalists. We shall return to this issue of how sport psychology is perceived by journalists in the fourth section of this chapter.

In summary, having explored the mental side of sport in general, and having examined the specific construct of mental toughness in athletes, there is one more question to address in this section of the chapter. Specifically, what factors influence the mental demands of a given sport?

What factors influence the mental demands of a given sport?

Although a considerable amount of research has been conducted on mental factors in athletic performance, surprisingly little discussion has taken place about the various factors that determine the mental challenge posed by a given athletic activity. What follows is a brief analysis of this important issue (see also Moran, 2000a).

At the outset, it is widely agreed that sports differ significantly in the *physical* demands that they make of performers. For example, sprinting requires a short burst of explosive power whereas marathon running demands not only great stamina but also the ability to maintain a steady pace throughout the race. Interestingly, research on marathon runners indicates that they can lose up to 8 per cent of their body mass during the race (Cooper, 2003). Perhaps not surprisingly, the psychological requirements of different sports also appear to vary widely. To illustrate, whereas some sports like weightlifting require short periods of intense concentration for a limited duration, other athletic activities like cycling demand sustained alertness for longer periods of time. But what causes such differences in the mental demands of these activities?

Among the most important determinants of the psychological demands of any sport are its nature and structure. For example, consider some differences between soccer and snooker. Whereas the former is a timed, physical contact, team-game, the latter is an untimed, non-contact, individual sport. These differences are likely to affect the mental challenges posed by these sports. For example, it seems plausible that whereas motivation, communication skills, and an ability to anticipate opponents' moves are vital for soccer players, snooker performers depend more on cognitive skills like concentration, decision making and the ability to recover mentally from errors. After all, a footballer can try to win the ball back off an opponent by chasing and tackling him or her, but a snooker player can only sit and watch while his or her opponent is potting balls on the table. In short, the structure of a sport can affect its psychological requirements. To illustrate this point, consider the phenomenon of sitting passively "in the chair" in snooker. Briefly, in this game, the player who is not scoring (or building breaks) at the snooker table has to sit and wait for his or her opponent to miss before returning to the table. Clearly, the challenge of sitting in the chair is to retain one's focus rather than becoming annoyed at oneself for previous mistakes. But what goes through snooker players' minds as they wait for their opponents? Stephen Hendry (the seven-times world champion snooker star) referred to "hoping you don't have to play a certain shot, dreading that you might" (cited in White, 2001, p. 18) when forced to watch and wait. Interestingly, not all snooker players feel as helpless as does Hendry in this situation. For example, Peter Ebdon, who won the world championship in 2002, claimed that although "the chair is the toughest place in sport . . . Well it is and it isn't. *It depends on what you do with your time there.* There's certain routines that you can be going through mentally which help you for when you get your chance" (cited in White, 2003, p. 20, italics mine). One of the most popular "chair routines" used by top players such as Steve Davis or Ken Doherty (cited in *Snooker: The World Championship*, 2003) is to imagine oneself playing the shots that one's opponent is confronted with (see also Chapter 5) so that one will be ready to recommence at the table when the opportunity arises. Another psychological technique that helps players to maintain their concentration is to scrutinise the layout of the balls facing one's opponent – hoping that one can anticipate precisely when s/he might miss a shot or lose position on the table. To summarise, most top snooker players use psychological strategies to prevent lapses in concentration in situations where passivity is likely (see also Chapter 4 on concentration).

Let us now consider the mental demands of a popular sport – golf. This sport is interesting because, as I mentioned earlier, many of its leading players are enthusiastic advocates of sport psychology. What is so special about golf from a psychological point of view?

Golf is a psychologically demanding game for at least three reasons. First, it is an untimed sport so players have to be prepared to play for as long as it takes (usually, a minimum of 3–4 hours) to complete a round or match. Sadly, many club-level and leisure players allow themselves to become upset at the apparently slow play of those ahead of them. Naturally, this self-generated annoyance usually hampers their performance. Second, golf is a tough sport mentally because players have to take full responsibility for their own performance on the course. They cannot be substituted if they are playing poorly. Unfortunately, many players try to evade this responsibility by making excuses: blaming course conditions, their clubs, the weather and/or the balls that they are using. In this regard, an old adage in sport psychology is relevant: "Winners are workers – only *losers* make excuses" (but see Box 1.2). Finally, the "stop-start" nature of golf means that players spend more time *thinking* about playing than actually hitting the ball. Indeed, some golf analysts believe that less than 20 per cent of the time on a course is devoted to hitting the ball. Usually, the remainder of the time is spent walking, talking, looking for balls, regretting mistakes, losing concentration and, of course, making excuses! Unfortunately, it is during this fallow time that players lose concentration either by thinking too far ahead or by regretting mistakes and/or lost opportunities in the past. Overall, this disjunction in golf between playing time and thinking time may explain why Sam Snead, a former player, once remarked that *thinking* was the biggest problem in the game (Moran, 2000a). In summary, golf is demanding mentally because it is an untimed, individual and discontinuous sport. In the light of these unique features, the mental challenge for golfers is to learn to concentrate on playing one shot at a time (see also Chapter 4). This challenge can be accomplished if golfers learn to *restructure* the game in their minds. For example, instead of perceiving golf as an eighteen-hole competition against others, people can be trained to see it as a *single-shot* contest between themselves and the target at which they are aiming. Using this technique of cognitive restructuring (see also Chapter 3), they can learn to shorten their focus so that they are concentrating only on the present shot. Before we conclude this section, let us return briefly to the ubiquitous phenomenon of excuse making in sport. Recently, Hodgkinson (2002) assembled a collection of excuses used by athletes and coaches (see Box 1.2).

Box 1.2 Some classic excuses in sport: can they be serious?

Athletes and coaches often make excuses to avoid taking personal responsibility for errors, mistakes or missed opportunities in sport. Recently, Hodgkinson (2002) presented some classic excuses in this field. Among them were:

- The suggestion that the grey colour of Manchester United's shirts prevented team-mates from seeing and passing to each other properly (Alex Ferguson, manager of Manchester United, after his team's 3–1 defeat by Southampton in 1996)
- The claim that "the balls were too bouncy"(Kenny Dalglish, then manager of Newcastle, after his team's 1–1 draw with Stevenage in an FA Cup match in 1998)
- The explanation that England's defeat by South Africa in 1999 in a cricket test match held in Johannesburg was due to "low cloud" conditions

Having scratched the surface of the mental dimension of sport, let us now introduce the discipline of sport and exercise psychology.

Sport and exercise psychology as an academic discipline

A common definition of sport psychology is that it is "a science in which the principles of psychology are applied in a sport or exercise setting" (R. H. Cox, 2002, p. 5). Although this definition may place excessive emphasis on the applied focus of the discipline, it implies that empirical research on mental aspects of athletic performance is at least as old as psychology itself. For example, in the nineteenth century, Triplett (1898) found that racing cyclists tended to perform at least 25 per cent faster when competing against other cyclists (or "pacemakers") than when performing alone against the clock. This discovery that individual athletic activity is facilitated by the presence of others became known as "social facilitation" and was attributed to the capacity of rival performers to "liberate latent energy not ordinarily available" (*ibid.*, p. 532). Interestingly, Triplett's research led to a robust empirical principle in social psychology. Specifically, the presence of other people tends to enhance the performance of well-learned skills but to impair the performance of poorly learned skills (Cashmore, 2002).

Unfortunately, despite having a research tradition spanning more than a century (see Brewer and Van Raalte, 2002; and McCullagh, 1995, for brief historical accounts), the field of sport psychology is difficult to define precisely. This is so because of the twin-track identity of the discipline (Feltz and Kontos, 2002). To explain, as we indicated in the previous section, sport and exercise psychology is not only regarded as a sub-field of mainstream psychology but also as one of the sport sciences. Indeed, Gill (2000) classified sport and exercise psychology as a "branch of exercise and sport science" (p. 7) rather than of psychology.

Despite this semantic difficulty of defining the discipline precisely, three characteristics of sport psychology are noteworthy. First, it is generally regarded as a science. As such, it is committed to the principle that its claims should be falsifiable or capable of being tested through objective and systematic methods of empirical inquiry (see Box 1.4). Second, sport psychology involves the study of *exercise* as well as of competitive athletic behaviour. In other words, physical activity undertaken for health and leisure is just as important to sport and exercise psychologists as is competitive sport. In formal recognition of this fact, the title of the *Journal of Sport Psychology* was changed to the *Journal of Sport and Exercise Psychology* in 1988. We shall explore the psychology of exercise and health in Chapter 8. Third, sport and exercise psychology is a *profession* as well as a science. Therefore, there are *applied* as well as theoretical dimensions to this discipline. So whereas some sport psychologists are engaged in basic research designed to establish how the mind works in a variety of athletic and exercise settings, others provide practical advice and training on performance enhancement and/or on healthy living. Recognising this distinction, in 1985, the Association for the Advancement of Applied Sport Psychology (AAASP) was established in order to cater for the growing interests of applied sport psychologists (see also Box 1.3). Each of these three key features of sport psychology – the commitment to scientific procedures, the emphasis on the study of exercise as well as sport, and the existence of an applied dimension to the discipline – will be emphasised throughout this book. In passing, it should be noted that the relationship between theorists and applied professionals in sport psychology has not always been harmonious. Thus Feltz and Kontos (2002) observed that some basic researchers in the field believe that professional services should not be provided to athletes and coaches until a solid body of knowledge has been established using empirical methods. On the other hand, many applied researchers argue that there is an urgent demand for psychological services within the sporting community and that such work should drive the theory and practice of sport psychology.

In spite of this debate between theorists and practitioners, applied sport psychology has grown rapidly in recent years. To illustrate, this sub-field has its own professional organisations (the AAASP), several associated journals (e.g., *The Journal of Applied Sport Psychology* and *The Sport Psychologist*) and over one hundred post-graduate training programmes in the United States, Australia, Britain, Canada and South Africa (see Sachs, Burke and Schrader, 2001). However, the vast majority of these programmes are located in exercise science departments rather than in departments of psychology – a fact which suggests that applied sport and exercise psychology has not yet been fully integrated into mainstream psychology. We shall deal with this issue of professional qualification and training in more detail in the next section of the chapter. At this point, however, let us outline briefly some key events in the history of the discipline.

A brief history of sport and exercise psychology

In the two decades which followed Triplett's (1898) research, investigators such as Swift (1910) and Lashley (1915) explored the determinants of sport skills such as ball-tossing and archery. Interestingly, such research was complemented by applied work in actual sport settings. For example, in the 1920s, the Chicago Cubs baseball team employed the services of a sport psychologist at the University of Illinois named Coleman Griffith. This researcher and practitioner is widely regarded as the progenitor of this discipline (see Green, 2003). Indeed, it was Griffith who had established the first sport psychology research facility, called the "Athletic Research

Laboratory", in the United States in 1925 (at the University of Illinois). Unfortunately, this laboratory closed in 1932 and despite Griffith's pioneering fusion of theory and practice in this field, research in sport psychology encountered a barren era between the 1920s and 1960s. It was during this latter decade, however, that sport psychology emerged as an independent discipline. Specifically, in 1965 the International Society of Sport Psychology was established by an Italian named Ferruccio Antonelli (LeUnes and Nation, 2002). This development heralded the arrival of sport psychology as a distinct sub-field of sport science. Unfortunately, within mainstream academic psychology, formal recognition of the burgeoning sub-field of sport psychology was slow to arrive. Indeed, it was not until 1986 that Division 47 (Exercise and Sport Psychology) was established by the American Psychological Association. A similar pattern of late recognition of sport psychology was apparent in Australia and Britain. For example, it was 1991 before the Board of Sport Psychologists was established within the Australian Psychological Society and 1993 before a sport and exercise psychology section was formed by the British Psychological Society. For a short summary of some key dates in the evolution of this discipline, see Box 1.3.

Box 1.3 Key dates in the history of sport and exercise psychology

Date	Significant event
1897–1898	Triplett's experimental research on psychological factors in cycling
1925	Coleman Roberts Griffith established the Athletic Research Laboratory in the University of Illinois
1965	Establishment of International Society of Sport Psychology (ISSP) / First International Congress of Sport Psychology held in Rome
1967	Establishment of North American Society for the Psychology of Sport and Physical Activity (NASPSPA)
1969	Establishment of Fédération Européenne de Psychologie des Sport et des Activités Corporelles (FEPSAC)
1970	Publication of first issue of *International Journal of Sport Psychology*
1979	Publication of first issue of *The Journal of Sport Psychology* (changed to *The Journal of Sport and Exercise Psychology* in 1988)
1986	Formation of Association for the Advancement of Applied Sport Psychology (AAASP)
1986	Publication of first issue of *The Sport Psychologist*
1986	Establishment of Division 47 of American Psychological Association on "Exercise and Sport Psychology"

1989	Publication of first issue of *Journal of Applied Sport Psychology*
1991	Formation of Board of Sport Psychologists within the Australian Psychological Society
1993	Establishment of "Sport and Exercise Psychology Section" of the British Psychological Society
2000	Publication of first issue of *Psychology of Sport and Exercise*
2003	Re-naming *International Journal of Sport Psychology* as *International Journal of Sport and Exercise Psychology*

As you can see from Box 1.3, the discipline of sport and exercise psychology has had many landmarks since Norman Triplett conducted his cycling studies over a century ago. Since the mid-1960s, however, many important developments have occurred in this field. Unfortunately, space restrictions in this chapter prevent a detailed analysis of these developments. For a more comprehensive account of the history of sport and exercise psychology, see Brewer and Van Raalte (2002), Feltz and Kontos (2002) and Gill (2000).

Research methods in sport and exercise psychology

In the previous section, I indicated that sport and exercise psychology is commonly regarded as an applied science. If so, what research methods does it use? As you might expect, there is a large toolbox of research methods available to sport and exercise psychologists. One way of classifying these techniques is to distinguish between traditional quantitative methods (where measurement and statistical analysis are used to make sense of the data) and more recently developed qualitative approaches (such as focus groups and grounded theory; see Camic, Rhodes and Yardley, 2003). Incidentally, reviews of qualitative methods in sport and exercise psychology have been undertaken by Culver, Gilbert and Trudel (2003) and Robson, Cripps and Steinberg (1996). Another way to classify research methods in this field is to distinguish between descriptive, correlational and experimental techniques (Passer and Smith, 2001). Let us now consider each of these three categories briefly.

To begin with, the aim of descriptive research is to record and analyse certain aspects of behaviour, especially in natural settings. Included in this category are such methods as case studies (which are intensive or in-depth analyses of individuals, groups or events), naturalistic observation (where researchers observe behaviour as it occurs in its own natural environment), survey research (where information is collected about the behaviour, experiences or attitudes of many people using a series of questions about the topic of interest) and psychometric testing (where differences between people on some psychological construct are assessed using specially designed, standardised instruments). For a useful source of information on tests and measures in sport and exercise psychology, see Duda (1998). Next, the purpose of correlational research is to measure the relationship or degree of association between two or more variables. For example, what is the relationship between athletes' anxiety levels and their performance in athletic competition? (see Chapter 3). Finally, the objective of experimental research is to determine cause-and-effect relationships between two or more variables. Using this method, a researcher tries to manipulate an independent variable under controlled conditions in order to study its effects on a dependent variable. For example, what is the relative efficacy of mental versus physical practice in the learning and performance of a motor skill (see Chapter 5)?

As you have probably encountered these various categories of research methods already in other academic courses (e.g., in your laboratory practicals and methodology courses), I shall provide only a brief outline of their strengths and weaknesses here. Therefore, in Box 1.4, I have summarised the main research methods used in sport and exercise psychology along with appropriate sample studies drawn from different areas of the field.

Sport and exercise psychology as a profession

In the previous section, we discussed sport and exercise psychology as an academic discipline. Let us now let examine its status as a profession. In this regard, three important questions need to be addressed. First, what exactly do sport psychologists do? Second, what is the best model for the provision of sport psychology services to clients such as athletes and coaches? Third, how can one qualify as a sport psychologist? Let us now consider each of these questions in turn (but see also Lavallee, Kremer, Moran and Williams, 2004, for a discussion of these issues).

What do sport psychologists do?

In an effort to address the issue of what sport psychologists do, the sport and exercise section of the British Psychological Society organised a symposium designed to explore the professional work and experiences of its members (Steinberg, Cockerill and Dewey, 1998). What emerged from this symposium was a fascinating spectrum of activities which ranged from the provision of mental skills training schedules for athletes (e.g., footballers, runners and racing drivers) to the design and implementation of health promotion programmes for non-athletic populations (e.g., to encourage people to engage in more regular physical activity). More generally, the professional activities of sport and exercise psychologists fall into three main categories: (i) applied consultancy work (including advice on performance enhancement as well as the provision of counselling and clinical psychology services); (ii) education; and (iii) research. Before we explore these functions, however, two cautions should be noted. First, there is considerable overlap between these three categories in practice (a point to which we shall return later in this section). Second, the majority of sport psychologists work only part-time in this field. Typically, the professional work from which they derive most of their income (i.e., their "day job") lies in some other area of psychology or sport science such as lecturing and research.

Box 1.4 Research methods in sport and exercise psychology

Method	Goal	Data obtained	Advantages	Limitations	Example
Experiments	To study cause–effect relationships by manipulation of certain variables and control of others	Quantitative – usually interval level of measurement	i Random assignment of Ss ii Precise control of independent variables iii Causal inference possible	i May be somewhat artificial – not always possible to generalise results beyond lab. setting ii Vulnerable to certain biases	MacMahon & Masters (2002) studied the effects of various secondary tasks on implicit motor skill performance
Surveys questionnaires and psychological tests	To measure people's attitudes, beliefs and/or abilities	Quantitative or qualitative	i Easy to administer, score and analyse ii Can be tailored to specific populations	i Limited to conscious experiences and processes ii Vulnerable to certain biases	Hall, Mack, Paivio & Hausenblas (1998) developed a test to measure imagery use in athletes
Interviews and focus groups	To explore people's knowledge and experiences of a topic "in depth"	Qualitative (main themes) and quantitative (e.g., frequency analysis of key words)	i Richness of data collected ii Flexible iii Can lead to "grounded theory"	i Very laborious and time-consuming to analyse ii Interviewer may contaminate findings	Jones, Hanton & Connaughton (2002) explored athletes' understanding of "mental toughness"
Case studies	To provide an intensive analysis of a single case or example	Qualitative	Can yield detailed information of a phenomenon over time	Difficult to generalise from findings	Krane, Greenleaf & Snow (1997) studied the motivation of an elite gymnast
Naturalistic observation	To observe and analyse naturally occurring behaviour in real-life settings	Qualitative	Can help to understand the nature and context of certain behaviour	i No experimental control over variables ii Presence of observer may influence findings	Muir (1991) conducted a participant observation study of behaviour in a tennis club

Applied consultancy work

This category of sport psychology services may be subdivided into two types of work: advice on performance enhancement and the provision of counselling/clinical psychology services. Let us consider these activities separately.

The most obvious reason why athletes consult sport psychologists is to gain practical advice on ways of improving their mental preparation and/or competitive performance. Such requests may come directly as self-referrals or indirectly through coaches, general practitioners, governing bodies of sports and/or national "carding schemes" whereby elite athletes may be given funded access to medical and sport science advisers. Typically, these consultations are motivated by a desire to realise some unfulfilled athletic potential and/or to gain a competitive edge over rival performers. Indeed, research suggests that a desire to perform better is the reason most frequently cited by athletes for their decision to consult sport psychologists. For example, Meyers (1997) reported that when he worked as an "on site" sport psychologist during the 1994 US Olympic Festival, most of his referrals concerned performance enhancement issues. As well as providing practical strategies to enhance athletic performance, sport psychologists are often asked to help athletes to resolve a heterogeneous array of alleged "psychological problems" (e.g., poor concentration, performance anxiety, low self-confidence) which tend to be self-diagnosed and vaguely expressed. Indeed, Clough *et al.* (2002) captured the frustration engendered by this unreliable referral system when they remarked that "being asked to solve a problem that is ill-conceived, ill-defined and ill-considered is the lifeblood of sport psychology. Coaches and athletes are more prone than most to using cliches, abbreviations, or shorthand phrases" (p. 32).

Let us now consider the second type of applied professional services that sport psychologists tend to provide for their clients – namely, consultations in the fields of counselling and clinical psychology. Recent years have witnessed a growth of research interest in the personal problems (e.g., alcohol abuse, stress and burnout, eating disorders) that may afflict those involved in sport and exercise. For example, a recent survey of professional soccer players in Britain for the BBC current affairs programme *Real Story* found that 46 per cent of them were aware of colleagues who used illegal recreational and/or performance-enhancing drugs on a regular basis (Jacob, 2003). Not surprisingly, such shocking findings have led to a call for the provision of medical and psychological services for athletes who suffer from drug and/or alcohol dependence problems. More generally, Lavallee and Cockerill (2002) published the proceedings of a workshop (organised by the British Psychological Society) which was designed to provide theoretical, practical and ethical guidelines for those involved in counselling people who are engaged in sport and exercise. Clearly, appropriate formal qualifications and a great deal of sensitivity are required by sport psychologists who offer such services because many athletes are afraid or embarrassed to seek professional help for personal problems. Typically, such performers fear the possibility of ridicule from their peers for seeking a consultation with a "shrink". Unfortunately, media coverage of sport psychology may serve only to exaggerate this problem due to the way in which this discipline is portrayed. For example, *The Times* (2002) reported recently that Graham Taylor (former manager of Aston Villa) called in "the shrinks" (p. 43) to offer psychological services to the players. In view of this caricature of the discipline, it is interesting to note that a scale has been developed by researchers to assess athletes' attitudes to seeking help from sport psychologists (see Martin, Kellmann, Lavallee and Page, 2002).

Education

Many sport and exercise psychologists are involved in educational aspects of the discipline. This professional role usually involves teaching students, athletes, coaches and perhaps business people about the principles, methods and findings of sport psychology. Such educational services are extremely important. For example, in the absence of accurate and up-to-date information conveyed by sport psychology professionals, myths and false assumptions about the discipline can arise. At a more practical level, coaches and managers are usually eager to obtain advice from psychologists about practical strategies for forging team spirit in their players (see also Chapter 7). Finally, there is an increasing demand for the services of sport and exercise psychologists in translating certain mental skills displayed by top athletes (e.g., goal-setting, coping with pressure) into practical life skills for business people.

Research

Research in sport psychology is extremely important because it can provide evidence-based answers to a number of practical questions. For example, is there a link between the way in which athletes prepare mentally for a competition and how they perform in it subsequently? What are the greatest mental challenges of a particular sport? Do relaxation tapes really work for athletes? What is the most effective way of promoting the benefits of physical activity among a sample of sedentary young people?

So far, we have seen that the work of sport and exercise psychologists falls into three main categories. Nevertheless, as I explained earlier, these categories overlap considerably in practice. To illustrate, consider the types of professional services which sport psychologists provide at the Olympic Games. In a fascinating paper on this issue, Terry, Hardy, Jones and Rodgers (1997) summarised their experiences as psychology consultants to the British team that competed in the 1996 Olympic Games in Atlanta. As you can see from Box 1.5, these services represented a mixture of performance-enhancement and educational activities.

> **Box 1.5** What do sport psychologists do at the Olympics? The British experience in 1996
>
> Four sport psychologists accompanied the British team to the 1996 Olympic Games in Atlanta (Terry *et al.*, 1997). These people performed two roles – namely, team psychologists (who worked exclusively with athletes from a specific sport) and "HQ psychologists" (who worked in the Olympic team

headquarters). In general, the former role was proactive and involved the provision of direct advice to athletes on performance enhancement. The latter role was mainly reactive and involved helping people to adjustment effectively to prevailing circumstances. Within these roles, certain critical junctures were identified as being important for the delivery of psychological services.

- **Before departure**
  Team psychologists helped athletes and coaches to prepare for the competitive environment by refining their pre-performance routines and by working on such issues as relaxation, concentration and effective teamwork. "What if?" training, or simulated preparation for various types of adversity, was used regularly.

- **Psychological work at the holding camp (HQ)**
  Most of the British team's athletes were based in a holding camp in Tallahassee, Florida. Two sport psychologists were stationed there for the full four weeks of camp training.

- **Olympic village**
  One of the sport psychologists worked in the Olympic village in Atlanta, providing a "drop in" service to interested athletes and coaches. Surprisingly, this strategy produced few referrals. What worked better was a referral route operating through medical and physiotherapy staff.

Recommendations
In their report, Terry *et al.* (1997) recommended that team psychologists should be appointed at least 18 months in advance of a trip to the Olympics. This suggestion sprang from the conclusion that the most satisfactory and successful psychological interventions were obtained in cases where "a good working relationship and mutual trust already existed" (p. 79). Not surprisingly, it seems that one cannot be an effective team psychologist unless one has established a solid relationship with the athletes involved. Unfortunately, many national Olympic organisations around the world have been slow to appreciate the value of accrediting sport psychologists to their travelling squads. How can this problem be overcome in your opinion?

In summary, this section shows that sport and exercise psychologists have multifaceted professional roles. Unfortunately, these roles cannot be performed adequately until an important question has been explored. Specifically, what model facilitates the optimal delivery of sport psychology services to athletes and coaches?

What is the best model for the delivery of psychological services to athletes?

Although discussion of the theoretical basis of service delivery may seem somewhat removed from the practical concerns of applied sport psychology, it has profound practical importance for the field. To explain, if sport psychologists work according to a traditional medical model, they will be expected to provide "quick fixes" and instant "cures" for athletes with problems in much the same way as physicians are expected to treat their patients through the prescription of suitable medication. What is wrong with this traditional medical model of service delivery and is there any alternative to it?

Unfortunately, there are at least three problems associated with a medical model of applied sport psychology (Kremer and Scully, 1998; Moran, 2000a). First, it places the burden of responsibility on the "expert" psychologist to "cure" whatever problems are presented by the athlete or coach. This situation may encourage clients to depend excessively on their sport psychologist, thereby impeding their growth towards self-reliance. Interestingly, in a recent discussion of his philosophy of service delivery, Gordin (2003) advocated the importance of empowering athletes when he remarked that "it is my intent to put myself out of a job with a client. That is, a goal of mine is to make the client self-sufficient and independent. Once these athletes have achieved independence, then the relationship is appropriately terminated or altered" (pp. 64–65). A second problem with the medical model of intervention is that the "expert" sport psychologist is often on shaky ground theoretically because many of the intervention techniques which s/he recommends have not been validated adequately. Finally, the distinction between "expert" and "client" ignores the fact that sportspeople, including athletes and coaches, are naïve psychologists in the sense that they have already developed informal theoretical intuitive psychological theories to account for the behaviour of their players (see Chapter 9 for information on the late Bill Shankley's attitude to injured soccer players). In these cases, such intuitive theories need to be deconstructed through discussion with sport psychologists before a client can be helped. Taken together, these three problems highlight the weaknesses of the traditional role of the medically oriented sport psychologist.

Fortunately, an alternative model has been proposed for the delivery of sport psychology services to athletes and coaches (see Kremer and Scully, 1998). Briefly, this model identifies the *coach* rather than the athlete as the primary target for psychological education. Accordingly, the role of the sport psychologist changes from that of a medical expert to that of a management consultant – somebody who works as part of a team with the coach/manager and his or her support staff. Of course, this new model does not eliminate the need for individual consultation. There will always be situations which warrant "one-to-one" consultations between athletes and sport psychologists. However, the adoption of Kremer and Scully's (1998) model does change one feature of the client–psychologist relationship. Specifically, it challenges the myth that sport psychologists are "shrinks" or "mind benders" who can provide instant solutions for athletes whose problems have baffled their coaches. Evaluating the model that underlies one's services is not the only self-appraisal task faced by sport and exercise psychologists. Increasingly, in this era of accountability

Figure 1.3 It is a myth that sport psychologists are "shrinks"

Box 1.6 Thinking critically about . . . evaluating the efficacy of sport psychology consultations

How can sport psychologists assess the efficacy of their professional work? At first glance, the answer to this question is simple. All they have to do is to evaluate their interventions and services empirically from time to time and publish the results accordingly. Unfortunately, for at least three reasons, this strategy has not proved popular in sport and exercise psychology. First, many practitioners are too busy to engage in evaluative activities. Second, until recently, few assessment tools were available for this purpose. Third, given certain inherent biases of the publication system, there is a danger that the only outcomes which sport psychologists might be willing to publish are *successful* ones. To illustrate, have you ever come across an article by a sport psychologist in which s/he revealed the complete *failure* of an intervention? Have you ever read a paper by a sport psychologist in which s/he referred to clients' failure to follow up on his or her advice? Given these problems, how can a sport psychologist evaluate his or her consultancy services? Recently, Anderson (2002) developed an instrument called the "Assessment of Consultant Effectiveness" (ACE) to help practitioners to assess the quality of their professional services. Briefly, this instrument asks clients to evaluate statements concerning "customer service" using a rating scale. Typical items include "The sport psychologist was a good listener" (item 5) or "The sport psychologist presented information in a clear and easy to understand way" (item 22).

Critical thinking questions
Is there any danger that clients may not tell the truth when answering this questionnaire? How can this problem be overcome? How could this instrument be validated? Can you think of any other ways of evaluating the efficacy of a sport psychologist's professional services?

and evidence-based practice, there is a need for psychologists to *demonstrate* the efficacy of the professional services that they provide. How can a sport psychologist tackle this question? This issue is examined in Box 1.6.

In this section of the chapter, we have explored the type of work that sport psychologists do as well as issues concerning the optimal delivery of psychological services to athletes and coaches. Now it is time to examine the question of how one can qualify as a "sport psychologist".

How can one qualify as a sport psychologist?

Earlier in this chapter, I introduced sport and exercise psychology as a hybrid discipline with roots in both psychology and sport science. Given this dual-discipline background, perhaps it is not surprising that there is no simple or universally agreed academic pathway to professional qualification in sport and exercise psychology at present. Not surprisingly, the crucial question of who is certified to call himself or herself a "sport psychologist" has been debated vigorously in such countries as Australia, Britain, Canada and the United States (see details of each country's position on this issue in Zizzi, Zaichkowsky and Perna, 2002). In most of these countries, there has been a disjunction between psychology associations and sport science organisations with regard to the issue of labelling and/or accrediting people as sport psychologists. For example, in the United States, anyone who receives a recognised doctoral degree in psychology qualifies for licensure (or statutory registration) as a "psychologist". Unfortunately, the American Psychological Association (APA) does not yet accredit programmes in *sport* psychology. Therefore, this organisation accepts that a psychologist's decision to claim a professional specialisation in sport psychology is a personal one which should only be taken in the light of full awareness of relevant APA ethical guidelines. For example, one of these guidelines stipulates that psychologists should work only within the boundaries of their competence. Working apart from the APA, sport science organisations have made important advances in accrediting sport psychology practitioners. For example, in the United States, the Association for the Advancement of Applied Sport Psychology (AAASP) developed a certification procedure for sport psychology in 1989. People who satisfy the criteria stipulated by AAASP (see details in Zizzi *et al.*, 2002) are entitled to call themselves "Certified Consultant, AAASP" – but not "Certified Sport Psychologist". This latter title is precluded because, as explained above, the term psychologist is protected by state licence in the United States. Similar certification processes have been established in Britain where the British

Association of Sport and Exercise Sciences (BASES) has a psychology section. So, how can one qualify as a sport psychologist in Britain?

According to Cockerill (2002), there are two general categories of people in Britain who use the title of "sport psychologist". The first category consists of people who have a recognised primary degree in psychology (i.e., one that confers eligibility for "Graduate Basis for Registration"(GBR) of the British Psychological Society), an eligibility for "Chartered Psychologist" status, and who have an interest or involvement in sport. Incidentally, to qualify as a chartered psychologist within the BPS, one needs to have a recognised primary degree in psychology as well as BPS-approved post-graduate training with a certain duration of supervised practice. The second general category of sport psychologists in Britain comprises people who do not have qualifications leading to "GBR" but who have completed, or are in the process of completing, the accreditation procedure established by the British Association of Sport and Exercise Sciences (BASES). To qualify for registration as a sport psychologist with BASES, one needs to have either a primary degree in psychology and a post-graduate degree in sport science or a primary degree in sport science with a post-graduate degree in psychology. In addition, BASES requires candidates to submit a portfolio of academic achievements and relevant supervised professional experience in the field. It is notable that the membership requirements of the Australian Psychological Society's College of Sport Psychologists are also stringent. Thus one needs four years of academic training in psychology (with an honours degree or its equivalent), additional undergraduate coursework in sports science, a two-year accredited master's degree in sport psychology, and a two-year period of specialised supervision in sport psychology (Bond, 2002).

Although the British Psychological Society has not yet accredited any academic training programmes in sport psychology, it is currently negotiating with BASES regarding the issue of who is entitled to be called a "sport psychologist". Recently, a European training programme in sport and exercise psychology was launched by the Fédération Européenne de Psychologie des Sport et des Activités Corporelles (FEPSAC). This modular programme, which is supported by funding from the European Union, is run through a network of university departments in Psychology, Physical Education and Sport Science. Further details of this course are available from the FEPSAC website (see Box 1.7). In summary, the issues of titles and certification in sport psychology are very complex. Perhaps this situation is to be expected, however, in view of the interdisciplinary foundations of sport and exercise psychology.

Where can I find out more about sport psychology?

If you would like to learn more about sport and exercise psychology using the internet, there are at least two options.

First, you could subscribe to an electronic bulletin board devoted to sport and exercise psychology. At present, there are two such bulletin boards in the field: Division 47 of the American Psychological Association and "SportPsy". Division 47 of the APA has an email list for members (remember that to join APA Division 47, you must be a member or affiliate of the APA and also request affiliation to Division

47). The purpose of this list is to post issues, questions and findings concerning research in sport and exercise psychology as well as related professional practice issues in this field. In order to join this list, you should send an email message to: listserv@lists.apa.org

Leave the subject field blank and type <subscribe div47 your name> in the body of the text. When your application is approved, you may send messages to the list by using the following address: div47@lists.apa.org

The SportPsy list has over 1,000 members and is maintained at Temple University. To join it, you should send the following command **in the command line**:

TELL LISTSERV AT LISTSERV.TEMPLE.EDU SUBSCRIBE SPORTPSY your name

Leave the subject field blank and type <subscribe sportpsy your name>

The second option is to consult the websites of some of the professional organisations listed in Box 1.7.

Box 1.7 Learning more about sport psychology: locating websites of professional organisations in the field

American Psychological Association – Division 47 (Exercise and Sport Psychology)
http://www.psyc.unt.edu/apadiv47/
Provides articles, information on the division, newsletter updates, membership news, book reviews and a conference calendar

Association for the Advancement of Applied Sport Psychology (AAASP)
http://www.aaasponline.org/index2.html
Aims to promote the development of psychological theory, research and intervention strategies in sport and exercise psychology

British Association of Sport and Exercise Sciences (BASES)
http://www.bases.org.uk
Aims to develop and spread knowledge about the application of science to sport and exercise

British Psychological Society (Sport and Exercise Psychology Section)
http://www.bps.org.uk/sub-syst/SPEX/about.cfm
Section aims to promote the development of psychology in sport and exercise through academic study and research

Fédération Européenne de Psychologie des Sports et des Activités Corporelles (FEPSAC; European Federation of Sport Psychology)
http://www.itp.lu.se/fepsac/
Aims to promote scientific, educational and professional work in sport psychology

---

International Society of Sport Psychology (ISSP)
http://www.phyed.duth.gr/sportpsy/international.html
Devoted to promoting research and development in the discipline of sport and exercise psychology

North American Society for Psychology of Sport and Physical Activity (NASPSPA)
http://www.naspspa.org/info/
An interdisciplinary association which aims to develop and advance the scientific study of human behaviour when individuals are engaged in sport and physical activity

Now that we have explored the scientific foundations and professional applications of sport and exercise psychology, let us consider its status as a discipline.

Current status of sport and exercise psychology: respect or scepticism?

At first glance, the field of sport and exercise psychology appears to be an intellectually challenging, vibrant and highly valued interdisciplinary enterprise. This conclusion is based on four strands of evidence.

First, since the 1970s, sport and exercise psychology has expanded its topical coverage as well as the range of populations at which its interventions have been aimed. To explain, whereas this discipline used to be concerned mainly with performance enhancement in sport performers, its scope has now enlarged to accommodate aspects of exercise and health in people of all ages – regardless of their athletic status. Second, the extent and quality of research in sport and exercise are indicated by the number of peer-reviewed journals in this field. To illustrate, a selection of scholarly journals containing the words "sport" and/or "exercise" is presented in Box 1.8.

Box 1.8 Selected journals in the field of sport and exercise psychology

International Journal of Sport and Exercise Psychology (published by the International Society of Sport Psychology, ISSP; first published in 1970 and re-named in 2003)

Journal of Applied Sport Psychology (published by the Association for the Advancement of Applied Sport Psychology, AAASP; first published in 1989)

Journal of Sport Behaviour (published by the United States Sports Academy; first published in 1978)

Journal of Sport and Exercise Psychology (published by the North American Society for the Psychology of Sport and Physical Activity, NASPSPA; first published in 1979)

Journal of Sports Sciences (published by Taylor & Francis Ltd.; first published in 1982)

Psychology of Sport and Exercise (published by Elsevier Publishers; first published in 2000)

Research Quarterly for Exercise and Sport (published by American Alliance for Health, Physical Education, Recreation and Dance; first published in 1930)

The Sport Psychologist (published by the International Society of Sport Psychology; first published in 1987)

The third reason for attributing a healthy status to sport and exercise psychology comes from the formal recognition of this discipline by mainstream psychology. In particular, as indicated in Box 1.3, professional psychological associations in the United States (in 1986), Australia (in 1991) and Britain (in 1993) have established special divisions or sections to cater for the needs of members who are interested in the application of psychology to sport and exercise settings. Finally, the practical value of sport psychology is evident from the increasing number of performers and coaches around the world who are using its services – mainly for performance enhancement (see LeUnes and Nation, 2002). But it is not just individual athletes who have emerged as enthusiastic advocates of sport psychology. Many countries competing at the Olympic Games employ sport psychologists as advisers (see Box 1.5 above) as do teams in baseball (Seppa, 1996), cricket (e.g., the Australian squad; see Wilde, 1998) and rugby (e.g., the Irish national team; see Thornley, 1997). In summary, the preceding strands of evidence suggest that sport and exercise psychology is now firmly established as a scientifically respectable and useful discipline. Unfortunately, this conclusion has been challenged by critics both from within and outside the discipline. Let us now consider briefly the nature and validity of their counter-arguments.

Within the discipline, Dishman (1983) argued that sport psychology is deeply flawed due to a combination of shaky theoretical foundations and unreliable intervention strategies. These sentiments were echoed by Morgan (1997) who bemoaned the absence of scientific evidence to support many of the intervention techniques promulgated by practitioners in this field. A similar point was made by Moran (1996) who noted that few concentration skills training programmes in applied sport psychology have been subjected to either conceptual or empirical evaluation. Augmenting these criticisms of theory and research in sport psychology are accounts of practitioners' disenchantment with the professional side of this discipline. For example, consider Meyers' (1997) candid account of his experiences as an "on site" sport psychologist at the US Olympic Festival. Working in this situation, he noted that although there was a clear demand for sport psychological services, "there exists little respect for what we do" (p. 466).

As indicated earlier in our analysis of the work of Hoberman (1992), criticisms have also been levelled at sport psychology from outside the field. For example, some athletes and journalists are sceptical of the value of the discipline. To illustrate, consider the dismissive attitude to sport psychologists displayed by Goran Ivanisevic, the former Wimbledon champion who observed that "You lie on a couch, they take your money, and you walk out more bananas than when you walk in" (cited in LeUnes and Nation, 2002, p. 18; see also Figure 1.3). Similar scepticism of the value of sport psychology is evident in professional football in England. For example, in 1997, a survey of forty-four football clubs was conducted by the BBC Radio 5 Live documentary team *On The Line*. Results showed that three-quarters of the clubs questioned had either never used, or would not ever consider using, a sport psychologist (see Bent, McIlroy, Mousley and Walsh, 2000). These clubs justified this decision by claiming that their own coaching staff, who are usually former professional players, knew best how to deal with the psychological needs of the footballers. Fortunately, Sven-Göran Eriksson, the current England team manager, does not share this view and has emphasised the importance of recruiting sport psychologists to deal with the mental side of football. Thus he suggested that "if we go into the heads of players we need a specialist to do it, but I believe that this is the future of the game" (cited in Every, 2002, p. 1).

What is the origin of this scepticism of sport psychology in football circles in Britain? One possibility is that it stems from a popular myth – the misidentification of psychology with psychiatry. Unfortunately, headlines that refer to managers who consult "shrinks" promulgate two potentially damaging ideas about sport psychology. First, by using the word "shrinks" (which is a popular slang abbreviation of the term "head shrinkers"), the headline suggests that sport psychologists are *psychiatrists*. In addition, it implies that they are consulted or called in only when there is a problem to be solved. It is worth noting that this view of sport psychology as a branch of psychiatry is based on the medical model that we explored in the previous section of this chapter. Perhaps it is this myth that players are "patients" who need to be "shrunk" by medical specialists that lies at the heart of certain journalists' scepticism of sport psychology. Unfortunately, as Box 1.9 shows, this discipline has also been associated in the popular mind with spoon bending and faith healing. In the light of this caricature of sport psychology as portrayed by some media, is it any wonder that Graham Taylor was pilloried in certain quarters for using a psychologist with the England team in the European Championships in 1992 (G. Taylor, 2002)?

Box 1.9 Thinking critically about . . . sport psychology, spoon bending and faith healing

Despite its scientific status, the discipline of sport and exercise psychology has not always received a universal welcome from the athletic community. To illustrate, consider two controversies which affected the public image of the field in the late 1990s as the England soccer team prepared to compete in the 1998 World Cup finals in France. First, Uri Geller, the famous entertainer,

---

claimed to have been hired by Glenn Hoddle (coach of the England soccer team at that time) and the English Football Association to use his "magic crystals" in order to prepare the England squad mentally for the tournament in France (Austin, 1998). Not surprisingly, this allegation attracted mirth and derision in equal measure. The second issue occurred when Hoddle decided to appoint a faith-healer named Eileen Drewery to his backroom staff. One of the reasons which Hoddle gave in justification for this decision was that Drewery "is a bit of a psychologist because she puts your mind at ease when she talks to you" (cited in Thorp, 1998, p. 5).

Critical thinking questions
Do you think that the public image of sport psychology is affected by incidents such as the ones described above? What are the similarities and differences between faith healing and applied sport psychology? If putting "your mind at ease" is all that footballers require to play well, does it matter whether or not a technique that achieves this purpose is accepted as "scientific"? How can sport psychologists change the popular image of their profession? List two to three practical strategies to address this issue.

Fortunately, in spite of the myths surrounding the discipline and the negative publicity engendered by the events described in Box 1.9, sport psychology has begun to make inroads into the world of professional football in Britain over the past few years. This upsurge of interest in psychology has been caused by three key changes in the sport.

First, improvements in the standard of coach education programmes have led to increased acceptance of the role that sport science (including psychology) plays in professional football. Put simply, if clubs are willing to accept the principle that regular physiological testing is a good way of maintaining physical fitness among players, then they should also accept the notion that footballers' mental fitness can be facilitated by advice from sport psychologists. Second, there has been an influx of foreign coaches and players into British football in recent years. These people have introduced indigenous players to the benefits of such sport scientific practices as "warming down" after games, adhering to a balanced diet, and preparing mentally for matches (Dixon, 2002). Third, and perhaps most importantly, the fact that successful coaches such as Sven-Göran Eriksson and Sir Alex Ferguson have employed sport psychologists (Winter, 2002a) has influenced other coaches to copy them. Mindful of these three developments, the Football Association in England recently launched a campaign to encourage football clubs in Britain to recruit more sport psychologists (*ibid.*). In summary, available evidence suggests that sport psychology in football is expanding not "shrinking" (Moran, 2002b).

To summarise this section, in spite of its struggle against certain persistent criticisms and misconceptions, sport and exercise psychology is making encouraging progress in establishing itself as a respected discipline. Of course, this conclusion must be tempered by awareness of at least two unresolved issues in the field. First, it is essential for the long-term viability of sport and exercise psychology that professional psychological organisations such as the American Psychological Association and the British Psychological Society should develop accreditation criteria for post-graduate training courses in this field. In addition, in an effort to safeguard the public against the possibility of malpractice, professional issues concerning titles and certification need to be addressed urgently. For a more extensive discussion of ethical issues in applied sport and exercise psychology, see Gordin (2003), Whelan, Meyers and Elkins (2002) and Woolfson (2002).

An idea for a research project on sport psychology

Here is an idea for a possible research project on the psychological aspects of sport. Its objectives are:

1   to find out what athletes mean by "mental preparation";
2   to establish how important it is to them; and
3   to estimate what proportion of their training time they devote to it on average.

To conduct this project, you will need an audio-cassette recorder or a mini-disc recorder and some volunteer athletes. Find three people who play different types of sports (e.g., a team-game, an individual game) who have been actively involved in competitive performance for at least five years. Request their permission to record your interview with them on the audio-cassette or mini-disc recorder. Then, ask them the following questions: "What does the term 'mental preparation' mean to you? On a scale of 0 (meaning 'not at all important') to 5 (meaning 'extremely important'), how important do you think that proper mental preparation is for successful performance in your sport? What sort of things do you do as physical training for your sport? What sort of things, if any, do you do as mental preparation for your sport? About what percentage of your training time do you devote to physical preparation? Give a rough percentage figure. And to mental preparation? Give an approximate percentage figure, please."

Compare and contrast the athletes' answers to your questions. You will probably discover that although these people think that mental preparation is important for optimal performance, they devote relatively little time to it. If this finding emerges, how do you interpret it? If not, what did the athletes say? Did the type of sport make a difference to the athletes' views?

Summary

- In this chapter, I have explained that sport and exercise psychology is both a science and a profession in which the principles and methods of psychology are applied in sport and exercise settings.
- The chapter began by investigating the nature and determinants of the mental side of sport as well as the construct of mental toughness in athletes.
- In the next section, I outlined the nature, history and research methods of the discipline of sport and exercise psychology.

- The third part of the chapter explored professional aspects of this field. Included here was a discussion of four key questions:

  1 What type of work do sport psychologists actually do?
  2 What is the best way to deliver sport psychology services to athletes and coaches?
  3 How can one qualify professionally as a sport psychologist? Where can one learn more about this field?
  4 The fourth section of the chapter provided a brief evaluation of the current status of sport and exercise psychology.

- This section addressed this question by assessing both the scientific standing of this discipline as well as people's perception of it.
- Finally, we provided a practical suggestion for a research project in this field.

EXPLORING ATHLETIC PERFORMANCE: KEY CONSTRUCTS

Overview

Part one of the book examined the nature of the discipline and profession of sport and exercise psychology. In Part two, I investigate the various psychological processes that affect individual athletes in their pursuit of excellence. Chapter 2 explores the psychology of motivation in athletes. Chapter 3 examines anxiety in sport performers. Chapter 4 addresses the topic of concentration and Chapter 5 tackles imagery processes in athletes. Finally in this part, Chapter 6 addresses the question of what determines expertise in sport.

GRIMSBY INSTITUTE OF
FURTHER & HIGHER EDUCATION
LIBRARIES

Motivation and goal-setting in sport

Motivation is a strange subject, it's not an exact science. Footballers are all different human beings. Some are self-motivators, they need to be left alone . . . For some, you need causes, your country, them and us, your religion. And those causes can be created by the manager . . . at Manchester United, we have to be better than everyone else . . . (Sir Alex Ferguson, Manager of Manchester United, cited in White, 1999, p. 26)

The manager gave us a great speech. He told us that if we lost, "you'll have to go up and get our losers' medals and you will be just six feet away from the European Cup but you won't be able to touch it. And for many of you that will be the closest you will ever get. Don't you dare come back in here without giving your all." (Teddy Sheringham, former member of Manchester United team which won the European Cup in 1999, cited in Thorp, 1999, p. 34)

Introduction

Motivation plays a crucial if somewhat misunderstood role in sport and exercise. The role is crucial in the sense that athletic success depends significantly on the willingness of sports performers to exert mental as well as physical effort in pursuit of excellence (see also Chapter 6). For example, Stephen Hendry, the seven-times world snooker champion observed that "if you are not committed mentally, then you might as well give up" (cited in McDermott, 2000, p. 20). The same principle holds true for exercise behaviour. In particular, a high degree of motivation is required to maintain involvement in physical activity programmes – a fact which explains why so many people drop out of exercise classes (see also Chapter 8). Despite these insights, the contribution of motivation to optimal performance in sport is widely misunderstood. For example, as Roberts (2001) pointed out, motivation is often confused with being "psyched up" (see also Chapter 3). Contrary to the experience of the former England soccer star Teddy Sheringham (see quote above), however, there is little research evidence that "psyching up" athletes by emphasising the disastrous consequences of failure is an effective ploy. Indeed, if anything, such a strategy may prove counter-productive because high levels of arousal are known to impair athletes' concentration skills (see Chapter 4). To illustrate, Webster (1984) reported that due to the effects of excessive anxiety, *not one* member of an Australian Rules football team could recall any of the coach's instructions in a vital game just *five minutes* after his rousing pre-match address! More recently, the issue of fear as a motivating factor in sport was raised by reports that Iraqi footballers were regularly beaten and tortured for losing matches under the regime of the late Uday Hussein, son of Saddam Hussein (Goldenberg, 2003) – a brutal practice which did nothing to enhance team morale or performance. Given this background of confusion about the role of motivation in sport and exercise, the present chapter will attempt to answer the following questions. What exactly does the term "motivation" mean? What types of motivation have been identified? What theoretical approaches have been used to explore this construct? How can athletes increase their motivation? Finally, what factors motivate people to participate in dangerous sports? In order to address these issues, the chapter is organised as follows.

To begin with, the nature and types of motivation in athletes will be considered. The second section of the chapter will present a brief overview of theoretical approaches to this construct in sport psychology. Special consideration will be given here to two influential cognitive models of motivational processes in athletes – achievement goal theory and attribution theory. The third section will explore the theory and practice of increasing motivation in athletes through goal-setting techniques. Next, I shall examine the motivational factors which impel some people to take part in risky activities in sport and exercise settings. Finally, some practical suggestions for possible research projects in the psychology of motivation will be provided.

Nature and types of motivation

As the term "motivation" is derived from the Latin word *movere* (meaning "to move"; Onions, 1996), it is concerned with those factors which initiate or energise behaviour. Within sport and exercise psychology, motivational issues are implicated when "a person undertakes a task at which he or she is evaluated or enters into competition with others, or attempts to attain some standard of excellence" (Roberts,

2001, p. 6). Unfortunately, as we have suggested already, the term motivation is plagued by a great deal of conceptual confusion. To illustrate, Box 2.1 presents some persistent myths surrounding this construct.

Box 2.1 Thinking critically about . . . popular understanding of "motivation"

According to Roberts (2001), motivation is one of the most misunderstood constructs in sport psychology for three main reasons. To begin with, it is often confused with arousal. As he pointed out, however, athletes cannot be motivated simply by "psyching" them up into a frenzy of adrenaline. If anything, arousal needs to be *channelled* in a specific direction for motivation to occur (see also Chapter 3). The second myth about motivation is that it can be enhanced through positive thinking. The assumption here is that if athletes can imagine themselves holding up the winner's trophy, their motivation will be strengthened. Unfortunately, research on goal-setting shows that people's objectives have to be controllable and realistic to be effective. Finally, some coaches believe that motivation is a genetically inherited characteristic – something that one either has or has not got. Again, this view is contradicted by research evidence which shows that motivation can be changed through appropriate instruction (see later in chapter). Given these popular misconceptions, is it any wonder that sport psychologists have to be careful when using the term motivation? After all, as Roberts (2001) concluded: "it is defined so broadly by some that it incorporates the whole field of psychology, so narrowly by others that it is almost useless as an organising construct" (p. 3).

Critical thinking questions
Do you agree with Roberts (2001) that motivation is widely misunderstood in sport? Why do you think that many people mistake a heightened state of arousal for motivation? Are there any distinctive behavioural signs or expressions of motivation? How would you design a study to explore athletes' understanding of motivation? Does the myth of motivation extend to people's understanding of the work that sport psychologists engage in with their clients? Why do many people mistakenly believe that sport psychology is mainly about motivating athletes to perform well?

In the light of the confusion surrounding motivational processes in sport, how should we approach this construct scientifically?

Traditionally, sport psychologists have distinguished between two different types of motivation – "intrinsic" and "extrinsic" (see review by Vallerand and Rousseau, 2001).

Intrinsic motivation refers to people's impetus to perform an activity "for itself and the pleasure and satisfaction derived from participation" (*ibid.*, p. 390). For example, some people love walking or running simply because it gives them feelings of fun and freedom and also because it enhances their subjective sense of well-being.

Anecdotally, it is precisely this sense of intrinsic joy or satisfaction which seems to characterise the motivation of top athletes in sports like swimming, golf and cricket. For example, consider the importance which the Australian Olympic gold medal winning swimmer Kieren Perkins attached to intrinsic influences in his sport when he said, "I always *race against myself to improve my own performances. The fact that I sometimes set world records in the process is a bonus. My personal best performance is the goal, not necessarily the world record*" (Clews and Gross, 1995, pp. 98–99; italics mine). A similar emphasis on intrinsic satisfaction is evident in Tiger Woods's observation that successful golfers "enjoy the serenity and the challenge of trying to beat their own personal records" (cited in Scott, 1999, p. 47). Finally, the Indian cricket star Sachin Tendulkar, who is the top run-scorer in World Cup history and is regarded as one of the finest batsmen of all time, claimed that "I don't set myself any targets. I just concentrate on trying to bat well . . . When I was a kid, I played cricket because I loved it and I still love it now" (cited in *Funday Times*, 2002, p. 12). Interestingly, a recent in-depth study of the motivational processes of elite track-and-field athletes (those who had finished in the top-ten at either the Olympic Games or the world championships) supported these anecdotal insights. Specifically, Mallett and Hanrahan (2003) interviewed these athletes in an effort to identify the factors which sustained their motivation to compete at the highest level. Results showed that these athletes were driven mainly by personal goals and achievements rather than by financial incentives. Nevertheless, the ego-oriented goal of defeating others remains a powerful source of motivation for many athletes. For example, Sam Lynch, who successfully defended his lightweight single sculls title at the World Rowing Championships in 2002, said afterwards, "I was aware that the conditions were fast but the title always comes first. You don't go for a world record in a race like this. It may come but *winning the title comes first*" (cited in R. T. Jones, 2002, p. 15, italics mine). Interestingly, according to Martens and Webber (2002), intrinsic motivation is associated with increased enjoyment of an activity, stronger sportspersonship (see also Chapter 7) and a reduced likelihood of dropping out from sport.

Extrinsic motivation applies whenever a person is involved in a task largely as a result of external factors or constraints. More specifically, this term refers to "engaging in an activity as a means to an end and not for its own sake" (Vallerand and Rousseau, 2001, p. 391). Typical extrinsic factors held to motivate athletes include money, trophies, praise and/or other forms of social approval from others. For example, a golfer would be regarded as extrinsically motivated if s/he joined a golf-club because s/he wanted to make new business contacts – not because s/he actually enjoyed the game of golf. In summary, extrinsic motivators are factors which influence a person to do something either because they provide a reward for such behaviour or because they provide some punishment or sanction for *not* doing it. In general, research shows that extrinsic motivation is associated with increased anxiety in, and increased likelihood of dropping out from, sporting activities (see Martens and Webber, 2002).

Theoretically, intrinsic and extrinsic motivation can be differentiated on at least three criteria (Vallerand and Fortier, 1998). First, consider the purpose of the activity. As indicated earlier, whereas intrinsically motivated activities are under-taken for their own sake, extrinsically motivated tasks are typically conducted for some perceived instrumental benefit. Second, although people who are intrinsically motivated tend to seek experiential rewards, those who are extrinsically motivated tend to be influenced more by social and/or objective rewards (e.g., money). Finally, Vallerand and Fortier (1998) proposed that intrinsically motivated performers tend to experience less pressure than extrinsically motivated counterparts when competing because the former people are largely concerned with the experience of participation itself.

Despite these theoretical distinctions, intrinsic and extrinsic motivation often overlap in real life. Indeed, as Box 2.2 shows, extrinsic rewards can affect intrinsic motivation under certain circumstances.

Box 2.2 Thinking critically about . . . how rewards can change people's motivation

The National Coaching Foundation (1996) presented an apocryphal tale which has a long history in psychology. This story portrays the principle that the withdrawal of rewards can change people's motivation in surprising ways.

An old man was plagued by teenagers playing football and making noise on the street outside his house. No matter what he said to them, they ignored him. In fact, the more he pleaded with them to stop, the more they persisted and the more obnoxiously they behaved. He was at his wits' end. Then one day, following a chat with a psychologist friend, he decided to try a new approach to the problem. Briefly, instead of scolding the boys, he decided to give them a *reward* (two euros each) for playing noisily outside his house. Of course, the boys were delighted with this decision. Imagine getting paid for doing something which they really enjoyed – making the old man's life miserable! When the boys returned the following evening, they received the same reward again – another two euros each. This practice puzzled the boys but they continued to wreak havoc on the old man. After a week, however, the man told them that he could not afford to pay each of them the two euros that they had been given previously. In fact, all he could manage was fifty cents each. This disappointed the boys a little but they continued to torment the man. Another week elapsed and this time, the old man reduced the reward to twenty cents each. Again, this was very frustrating to the boys who had grown used to receiving a larger reward. Eventually, the old man reduced the reward to two cents each – at which time, the leader of the boys grew very angry. Shouting at the old man, he said, "We've had enough of your meanness. If you think that we're going to play football for your entertainment outside your house for two cents, then you've got another think coming! We're off!" Clearly, the moral of this tale is that when the old man removed extrinsic motivation for the football, the boys lost interest in doing what they had done previously for nothing.

Critical thinking questions

Do you think that this story has any relevance for understanding why highly paid sports performers sometimes lose their motivation? From your knowledge of other areas of psychology (e.g., behaviour modification), can you think of any other explanation of the boys' loss of motivation? Can cognitive evaluation theory (see text for description) offer any insights into what happened in this story?

As you can see from Box 2.2, if people who are performing an activity for the sheer fun of it are given external rewards, their level of intrinsic motivation may decrease (Deci, 1971). Interestingly, there is evidence that athletes who engage in sporting activity to receive a trophy tend to show a subsequent decrease in intrinsic motivation as measured by self-report scales (Vallerand and Rousseau, 2001). In an effort to explain this somewhat surprising finding, cognitive evaluation theory (Deci and Ryan, 1991) suggested that the way in which rewards are perceived must be considered. Briefly, this theory assumes that rewards can fulfil one of two functions: "controlling" (i.e., those which influence behaviour) or "informational" (i.e., those which provide feedback about the performer's level of performance on a given task). Depending on how athletes perceive rewards, their intrinsic motivation may be either enhanced or reduced. For example, if they believe that their sporting behaviour is controlled by external rewards, their level of intrinsic motivation may decline. On the other hand, if rewards are perceived as merely providing feedback, then intrinsic motivation will probably increase. According to cognitive evaluation theory, controlling rewards tend to impair intrinsic motivation whereas informational rewards may strengthen it. Before we conclude this section, it is important to consider the relationship between praise (which we can define as communicating a positive evaluation of another person's performance or attributes to him/her) and motivation. It has long been assumed that praise enhances children's motivation. But is this really true? In a recent critique of this claim, Henderlong and Lepper (2002) argued that when praise is perceived as being sincere, it is beneficial to motivation as long as it conveys attainable standards and expectations and encourages people to make "attributions" (see later in chapter) to controllable causes. Interestingly, praise may inadvertently undermine children's motivation – perhaps because it encourages invidious social comparison processes.

Having considered the nature and types of motivation, let us now review the main theoretical approaches to this construct in sport and exercise psychology.

Theories of motivation: from personality to cognition

Historically, two major theoretical approaches have dominated research on motivational processes in sport and exercise over the past fifty years – the personality model (epitomised by research on individual differences in people's need for achievement) and two social-cognitive models (including the goal-orientation approach and attribution theory). Perhaps the most important difference between these two approaches is that whereas personality theorists view people as being driven by deep-seated psychological needs, social-cognitive researchers are more concerned with understanding how people's thoughts and perceptions guide their behaviour. Another difference between these approaches is that whereas personality theorists are concerned mainly with the origins of people's achievement strivings (i.e., the past determinants of their needs), cognitive motivational researchers are more interested in people's choice of future actions (Roberts, 2001). Let us now review the theoretical rationale of each of these approaches in more detail.

The personality approach

Initially, sport psychologists tried to account for athletes' motivational processes by referring to two types of variables – innate instincts and learned drives. Superficially, such theories seem plausible. For example, aggressive behaviour on the football field is commonly attributed to the possession of an aggressive nature. But on closer inspection, this approach is flawed by circularity of reasoning. The difficulty here is that any scientific explanation for a phenomenon must be independent of the phenomenon itself. Otherwise, one unknown variable is used to "explain" another. This problem of proposing circular explanations for people's behaviour has a long history and was satirised by Molière in *La Malade Imaginaire* when he made fun of doctors who had suggested that what gives opium its soporific quality is its "virtus dormitiva" – or soporific quality! In a similar vein, aggressive actions cannot be explained adequately by appealing to hypothetical aggressive instincts – because the existence of these instincts depends on evidence of aggressive behaviour. On logical grounds, therefore, instinct theories of motivation have been discredited significantly in psychology.

Following the demise of instinct theory, sport psychologists turned to *personality traits* in an effort to account for motivational phenomena. One trait of particular interest was a construct called "need for achievement" (see McClelland, Atkinson, Clark and Lowell, 1953). Briefly, this trait was believed to be elicited by situations involving approach–avoidance conflicts. In such situations, people face a dilemma in which their natural desire to achieve success (i.e., their "need to achieve") is challenged by their fear of failure. Theoretically, athletes were said to have a relatively high level of achievement motivation if their need to achieve was greater than their fear of failure. Conversely, they were alleged to have a relatively low level of achievement motivation when their fear of failure exceeded their desire to succeed. According to McClelland and his colleagues, people with high achievement needs are impelled to seek challenging but realistic objectives for their performance in competitive settings. Applied to sport, this principle suggests that athletes who have a high need to achieve should prefer to compete against opponents of a similar, or slightly higher, level of ability. By contrast, athletes with low achievement motivation tend to avoid challenging situations and should prefer to compete against opponents of lower ability levels. Despite its intuitive appeal, this theory has made little progress in accounting for the motivational behaviour of sport performers. This situation is attributable to two main problems. First, there is a dearth of valid instruments available for the measurement of achievement motivation in athletes (Roberts, Spink and Pemberton, 1999). In addition, researchers have criticised the assumption in traditional achievement motivation theory that success and failure may be defined objectively. Thus Maehr and Nicholls (1980) argued that these variables are largely subjective because they are usually defined in relation to people's *perception* of goal achievement. For example, whereas some athletes may regard "success" as being defined by defeating an opponent or winning a competition, others may perceive it in relation to achieving a "personal best" performance or impressing their coach or parents.

Recognition of this subjective influence on people's achievement strivings influenced researchers to switch from a personality-based to a social-cognitive approach in the study of motivation in athletes. This change in emphasis had important theoretical implications for sport psychology. As Kremer, Sheehy, Reilly, Trew and Muldoon (2003) observed, it "switched attention from the 'what' or content of motivation to the 'why' or process whereby we are or are not motivated" (p. 188). Within the social-cognitive paradigm of motivation research, two conceptual models deserve special mention: achievement goal theory and attribution theory. Let us now examine each of these approaches briefly.

The social-cognitive approach: achievement goal theory

The main assumption of the social-cognitive approach to motivation in sport is that athletes' behaviour in achievement situations is a consequence of their perception of "success" in different contexts (Roberts, 2001). Put differently, this approach suggests that in order to understand athletes' motivation, we need to explore what success means to them. Adopting this subjective approach, Maehr and Nicholls (1980) proposed that success and failure "are not concrete events. They are psychological states consequent on perception of reaching or not reaching goals" (p. 228). Within this paradigm, perhaps the most influential model has been "achievement goal" theory (see reviews by Duda, 2001; Duda and Hall, 2001; Weiss and Ferrer-Caja, 2002). Since this latter model has been hailed as "the most important conceptual avenue to address motivation in sport and physical education" (Roberts, 2001, p. 10), we need to examine its central propositions more closely.

Achievement goal theory postulates that two main types of motivation (or "goal orientations") may be identified in athletes depending on how they interpret the goal of achievement (or success). The first type of motivation is called a "task orientation". With this outlook, the athlete is interested mainly in subjective indices of success such as skill learning, mastery of challenges and self-improvement. For example, a task-oriented athlete may perceive herself or himself to be successful if s/he can perform a specific sport skill (e.g., serving a tennis ball) better today than s/he did three weeks ago. The second type of motivation is called an "ego orientation" and stems from a view of success that is normative or defined in relation to the attainments of other people. For example, an ego-oriented athlete regards herself or himself as successful only if s/he performs better than others. In other words, such a person is interested only in demonstrating superior ability to others. Therefore, winning and beating others are the main preoccupations of ego-oriented athletes.

These goal orientations are assumed to be independent. Therefore, a person may achieve a high or a low score on either goal orientation or both at the same time. What does research reveal about the correlates of these two motives?

According to Lemyre, Roberts and Ommundsen (2002), task-oriented athletes perceive achievement in sport in self-referenced terms involving skill improvement/ mastery and technical development. As a consequence, they tend to be intrinsically interested in the task, willing to expend effort in persisting with it and, above all, guided by personal standards of achievement rather than by prevailing social norms. Conversely, ego-oriented athletes strive to "demonstrate superior normative ability, or avoid the demonstration of incompetence at the task at hand" (p. 122). In other words, they judge their own success by the degree to which they can perform better than others. Thus winning and defeating others is their primary concern in athletic situations. This description of ego-oriented performers brings to mind a quotation attributed to the writer Gore Vidal: "it's not enough to succeed – others must fail!" (cited in McErlane, 2002, p. 3).

Having outlined briefly what these two goal orientations involve, let us now consider how they can be measured psychologically before sketching some general findings in this field.

Measuring achievement goal orientations

Task and ego goal orientations may be assessed using questionnaires such as the "Task and Ego Orientation in Sport Questionnaire" (TEOSQ; Duda and Nicholls, 1992; see also review by Duda and Whitehead, 1998) and/or the "Perceptions of Success Questionnaire" (POSQ; Roberts, Treasure and Balague, 1998). The TEOSQ consists of thirteen items – seven of which measure a task orientation and six of which assess an ego orientation. Participants are required to respond to the generic stem "I feel most successful in my sport when . . ." using a five-point Likert scale. Responses range from 1 (strongly disagree) to 5 (strongly agree). Typical items in the task orientation scale are "I learn a new skill by trying hard" or "I do my very best". Similarly, typical items on the ego orientation scale include "The others can't do as well as me" or "I'm the best". Psychometric research indicates that these scales possess adequate reliability (Duda and Whitehead, 1998). The POSQ is a twelve-item test of task and ego orientation with six items in each sub-scale. In this test, the stem item is "When playing my sport, I feel most successful when . . .". Typical items in the task orientation sub-scale include: "I work hard" (item 1) or "I master something I couldn't do before". Meanwhile, the ego orientation sub-scale comprises items such as "I am the best" or "I accomplish something others can't do". As with the TEOSQ, there is evidence of acceptable validity and reliability for the POSQ (Harwood, 2002).

Some research findings on achievement goal theory

A number of predictions from achievement goal theory have been tested by researchers. First, children who hold task-oriented goals (e.g., wanting to learn new skills) should show persistence in sport situations whereas more ego-motivated counterparts may drop out of sport at an earlier stage. Some support for this prediction has been found (see review by Weiss and Ferrer-Caja, 2002). Second, achievement goal theory predicts that athletes with different goal orientations will have different beliefs about the causes of their success. As in the previous case, this hypothesis has received some empirical support. Thus task-oriented athletes tend to regard athletic success as being determined significantly by the expenditure of effort. By contrast, athletes with an ego orientation typically believe that success is achieved mainly by having high ability (Roberts, 2001). Interestingly, the belief that effort rather than ability leads to success may help to explain why task-oriented athletes tend to persist longer in sport than do ego-oriented counterparts. A third trend in research findings in this field is that athletes' goal orientations are related to the way in which they cope with anxiety. For example, Ntoumanis, Biddle and Haddock (1999) discovered that when exposed to stressful situations, task-oriented student athletes tended to use problem-solving strategies (e.g., exerting more effort, seeking social support) whereas those with a predominant ego orientation tended to rely on emotion-focused coping strategies (e.g., venting their emotions). Furthermore, a task orientation was found to be negatively associated with thoughts about wanting to escape from a losing situation in sport whereas an ego orientation was positively associated with such thoughts (Hatzigeorgiadis, 2002).

So far, we have examined the predictions of achievement goal theory in sport as if no moderating variables were involved. Unfortunately, the impact of situational factors in this field needs to be considered carefully. Not surprisingly, therefore, researchers in this field have postulated that an intervening variable called "motivational climate" regulates the relationship between goal orientation and athletic performance. According to Ames (1992), motivational climate refers to the perceived structure of the achievement environment as mediated by the coach's attitudes and behaviour. In general, two types of climate may be identified. A "mastery" climate is perceived when the coach places the emphasis on personal effort and skill development. In such an environment, mistakes are regarded as sources of feedback and learning. By contrast, an "ego-oriented" motivational climate is said to prevail when athletes are compared with, and pitted against, each other and when their mistakes are criticised and punished (Duda and Pensgaard, 2002). A scale has been developed by Walling, Duda and Chi (1993) to measure the "Perceived Motivational Climate in Sport".

Several trends are evident from research findings on motivational climates in sport. To begin with, available evidence (over 14 studies based on about 4,500 participants) suggests that a task-orientation or mastery climate is correlated significantly positively with athletes' satisfaction and intrinsic motivation (r of approximately 0.70). Next, an ego-oriented climate is typically correlated negatively with similar motivational indices (approximate $r = 0.3$) (Harwood and Biddle, 2002). One possible reason for the perceived advantage of the task-oriented climate over the ego-oriented one is that in the former, the athlete is encouraged to focus on factors within his or her control whereas in the latter, athletes tend to use social comparison processes when assessing their own competence (Duda and Hall, 2001). Generally, most achievement goal theorists (e.g., Ames, 1992; Nicholls, 1992) advocate the importance of cultivating a task-oriented climate in which athletes are taught to value effort, skill-mastery and intrinsic motivation rather than an ego-oriented climate in which the goal of defeating others is paramount. Theoretically, task-oriented motivational climates can be cultivated by the provision of coaching feedback that focuses on athletes' performance relative to self-referenced criteria of achievement and improvement. The value of an ego-oriented climate should not be dismissed completely, however. Thus Hardy, Jones and Gould (1996) argued that some degree of ego involvement is a necessary prerequisite of success for any elite athlete.

Having sketched the nature, measurement and predictions of achievement goal theory, it is time to evaluate its contribution to motivational research in sport. In Box 2.3, we present a brief critical appraisal of this theory.

Box 2.3 Thinking critically about . . . achievement goal theory in sport

According to Duda and Hall (2001), achievement goal theory is "a major theoretical paradigm in sport psychology" (p. 417). Although this claim may be true, the theory itself suffers from a number of limitations which can be specified as follows.

First, as Duda and Hall (2001) acknowledged, achievement goal theorists are rather vague about the ways in which athletes' goal orientations interact with situational factors such as perceived motivational climate in order to determine motivational behaviour. In addition, a preoccupation with task- and ego-oriented goal orientations has led to the neglect of *other* possible goal perspectives in sport such as affiliative needs. A third problem with achievement goal theory was noted by Kremer and Busby (1998) in relation to understanding participant motivation – the question of why some people persist with physical activity whereas other people drop out of it. In particular, these authors pointed out that it is somewhat naïve to expect that task and ego orientations do not overlap considerably in real life. For example, whereas some people may initially involve themselves in physical activity for task-oriented reasons (such as losing weight), they may learn to love such activity for its own sake over time. In other words, people's motivational orientation is neither fixed nor static. A fourth problem with achievement goal theory in sport psychology is that although there have been many studies on athletes' goal orientations, there have been few studies on athletes' "goal states" – or the type of achievement goals that athletes pursue in specific sport situations (Harwood and Biddle, 2002). Finally, as Harwood (2002) pointed out, nomothetic measures of goal orientation such as the TEOSQ (Duda and Nicholls, 1992) are often used inappropriately for the purposes of quantitative idiographic assessment of individual athletes even though such tests are poor at identifying the differences between high, moderate and low task-orientation scores. Furthermore, there is some evidence (Harwood, 2002) that athletes' goal orientations may be more context-specific than had previously been realised. For example, an athlete's goal orientation in training may differ significantly from that which s/he displays in competitive settings. Also, as Roberts (2001) acknowledged, athletes may shift their goal orientation within a game. To illustrate, a tennis player may begin a match with the ego-related aim of defeating an opponent but may soon realise that this will probably prove impossible. So, gradually, this player may choose instead to disregard the score and use the game as an opportunity to practise some new technical skills that s/he has acquired. In summary, achievement goal theory is plagued by conceptual and methodological issues.

Critical thinking questions
Does a typology like task- versus ego-oriented motivation really explain anything – or is it merely a convenient way of classifying behaviour? What specific predictions does goal achievement theory make about the relationship between goal orientation and athletic performance? As there are many anecdotal examples of elite athletes with prominent ego orientations (e.g., John McEnroe), is this type of goal perspective necessarily a bad thing for athletes?

Having reviewed research on achievement goal theory, let us now turn to the second of the social-cognitive approaches to motivation in sport psychology – namely, attribution theory or the study of how people construct explanations for the successes and failures which they experience.

Social-cognitive approach: attribution theory

Attribution theory is a vibrant research field in mainstream psychology that explores people's explanations for the causes of events and behaviour. Although space limitations preclude detailed coverage of this field, see Biddle and Hanrahan (1998), Biddle, Hanrahan and Sellars (2001) and McAuley and Blissmer (2002) for recent reviews of attributional research in sport psychology. Before outlining the attributional approach to motivation in athletes, some background information on this theory is required.

Put simply, the term attribution (which is associated with Heider, 1958, one of the progenitors of this field) refers to the cause or reason which people propose when they try to explain why something happened to them. For example, a tennis player may attribute her victory over an opponent in a long match to her own "never say die" attitude on court. Conversely, the manager of a football team may ascribe a defeat to some misfortune over which s/he had no control (e.g., a series of unfair refereeing decisions during the match). There is an important difference between these two examples of attribution, however. In the first case, the tennis player's attribution is made to a *personal* quality – namely, her high motivation – whereas in the second case, the football manager's attribution is made to an external cause (the referee). This distinction highlights the difference between internal or "dispositional" attributions (i.e., explanations that invoke stable individual personality characteristics of the person in question) and external or "situational" attributions (i.e., explanations that refer to environmental causes of a given outcome or event). Attributions may also vary in dimensions other than this one of internal versus external locus of causality. Thus some attribution theorists postulate that people's explanations for events vary in stability (i.e., whether the perceived cause is consistent or variable over time) as well as controllability (i.e., the degree to which the person involved – the "actor" – could exert personal influence over the outcome in question).

Some research findings on attribution theory

In sport and exercise psychology, one of the earliest attributional questions addressed was whether or not winners differ from losers in the type of explanation which they provide for their sporting behaviour. As expected, research findings have generally supported this hypothesis (see Biddle and Hanrahan, 1998). Specifically, in contrast to their less successful counterparts, winners in sport tend to favour attributions to internal and personally controllable factors such as degree of preparation or amount of practice conducted. Such attributions for success are important because they may be predictive of *future* athletic achievement. For example, if a young sprinter attributes a sequence of poor performances to a lack of ability (a relatively stable internal factor) rather than to the high quality of his or her opponents (a variable external factor), then s/he may become demoralised and lose motivation. In this way, attribution theory, or the study of how people construct explanations for their successes and failures, has a number of practical implications for everyday life. To illustrate, consider the common finding that people tend to accept personal responsibility for successful outcomes but blame others for significant failures (the so-called "credit for success, blame for failure" tendency). For example, a student who passes an exam is likely to attribute this result to internal factors like hard work or high intelligence but a student who fails an exam may explain it with reference to bad luck or being asked the "wrong" questions. In a similar vein, managers of losing teams tend to make excuses for poor results (see Figure 2.1).

Figure 2.1 Managers of losing teams tend to make excuses

Why do managers tend to make excuses for poor results or performances by their teams? One obvious explanation is that managers may use excuses in order to preserve their sense of self-esteem in the fickle world of sporting success. Another possible explanation is that excuses help people to present a favourable image to others. In order to explore further this tendency for people to internalise their successes and to externalise their failures, try the research exercise in Box 2.4.

Box 2.4 Exploring the self-serving bias by analysing sports reports in newspapers (based on McIlveen, 1992)

The "self-serving" attributional bias is a tendency for people to make internal attributions for success and external attributions for failure. They do this mainly to protect their self-esteem. But as this tendency has been usually tested using laboratory paradigms in which the participants have little personal interest in the outcomes under consideration, it is difficult to generalise such research to everyday life settings. This problem can be overcome, however, by taking advantage of a naturally occurring situation in which people are asked to give explanations for events which occured in their lives and which affect them in significant ways (Lau and Russell, 1980). A good example of such a situation is the post match interview with football managers. In this situation, self-serving biases are likely to occur as managers try to explain the apparent causes of match outcomes (see McIlveen, 1992).

Hypothesis
That victories in football matches will be attributed more frequently to internal than to external factors whereas defeats will be attributed more frequently to external than to internal factors.

Instructions
The first step in this exercise is to locate possible attributional content in newspaper coverage of football matches. In particular, you should try to find twenty attributions for team success or failure in matches involving the Premiership and/or First Division in England. Both tabloid and broadsheet daily newspapers should be consulted in this regard. Look out especially for quotations from players or managers that contain a possible explanation for the outcome of the match. The match result could be coded crudely as a success if the attributor's team won the match and a failure if the team lost the match. The perceived cause of the attribution should be deemed internal if the player or manager referred to something personal about the team (e.g., its character or ability) in the explanation provided. Conversely, the locus of causality may be deemed external if the player or manager attributed the result to something *outside* the team or its players (e.g., bad weather).

Analysis
A 2×2 contingency table should be constructed in which outcome (success or failure) and perceived cause (internal or external) are the row and column

variables, respectively. Next, enter the number of attributions that fall into each of the four categories in this table. Then, using a chi-square test (check your statistics book/notes to find out how to use this test), work out the statistical relationship between match outcome and type of attribution. If the self-serving bias is present, we would expect a significantly higher proportion of internal than external attributions for successful results and a significantly higher proportion of external than internal attributions for failure outcomes.

Issues for discussion
Are success and failure objective events? How would achievement goal theorists answer this question? In any case, can we be sure that people's attributions expressed in public situations reflect what they really believe?

So far, we have presented attribution theory as a powerful theory of people's attempt to make sense of their world. But this theory suffers from several limitations.

Weaknesses of attribution theory

At least three weaknesses have been identified in the application of attribution theory to sport (see Biddle, Hanrahan and Sellars, 2001). First, it seems clear that athletic success and failure are neither objective events nor synonymous with winning and losing, respectively. To illustrate, imagine interviewing an athlete who won a competitive race – but by a very close margin. Superficially, this performer embodies a winning mentality. But what if this person's opponents were of a low athletic standard? In this case, the athlete may not regard barely winning a race against a poor field as being a successful performance at all. Therefore, Biddle *et al.* (2001) argued that a win is not always perceived as being a success and a loss is not always seen as an index of failure. The practical implication of this principle is that attribution researchers in sport and exercise psychology now tend to use *subjective* indices of success and failure whenever possible. A second problem for attribution theory in sport is that researchers cannot always be sure about what participants mean by certain words or phrases. For example, if a golfer says that his or her opponent "played better" than s/he did in a match-play event, does this signal a stable attribution (such that "my opponent is likely to defeat me again because s/he is simply a better player") or an unstable attribution ("my opponent defeated me on the day – but I believe that I can defeat him/her the next time we play")? Clearly, researchers in this field should adopt a painstaking approach when investigating what participants mean in using certain phrases (Biddle *et al.*, 2001). A third complication for attribution research in sport is that individual differences in explanatory tendencies may affect the attributions that athletes make. Indeed, research suggests that there is a link between the way in which athletes tend to explain events (their "attributional style") and their motivation to compete. Put simply, optimism and pessimism have motivational consequences. For example, when sport performers habitually explain negative outcomes (such as losing a match) by references to personal factors (i.e., to perceived causes which are internal, stable and global, such as "it's down to me; I can't change it and it seems to affect my whole life"), they are said to display a "*pessimistic*" explanatory style. In this frame of mind, people may behave as if they are powerless to change their situation. Not surprisingly, this despondency often leads to a loss in motivation. By contrast, when athletes attribute negative outcomes to external, unstable and specific causes (e.g., "my defeat was just a freak occurrence and it doesn't affect the most important things in my life"), they are displaying an "*optimistic*" explanatory style – which helps them to learn from their defeat and to work harder in the future. Clearly, certain athletes can achieve a healthy resilience by thinking optimistically in the face of adversity. Why does optimism make athletes more resilient? One possible explanation (Seligman, 1998) is that an optimistic outlook allows athletes to keep their confidence levels high – encouraging them to believe that they have the ability to overcome any temporary setbacks. Put simply, therefore, athletes with low motivation tend to interpret setbacks as being permanent. On the other hand, optimists tend to believe that positive outcomes (e.g., winning a football match) are not caused by luck but have causes that are relatively permanent in nature (such as ability).

Attributional style and athletic performance

As explained earlier, the term attributional style or "explanatory style" (ES) refers to people's tendency to offer similar kinds of explanations for different events in their lives. More precisely, it reflects "how people habitually explain the causes of events" (Peterson, Buchanan and Seligman, 1995, p. 19). It can be measured using a general self-report instrument called the "Attributional Style Questionnaire" (ASQ; Peterson, Semmel, Von Baeyer, Abramson, Metalsky and Seligman, 1982). This questionnaire requires people to identify causes for twelve hypothetical situations (involving six "good" outcomes and six "bad" outcomes) and to rate these causes along three bipolar dimensions: locus of causality, stability and globality. As explained earlier, the first of these dimensions refers to whether the alleged causal event is internal (due to the person involved) or external (due to someone else). The second dimension relates to whether the cause in question is stable (or likely to last for the foreseeable future) or unstable (i.e., short-lived). The third dimension refers to whether it is global (i.e., likely to affect every aspect of one's life) or specific (i.e., or highly circumscribed in its effects). Although the ASQ is psychometrically adequate, it is not designed specifically for athletic populations. Therefore, an alternative test called the Sport Attributional Style Scale (SASS; Hanrahan, Grove and Hattie, 1989) was devised for use in sport and exercise settings. This sixteen-item scale is also available in a shortened (ten-item) format (Hanrahan and Grove, 1990). In general, psychometric evidence in support of the SASS has been encouraging (Biddle and Hanrahan, 1998). For example, most of its sub-scales appear to be correlated significantly with those of the criterion instrument, the Attributional Style Questionnaire (ASQ).

Research on the relationship between explanatory style and athletic performance has generated some interesting findings. For example, Seligman, Nolen-Hoeksema, Thornton and Thornton (1990) discovered that university swimmers with a pessimistic explanatory style (ES) were more likely to perform below the level of coaches' expectations during the season than were swimmers with a more optimistic outlook. In fact, the pessimists on the Attributional Style Questionnaire had about twice as many unexpectedly poor swims as did their optimistic colleagues. In the same study, pessimistic swimmers were less likely to "bounce back" from simulated defeats than were optimistic counterparts. Third, the explanatory style scores of the swimmers were significantly predictive of swimming performance even after coaches' judgements of ability to overcome a setback had been controlled for in the data analysis. Interestingly, these findings show that explanatory style is quite separate from athletic ability. Thus pessimistic ES profiles were as prevalent among high-level as among low-level performers. One implication of this finding is that a successful performance by itself will not engender confidence in an athlete. In other words, a sports performer has to *learn* to attribute successful events constructively in order to benefit optimally from them.

In another series of studies, Rettew and Reivich (1995) explored the correlates of explanatory style in a sample of professional athletes drawn from team sports such as basketball and baseball. Briefly, these authors found that basketball teams with relatively optimistic ES scores tended to perform significantly better than did those with a more pessimistic outlook. However, ES did not predict overall win percentage. Likewise, baseball teams with an optimistic ES profile tended to win more games than did their more pessimistic colleagues. Taken together, these studies show that explanatory style can predict certain aspects of team performance in sport – even when athletic ability levels are taken into consideration. A practical implication of these findings concerns attributional retraining. Specifically, Rettew and Reivich (1995) suggest that the most helpful ES in terms of future athletic success is one "that motivates the individual to continue doing whatever he or she does when things are going well but galvanises the player when things are not going well" (pp. 185).

So far, our discussion of attributional styles has been largely theoretical. But for a practical insight into this topic, try the exercise in Box 2.5.

Box 2.5 What is your typical explanatory style?

When something unpleasant or negative happens to you (e.g., failing an examination), ask yourself the following questions. First, what do you think was the main cause of the event? More precisely, are you responsible for it or is it due to some external circumstances? This question relates to the internal–external attributional dimension. Second, do you think that the cause will persist in the future? This question concerns the permanence of the attribution. Finally, there is the pervasiveness issue. How much will this event affect other areas of your life? By the way, if you cannot see the difference between "permanence" and "pervasiveness", then try thinking of the former as relating to time and the latter to space.

Overall, if you attributed the event to yourself (Q.1) and to things which will not change in the future (Q. 2) and if you believe that it affects all of your life (Q. 3), then you probably have a *pessimistic* explanatory style. If so, then you have a tendency to explain misfortune by saying "it's my fault" (person-alisation), "it will never change" (permanence) and "it's going to ruin my whole life" (pervasiveness). Optimists, on the other hand, tend to interpret setbacks as being caused by temporary circumstances which may change in the future.

Before we conclude this section of the chapter, I would like to explore the coaching implications of research on explanatory styles.

Implications of research on explanatory styles

According to Seligman (1998), research on attributional style has several practical implications for sport performance. First, an optimistic explanatory style is not something that is immediately apparent to coaches. As this author put it, the ASQ "measures something you can't. It predicts success beyond experienced coaches' judgements and handicappers' expertise" (p. 166). Second, athletes' or players' levels of optimism have implications for when to use them in team events. Thus, in general, pessimistic players should be used only after they have done well – not when they are in a run of poor form. Third, in talent search programmes, optimists may be better bets than pessimists as they will probably perform better in the long run. Finally, pessimistic athletes can be trained to become more optimistic. As Seligman put it, "unlike IQ or your waistline, pessimism is one of those characteristics that is entirely changeable" (cited in DeAngelis, 1996, p. 33).

Having learned about the nature of athletes' attributional tendencies, can these thinking patterns be changed through professional intervention? On the basis that this practice has produced some encouraging results in clinical psychology (see Fosterling, 1988), attributional retraining may be worth trying in sport settings. For example, if a coach could change a lazy athlete's tendency to make attributions to unstable/internal dimensions, then such a performer may discover that the expenditure of additional effort is helpful. Conversely, performers who are prone to "depressogenic" attributions (e.g., by ascribing unwanted outcomes to stable/internal factors) may be helped by encouraging them to externalise their explanations. In general, coaches can help athletes to become more self-reliant by helping them to decrease their tendency to use external attributions after poor performances and instead to use internal attributions. For example, a golfer may confide in her coach that she had been lucky to get away with a bunker shot that barely skimmed the rim of the bunker before landing on the green. This attribution to an external unstable factor (e.g., luck) may erode a player's confidence over time. But if the golfer could be trained to rephrase this attribution to an internal source (e.g., "If I concentrate on getting more elevation on my sand shots, I will become a much better bunker player"), then she will probably be more motivated to practise her bunker play more assiduously.

In a study of this topic, Orbach, Singer and Price (1999) investigated the effects of an attributional training programme on the manner in which thirty-five tennis players explained failure on a tennis skills test. Performers were assigned to one of three treatment groups: those involving controllable and unstable attributions (CU group), those involving uncontrollable and stable attributions (US group) and those in a non-attributional control condition. Results showed that not only is it possible to alter people's attributions for their performance – but that such modified attributions remained stable for at least three weeks afterwards. Interestingly, attributional retraining has also been applied successfully to young athletes. Thus Sinnott and Biddle (1998) tested twelve children whose ages ranged between 11 and 12 years. Half of these children rated their performance on a ball-dribbling task as being poor while the other half rated themselves as performing this skill successfully. Following attributional retraining, the former group showed significant increases not only in their self-ratings but also in their level of intrinsic motivation (see Chapter 2). Although the potential value of attributional retraining is impressive, a great deal of additional research is required to evaluate the nature and scope of this phenomenon in sport and exercise psychology.

Now that we have explored the nature of motivation and some theoretical perspectives on it, let us turn to the question of how it can be increased in athletes.

Increasing motivation in athletes: goal-setting in sport

Effective motivation requires direction as well as drive or energy. To understand this idea, consider the following analogy. Imagine a car being driven around in circles in a carpark. Although its engine is in perfect working order, the vehicle is not actually going anywhere. Clearly, what is needed is a signpost that can direct the driver out of the carpark and towards his or her destination. By analogy, athletes require a map or signpost which will channel their motivational energy effectively. One way of providing this signpost is through a procedure called "goal-setting" (see reviews by Burton and Naylor, 2002; Weinberg, 2002). As we shall see, this procedure is "a highly consistent and a robust performance enhancement strategy" (Burton and Naylor, 2002, p. 463) that is alleged to enhance motivation in athletes.

What is goal-setting?

A goal is a target or objective which people strive to attain. For example, it might be winning a match, losing weight or being selected for a club team or national squad (Weinberg, 2002). So, goal-setting is the process by which people establish desirable objectives for their actions.

Within sport and exercise psychology, research on goal-setting has been influenced by two distinct theoretical traditions: cognitive psychology and organisational psychology. To illustrate the former lineage, cognitive researchers such as Tolman (1932) proclaimed that human actions are understood best as the outcome of internally represented conscious goals rather than as the product of environmental forces. The organisational roots of research in this field come from theorists like Taylor (1911/1967) and Locke and Latham (1985) who extolled the merits of goal-setting for performance enhancement. To illustrate, in an early review of this topic within organisational psychology, Locke, Shaw, Saari and Latham (1981) concluded that "the beneficial effect of goal-setting on task performance is one of the most replicable findings in the psychological literature. Ninety per cent of the studies showed positive or partially positive effects" (p. 145). Later Locke and Latham (1990) claimed that of 201 studies on goal-setting, positive effects on performance were shown for 183 of them – resulting in an estimate of 91 per cent success rate for goal-setting. Equivalent (if more modest) claims about the efficacy of goal-setting also emerged from studies in sport settings. Thus Burton, Naylor and Holliday (2001) reported that forty-four out of fifty-six published studies (almost 79 per cent) yielded moderate to strong effects of goal-setting on athletic performance. From a cursory inspection of these figures, it appears that the effects of goal-setting in sport are not quite as impressive as they are in organisational settings. We shall return to this issue later. At this stage, however, we need to explore what psychological research reveals about goal-setting in athletes.

Types of goals

Three main types of goals have been identified in sport and exercise psychology research (Weinberg, 2002). First, "outcome" or result goals are objective targets such as winning a competition, defeating an opponent or achieving a desired finishing position (e.g., making the cut in a golf tournament). What is not often appreciated about such goals, however, is the extent to which their achievement depends on the ability and performance of one's opponents. For example, a tennis player could play the best game of his or her life but still lose a match because the opposing player has played better on the day. The second type of objective encountered in sport is the "performance" goal. This goal designates the attainment of a personal standard of competence with regard to technique (e.g., learning to hit a top-spin backhand in tennis), effort (e.g., "giving 100 per cent effort at all times in a match"), time (running a marathon in less than four hours) distance and/or height (in certain athletic events). Unlike its predecessor, the characteristic feature of performance goals is that they are largely under the control of the performer. For example, a golfer could set as her performance goal the task of putting to within 30 cm of the hole every time she is on the green. Nobody can stop the player from achieving this level of accuracy because putting is a self-paced skill. The third type of target studied in sport psychology is the "process" goal – or a behavioural strategy by which an athlete executes a particular skill. For example, in golf, a process goal in putting might be to keep one's head steady while taking a slow backswing.

As they can be controlled directly, performance and process goals are usually regarded as being more motivational for athletes than are result goals. For example, Weinberg (2002) exhorted people "to set goals that are based on their own levels of performance rather than on the outcome of winning and losing" (p. 38). Likewise, Orlick (1986) proclaimed that "day-to-day goals for training and for competition should focus on the means by which you can draw out your own potential. Daily goals should be aimed at the improvement of personal control over your performance, yourself, and the obstacles you face" (p. 10). In a similar vein, Gould (1998) proposed that athletes should "set process and performance goals as opposed to outcome goals" (p. 187) and Hodge and McKenzie (1999) advised athletes to "set performance goals rather than outcome goals" (p. 31). Unfortunately, this emphasis on performance goals is not completely supported by research findings. For example, a quantitative literature review by Kyllo and Landers (1995) found that performance goals were no more effective than result goals in enhancing skills. But why exactly should goals motivate athletes and improve their performance?

Why should goals enhance performance?

Goal-setting is believed to affect athletic performance in at least five ways (Locke and Latham, 2002; Weinberg, 2002). First, goals serve to focus and direct attention towards relevant actions. For example, if an athlete is told that unless she becomes fitter she will be dropped from a basketball team, she may not know what action to take. But if she is advised to improve her performance on a specific index of fitness such as the "bleep test" by a certain date, then she is clearer about what is expected of her. Likewise, a tennis player who tries to achieve at least 70 per cent accuracy on his first serve should be less distractible on court than a player who has no objective for the match. Second, goals help to elicit effort and commitment from athletes. Presumably, that is why coaches give "pep talks" at half-time in football matches (see Chapter 3): to remind players what they are striving for collectively. Third, goals provide incentives that may foster persistence in athletes, especially if they can measure their progress towards the targets in question. For example, a weekly fitness chart could be maintained for all members of a squad in order to encourage them to adhere to prescribed training regimes. According to Burton *et al.* (2001), the preceding theoretical mechanisms may explain why goals tend to have impressive short-term influences on athletic performance. But how do they enhance the development of new strategies over a longer period of time? This leads us to the fourth putative mechanism of goal-setting effects. Specifically, goals may work simply because they help athletes to break large problems into smaller components and then develop action plans for dealing with these sub-goals. For example, a golfer who wants to achieve greater accuracy off the tee may go to the driving range to hit a bucket of balls at a designated target. In so doing, s/he has begun to practise using a problem-solving approach to the game. Fifth, goals may influence athletic performance indirectly by boosting athletes' self-confidence (e.g., "I'm delighted to have achieved that goal – it restores my faith in my own ability") as well as their sense of satisfaction ("That win felt really great"). This latter possibility that goals may influence performance through the mediation of cognitive factors reminds us of the achievement goal theory that we mentioned earlier in this chapter. As you may recall, this theory proposes that athletes' motivational behaviour is influenced by their goal orientation (whether task- or ego-related) as well as by their perception of their own athletic ability.

Research on goal-setting in sport and exercise psychology: principles, findings and issues

Goal-setting is not only one of the most widely used performance-enhancement techniques in sport and exercise psychology but also one of the most extensively researched. The typical paradigm for such research involves a comparison between the performance of people who have been instructed to set goals according to certain criteria (e.g., specific goals) with that of counterparts who have been told simply to "do your best". Often, a third sample of participants is used: a control group of people who are given no advice on goal-setting. Using this paradigm, researchers have sought to explore the characteristics of goals that make them most effective in sport settings. This topic is known as "goal attribute" research (Burton and Naylor, 2002).

Based largely on organisational psychology (see Locke and Latham, 1985), various theoretical principles have been postulated in an effort to guide research on goal-setting in sport (Weinberg, 2002). First, the more specific the goal, the more likely it is to be effective. Second, goals are alleged to work best when they are realistic but challenging. Third, goals should be written down to ensure maximum compliance. Fourth, separate goals should be established for practice and competition. Finally, progress towards goal achievement should be evaluated regularly for optimal benefits to occur. Have these principles been supported? In testing these ideas, the following general findings have emerged (see comprehensive reviews by Burton *et al.*, 2001; Burton and Naylor, 2002; Hall and Kerr, 2001; Weinberg, 2002).

First, although goal-setting is one of the most widely used interventions in applied sport psychology, most athletes rate goals as being "only moderately effective" (Burton *et al.*, 2001, p. 497) facilitators of performance. This is largely because sport performers are not entirely clear about how best to maximise the effectiveness of their goals. In the next section of this chapter, we shall consider some practical ways of setting effective goals. Second, there is general agreement among researchers that specific goals are more effective than general goals, vague goals or no goals at all (Hall and Kerr, 2001). This finding, which is called the "goal specificity" effect, may be attributable to the greater precision of specific goals than general goals. However, an important caveat must be noted here. To explain, research on goal-setting in sport shows that it may not provide any incremental benefits to athletes who are *already* motivated to do their best (a phenomenon called the "ceiling effect"; see also Box 2.6). This point is illustrated by the fact that not all top athletes set goals for their performance. For example, as we learned earlier in this chapter, the Indian batsman Sachin Tendulkar claimed that he does not set any goals before matches. Another complicating factor here is that the complexity of the skill in question may serve as a mediating variable. Thus Burton (1989) investigated the effects of specific versus general goals on basketball skills of varying degrees of complexity. Results showed that although specific goals *did* enhance performance relative to general goals as predicted, this benefit was mediated by the level of complexity of the task – a fact which had not been predicted. As a third general finding in goal-setting research, Burton *et al.* (2001) claim that performance goals are more effective than result goals in improving athletic performance –

presumably because the former type of goals facilitate improved concentration processes in athletes (see also Chapter 4 for a discussion of goal-setting as a concentration technique). It should be noted, however, that goal-setting practice studies show that athletes tend to set both types of goals – performance and result – equally often (*ibid.*). A fourth general finding in the goal-setting research literature is that athletes and coaches are not systematic in writing down their goals (Weinberg, 2002). Fifth, research has accumulated on the "goal proximity" prediction – namely, the suggestion that short-term goals should be more effective motivationally than long-term goals. Surprisingly, this hypothesis has received only modest support in sport and exercise psychology (Hall and Kerr, 2001). Sixth, a number of practical barriers appear to hamper goal-setting practices among athletes. These barriers include such factors as a lack of time and distractions arising from social relationships (Weinberg, 2002). Seventh, the relationship between goals and performance is mediated by a host of intervening variables. For example, the level of ability of the performer, the extent to which s/he is committed to the goal, and the quantity and quality of feedback provided are all important factors in moderating the influence of goals on performance (Hall and Kerr, 2001). Finally, research evidence is accumulating to suggest that goal-setting skills can be taught to athletes. Thus Swain and Jones (1995) used a single-subject, multiple-baseline research design to examine the effects of a goal-setting intervention programme on the selected basketball skills (e.g., getting rebounds) of four elite university performers over a series of sixteen matches in a competitive season. Results showed that the intervention yielded significant positive effects on the targeted basketball skills for three out of four of the participants in the study.

In addition to the preceding findings, research in sport and exercise psychology has yielded two recurrent themes: "first, goals work well in sport, but not as well as in business; second, goal-setting is a paradox because this simple technique is somewhat more complicated than it looks" (Burton *et al.*, 2001, p. 497). Overall, such research indicates that although goal-setting affects performance, many of its principles derived from organisational contexts do not generalise to athletic domains. For example, setting specific goals is not always more effective in sport than is the practice of exhorting people to do their best. Having summarised the main principles and findings in this field, let us conclude this section by evaluating some unresolved issues in goal-setting research.

One of the most contentious issues in this field is the fact that goal-setting seems to be more effective in business settings than in sport. In an effort to explain this anomaly, Locke (1991) suggested that methodological factors may be involved. Specifically, he claimed that perhaps participants in the "no goal" and the "do your best" goal conditions actually set goals for themselves spontaneously. Also, there are many important conceptual differences between the fields of work and sport. For example, consider the issue of choice. To explain, Hall and Kerr (2001) noted that whereas most athletes have chosen to invest time and effort in pursuit of their sporting goals, the decision about whether or not to work is far less influenced by personal factors. In short, people *choose* to play sport – but they *have* to work, for economic reasons. This is why Weinberg and Weigand (1996) suggested that as they have chosen to participate in their chosen activities, sports performers are usually more motivated than average workers. Another problem with goal-setting studies in sport is that they are rather atheoretical. To explain, few researchers in this field have attempted to find out *why* people set the goals that they do. As Hall and Kerr (2001) observed, few investigators have studied "the causes underlying the particular goals an individual might adopt" (p. 186).

Having outlined relevant theory and research on goal-setting in sport, we should now consider some practical applications.

Practical application: motivational properties of goals

As we indicated earlier, goal-attribute research suggests that certain properties of goals should energise the behaviour of athletes. In particular, three characteristics of goals have been deemed to be especially motivational. These properties concern goal specificity, goal challenge and goal proximity (Bandura, 1997).

Goal specificity

Evidence suggests that goals which are stated in clear, specific and attainable terms tend to elicit more effort and better performance than do goals which are in more vague terms. For example, a golfer who is told to "drive the ball straight down the fairway – but don't worry about the distance you achieve" should try harder than someone who is told simply to "do your best". In this regard, Weinberg, Stitcher and Richardson (1994) found that college lacrosse players who had been given specific tasks to achieve during a season performed significantly better than did counterparts assigned to "do your best" goals.

Goal challenge or difficulty

According to Locke and Latham (1990), the more challenging the level of a goal in organisational settings, the more motivation it elicits. This principle does not seem to apply to sport, however. Thus surveys of goal-setting practices in athletes (reviewed in Burton and Naylor, 2002) indicated that sports performers are motivated best by *moderately* challenging goals.

Goal proximity

The issue of how far into the future goals are projected tends to affect people's motivation. Thus Bandura (1997) claimed that whereas "proximal" or short-term goals mobilise effort and persistence effectively, "distal goals alone are too far removed in time to provide effective incentives and guides for present action" (p. 134).

In addition to these features, goals should be stated positively as much as possible. For example, in soccer, it is better for a striker to set a positive goal such as "I am going to practise timing my runs into the box" than a negative goal such as

"I must try not to get caught off-side so often". The reason for this advice is that a goal which is stated positively tells the person what to do, whereas a negatively stated goal does not provide such explicit guidance.

Does goal-setting really work?

A rigorous "meta-analytic" review on the effects of goal-setting was conducted by Kyllo and Landers (1995) using data from thirty-six studies in this field. Briefly, meta-analysis is a quantitative statistical technique which combines the results of a large number of studies in order to determine the overall size of a statistical effect. According to Kyllo and Landers (1995), goal-setting was effective in enhancing performance in sport over baseline measures by about one third of a standard deviation (mean effect size of 0.34). This effect was increased when goals of a moderate level of difficulty were used. Also, as mentioned earlier, these researchers found that the greatest effects were obtained when the goals were result-based (which contradicts the received wisdom that performance goals work best), moderately difficult and agreed by the athletes themselves (i.e., self-set) rather than imposed from outside.

Earlier, we learned that most studies on goal-setting have been based on the theories of Locke and Latham (1985, 2002) in organisational psychology. These authors predicted that relative to either "no goal" or vague "do your best" instructions, athletes' performance should be enhanced when they use goals that are specific, short-term and difficult yet realistic. Unfortunately, research designed to test Locke and Latham's predictions in sport has produced equivocal findings. For example, several studies have failed to establish the allegedly beneficial effects of specific and realistic goals on people's performance of motor tasks. Thus Weinberg, Bruya, Garland and Jackson (1990) found that the performance of hand strength and "sit-up" tasks was related neither to goal difficulty nor to goal specificity. In an effort to explain this anomaly, a variety of conceptual and methodological issues in research on goal-setting in sport may be identified (Weinberg, 2002). These issues are discussed in Box 2.6.

Box 2.6 Thinking critically about . . . research on goal-setting in sport

Sport psychology is replete with claims about the value of goal-setting as a performance-enhancement strategy in sport. Thus Hall and Kerr (2001) asserted that "not only is the efficacy of goal setting assumed; it is also claimed that the technique is a fundamental psychological skill that all athletes must develop if they are to maximize athletic potential" (p. 183). But are these claims warranted by available evidence? How well do the goal-setting principles emerging from organisational settings apply to the world of sport? Although Locke (1991) claimed that goal-setting effects in sport are similar to those in business, Weinberg, Bruya and Jackson (1985) argued that there are significant differences between these two spheres. For example, Kremer and Scully (1994) observed that the extrinsic rewards arising from the world of work "stand in contrast to the intrinsic motivators which have been identified as being so crucial to maintaining an interest in amateur sport" (p. 145). Other problems in this field come from the following methodological flaws in research on goal-setting (see Burton *et al.*, 2001, and Burton and Naylor, 2002):

i Possible "ceiling effects"
There is evidence that the goal effectiveness curve flattens out or reaches a ceiling as people approach the limits of their ability. In other words, ability factors restrict the amount of improvement that can be made through goal-setting.

ii Complexity of task or skill
Goal-setting effects may not be noticeable when the tasks used to assess them require complex skills. In fact, research indicates that as tasks become more complex, athletes must learn to adopt strategic plans to extract maximum benefit from goal-setting practices (Hall and Kerr, 2001).

iii Individual differences
The relationship between goal-setting and performance may be moderated by strategic factors. Thus Burton *et al.* (2001) claimed that such factors as self-efficacy can affect the impact of goal-setting practices on skilled performance.

iv Spontaneous goal-setting in control group
In the typical experimental paradigm used to study goal-setting effects (see earlier in chapter), it is difficult to ensure that participants in control groups do not set goals spontaneously for themselves. Indeed, there is evidence (Weinberg *et al.*, 1985) that over 80 per cent of participants in a "no goal" control group admitted later that they had set goals for themselves.

Critical thinking questions
What are the similarities and differences between goal-setting processes in business and sport? What factors could account for the tendency for goal-setting to be less effective in sport than in business contexts? In sport, is it possible to eliminate the possibility of spontaneous goal-setting among people in control groups? Why do you think so few studies on goal-setting have used athletes studied in field settings?

Future directions in research on goal-setting

According to Burton *et al.* (2001) and Burton and Naylor (2002), the following new directions can be sketched for research on goal-setting in athletes. First, more research is required to establish the optimal level of goal difficulty for athletes in specific types of sports. Second, little is known, at present, about the relationship between the frequency with which people monitor their goal-setting behaviour and the efficacy of their goals. Third, additional research needs to be conducted on the issue of goal commitment or the degree to which people act on and/or otherwise pursue the goals that they endorse verbally. Fourth, goal-setting researchers need to move on from studying atheoretical questions such as "what types of goals are most effective?" to investigating the psychological mechanisms underlying the motivational effects of goals on specific sport skills. Finally, more longitudinal field studies are required to establish the actual goal-setting practices of athletes and coaches over the course of a competitive season.

Practical goal-setting: the SMART approach

To be effective as a motivational technique, goal-setting should be conducted according to sound psychological principles. These principles are encapsulated in the acronym "SMART" (Bull, Albinson and Shambrook, 1996). The SMART approach to goal-setting is illustrated in Box 2.7 with regard to the task of motivating oneself to exercise more regularly (see also Chapter 8).

Box 2.7 The SMART approach to goal-setting (based on Bull *et al.*, 1996)

How can you motivate yourself to take physical exercise more regularly? One way of achieving this goal is to use the SMART approach to goal-setting. This approach is based on the idea that goal-setting works best when it follows certain principles that are captured by the acronym "SMART". The SMART approach can be applied to your exercise behaviour as follows.

S = specific
The clearer and more specific your goal is, the more likely you are to achieve it. For example, "I want to visit the gym three times a week for the next three months" is better than saying "I would like to become fitter in the future".

M = measurable
If you cannot measure your progress towards your goal, then you will quickly lose interest in it. So it is important to keep a record of your progress towards your fitness objective. For example, you could measure the length of time it takes you to run a mile and then try to improve on it every three weeks.

A = action-related
Unless you identify a number of stepping stones (i.e., tasks which take you a step nearer to your goal and which involve specific actions that are under your control) for your goals, you may feel confused about what to do next. One action step is to join a gym and a second is to get a weekly assessment of your progress from a qualified fitness instructor.

R = realistic
Your goals should be realistic for your present level of health and fitness. Therefore, it is important that you get a full health check-up before you begin an exercise programme so that your fitness level and exercise aspirations can be assessed. Otherwise, your fitness goals may be unrealistic.

T = timetabled
In order to motivate yourself to exercise regularly, you must build some daily physical activity into your timetable. Planned exercise is the key to better fitness levels (see also Chapter 8).

So far in this chapter, we have explored the nature and types of motivation, various theoretical approaches to the study of this construct and a strategy (goal-setting) that attempts to increase motivation in athletes. The final section will address a rather puzzling question in this field. What motivates people to participate in dangerous sports? This question is perplexing because involvement in risky sports is counter-intuitive. After all, dangerous sports elicit fear – and fear is supposed to dissuade people from danger, not attract them to it (Piët, 1987). So, why do people engage in sporting behaviour that does not seem to make any psychological sense?

What motivates people to take part in risky sports?

On 12 October 2002, a young woman named Audrey Mestre was drowned as she attempted to set a target depth of 558 feet in the ancient but highly dangerous sport of "no limits free diving" in which participants plunge as deeply as possible into the ocean without the aid of breathing apparatus (Duggan, 2002). What motivated her to push her body to the limit of its physiological endurance? More generally, why do people risk their lives by taking part in such dangerous (or "extreme") sports as mountain-climbing, ballooning, hang-gliding, parachute-jumping, white-water kayaking, sky-diving or motorcycle racing? At least three psychological theories have been proposed to answer this question.

First, some theorists believe that dangerous activities offer people an escape from a world that the writer Al Alvarez describes as increasingly "constricted by comfort" (cited in Delingpole, 2001, p. 5). According to this theory, many people feel excessively cosseted by the materialistic comforts of our contemporary society and hence seek dangerous experiences in an effort to fill a gap in their lives. As western city life "is now tame and increasingly controlled" (Vidal, 2001, p. 2), some people look for danger in outdoor experiences. Therefore, risk-taking behaviour may represent a conscious backlash against the bland and sterile security of everyday life. Although this theory is speculative, it seems plausible that alienated people may experience a heightened state of awareness when they are faced with the prospect of injury or death. Indeed, Schrader and Wann (1999) suggested that one way to achieve the illusion of control over one's mortality is by "cheating death" (p. 427) through involvement in high-risk activities.

A second theory of risk-taking behaviour is the proposition that it stems from a personality trait called "sensation seeking". According to Zuckerman (1979), this trait involves the "need for varied, novel and complex sensations and experiences and the willingness to take physical and social risks for the sake of such experiences" (p. 10). Originally, Zuckerman speculated that people who participated in risky sports were high sensation seekers who displayed a tendency to underestimate the dangers posed by these sports. More recently, however, he revised this view by suggesting instead that sensation seekers are actually accurate in their risk assessment – even though they apparently believe that the rewards of arousal outweigh the degree of risk involved by the activity in question (Zuckerman, 1994). This trait of sensation seeking can be measured using the "Sensation Seeking Scale" (Zuckerman, 1984) which assesses such dimensions of the construct as "thrill and adventure seeking" (the desire to engage in adventurous activities), "experience seeking" (the tendency to seek arousal through mental and sensory means), "disinhibition" (seeking a release through such activities as drinking and gambling) and "boredom susceptibility" (an aversion to monotony). For a critical perspective on this test, see Box 2.8.

Box 2.8 Thinking critically about . . . sensation seeking in sport

What factors are associated with people's involvement in risky sporting activities? Schrader and Wann (1999) investigated the role of variables such as gender, "death anxiety" (i.e., the degree to which one feels that one can cheat death by participating in high-risk activities) and sensation seeking (Zuckerman, 1979) in people's involvement in dangerous sports. Results showed that only two variables accounted for significant amounts of variance in thrill-seeking behaviour. These variables were gender and sensation seeking. More precisely, the authors found that a much higher proportion of males (about 62 per cent) than females (approximately 37 per cent) participated in high-risk recreation activities. In addition, sensation seeking (as measured by Zuckerman's, 1979, Sensation Seeking Scale) was significantly associated with involvement in high-risk activities.

Critical thinking questions
Do you think that correlations between risk-taking behaviour and personality variables really explain anything? After all, to say that someone chooses dangerous sports because s/he enjoys the thrill of danger seems rather circular. Furthermore, how can we be sure that participants regard their chosen athletic behaviour as "risky" unless we assess their perceptions of it? What other implicit assumptions do researchers in this field make? Why do you think that proportionately more males than females tend to participate in risky sporting activities? If thrill-seeking behaviour is as addictive as is often claimed (Vidal, 2001), then why do people tend to choose *only one* outlet for their risky behaviour? For example, why do rock-climbers rarely become interested in other dangerous sports like motor-racing or bungee-jumping?

The third theoretical approach to risky behaviour in sports comes from the cognitive tradition. To illustrate, consider the idiosyncratic ways in which people estimate the risks associated with certain activities. Thus Kerr (1997) noted that athletes who participate in dangerous sports often confess to a fear of participating in *other* sports which are equally dangerous. Thus Carl Llewellyn, a British National Hunt jockey who has suffered a catalogue of serious injuries in his sport, confessed to being petrified of activities like bungee-jumping. Presumably, familiarity with the risks of one's sport blinds one to the dangers which they pose. In an effort to explain this phenomenon, Kerr (1997) speculated that athletes who take part in dangerous sports tend to construct subjective "protective frames" which give them a feeling of invincibility – although such frames do not appear to extend to less familiar sports.

Before we conclude this section, it is worth noting that there may be a neurochemical basis to risk-taking behaviour. Thus Zorpette (1999) claimed that such behaviour is addictive physiologically because dopamine is released by the brain as a chemical reward for experiencing dangerous situations. As yet, however, there have been few systematic attempts to explore the brains of "thrill-seekers" using neuroscientific imaging technology.

Ideas for research projects on motivation in athletes

Here are six ideas for possible research projects on motivation in athletes.

1   Is there a relationship between the motivation of an athlete and the type of sport which s/he plays? To answer this question, you could compare and contrast the motivation of performers from individual and team sports using a questionnaire such as the "Sport Motivation Scale" (Martens and Webber, 2002).

2   What factors sustain the motivation of elite athletes who still compete at a high level? Apart from a recent study by Mallett and Hanrahan (2003), little research has been conducted on this question.

3   Have you ever wondered about the factors that motivate aspiring marathon runners to put themselves through such arduous training schedules? If so, then you could replicate a study by Ogles and Masters (2003) on the motives of people who participate in marathons.

4   Do the coping strategies of task-oriented athletes differ from those used by ego-oriented athletes in stressful situations (see Pensgaard and Roberts, 2003)?

5   Relatively little is known about the actual goal-setting practices of athletes who have been tested in field settings. As we indicated earlier, most goal-setting studies have been conducted in laboratory settings on non-athlete samples. In view of this gap in the research literature, you may wish to investigate the goal-setting practices of athletes of different levels of ability over a six-week period during their competitive season. A useful starting point for this project is a study conducted by Burton, Weinberg, Yukelson and Weigand (1998) on the goal-setting practices of collegiate athletes.

6   In the light of the results reported by Schrader and Wann (1999), it may be interesting to find out if the gender differences in risky sport involvement apply to other dangerous sports and also to non-sporting risky activities.

Summary

- Motivation plays a vital but often misunderstood role in sport and exercise. The role is critical because athletic success depends significantly on people's willingness to exert mental as well as physical effort in pursuit of excellence. Unfortunately, the role of motivation in sport is also potentially confusing because of certain myths that surround this term (e.g., the idea that being "psyched up" is synonymous with being appropriately motivated for competitive action). Therefore, the purpose of this chapter was to examine selected theories and research on motivational processes in athletes. It began with a clarification of the nature and types of motivation.
- The second part of the chapter provided a brief overview of two influential cognitive models of motivational processes in athletes: achievement goal theory and attribution theory.
- The third section examined the theory and practice of goal-setting as a motivational strategy in sport. This section concluded with a discussion of some key conceptual and methodological issues affecting research in this field.
- After that, we considered the motivational factors which impel some people to take part in dangerous athletic pursuits.
- Finally, six practical suggestions were presented for possible research projects on the psychology of motivation in sport.

Chapter 3

"Psyching up" and calming down: anxiety in sport

The first round often provides the most panic-stricken snooker you'll ever see. When the lights go up it feels that you're wearing a rabbit-skin waistcoat, no matter how much experience you've got. It feels as if you're playing with someone else's arm. (Steve Davis, former world champion snooker player, cited in Everton, 1998, p. 24)

When you go to hit your first shot, you can't see the ball even though you are standing over it. You have to tell yourself to hit it, though you're looking down and it's gone all blurred. The funny thing about the Ryder Cup is that a certain level of pressure stays throughout the whole week. Normally, that sort of pressure comes and goes in tournaments and you really only feel it on the last nine holes. But at the Ryder Cup, it's there all week, even in the practice rounds. That's why it's so intense. (Golfer Pádraig Harrington on the anxiety associated with playing in the Ryder Cup; cited in MacGinty, 2002, p. 19)

There is nothing you can do about nerves. If you're not nervous then there is something wrong with you. Nerves create adrenaline and I told them to use that, use it in your own advantageous way, to make you feel better, get pumped up; just get psyched up. (Sam Torrance, captain of the victorious 2002 European Ryder Cup team, cited in O'Sullivan, 2002a, p. 19)

Introduction

Competitive sport can make even the world's most successful athlete feel nervous. For example, the quotations above bear eloquent testimony to the anxiety experienced by such seasoned performers as the six-times world champion snooker player Steve Davis (when performing at the Crucible in Sheffield) and the world top-ten golfer Pádraig Harrington (when playing for Europe in the 2002 Ryder Cup match against the United States) in pressure situations (see Figure 3.1)

Figure 3.1 According to Pádraig Harrington, playing in the Ryder Cup can be a nerve-racking experience
Source: courtesy of Inpho Photography

As Harrington revealed, most athletes have discovered from personal experience that if they wish to perform consistently well in competition, they must learn to control their arousal levels effectively. Put simply, they have to be able to "psych themselves up" (see Chapter 2) or else calm themselves down as required by the situation. Indeed, some sports challenge the performer to alternate regularly between these two mental states within the same competition. For example, gymnasts must be able to energise themselves before attempting a vault exercise but must relax when preparing for a routine on the beam. Otherwise, they may slip – as happened to Andrea Raducan, the 2000 Olympic gymnastics champion, who fell off the balance beam at the 2002 world championships in Hungary (Sarkar, 2002). Interestingly, the importance of arousal control in sport was highlighted by Mike Atherton, a former captain of England's cricket team, who observed that

> there are two sorts of player: those who are quite placid people . . . who need an adrenaline flow to get them up for it, and so find nerves a real help. And then there are those who are naturally hyper for whom that additional flow may not be such a good thing. When I look at players now I can see who fits into which category and then *their ability to cope depends on whether they can either bring themselves up or take themselves down.* (cited in Selvey, 1998, p. 2; italics mine)

Similar sentiments were expressed by Sam Torrance, the captain of the victorious European golf team before the 2002 Ryder Cup, when he urged his players to use their nervous energy effectively (see quote at the beginning of this chapter). Given the importance of anxiety control in sport, how can athletes manage to calm themselves down before or during a competition? More generally, what does "anxiety" mean to athletes and does it help or hinder their performance? What causes it and how can it be measured in sport settings? The purpose of this chapter is to provide answers to these and other questions raised by the study of arousal and anxiety in sport.

The chapter is organised as follows. The first section will explore the nature, causes and types of anxiety in sport performers as well as its meaning for the athletes themselves. In the second section, various ways of measuring anxiety in athletes will be evaluated briefly. The third part of the chapter will review research findings on the relationship between anxiety and athletic performance. This section will also feature a discussion of the nature and causes of "choking" under pressure in sport. In the next part, the topic of anxiety *control* will be addressed. This section will provide several practical techniques used by athletes to cope with pressure situations in sport. The fifth section will indicate some unresolved issues and new directions in research on anxiety in athletes. Finally, I shall present a practical suggestion for a research project in this field.

Anxiety in athletes

According to Onions (1996), the term anxiety is derived from the Latin word *angere*, meaning "to choke". This Latin root is interesting because choking under pressure is widespread in sport (see later in chapter). In sport psychology, anxiety refers to an unpleasant emotion which is characterised by vague but persistent feelings of apprehension and dread (Cashmore, 2002). A similar view of this construct was provided by Buckworth and Dishman (2002) who defined anxiety as a state of "worry, apprehension, or tension that often occurs in the absence of real or obvious danger" (p. 116). Typically, the tension felt by anxious people is accompanied by a heightened state of physiological arousal mediated by the autonomic nervous system.

In order to understand anxiety properly, we need to explore its psychological components and also to distinguish it from similar constructs such as "fear" (a brief emotional reaction to a stimulus that is perceived as threatening; Cashmore, 2002) and "arousal" (a diffuse state of bodily alertness or "readiness"; *ibid.*). The latter distinctions are very important because anxiety research in sport has been plagued by conceptual confusion (Gould, Greenleaf and Krane, 2002; Woodman and Hardy, 2001; Zaichkowsky and Baltzell, 2001). For example, some researchers have used the terms anxiety and arousal interchangeably even though these constructs have different meanings.

Components of anxiety: cognitive, somatic and behavioural

Most psychologists regard anxiety as a multidimensional construct with at least three dimensions or components: mental (or "cognitive"), physical (or "somatic") and behavioural (Gould *et al.*, 2002). Let us now examine each of these components in turn.

First, cognitive anxiety involves worrying or having negative expectations about some impending situation or performance and engaging in task-irrelevant thinking as a consequence (see also Chapter 4 on concentration in athletes). More precisely, it refers to "negative expectations and cognitive concerns about oneself, the situation at hand and potential consequences" (Morris, Davis and Hutchings, 1981, p. 541). But what do athletes worry about in sport? Although little research has been conducted on this issue, Dunn (1999) and Dunn and Syrotuik (2003) discovered four main themes in an analysis of cognitive anxiety in intercollegiate ice-hockey players. These themes were a fear of performance failure, apprehension about negative evaluation by others, concerns about physical injury or danger, and an unspecified fear of the unknown. On average, the players in this study were more concerned about performance failure and negative evaluation by others than about the other two worry domains. In general, cognitive anxiety has a debilitating effect on athletic performance (Cashmore, 2002). We shall return to this issue in the third section of the chapter when we explore why some athletes "choke" under pressure. By the way, cognitive anxiety about future performance is also widespread among performers other than athletes. For example, performance anxiety or stage fright has blighted the careers of such talented people as the singer Barbra Streisand who forgot the words of one of her songs during a concert in Central Park, New York, in front of 135,000 people – an event which prompted her to avoid singing "live" for another twenty-seven years (Sutcliffe, 1997). Similar problems of excessive anxiety have been documented in the cases of actors Vanessa Redgrave, Derek Jacobi and Stephen Fry (Harlow, 1999).

The second component of the construct of anxiety involves somatic or bodily processes. Somatic anxiety refers to the *physical* manifestation of anxiety and may be defined as "one's perception of the physiological-affective elements of the anxiety experience, that is, indications of autonomic arousal and unpleasant feeling states such as nervousness and tension" (Morris *et al.*, 1981, p. 541). In sport, this component of anxiety is apparent when an athlete is afflicted by such physical symptoms as increased perspiration, a pounding heart, rapid shallow breathing, clammy hands and a feeling of "butterflies" in the stomach. Whereas cognitive anxiety is characterised by negative thoughts and worries, somatic anxiety is associated with signs of autonomic arousal. It should be noted, however, that some researchers (e.g., Kerr, 1997) have suggested that increases in physiological arousal may accompany emotions other than anxiety. In particular, excitement and anger appear to have physiological substrates similar to those of anxiety (see also Box 3.3). The third component of anxiety is behavioural. In this domain, indices of anxiety include tense facial expressions, changes in communication patterns (e.g., unusually rapid speech delivery) and agitation and restlessness (Gould *et al.*, 2002). Surprisingly, relatively little research has been conducted on the behavioural manifestations of anxiety in athletes – mainly because of the dearth of suitable checklists for the assessment of such phenomena. Nevertheless, it is widely believed that anxiety produces jerky and inefficient muscular movements in athletes.

Before we conclude this section, an important theoretical issue needs to be addressed concerning the tri-dimensional nature of anxiety. Specifically, given the inextricable links between mind and body in sport, is it valid to postulate that cognitive and somatic anxiety are truly separate dimensions of this construct? There are at least two sources of evidence to support this distinction (Burton, 1998). First, factor analyses of self-report state anxiety scales tend to reveal a multidimensional rather than a unidimensional structure. Second, there are grounds for believing that cognitive and somatic anxiety emanate from different types of pre-competitive patterns. For example, research suggests that whereas cognitive anxiety remains relatively high and stable prior to competition for most athletes, somatic anxiety tends to remain low until one or two days before the event – at which point it increases steadily before peaking at the start of a competition. After that, it tends to dissipate rapidly (Woodman and Hardy, 2001). With regard to this issue, Fenz and Epstein (1967) explored the temporal pattern of physiological arousal responses among expert and novice sky-divers prior to performance. Results showed that in the expert performers, peak arousal levels were reached significantly in advance of the jump. By contrast, the physiological arousal of the novice parachutists started at a relatively low level but increased progressively in the time leading up to the jump. In summary, evidence from psychometric studies of self-report scales and that from studies of changes in the pattern of athletes' affect over time suggests that cognitive and somatic anxiety are in fact independent dimensions of anxiety.

Anxiety, fear and arousal

So far, we have been using the terms anxiety, arousal and fear quite loosely. Let us now distinguish between them more precisely. Anxiety is believed to differ from fear in lasting longer (Buckworth and Dishman, 2002) and in tending to be more undifferentiated than fear – because people can be anxious about something that is not physically present or immediately perceptible. Despite these differences, however, anxiety is similar to a fear in some ways. To explain, anxiety is elicited whenever people interpret a particular person, event or situation as posing a *threat* to them in some way. This perception of threat may be based on realistic or imaginary fears – although the distinction between these two factors is often blurred in everyday life. For example, if you are a tennis player and serving at match-point in your local club championship, you will probably feel a little anxious – even though your feelings in this case are disproportionate to the physical danger involved in the situation, unless your opponent has a reputation for being physically violent on court! But if you are a novice parachutist facing your first jump with no instructor around, you may have every reason to feel nervous because of the potential danger to your life. Let us turn now to the distinction between anxiety and arousal.

In psychology, the term "arousal" refers to a type of bodily energy which primes or prepares us for emergency action. For example, when we are threatened physically, our body's sympathetic nervous system prepares us either to confront the source of danger or to run away from it. This "fight or flight" response triggers such bodily reactions as a faster heart beat, release of glucose into the bloodstream and heightened levels of arousal. But what does "arousal" involve? According to Gould *et al.* (2002), it is a "general physiological and psychological activation of the organism which varies on a continuum from deep sleep to intense excitement" (p. 227). In other words, arousal is an undifferentiated somatic state which prepares people to respond to anticipated demands for action (Whelan, Epkins and Meyers, 1990). Physiologically, feelings of arousal are mediated by the sympathetic nervous system. Thus when we become aroused, our brain's reticular activating system triggers the release of biochemical substances like epinephrine and norepinephrine into the bloodstream so that our body is energised appropriately for action. Therefore, anxiety can be distinguished from arousal as follows. Although arousal involves undifferentiated bodily energy, anxiety is an emotional label for a *particular type* of arousal experience (Hardy, Jones and Gould, 1996). This view is endorsed in a model of arousal developed by Gould *et al.* (2002). In this model, cognitive anxiety is believed to emerge from the interpretation or appraisal of arousal. Therefore, anxiety can be regarded as *negatively interpreted* arousal. This proposition raises the question of individual differences in arousal interpretation.

It has long been known that athletes differ from each other in the labels that they attach to arousal states. Thus certain bodily symptoms (e.g., rapid heart beat, shortness of breath) may be perceived as "pleasant excitement" by one athlete but regarded as unpleasant anxiety by another performer. To illustrate a *positive* interpretation of an arousal state, consider how the tennis star Andre Agassi felt about his opening match in the 2002 US Open: "Going out there I was pretty nervous, and excited, and I felt like I controlled everything that I wanted to. That's a good sign" (cited in Wood, 2002, p. S5). Notice that he labelled his nervousness as excitement. In a similar vein, Tiger Woods revealed that "the challenge is hitting good golf shots when you have to . . . to do it when the nerves are fluttering, the heart pounding, the palms sweating . . . that's the *thrill*" (cited in D. Davies, 2001, p. 26; italics mine) (see Figure 3.2).

These comments by Agassi and Woods highlight the role that perception plays in the emotional experiences of elite athletes. For example, a low level of arousal may be experienced either as a relaxed state of readiness or as an undesirable "flat", lethargic or sluggish feeling. This idea that athletes' arousal levels may be *interpreted* in either positive or negative terms raises the issue of what anxiety means to sport performers.

Figure 3.2 Tiger Woods has learned to perceive pressure situations as exciting
Source: courtesy of Inpho Photography

Athletes' interpretation of anxiety symptoms: help or hindrance?

Traditionally, arousal and anxiety have been regarded as factors to be controlled in case they hampered athletic performance. However, this assumption was challenged by research which showed that, in many athletic situations, it is not the *amount* of arousal that affects performance but the way in which such arousal is interpreted. For example, Mahoney and Avener (1977) found that successful gymnasts (i.e., those who qualified for the 1976 US Olympic squad) tended to perceive pre-competitive arousal as a form of anticipatory excitement – a view which apparently facilitated their subsequent performance. Conversely, less successful counterparts (i.e., athletes who failed to qualify for the US team) tended to treat their arousal levels negatively, interpreting them as unwelcome signs of impending failure. Influenced by this finding, G. Jones and Swain (1992), G. Jones and Swain (1995) and Hanton and Jones (1999) showed that somatic symptoms of anxiety can have either a facilitative effect or a debilitative effect on sport performance depending on how the athlete perceives them. Thus a performer who interprets sweaty palms as a sign of uncertainty is experiencing debilitative anxiety whereas someone who regards similar symptoms as a sign of readiness to do well is experiencing facilitative anxiety (as in the cases of Andre Agassi and Tiger Woods above). Although this "directional perception" theory of anxiety in sport seems plausible, it is controversial due to the terminology involved. For example, G. Jones and Hanton (2001) acknowledged that the term "facilitative anxiety" seems like an oxymoron. To explain, as the term "anxiety" has negative connotations, and as it is difficult to distinguish between somatic anxiety and other emotions (Kerr, 1997), then perhaps athletes who label "anxiety" symptoms as facilitative may not be experiencing anxiety at all – but rather, a sense of excitement or challenge (see the preceding quote from Tiger Woods). Despite this controversy about terminology, G. Jones and Swain (1995) highlighted the importance of taking athletes' interpretations of their bodily feelings into account when they found that elite cricketers interpreted their arousal symptoms as being more facilitative of competitive performance than did less successful counterparts. To summarise, the way in which athletes *label* their arousal levels (if not their anxiety) seems to play a significant role in whether they feel challenged or overwhelmed by pressure situations.

This idea that a given level of arousal is amenable to different interpretative labels has significant theoretical and practical implications. For example, on the theoretical side, it suggests that attempts to measure anxiety should include indices of *direction* or interpretation as well as of intensity. With regard to practical implications, directionality effects highlight the importance of teaching athletes to "re-frame" their physiological symptoms constructively. For example, Hanton and Jones (1999) reported that elite swimmers benefited from learning to interpret pre-race anxiety symptoms in a positive manner. As these authors put it so memorably, the elite swimmers in their study had learned to make their butterflies "fly in formation"! In an effort to explore the meaning of anxiety to athletes, try the exercise in Box 3.1.

Box 3.1 Exploring the meaning of anxiety to athletes

The purpose of this exercise is to explore what performance anxiety means to athletes and to investigate how they cope with it. In order to complete this exercise, you will need to interview three competitive athletes – preferably from different sports. Before you begin, however, please ensure that these participants have been informed about the purpose of the study and have consented to have their views recorded and analysed. Then, using an audio-cassette or a mini-disc recorder, ask them the following questions:

- What does the word "anxiety" mean to you? Do you think that it is helpful or harmful to your performance?
- On a scale of 0 (meaning "not at all important") to 5 (meaning "extremely important"), how important do you think that the ability to control anxiety is for successful performance in your sport?
- Do you prefer to be "psyched up" or calm before a competitive event in your sport? Why? Please explain.
- What things make you anxious *before* a competition? How do these factors affect your performance? Explain.

- What things make you anxious *during* a competition? How do these factors affect your performance? Explain.
- What techniques do you use, if any, to cope with anxiety in your sport? Where did you learn these techniques?

Analysis
Do the athletes differ in their understanding of anxiety? If so, are these differences related to the sports that they play? From the athletes' experiences, what factors make them anxious before and/or during competition? Do the athletes use any specific techniques to cope with anxiety? If so, where did they learn these techniques?

In summary, we have learned so far that anxiety is a multidimensional construct with cognitive, somatic and behavioural components. In addition, we have discovered that this construct can be distinguished from fear and arousal experiences. Third, we saw how athletes differed in the way in which they interpret their arousal levels as being either facilitative or debilitative of their sport performance. At this stage, however, we need to tackle the question of whether or not different types of anxiety can be identified.

Types of anxiety: state and trait

Since the seminal research of Spielberger (1966), a distinction has been drawn by psychologists between anxiety as a mood state ("state" anxiety) and anxiety as a personality characteristic ("trait" anxiety). Whereas the former term (also known as "A-state") describes transient, situation-specific feelings of fear, worry and physiological arousal, the latter one (also called "A-trait") refers to a relatively stable personality trait (or chronic pre-disposition) which is characterised by a tendency to perceive certain situations as anxiety-provoking. Thus as Spielberger (1966) explained, state anxiety may be defined as "subjective, consciously perceived feelings of tension and apprehension" (p. 17) whereas trait anxiety refers to a general disposition among people to feel anxious in certain environmental situations (e.g., when playing an important match). Applied to sport, the concept of state anxiety may be used to describe situations in which an athlete's feelings of tension may change during a match. Thus a footballer may feel nervous in the dressing-room before an important match but may become calmer once the competitive action begins. On the other hand, a player who scores highly on trait anxiety may feel pessimistic most of the time. Another way of explaining this distinction is to say that trait anxiety is a predisposition to experience state anxiety under certain circumstances. According to this view, athletes who display a high degree of trait anxiety are more likely to interpret sport situations as threatening than are less anxious counterparts.

What causes anxiety in athletes?

Many factors induce feelings of anxiety in athletes. Unfortunately, due to space restrictions, this section contains only a brief list of possible determinants of anxiety in sport performers (but see Woodman and Hardy, 2001, for more detailed accounts of this issue).

Perceived importance of the competition

In general, the more importance is attached to a forthcoming competition by an athlete, the more anxiety s/he is likely to experience in it.

Predispositions: trait anxiety

Many sport psychologists (e.g., Anshel, 1995) believe that athletes' levels of trait anxiety are important determinants of the amount of state anxiety which they are likely to experience in a given situation. But, as we indicated in Chapter 2, it is not valid to use a personality trait as an "explanation" for a mental state. After all, one cannot explain aggressive behaviour by saying that a person has an "aggressive" personality. Clearly, we must be careful to avoid circular reasoning when seeking to explain why athletes become anxious in certain situations. Nevertheless, research suggests some reasons why athletes differ in their level of pre-competitive trait anxiety (see Box 3.2).

Box 3.2 Thinking critically about . . . why athletes might differ in pre-competitive anxiety

Why do athletes differ so much from each other in the amount of pre-competitive anxiety which they display? According to Wann (1997), research on this question has identified at least three key mediating variables. First, the level of competitiveness of the athlete appears to be important. In particular, athletes who are relatively low in competitiveness tend to show a steady increase in cognitive anxiety before an important competition whereas those who score highly on it tend to show a stable pattern of pre-competitive cognitive anxiety. Second, the type of sport seems to make a difference. Thus athletes who participate in endurance sports tend to display lower levels of pre-competitive anxiety than do athletes competing in other track-and-field sports. Finally, gender may play a role. Specifically, whereas cognitive anxiety levels tend to remains relatively stable for male athletes, they tend to increase in female performers as a competition approaches.

Critical thinking questions
Do these general principles make sense to you? If not, which of them do you find it hard to believe and why? Is it valid to compare the possible determinants of pre-competitive anxiety in athletes from different sports?

Attributions/expectations

As I explained in Chapter 2, a tendency to attribute successful outcomes to external and unstable factors (e.g., luck) and to attribute unsuccessful outcomes to internal and stable factors (e.g., low levels of skill) is likely to induce anxiety in athletes. Perceptions of audience expectations are also important determinants of performance anxiety. For example, the soprano June Anderson said that "in the beginning of your career . . . nobody knows who you are, and they don't have any expectations. There's less to lose. Later on, when you're known, people are coming to see you, and they have certain expectations. You have a lot to lose" (cited in Blau, 1998, p. 17).

Perfectionism

Athletes who set impossibly high standards for their performances may feel anxious when things fail to go smoothly for them. Interestingly, Frost and Henderson (1991) discovered that athletes who displayed a significant concern for their mistakes (which is associated with perfectionism) tended to experience more anxiety than did less perfectionistic colleagues. A similar problem is apparent in the performing arts. For example, the pianist Louis Lortie attributed stage fright and other forms of anxiety to the fact that "we were brought up with the idea that there shouldn't be mistakes" (cited in Blau, 1998, p 17).

Fear of failure

Many athletes are indoctrinated to adopt a "win at all costs" attitude, which ultimately makes them vulnerable to performance anxiety. If they believe that their self-esteem is tied inextricably to what they achieve, they are especially likely to become nervous at the prospect of defeat as it constitutes a threat to their self-worth.

Lack of confidence

Some sport psychologists have speculated that athletes who have little confidence in their own abilities are likely to experience high levels of anxiety in competitive situations. This hypothesis is supported by research (e.g., Martin and Gill, 1991) which shows that runners who scored highly in self-confidence reported experiencing little cognitive anxiety.

In summary, at least three conclusions have emerged from studying anxiety in athletes. First, even the world's best athletes get nervous before competition. Second, many athletes and coaches believe that competitive performance is determined significantly by the ability to control and channel one's nervous energy effectively. Finally, we have learned that anxiety tends to affect people at different levels – via their thinking, feeling and behaviour. In short, anxiety causes athletes to think pessimistically about the future and to feel tense and agitated.

Measuring anxiety in athletes

In the previous section, we learned that the construct of anxiety has three different dimensions: cognitive, somatic and behavioural. Within sport psychology, attempts to measure anxiety have focused largely on the first and second of these dimensions, with virtually no research available on the behavioural aspect of this construct. Of the measures developed, the most popular tools for anxiety assessment have been self-report scales – probably as a result of the availability and convenience of these instruments (see R. E. Smith, Smoll and Wiechman, 1998, for a review of anxiety measurement in sport performers).

Physiological measures

As anxiety is analogous to a fear reaction, it has a strong physiological basis. Thus Spielberger (1966) proposed that anxiety states are "accompanied by or associated with activation of the autonomic nervous system" (p. 17). As we have seen, this activation results in such typical symptoms of anxiety as elevated heart rate, increased blood pressure, fast and shallow breathing, sweaty palms and tense musculature. If such indices could be measured conveniently, they would facilitate research in this area as they are relatively unaffected by response sets such as people's tendency to guess the purposes of questionnaire items so that they can present themselves in a maximally desirable light (a tendency called "social desirability"). Unfortunately, physiological measures of anxiety are relatively rare in sport psychology for at least five reasons. First, there is no single, universally agreed physiological index of anxiety. Second, as athletes differ in the way in which they interpret autonomic arousal (i.e., as facilitative or debilitative of their performance), physiological measures of anxiety are of limited value. Third, these measures assess arousal not anxiety. Fourth, physiological indices of arousal are not highly intercorrelated, a fact which suggests that they are not all measuring the same construct. Finally, physiological assessment of athletes is time-consuming and inconvenient. For these reasons, researchers in sport psychology have tended to use self-report rather than physiological instruments to measure anxiety states in athletes.

Self-report instruments

Given their simplicity, brevity and convenience, paper-and-pencil tests of anxiety have proliferated in sport psychology research. Among the most popular self-report instruments in this field are such trait anxiety measures as the "Sport Competition Anxiety Test" (SCAT; Martens, 1977) and the "Sport Anxiety Scale" (SAS; R. E. Smith, Smoll and Schutz, 1990) as well as such state anxiety tools as the "Competitive State Anxiety Inventory-2" (CSAI-2; Martens, Burton, Vealey, Bump and Smith, 1990) and the "Mental Readiness Form" (MRF; Krane, 1994). In general, these scales have focused largely on the measurement of anxiety intensity in athletes rather than on how anxiety is interpreted by them.

The "Sport Competition Anxiety Scale" (SCAT; Martens, 1977)

The Sport Competition Anxiety Scale (SCAT) is a ten-item inventory which purports to measure trait anxiety in sport performers. Parallel versions of this test are available for children (aged 10–14 years) and for adults (of 15 years and above). Typical items include "When I compete I worry about making mistakes" and "Before I compete I get a queasy feeling in my stomach". Respondents are required to indicate their agreement with each item by selecting their preferred answer from the three categories of "hardly ever", "sometimes" and "often". Reverse scoring is used on certain items (e.g., "Before I compete I feel calm") and overall test scores can range from 10 to 30. Internal consistency coefficients range from 0.8 to 0.9 and test-retest reliability values cluster around 0.77 (R. E. Smith *et al.*, 1998). Validation studies suggest that the SCAT is mainly a measure of somatic anxiety (*ibid.*). Evidence of convergent validity comes from studies which show that the test is correlated moderately with various general anxiety inventories. Overall, R. E. Smith *et al.* (1998) concluded that although the SCAT "has been a very important research tool within sport psychology" (p. 117), it needs to be revised as a multidimensional test, reflecting the distinction between somatic and cognitive anxiety.

The "Sport Anxiety Scale" (SAS; R. E. Smith et al., 1990)

The "Sport Anxiety Scale" (SAS; R. E. Smith *et al.*, 1990) is a sport-specific multidimensional test of cognitive and somatic trait anxiety. It contains twenty-one items which are divided into three sub-scales: somatic anxiety (nine items such as "I feel nervous"), worry (seven items such as "I have self-doubts") and a "concentration disruption" (five items such as "My mind wanders during sport competition") sub-scale. Reliability data for this scale are encouraging, with internal consistency estimated at between 0.88 (somatic anxiety), 0.87 (worry) and 0.69 (concentration–disruption) (Dunn, Causgrove Dunn, Wilson, and Syrotuik, 2000) and test-retest figures at 0.77 for an inter-test interval of eighteen days (Smith *et al.*, 1990). Evidence of convergent validity for this scale was reported by Smith *et al.* (1990) who calculated significant correlations (ranging between 0.47 and 0.81) between its sub-scales and the Sport Competition Anxiety Test (SCAT; Martens, 1977). Discriminant validity for the SAS is supported by evidence of low correlations between it and general mental health measures (see Smith *et al.*, 1998). Factor analyses have also confirmed that the SAS assesses three separate dimensions: somatic anxiety, cognitive anxiety/worry, and concentration–disruption (Dunn *et al.*, 2000).

The "Competitive State Anxiety Inventory-2" (CSAI-2; Martens et al., 1990)

The "Competitive State Anxiety Inventory-2" (CSAI-2; Martens *et al.*, 1990) is a test of state anxiety. It comprises twenty-seven items which are divided into three sub-scales (with each containing nine items): cognitive anxiety, somatic anxiety and self-confidence. Typical items in the somatic anxiety sub-scale include "I feel nervous" and "My body feels tense". A sample item in the cognitive anxiety sub-scale is "I am concerned about losing". The "self-confidence" sub-scale is included in the test because a lack of confidence is believed to be a sign of cognitive anxiety (*ibid.*). On a four-point scale (with 1 = "not at all" and 4 = "very much so"), respondents are required to rate the intensity of their anxiety experiences prior to competition. Following a review of forty-nine studies using the CSAI-2, Burton (1998) reported that internal consistency estimates for these three sub-scales ranged from 0.76 to 0.91.

In the previous section of the chapter, we indicated the importance of athletes' interpretations of their arousal symptoms. In this regard, the CSAI-2 is hampered by a significant methodological deficiency – namely, its neglect of the issue of "*direction*" or personal meaning of anxiety symptoms for athletes (G. Jones, 1995). To rectify this problem, some researchers advocate the addition of a *directional* measure to all "intensity" indices of anxiety (G. Jones and Swain, 1992). In this case, respondents may be required first to complete the CSAI-2 in order to elicit the intensity with which they experience the twenty-seven symptoms listed in this test. Then, they may be asked to rate the degree to which the experienced intensity of each symptom is facilitative or debilitative of their subsequent athletic performance. A seven-item Likert response scale is used, with values ranging from –3 (indicating "very negative") to +3 (indicating "very positive"). To illustrate, an athlete might respond with a maximum "4" to the statement "I am concerned about losing" but might then rate this concern with a +3 on the interpretation scale. Through these scores, the performer is indicating that s/he feels that this concern about losing is likely to have a facilitative effect on his/her forthcoming performance. With this modification, CSAI-2 "direction of anxiety" scores can vary between –27 and +27. Internal consistency reliability estimates for this facilitative/debilitative measure range from 0.72 (for the somatic anxiety sub-scale) to 0.83 (for the cognitive anxiety sub-scale) (Swain and Jones, 1996). When this "directional modification" scale has been used in conjunction with the CSAI-2, the resulting instrument is called the "DM-CSAI-2" (Burton, 1998) or the CSAI-2(d) (M. V. Jones and Uphill, 2003). But how valid is this procedure? See Box 3.3.

Box 3.3 Thinking critically about . . . research on direction of anxiety

In sport psychology, the term "direction of anxiety" refers to whether an athlete sees anxiety as facilitative or debilitative of athletic performance. To indicate the value of this variable, G. Jones and Swain (1992) added a Likert scale of directionality to each item of the Competitive State Anxiety Inventory-2 to explore the degree to which athletes viewed anxiety as facilitative of their performance. They also administered a test of competitiveness to each athlete. Results showed that highly competitive athletes believed more significantly in the facilitative effects of anxiety than did less successful counterparts. Another study by G. Jones, Hanton and Swain (1994) found that successful swimmers viewed their anxiety as being more facilitative of performance than did less successful swimmers – even though the groups did not differ significantly on anxiety intensity. Based on such evidence, G. Jones (1995) recommended the "directional modification" of the Competitive State Anxiety Inventory-2. Recently, however, conceptual and methodological criticisms of direction of anxiety have been raised – as well as an alternative model of the relationship between arousal and performance.

First, Burton (1998) has queried the rationale underlying G. Jones's approach. In particular, he wondered whether or not anxiety can ever be regarded as "facilitative". Is it possible that researchers have been confusing somatic anxiety with more positive emotional states such as excitement or challenge (see also Kerr, 1997)? Burton (1998) argued that cognitive appraisal processes determine whether people experience a positive emotion, such as excitement/challenge, or a negative emotion, such as anxiety, when they are aroused in athletic competition. Clearly, more research is required to distinguish between the different emotional experiences of athletes (but see Hanin, 2000). The second weakness of G. Jones's approach is that measurement of direction of anxiety relies on self-report data. As indicated in Chapter 1, however, people are not always reliable judges of their own behaviour. Therefore, we should not assume that athletes are always correct when they tell us that anxiety had a *facilitative* effect on their performance. Finally, "reversal theory" (a conceptual model of motivation and emotion which suggests that people switch back and forth between different frames of mind: see Kerr, 1997) also highlights the importance of individual differences in the interpretation of arousal symptoms. For example, when athletes are in a "telic state" (i.e., highly task-oriented), high arousal may be interpreted as unpleasant anxiety whereas low anxiety may be interpreted as pleasant relaxation. By contrast, athletes who are in a "paratelic state" (characterised by a fun-loving, present-centred focus) may regard high arousal as pleasantly exciting whereas they may perceive low arousal as unpleasant boredom). In summary, despite its intuitive plausibility, the concept of direction of anxiety has not been validated adequately in sport psychology.

Critical thinking questions

Can you think of a way of assessing whether anxiety facilitates or hampers athletic performance without using a quantitative research design or self-report scales? In particular, would qualitative research methodology (see Chapter 1) offer a viable alternative to the self-report approach? How could you validate athletes' insights into their own emotional experiences? Can reversal theory help to explain why athletes may switch from perceiving anxiety as facilitative to perceiving it as debilitative of their performance (see Hudson and Walker, 2002)?

Despite the issues raised in Box 3.3, several studies have supported the validity of the DM-CSAI-2. For example, G. Jones *et al.* (1994) discovered that elite swimmers reported that they had interpreted cognitive and somatic anxiety as being more

tative of their performance than did their less successful counterparts. Not
isingly, a significant proportion of the non-elite swimmers reported anxiety as
being debilitative to their performance. Before we conclude this section, it should
be noted that concern has been expressed recently about the psychometric
adequacy of the CSAI-2. Briefly, Craft, Magyar, Becker and Feltz (2003) conducted
a recent meta-analysis of the association between this test and athletic performance.
Unfortunately, relationships between the three sub-scales (cognitive anxiety,
somatic anxiety and self-confidence) and sport performance were generally weak –
thereby raising doubts about the construct validity of the CSAI-2. Let us now
consider in more detail the issue of how anxiety affects athletic performance.

Arousal, anxiety and athletic performance

At the beginning of this chapter, we suggested that the ability to regulate one's
arousal level is a vital determinant of success in sport. Endorsing this principle, many
athletes and coaches have developed informal methods of either energising themselves or lowering their arousal levels before important competitions. For example,
athletes who are involved in sports which require strength and power (e.g., wrestling
and weightlifting) and/or physical contact (e.g., soccer, rugby) tend to favour
"psych up" strategies such as listening to inspirational music in the hours or minutes
before the competition begins. According to Dr Neil Todd (cited in Tyldesley, 2003),
rhythm is "a key element of psyching people up . . . It can provide a mental edge"
(p. S3). Apparently, the song used most frequently by Premiership soccer players
during the 2002–2003 season was "Lose Yourself" by Eminem (*ibid.*). Of course,
music is not the only "psych up" strategy used in sport (see Zaichkowsky and
Baltzell, 2001). Thus some coaches believe that if players are taunted or made *angry*
before they compete, their performance will be improved. For example, Laurent
Seigne, the French rugby coach, is reported to have punched members of his
team, Brive, before a match in order to psych them up appropriately (S. Jones, 1997)!
As yet, however, this theory has not been tested empirically in sport psychology
– and ethical prohibitions make this possibility unlikely if not impossible! Arousal
regulation strategies are also used in precision sports such as golf, snooker and
archery where performers need to calm down in order to play well. For example,
the American archer Darrell Pace, twice an Olympic gold medal-winner, extolled
the benefits of a controlled breathing technique as a preparation strategy before
competitions. In this breathing technique, Pace synchronised the pattern of his
inhalations and exhalations with covert repetition of the word "relax" (Vealey and
Walter, 1994).

Although the preceding anecdotal examples are useful in highlighting the
importance of arousal control to athletes, they do not illuminate the relationship
between anxiety and performance. Fortunately, there is a considerable empirical
research literature on this topic (e.g., see reviews by Gould *et al.*, 2002; Zaichkowsky
and Baltzell, 2001). Let us now evaluate the main theories and findings emerging
from this research literature.

Theories of arousal/anxiety–performance relationships

Since the early 1900s, a considerable amount of psychological research has been conducted on the relationship between people's arousal levels and their subsequent performance on skilled tasks. In general, this research has been influenced by four main theories: "Drive theory" (based on Hull, 1943); the "inverted-U" hypothesis (based on Yerkes and Dodson, 1908); more recently, "catastrophe theory" (e.g., Hardy, 1990, 1996; Hardy and Parfitt, 1991); and the "conscious processing" hypothesis (Masters, 1992). Although the earlier theories (e.g., drive theory, the "inverted-U" hypothesis) applied mainly to *arousal*-performance relationships, the more recent ones (e.g., catastrophe theory, the "conscious processing" hypothesis) deal more with *anxiety*-performance relationships. Details of other approaches such as the "individual zones of optimal functioning" hypothesis (Hanin, 1997) and "reversal theory" (Kerr, 1997) may be found in Gould *et al.* (2002) and Zaichkowsky and Baltzell (2001).

Drive theory

In learning theory, a "drive" is regarded as a psychological state of arousal that is created by an imbalance in the homeostatic mechanisms of the body and that impels the organism to take ameliorative action. In general, two types of drives have been identified (Cashmore, 2002). Primary drives arise from the pursuit of basic biological needs such as eating, drinking and restoring homeostasis (or the internal equilibrium of the body). Secondary drives are stimuli (e.g., earning money, winning titles) that acquire the motivational characteristics of primary drives as a result of conditioning or other forms of learning. Applied to sport, drive theory postulates a positive and linear relationship between arousal level and performance. In other words, the more aroused an athlete is, the better his or her performance should be. Initially, support for this theory was claimed by researchers like Oxendine (1984) who argued that in power and/or speed sports such as weightlifting or sprinting, a high level of arousal tends to enhance athletic performance. Although superficially plausible, this theory does not stand up to scientific scrutiny. For example, consider the problem of false starts in sprinting. Here, an athlete may become so aroused physiologically that s/he anticipates wrongly and ends up "jumping the gun". Indeed, this very problem occurred in the 1996 Olympic Games when the British sprinter Linford Christie made *two* false starts in the 100 m race and was subsequently disqualified. In an effort to counteract this problem of over-anticipation, official starters in sprint competitions tend to use variable foreperiods before firing their pistols. Similar problems stemming from over-arousal can occur in weightlifting when athletes fail to "chalk up" before lifting the barbell. In team sports, over-arousal may be prompted by rousing "pep talks" delivered by a coach to his or her players before a game. On the one hand, such talks may capture the attention of the players, especially if they refer to alleged insults by opponents. Thus Jeremy Guscott, the former England and Lions rugby player, remarked that "nothing is a better motivator than being bad-mouthed by the opposition" (Guscott, 1997, p. 44). On the other hand, there is little or no empirical evidence to indicate that pep talks channel players' arousal effectively. Recall from Chapter 2 that motivation requires *direction* as well as intensity. Clearly, the problem with rousing pep talks is that they usually lack this important directional component (Anshel, 1995).

The "inverted-U" hypothesis

According to the "inverted-U" hypothesis (Oxendine, 1984), the relationship between arousal and performance is curvilinear rather than linear. In other words, increased arousal is postulated to improve skilled performance up to a certain point, beyond which further increases in arousal may impair it. To illustrate this theory, imagine being required to sit an examination just after you wake up (low arousal) or after you have run a marathon (high arousal). At both of these extreme ends of the arousal continuum, your academic performance would probably be poor. On the other hand, if you had a good night's sleep and felt properly prepared for the exam, you should perform at your best. This proposition that arousal has diminishing returns on task performance is derived from the Yerkes–Dodson law (Yerkes and Dodson, 1908). Briefly, this law proposed that there is an optimal level of arousal for performance on any task. Specifically, performance tends to be poor at low or high levels of arousal but is best at intermediate levels of arousal. A summary of the Yerkes–Dodson law is presented in Box 3.4.

Box 3.4 Of mice and men (and women) ... the "Yerkes–Dodson law"

Although the Yerkes–Dodson law is widely cited in sport psychology, its origins lie in research on animal learning in the early 1900s. Specifically, in 1908, Robert Yerkes and John Dodson reported experiments on the relationship between arousal level and task difficulty. Briefly, they devised a paradigm in which mice could avoid electrical shocks by entering the brighter of two compartments. Arousal level was varied by changing the intensity of the electrical shocks administered to the mice. Task difficulty was manipulated by varying the contrast in brightness between the two compartments. Results showed that the amount of practice required by the mice to learn the discrimination task increased as the difference in brightness between the compartments decreased. In other words, when the task was easy (i.e., when the brighter compartment was easy to identify), the mice performed best at high levels of arousal (i.e., larger electric shocks). However, when the task was difficult (i.e., when there was little difference between the brightness of the two compartments), the mice performed best at low levels of arousal (i.e., small electrical shocks). These findings led Yerkes and Dodson (1908) to conclude that "an easily acquired habit, that is, one which does not demand difficult sense discrimination or complex associations, may readily be formed under strong stimulation, whereas a difficult habit may be acquired readily only under relatively weak stimulation" (pp. 481–482). Thus the Yerkes–Dodson law consists of two parts.

Part one suggests that people's performance on skilled tasks is best when their level of arousal is intermediate and that it deteriorates as their arousal either increases or decreases from that optimal level. In other words, the relationship between arousal and performance looks like an inverted "U". For example, as when you are either drowsy (under-aroused) or very excited (over-aroused), it is difficult to do an exam to the best of your ability. Part two of the Yerkes–Dodson law suggests that as the complexity of a skill increases, the amount of arousal required for optimal performance of it *decreases*. In other words, the performance of difficult tasks decreases as arousal increases whereas the performance of easy tasks increases as arousal increases. In summary, the Yerkes–Dodson law suggests that optimal performance occurs when people's arousal levels are intermediate in strength. Further details of this law may be found in Teigen (1994).

If the Yerkes–Dodson theory is correct, then athletic performance that occurs under conditions of either high or low arousal should be inferior to that displayed at intermediate levels. This hypothesis has received some empirical support. For example, Klavora (1978) found that within a sample of high-school basketball players, the highest levels of performance were displayed by people who had reported moderate levels of somatic anxiety. More generally, Landers and Boutcher (1998) concluded that "the inverted-U hypothesis seems to generalise across field and experimental situations" (p. 205).

Unfortunately, despite its plausibility, the Yerkes–Dodson principle is difficult to test empirically for several reasons. First, as we learned earlier, it is not easy to devise or agree on a satisfactory independent measure of the construct of arousal. As a result, researchers find it difficult to decide whether a given arousal level is too low or too high for a performer. Second, there is an inherent flaw at the heart of this law. In particular, as researchers cannot predict in advance the point of diminishing returns for the effects of arousal on skilled performance, the inverted-U hypothesis is "immune to falsification" (Neiss, 1988, p. 353). Finally, researchers disagree about the best way in which to induce different levels of arousal in participants. For ethical reasons, contemporary investigators cannot use electric shocks or other forms of aversive stimuli for this purpose – unlike their predecessors Yerkes and Dodson (1908). In summary, the inverted-U theory has several flaws as a possible explanation of the link between arousal and performance. Perhaps most significantly, it does not elucidate putative theoretical mechanisms which might account for the link between arousal and performance. Thus the inverted-U is "a general prediction, not a theory that explains how, why, or precisely when arousal affects performance" (Gould *et al.*, 2002, p. 214). Unfortunately, despite these limitations, this hypothesis has been promulgated as an established fact by some applied sport psychologists. To illustrate, Winter and Martin (1991) used it to justify their advice to tennis players on "controlling 'psych' levels" (p. 17).

Catastrophe theory

The catastrophe theory of anxiety (e.g., Hardy, 1990; 1996; Hardy and Parfitt, 1991) is different from the two previous arousal-performance models in proposing that physiological arousal *interacts* with certain aspects of anxiety (in this case, cognitive state anxiety or worry) to influence athletic performance. More precisely, this theory postulates that arousal is associated with athletic performance in a manner described by the "inverted-U" curve – but only when athletes have low cognitive state anxiety (i.e., when they are not worried). When cognitive anxiety is high, however, increases in arousal tend to improve performance up to a certain point beyond which further increases may produce a swift, dramatic and discontinuous (hence the term "catastrophic") decline in performance rather than a slow or gradual deterioration. Therefore, the cornerstone of catastrophe theory is the assumption that arousal may have different effects on athletic performance depending on the prevailing level of cognitive anxiety in the performer.

Based on this assumption, at least two predictions are possible (Gould *et al.*, 2002). First, the interaction of physiological arousal and cognitive state anxiety will determine athletic performance more than will the absolute value of either variable alone. Thus high cognitive anxiety should enhance performance at low levels of physiological arousal but should hinder performance at relatively higher levels of arousal. This prediction is interesting because it suggests that, contrary to popular opinion, cognitive anxiety does not always hamper performance (Hardy, 1997). The second prediction is that when an athlete experiences high cognitive anxiety, the arousal-performance curve should follow a different path under conditions of increasing versus decreasing physiological arousal (a phenomenon known as "hysteresis"). Although catastrophe theory has received some support in sport psychology (see Edwards, Kingston, Hardy and Gould, 2002; Woodman and Hardy, 2001), its complexity (e.g., three-dimensional nature) renders it difficult to test. Nevertheless, it is an intriguing model which deserves additional empirical scrutiny.

Conscious processing hypothesis

The conscious processing hypothesis (Masters, 1992) was spawned by the well-known "paralysis-by-analysis" phenomenon whereby skilled performance tends to deteriorate whenever people try to exert conscious control over movements that had previously been under automatic control (see Figure 3.3).

Strictly speaking, the conscious processing hypothesis applies more to the association between anxiety and performance than to arousal-performance relationships. Specifically, it proposes that when athletes experience increases in their anxiety levels, they attempt to control their performance by consciously controlling their movements using explicit rules rather than automatic habits. If this theory is correct, then anxiety should have differential effects on skilled performance – depending on how the skill had been acquired originally (i.e., whether it had been learned explicitly or implicitly).

In an effort to test this prediction using the skill of golf putting, Masters (1992) devised an intriguing experimental paradigm. Briefly, participants were required to

Figure 3.3 Over-analysis can unravel people's sport skills

perform putting skills in both training and testing phases. Two conditions were crucial to the experiment. In the explicit condition, participants were instructed to read coaching manuals on golf putting. Conversely, in the implicit condition, participants were given no instructions but had to putt golf balls while performing a secondary task which had been designed to prevent them from thinking about the instructions on putting. There were four training sessions in which participants had to try to hole 100 golf balls. The number of putts holed was measured in each case. After the fourth training session, a source of stress was introduced. This stress was induced by a combination of evaluation apprehension (e.g., requesting an alleged golfing expert to judge their putting performance) and financial inducement. Results suggested that the implicit learning group showed no deterioration in performance under stress in contrast to the golfers in the explicit learning condition. Masters (1992) interpreted this to mean that the skills of athletes with a small pool of explicit knowledge were less likely to fail than were those of performers with relatively larger amounts of explicit knowledge. In other words, the prediction of the conscious processing theory was corroborated. Anxiety appears to have different effects on performance depending on how the skill was acquired in the first place (i.e., through explicit or implicit learning). To summarise, the conscious processing hypothesis predicts that athletes whose cognitive anxiety increases will tend to revert to conscious control of normally automatic skills. This theory has received some empirical support (see review in Woodman and Hardy, 2001).

Conclusions about arousal/anxiety–performance relationship

At least three general conclusions have emerged from the preceding theories and research (Weinberg and Gould, 1999). First, anxiety and arousal are multi-dimensional constructs which do not have simple linear relationships with athletic performance. Second, increases in physiological arousal and cognitive state anxiety do not inevitably lead to a deterioration in athletic performance. Recall that the effects of both of these variables depend crucially on how the performer *interprets* the perceived changes in arousal. For example, increased arousal may be perceived as energising rather than overwhelming and hence facilitative of performance. Third, the interaction between arousal and cognitive anxiety seems to be more important in determining performance than is the absolute value of either variable on its own. With these general conclusions in mind, let us now consider what happens when anxiety hampers athletic performance.

Performance anxiety in sport: "choking" under pressure

Earlier in the chapter, we learned that the term anxiety is derived from the Latin word *"angere"* which means "to choke". Not surprisingly, the phenomenon of "choking under pressure", whereby athletic performance is suddenly impaired by intense anxiety, has attracted both popular interest (e.g., Coop and Morrice, 2002; Dobson, 1998) and scientific scrutiny (e.g., Graydon, 2002). Interestingly, the term "choking" is so widely known in athletic performance that it has a variety of sport-specific synonyms, such as "icing" (in basketball), "dartitis" (in darts) and the "yips" (in golf). Although it affects athletes of all levels of ability and/or experience, choking is especially prevalent among performers of precision sports such as golf, tennis, snooker, darts and cricket. To illustrate, current stars like John Daly (golf) and former world-class athletes like Rod Laver and John McEnroe (both tennis) and Lee Trevino and Tom Watson have all admitted publicly that they have choked psychologically in certain pressure situations.

Unfortunately, choking is not only debilitating but can affect athletes over a long period of time. For example, the Welsh golfer Ian Woosnam admitted that he had suffered from the "yips" for three years. More precisely, he said that "it got to the stage where the right hand would suddenly jerk into action and you'd putt to the left . . . Then, as it goes on, you don't know where the right path is and you get even more tense. I was suffering so much when I got onto the green I was feeling physically sick" (cited in White, 2002b, p. 22). Fortunately, this problem disappeared when he made a technical adjustment to his stroke by switching to a "broom handle" putter. Similarly, Eric Bristow, who won the world darts championship five times, choked so badly at times that he could not release the dart from his fingers. It took him years to overcome this problem (Middleton, 1996). Other athletes have not been so lucky. For example, the former snooker star Patsy Fagan had to abandon the sport because of his failure to overcome anxiety problems which affected his cueing action (Dobson, 1998). Less dramatically, anxiety has prompted remarkable collapses in the performance of such athletes as Jana Novotna and Greg Norman. To illustrate, consider what happened in the 1993 Wimbledon Ladies' Singles final between Jana Novotna (the Czech Republic) and Steffi Graf (Germany). Serving at 4–1 in the third set, with a point for 5–1, Novotna began to lose control. She produced a double-fault and some wild shots to lose that game. Later, she served *three* consecutive double-faults in her anxiety to increase her 4–3 lead over Graf (Thornley, 1993, p. 6). Interestingly, Novotna played in a similar fashion in the third round of the 1995 French Open championship in Paris when she lost a match to the American player Chanda Rubin despite having 9 match points when leading 5–0, 40–0 in the third set. In a similar vein, the golfer Greg Norman surrendered a *six-shot* lead in the final round of the 1996 US Masters' championship in Augusta to lose to Nick Faldo. More recently, the American golfer John Daly admitted that "when the heat was on, I choked" (*The Title*, 1998, p. 8) in the 1998 golf World Cup in New Zealand. Interestingly, in the case of Daly, a curious moderating factor was at work – namely, the effects of alcohol. Thus Daly believed that the effects of anxiety on his golf performance had been intensified by the fact that he had given up drinking before the tournament. Ironically, Daly's sobriety had caused him to feel more nervous than he would have been in the past: "Usually, when I have that situation I don't feel the pressure, I usually just knock them in. But now it's totally different. I guess I used to be so drunk I didn't care. Now it's tough, I feel all the nerves and the pressure more than ever" (*ibid.*, p. 8). In summary, the preceding examples show clearly that choking is a potentially significant problem for many athletes. But what do we really know about the nature and causes of this problem?

What is choking?

The term choking is used by sport psychologists to refer to a phenomenon in which athletic performance is impaired suddenly by anxiety. Technically, it involves "the failure of normally expert skill under pressure" (Masters, 1992, p. 344) or "the occurrence of suboptimal performance under pressure conditions" (Baumeister and Showers, 1986, p. 362). What makes this mental state intriguing psychologically is that it stems from a motivational paradox. To explain, in the pressure situations that prompt choking, the more effort the athlete puts into his or her performance, the *worse* it becomes. Put simply, choking occurs paradoxically because people try *too* hard to perform well.

The symptoms of choking are similar to those of any arousal state (see earlier in chapter). To begin with, they include tense muscles, shaky limbs, rapid heart and pulse rates, shortness of breath, butterflies in the stomach, "racing" thoughts and feelings of panic. In addition, choking may involve the sensation that one cannot complete the stroke or movement that one intends. For example, golfers who suffer from the "yips" often feel themselves getting tense over the ball and cannot complete a putting stroke due to interference from sudden involuntary movements. Likewise, bowlers in cricket who suffer from anxiety attacks suddenly feel as if they cannot release the ball. For example, Phil Edmonds, the former Middlesex and England bowler, was so badly afflicted with anxiety that he ended up standing in the crease and lobbing the ball at the batter's end (Middleton, 1996). Choking reactions may also be characterised by a tiny muscular spasm that occurs just as the stroke is about to be executed – even in practice situations. For example, Eric Bristow, a world champion in darts for three consecutive years, revealed that "I had it so bad I was even getting it when I was practising . . . It took me six or seven years to sort it out" (cited in Dobson, 1998, p. 16). Before concluding this section, it should be noted that choking seems to occur more frequently in untimed individual sports (e.g., golf, tennis) than in timed team-games (e.g., football, rugby). As yet, however, the precise reasons for this phenomenon remain unknown.

Happily, some progress has been made recently in understanding the aetiology of the "yips" in golf. Briefly, Smith, Adler, Crews, Wharen, Laskowski, Barnes, Bell *et al.* (2003) distinguished between two types of yips phenomena on the basis of whether they were caused by neurological or psychological factors. On the one hand, the yips "type 1" was postulated to reflect a neurological condition called "dystonia" in which a deterioration occurs in the motor pathways involving the basal ganglia. On the other hand, the yips "type 2" probably results from severe performance anxiety or choking. Interestingly, these authors speculated that golfers who suffer from the neurologically mediated type 1 yips may have to learn a new stance or else switch to a longer putter as the prognosis for this condition is poor.

What causes choking in sport?

In contemporary sport psychology, choking is regarded as an anxiety-based attentional difficulty (see also Chapter 4) rather than as a personality problem. This distinction is important because it suggests that the propensity to choke is not a character flaw but a cognitive problem arising from an interaction between anxiety and attention. If this attentional perspective is correct, then any athlete, regardless of his or her personality, can choke if s/he concentrates on the "wrong" target – anything which is outside his or her control or which is irrelevant to the task at hand. But what psychological mechanisms could underlie this choking effect?

According to Graydon (2002), two main theoretical accounts of choking have been postulated in recent years – the "self-consciousness" approach (Baumeister, 1984; Baumeister and Showers, 1986) and "processing efficiency" theory (Eysenck and Calvo, 1992). According to the self-consciousness model, when people experience a great deal of pressure to perform well they tend to think more about themselves and the importance of the event in which they are competing than they would normally. This excessive self-consciousness causes people to attempt to gain conscious control over previously automatic skills – just as a novice would do. As a result of this attempt to invest automatic processes with conscious control, skilled performance tends to unravel. According to some athletes, this unravelling of skill may be caused by thinking too much as one gets older. For example, consider Ian Woosnam's experience of trying to correct his putting stroke in golf. In particular, he said that "putting shouldn't be hard . . . but that's where the mind comes in. So much is running through your mind – hold it this way, keep the blade square – whereas when you're young, you just get hold of it and hit it. When you get old too much goes through your mind" (cited in White, 2002b, p. 22). This self-consciousness approach is similar to the conscious processing hypothesis (Masters, 1992) discussed in the previous section. Indeed, this latter hypothesis suggests that under pressure, "the individual begins thinking about how he or she is executing the skill, and endeavours to operate it with his or her explicit knowledge of its mechanics" (Masters, 1992, p. 345).

The second theoretical approach to choking, which is called processing efficiency theory (Eysenck and Calvo, 1992), suggests that anxious athletes may try to maintain their level of performance by investing extra effort in it. Although this increased effort investment may appear to generate immediate benefits, it soon reaches a point of diminishing returns. At this stage, the athlete may conclude that too much effort is required and so, s/he gives up. At that point, his or her performance deteriorates rapidly. Unfortunately, as Graydon (2002) pointed out, this theory is hampered by the difficulty of measuring mental effort objectively. For a brief account of psychological explanations of choking, see Box 3.5.

Box 3.5 Thinking critically about . . . explanations of choking behaviour in athletes

At first glance, choking in sport can be explained by attributing it to a nervous personality disposition. But as we learned in Chapter 2, trait explanations of behaviour are rather dubious. Logically, traits are inferences from, rather than causes of, behaviour. Therefore, there is always a danger of circularity when "explaining" behaviour using traits (e.g., "she acted nervously because she is an anxious person"). Instead of explaining choking in terms of anxiety-proneness, modern sport psychology researchers tend to consider it as an attentional problem. Specifically, it seems to be caused by focusing on oneself when one should be concentrating on the task at hand. To illustrate this approach, consider the research of Roy Baumeister in this field (see Azar, 1996, p. 21). To begin with, Baumeister (1984) began by distinguishing between sports that are dominated primarily by skill (e.g., golf, gymnastics) and those which require sustained effort (e.g., running, weightlifting). According to him, the pressure of a competition can facilitate performance of an "effortful" skill but can impede the performance of a precision skill. This theory was tested using simulated pressure situations in laboratory conditions. For example, Baumeister devised an effortful task by timing the speed and accuracy with which college students could arrange a deck of cards in numerical order. However, he introduced a pressure component into this task by telling the respondents that if they did better than their previous score, he would pay them $5. In general, results showed an improvement in sport performance in the pressure group. But when Baumeister used a skilful task (e.g., playing a videogame), different findings emerged. Thus Baumeister suggested that although pressure from competition or from public scrutiny makes people try harder on effortful tasks, it does not make them perform better on skill-based tasks. This happens because pressure tends to make people pay attention to automatic (i.e., highly practised) aspects of a given task. But here the picture becomes more complex. To explain, Baumeister proposes that athletes who are used to focusing on themselves choke less frequently than do counterparts who engage in less self-focused observation. In other words, pressure does not alter the chronic self-focus achieved by some people – but it *does* affect the behaviour of people who do not normally concentrate on their own actions.

Critical thinking questions
Can you think of any alternative explanation of Baumeister's results? Do you agree with him that excessive self-awareness is the main cause of choking in athletes? Why do you think choking is more prevalent in untimed individual sports rather than timed group sports?

In summary, we have learned that choking under pressure is a pervasive problem in sport. Unfortunately, no consensus has been reached as yet about the theoretical mechanisms that cause it. Nevertheless, most theories of this phenomenon agree that anxiety impairs performance by inducing the athlete to think too much, thereby regressing to an earlier stage of skill acquisition. By the way, some helpful practical tips on how to counteract choking are provided by Coop and Morrice (2002). This leads us to the next section of the chapter which explains how athletes can learn to control anxiety and cope with pressure situations in sport.

Controlling anxiety in sport: coping with pressure situations

Given the ubiquity of performance anxiety in sport, it is not surprising that psychologists have devised a variety of strategies in an effort to reduce athletes' pre-competitive anxiety levels. Before describing these techniques, however, we need to explain two key points. First, we must distinguish between pressure *situations* and pressure *reactions* in sport. This distinction is extremely important in applied sport psychology because athletes need to be trained to understand that they do not automatically have to experience "pressure" (i.e., an anxiety response) in pressure situations. Second, we need to understand what effective anxiety control or "coping" involves psychologically. In this regard, coping usually refers to any efforts which a person makes to master, reduce or otherwise tolerate pressure. These efforts fall into two main categories. On the one hand, some athletes like to confront the pressure situation directly. This strategy is known as "problem-focused" coping and involves such activities as obtaining as much information as possible about the pressure to be faced or forming a plan of action designed to reduce it. Alternatively, in "emotion-focused" coping, sports performers actively seek to change their interpretation of, and reaction to, the pressure situation in question. Therefore, they may use one of the many intervention strategies recommended by sport psychologists for anxiety reduction (see Gordin, 1998; Williams and Harris, 1998). Typically, problem-focused coping techniques are advisable when preparing for controllable sources of pressure whereas emotion-focused strategies are usually more appropriate when the pressure situation is uncontrollable.

With these two ideas in mind – that pressure lies in the mind of the beholder and that different strategies are available to facilitate active coping – here is a summary of some of the most popular techniques used by athletes to deal with unwanted anxiety in sport.

Understanding the experience of pressure

According to psychologists, we experience pressure and concomitant anxiety symptoms whenever we believe that a current or impending situation threatens us in some way. For example, a soccer player might be apprehensive about making a mistake in an important match in front of his or her home supporters. Alternatively, a swimmer may feel tense at the prospect of competing under the watchful eye of a feared coach. More generally, whenever there is a discrepancy between what we think we can do (i.e., our assessment of our own abilities) and what we believe we are *expected* to do (i.e., the perceived demands of the situation), we put *ourselves* under pressure. Psychologically, therefore, pressure is a subjective interpretation of certain objective circumstances (the "pressure situation"). Another point to note is that although we cannot change a pressure situation, we *can* change our reaction to it. Specifically, by restructuring the situation in our minds, we can learn to interpret it as a challenge to our abilities rather than as a threat to our well-being. To illustrate, consider what Jack Nicklaus, who is statistically the greatest golfer ever by virtue of winning eighteen major tournaments, revealed about the distinction between feeling nervous and excited. Specifically, he said,

> Sure, you're nervous, but that's the difference between being able to win and not being able to win. And that's the fun of it, to put yourself in the position of being nervous, being excited. I never look on it as pressure. I look on it as fun and excitement. That's why you're doing it. (cited in Gilleece, 1996, p. 7)

Unfortunately, this skill of perceiving pressure situations as *challenges* does not normally develop spontaneously in athletes. It can be cultivated through specialist advice and training, however. To learn the rudiments of cognitive restructuring in practical terms, try the exercise in Box 3.6.

Box 3.6 Cognitive restructuring in action: turning a pressure situation into a challenge

The purpose of this exercise is to show you how to use a technique called cognitive restructuring to turn a feared pressure situation into a manageable challenge (based on Moran, 1998). To begin, think of a situation in your sport or daily life that usually makes you feel anxious. Now, describe this situation by finishing the following sentence:

"I hate the pressure of . . .".

Fill in the missing words with reference to the pressure situation you have experienced. For example, you might write down "I hate the pressure of serving for the match when playing tennis". Alternatively, it could be "I hate the pressure of facing exams when I have not studied for them".

Now, think of this pressure situation again. This time, however, I would like you to *restructure* it in your head so that you think about it differently:

"I love the challenge of . . .".

Please note that you are not allowed to simply repeat what you wrote before. For example, you cannot say "I love the challenge of serving for the match when playing tennis". Instead, you have to pick something else to focus on in that pressure situation besides the fear of making mistakes. As we shall see in Chapter 4, the secret of maintaining your focus under pressure is to concentrate on something that is specific, relevant and under your own control. Usually, that means concentrating on some aspect of your *preparation* for the feared situation. For example, you could write "I love the challenge of preparing in the same way for every serve – no matter what the score is in the match". Notice how restructuring a situation can make you feel differently about it. You no longer see it as something to fear but as something which challenges your skills.

Having learned how athletes can restructure pressures as challenges, our next step is to examine some practical techniques for reducing anxiety in pressure situations.

Becoming more aware of anxiety: interpreting arousal signals constructively

Despite their talent and experience, many athletes have a poor understanding of what their body is telling them when they are anxious. In particular, they need to be educated to realise that anxiety is not necessarily a bad thing but merely a sign that they *care* about the results of what they are doing. Without such education, athletes tend to make the mistake of misinterpreting physical signs of *readiness* (e.g., a rapid heart beat, a surge of adrenaline) as harbingers of impending disaster. Therefore, sport performers must learn to perceive somatic arousal as an essential prerequisite of a good performance. Some players realise this intuitively when they concede that they cannot play well unless they feel appropriately "juiced" or pumped up for a contest. In summary, the first step in helping athletes to cope with anxiety is to educate them as to what it means and how to detect it. The psychological principle here is that awareness precedes control of psychological states.

Using physical relaxation techniques: lowering shoulders, slowing down and breathing deeply

In the heat of competition, athletes tend to speed up their behaviour. The obvious solution to this problem is to encourage them to slow down and relax whenever tension strikes. Of course, this advice must be tailored to the demands of the particular sport in question. Indeed, the feasibility of using physical relaxation techniques such as progressive muscular relaxation (see practical tips offered by Williams and Harris, 1998) depends heavily on the amount of "break time" offered by the sport in question. For example, in stop-start, untimed sports like golf or tennis, there are moments where it may be possible to lower one's shoulders, flap out the tension from one's arms and engage in deep-breathing exercises. Interestingly, some professional tennis players use a relaxation strategy whereby they visualise an imaginary area (e.g., behind the baseline of a tennis court) which serves as a relaxation zone where they can switch off mentally during breaks in play (see also Chapter 5 for a discussion of mental imagery in sport). However, this procedure may be impossible to use in athletic activities where play is fast and continuous (e.g., hockey). Also, another caution is necessary when teaching relaxation skills to athletes. In my experience, relaxation tapes do not work effectively with many sport performers as they are perceived as being too passive (see Box 3.7).

Box 3.7 Thinking critically about . . . using relaxation tapes with athletes

Relaxation tapes are often recommended to athletes who suffer from excessive anxiety. But do these tapes really work? Unfortunately, in my experience, such tapes are rarely effective with athletes. In fact, I recall seeing one anxious performer trying to "fast forward" his way through a relaxation tape!

Critical thinking questions
If anxiety has at least three different components (i.e., cognitive, somatic, behavioural), are all of them affected by a relaxation tape? If not, what aspects of anxiety are omitted? What are the differences between the situation in which athletes might listen to a relaxation tape and the competitive situation in which they become anxious? How can such differences be minimised? Using an automated database such as PsycINFO, can you locate any published research which evaluates the efficacy of relaxation tapes?

Giving oneself specific instructions

Anxiety is unhelpful because it makes people focus on what might go *wrong* (i.e., possible negative consequences) rather than on what exactly they have to do (the immediate challenge of the situation). Therefore, a useful way to counteract pressure in a competition is to ask oneself: "What exactly do I have to do right now?" By focusing on what they have to do, athletes can learn to avoid the trap of confusing the *facts* of the situation (e.g., "we're 1–0 down with ten minutes to go") with an anxious *interpretation* of those facts ("it's no use, we're going to lose"). Therefore, when athletes experience pressure, they should give themselves specific commands which help them to focus on actions that can be performed immediately.

Adhering to pre-performance routines

Most athletes use "pre-performance routines", or systematic sequences of pre-paratory thoughts and actions, in an effort to concentrate optimally before they execute important skills (e.g., golf putts, penalty-kicks; see also Chapter 4). Briefly, these routines serve as a cocoon against the adverse effects of anxiety. In particular, by concentrating on each step of the routine, athletes learn to focus on only what they can control – a vital principle of anxiety control.

Constructive thinking: encouraging oneself

When sports performers are anxious, their "self-talk" (i.e., what they say to them-selves inside their heads – see also Chapter 4) tends to become hostile and sarcastic. Although such frustration is understandable, it is *never* helpful to the person involved and may even make the situation worse. So, athletes need to talk to themselves with two objectives: to encourage themselves for their efforts (positive reinforcement) and to instruct themselves on what to do next (guidance). For example, an anxious tennis player might say, "Come on, this point now: go cross-court on the next return of serve".

Simulation training

One of the best ways of developing mental toughness (see Chapter 1) is to inoculate oneself against anxiety by practising under simulated pressure situations in training. For example, Miller (1997) described how, as part of their training for gold-medal success in the 1988 Olympics, the Australian women's hockey team practised under such adversity as gamesmanship (especially verbal "sledging") and adverse umpiring decisions. The concept of simulation training is discussed in more detail in Chapter 4.

In summary, this section of the chapter suggests that athletes can learn to cope with pressure situations by using at least four psychological strategies. First, they must be trained to believe that pressure lies in the eye of the beholder. Therefore, they must be taught to cognitively restructure competitive events so that they can be perceived as opportunities to display their talents (the challenge response) rather than as potential sources of failure (the fear response). Second, athletes must learn for themselves that systematic preparation tends to reduce pressure. One way of doing this is to use simulation training and mental rehearsal (or "visualisation" – see also Chapter 5) to inure themselves against anticipated difficulties. Third, anxious athletes can benefit from using self-talk techniques to guide themselves through pressure situations. Finally, when anxiety strikes, athletes must be prepared to deepen their routines and to use physical relaxation procedures in accordance with the temporal demands of the sport that they are performing.

Unresolved issues and new directions in research on anxiety in athletes

Despite a long tradition of research on anxiety in athletes, many issues remain unresolved in this field. Identification of these issues can help us to outline areas for further research on anxiety in sport performers (see also Gould *et al.*, 2002; Woodman and Hardy, 2001; Zaichkowsky and Baltzell, 2001).

First, the fact that researchers tend to use terms such as arousal, fear, anxiety and stress interchangeably in sport psychology suggests that greater conceptual rigour is required throughout this field. Fortunately, some progress in this regard is evident with the development of a model designed to clarify the relationship between arousal-related constructs (see Gould *et al.*, 2002). Second, idiographic research designs (i.e., ones which reflect the uniqueness or individuality of the phenomena of interest – Cashmore, 2002) are required to augment the traditional nomothetic approach (i.e., the search for general principles of psychology based on large samples of participants) to anxiety in sport. A good example of the idiographic approach comes from a recent interview study by Edwards *et al.* (2002) on the catastrophic experiences of elite athletes when choking competitively. Qualitative methodology such as focus groups (see Chapter 1) could be especially useful in exploring the meaning of anxiety to athletes. Third, little research has been conducted to date on the question of how cognitive anxiety and physiological arousal interact to affect performance in sport. Fourth, apart from anecdotal insights yielded by athletes and coaches, virtually nothing is known about the effects of emotions like anger or revenge on sport performance. Finally, surprisingly little research has been conducted on the anxiety experienced by athletes close to and during competitive performance (Thomas, Hanton and Jones, 2002). Field studies in this area are particularly welcome.

Ideas for research projects on anxiety in athletes

Here are five ideas for research projects on anxiety in athletes.

1 Based on the research of Thomas *et al.* (2002), you could investigate possible changes in athletes' experiences of arousal and anxiety in the days preceding a competitive match. As yet, little is known about the time course of these constructs among athletes in field settings. Of course, in such a study, you would have to be extremely careful to be as unobtrusive as possible in your data collection to prevent possible interference with the athletes' preparation.

2 It would be helpful to explore the extent to which athletes' anxiety experiences change during a series of competitive encounters (e.g., over the rounds of a

strokeplay tournament in golf). Few studies have been conducted on this topic (but see Butt, Weinberg and Horn, 2003).

3   It would be interesting to compare and contrast the sources of worry (cognitive anxiety) experienced by athletes in different sports (see Dunn, 1999; Dunn and Syrotuik, 2003). For example, do players involved in physical contact sports such as soccer or rugby have different worries from those of equivalent age and ability who are involved in non-contact sports such as golf or tennis?

4   You could evaluate the psychometric adequacy of one of the self-report anxiety scales described in this chapter. Surprisingly little data on these tests have been gathered from elite athletes.

5   It would be interesting to attempt a replication of Masters' (1992) study on the differential effects of anxiety on a skill acquired under either implicit or explicit learning. The hypothesis to be tested is that a golf putt that has been learned *implicitly* will be significantly more resistant to the effects of pressure than will one that has been learned explicitly (*ibid.*).

Summary

It is widely agreed that athletic success depends significantly on the ability to regulate one's arousal levels effectively. Put simply, sport performers need to know how and when to either psych themselves up or to calm themselves down in competitive situations.

- In the first section of the chapter, we examined the nature, causes and types of anxiety experienced by athletes. We also distinguished between anxiety and related constructs such as fear and arousal and explored the question of whether anxiety facilitates or impairs performance in sport.
- The second section of the chapter reviewed the most popular instruments available for the measurement of anxiety in athletes.
- Next, theories and research on the relationship between arousal, anxiety and performance were examined. This section also contained a brief discussion of the nature and causes of choking under pressure in sports.
- The fourth part of the chapter addressed the practical issue of how to control anxiety and cope effectively with pressure situations in sport.
- Finally, some unresolved issues on anxiety in athletes were identified along with several potentially fruitful new directions for future research in this field.

Chapter 4

Staying focused in sport: concentration in sport performers

I have learned to cut out all the unnecessary thoughts . . . on the track. I simply concentrate. I concentrate on the tangible – on the track, on the race, on the blocks, on the things I have to do. The crowd fades away and the other athletes disappear and now it's just me and this one lane. (Michael Johnson, three times Olympic gold-medallist in 400 m, and nine times a world athletics gold-medallist, cited in Miller, 1997, p. 64)

I was in my own little world, focusing on every shot. I wasn't thinking of what score I was on or anything . . . But today was probably as good as I have ever played. (Darren Clarke, Ryder Cup golfer, after he had shot a record-equalling 60 in the 1999 European Open championship in Kildare, Ireland, cited in Otway, 1999, p. 13)

At 16–16, I was singing songs in my head. I was singing Tom Jones' Delilah. I just tried to take my mind off the arena, the crowd, everything. (Mark Williams, 2003 world snooker champion, after he had defeated Ken Doherty 18–16 in the final, cited in Everton, 2003, p. 31)

Introduction

Most athletes have discovered from personal experience that "concentration", or the ability to focus effectively on the task at hand while ignoring distractions (Schmid and

Peper, 1998), is a vital prerequisite of successful performance in sport. For example, Garry Sobers, the former West Indies cricket star, proclaimed that "on the cricket field, you have to have a concentration that you can rely on to take you beyond the average" (cited in White, 2002a, p. 20). A similar testimonial to the value of concentration came from the Ryder Cup golfer Darren Clarke (see the quotation above) whose career-best round of 60 in the 1999 European Open championship coincided with a deliberate effort to focus on only one shot at a time. By contrast, Stephen Hendry, the snooker star, ascribed his narrow defeat (18–17) by Peter Ebdon in the 2002 world championship final to a lapse in concentration in the deciding frame of the match: "The one thing you want in the last frame is a chance and I had three but I bottled it . . . My concentration went" (cited in Everton, 2002, p. 25). Not only do these quotations highlight the value of focusing ability to athletes but they also indicate that top sports performers have developed rich informal theories about how their concentration systems work in competitive situations. To illustrate, Sobers proposed that "concentration's like a shower. You don't turn it on until you want to bathe . . . You don't walk out of the shower and leave it running. You turn it off, you turn it on . . . It has to be fresh and ready when you need it" (cited in White, 2002a, p. 20). Perhaps not surprisingly, these intuitive theories are often accompanied by idiosyncratic concentration techniques. For example, the snooker player Mark Williams raised a few eyebrows when he revealed that he had sung "Delilah" silently to himself in an effort to block out negative thoughts towards the end of his classic match against Ken Doherty in the 2003 world championship final. But can psychological techniques help athletes to turn on and turn off their concentration systems like a shower? What other strategies can they use to achieve and maintain an optimal focus for competition? What is concentration anyway and why do athletes lose it so easily in competitive situations?

The purpose of this chapter is to answer these and other relevant questions using the principles and findings of cognitive sport psychology: that part of the discipline that is concerned with understanding how the mind works in athletic situations. In order to achieve this objective, the chapter is organised as follows. To begin with, I shall explore the nature, dimensions and importance of concentration in sport psychology. Then I shall outline briefly the principal methods used by psychologists to measure attentional processes (including concentration) in athletes. The third section of the chapter will summarise some key principles of effective concentration that have emerged from research on attention in sport performers. Next, I shall address the question of why athletes are vulnerable to lapses or loss of concentration. In the fifth section, I shall review various practical exercises and psychological techniques that are alleged to improve concentration skills in athletes. The sixth section will outline some old problems and new directions for research in this field. Finally, I shall suggest some ideas for possible research projects on concentration in athletes.

Nature and importance of concentration in sport psychology

In cognitive sport psychology, concentration is regarded as one component of the multidimensional construct of "attention" (Moran, 1996). For cognitive psychologists, this latter construct refers to "a concentration of mental activity" (Matlin, 2002, p. 51) or the "concentration of mental effort on sensory or mental events" (Solso, 1998, p. 130). Let us now consider the main dimensions and types of attention before examining the special importance of concentration in sport.

Dimensions of attention

At least three separate dimensions of attention have been identified by cognitive psychologists. The first one is called "concentration" and refers to a person's ability to exert deliberate mental effort on what is most important in any given situation. For example, football players concentrate when they attempt to absorb coaching instructions delivered before an important match. The second dimension of attention denotes a skill in selective perception – namely, the ability to "zoom in" on task-relevant information while ignoring potential distractions. In other words, this dimension refers to the ability to discriminate relevant stimuli (targets) from irrelevant stimuli (distractors) that compete for our attention. To illustrate, a tennis player who is preparing to smash a lob from his or her opponent must learn to focus only on the flight of the ball, not on the distracting movement of the player(s) on the other side of the net. The third dimension of attention refers to a form of mental time-sharing ability whereby athletes learn, as a result of extensive practice, to perform two or more concurrent actions equally well. For example, a skilful basketball player can dribble with the ball while simultaneously looking around for a team-mate who is in a good position to receive a pass. As you can see, the construct of attention refers to at least three different cognitive processes: concentration or effortful awareness, selectivity of perception, and/or the ability to co-ordinate two or more actions at the same time. A fourth dimension of attention called "vigilance" has also been postulated (De Weerd, 2002). This dimension designates a person's ability to orient attention and respond to randomly occurring relevant stimuli over an extended period of time.

Unfortunately, occasionally the multidimensional nature of attention has spawned conceptual confusion among sport psychologists. For example, Gauron (1984) appeared to suggest that mental time-sharing is a weakness or pathology rather than a skill when he claimed that athletes could *"suffer* from divided attention" (p. 43, italics mine). Perhaps this author failed to grasp the fact that repeated practice enables people to spread their attentional resources between concurrent activities – often without any deterioration in performance. Incidentally, research shows that people are capable of doing two or more things at the same time provided that at least one of them is highly practiced and the tasks operate in different sensory modalities (Matlin, 2002). If neither task has been practised sufficiently and/or if the concurrent activities in question take place in the same sensory system, then errors will probably occur. In Box 5.3 in Chapter 5, we examine a practical implication of this principle when we explain why it is dangerous to drive a car while listening to a football match on the radio.

Since the 1950s, a number of metaphors have been coined by cognitive psychologists to describe the selective and divided dimensions of attention. For example, according to the "spotlight" metaphor (see review by Fernandez-Duque and Johnson, 1999), selective attention resembles a mental beam which illuminates targets that are located either in the external world around us or else in the subjective domain of our own thoughts and feelings. This idea of specifying a target for one's attentional spotlight is important practically as well as theoretically because it is only recently that sport psychologists have begun to explore the question of what exactly athletes should focus on when they are exhorted to "concentrate" by their coaches (see Mallett and Hanrahan, 1997; Singer, 2000). Unfortunately, the spotlight metaphor of attention is plagued by two main problems. First, it has not adequately explained the mechanisms by which executive control of one's attentional focus is achieved. Put simply, who or what is directing the spotlight? This question is difficult to answer without postulating a homunculus. Second, the spotlight metaphor neglects the issue of what lies *outside* the beam of our concentration. Therefore, it ignores the possibility that unconscious factors can affect people's attentional processes. Interestingly, such factors have attracted increasing scrutiny from cognitive scientists in recent years. Thus Nadel and Piattelli-Palmarini (2002) remarked that although cognitive science began with the assumption that cognition was limited to conscious processes, "much of the domain is now concerned with phenomena that lie behind the vale of consciousness" (p. xxvi). We shall return to this issue later in the chapter when we consider how unconscious sources of distraction can affect athletes.

Metaphors have also been coined for divided attention. Thus the fact that people can sometimes do two or more concurrent tasks equally well suggests that attention is a "resource" or pool of mental energy (Kahneman, 1973). This pool is believed to be available for allocation to competing tasks depending on various strategic principles. For example, motivation, practice and arousal are held to increase spare attentional capacity whereas task difficulty is believed to reduce it (*ibid.*). Unfortunately, the resource metaphor of divided attention is somewhat simplistic. Thus Navon and Gopher (1979) have argued that people may have multiple attentional resources rather than a single pool of undifferentiated mental energy. Each of these multiple pools may have its own functions and limits. For example, Schmidt and Lee (1999) discovered that the attentional resources required for a motor skill such as selecting a finger movement may be separate from those which regulate a verbal skill such as the pronunciation of a word. Although intuitively appealing, multiple resource theories of attention have been criticised on the grounds of being "inherently untestable" (Palmeri, 2002, p. 298). To explain, virtually any pattern of task interference can be "explained" *post hoc* by attributing it to the existence of multiple pools of attentional resources.

In general, cognitive models of attention, whether based on spotlight or resource metaphors, have two major limitations. First, they have focused mainly on external (or environmental) determinants of attention and have largely overlooked internal factors (e.g., thoughts and feelings) which can distract athletes. For example, consider what happened to Sonia O'Sullivan, the 2000 Olympic silver-medallist in the 5,000 m event in Sydney, who allowed her concentration to slip in the 10,000 m race at the Games. According to her post-event interview, the thought of the medal she had won prevented her from focusing properly in the next race: "If I hadn't already got a medal, I might have fought a bit harder. But when you have a medal already, maybe you think about that medal for a moment. It probably was only for a lap . . . but that is all it takes for a race to get away from you" (cited in Curtis, 2000, p. 29). Of course, as we indicated in Chapter 1, athletes' insights into their own mental processes are not always reliable or valid from a researcher's perspective. The second weakness of cognitive models of attention is that they ignore the influence of emotional states. This neglect of the affective dimension of behaviour is lamentable because it is widely known in sport psychology that anxiety impairs attentional processes. For example, the phenomenon of choking under pressure (whereby nervousness causes a sudden deterioration of athletic performance; see also Chapter 3) illustrates how the beam of one's attentional spotlight can be directed *inwards* when it should be focused only on the task at hand. For a comprehensive account of the role of emotional factors in sport, see Hanin (2000).

To summarise, this section of the chapter highlighted two important ideas. First, concentration is just one aspect of the multidimensional construct of attention. In particular, it refers to the ability to pay attention to the task at hand while ignoring distractions from internal as well as external sources. In addition, despite their plausibility, cognitive metaphors of attention have certain limitations which hamper theories and research on concentration in athletes. Having sketched the nature of concentration, let us now consider its importance for optimal athletic performance.

Importance of concentration in sport

The importance of concentration in sport is indicated by at least three sources of evidence: anecdotal, descriptive and experimental (see Chapter 1 for a discussion of the main research methods used in sport and exercise psychology).

First, as the anecdotal examples at the beginning of this chapter reveal so graphically, many top athletes attest to the value of focusing skills in sport. To illustrate, Michael Johnson, the multiple Olympic gold-medallist, attributed much of his athletic success to an extraordinary skill in selective attention which enabled him to block out potential distractions on the track. Secondly, descriptive studies in the form of athlete surveys indicate the importance of concentration to sport performance. For example, Durand-Bush, Salmela and Green-Demers (2001) discovered that focusing skills were regarded as crucial to success by a large sample ($n = 335$) of athletes in their study. Unfortunately, this survey did not explore in depth what the term "focusing" meant to athletes. Therefore we cannot be sure that athletes and researchers were referring to the same cognitive construct in this study. Another source of descriptive evidence on the value of concentration in sport comes from studies of "flow" states or "peak performance" experience of athletes. These experiences refer to coveted yet elusive occasions during which the physical, technical, tactical and psychological components of sporting performance (see Figure 1.2) intertwine perfectly for the athlete in question. Given the importance of such experiences to athletes, it is not surprising that they have attracted considerable research interest from psychologists (see Carr, 2004; Jackson, 1996; Kimiecik and Jackson, 2002; Nakamura and Csikszentmihalyi, 2002). Interestingly, a key finding from such research is that flow experiences emanate mainly from a *cognitive* source – namely, a heightened state of concentration. Indeed, Jackson, Thomas, Marsh and Smethurst (2001) defined flow as a "state of concentration so focused that it amounts to absolute absorption in an activity" (p. 130). In summary, studies of peak performance suggest that athletes tend to perform optimally when they are totally absorbed in the task at hand. This state of mind is epitomised in a quote from the golfer Darren Clarke who remarked after a tournament victory that his ball had seemed to be "on the club-face for so long I could almost tell it where I wanted it to go" (cited in Kimmage, 1998, p. 29L) (see Figure 4.1). Unfortunately, research on flow states in sport is plagued by some conceptual and methodological problems that are summarised in Box 4.1.

Figure 4.1 In the zone . . . Darren Clarke is totally focused on the task at hand
Source: courtesy of Inpho Photography

Box 4.1 Thinking critically about . . . flow states in sport

Flow states or peak performance experiences tend to occur when people become absorbed in challenging tasks that demand intense concentration and commitment (see review in Kimiecik and Jackson, 2002). In such desirable but fleeting states of mind, performers become so deeply immersed in the activities of the present moment that they lose track of time, feel highly alert and experience a temporary sense of euphoria and joy. Research in this field was pioneered by a Hungarian psychologist named Mihalyi Csikszentmihalyi (pronounced "chick-sent-me-hai") who set out to explore the reasons why some people pursue activities (e.g., painting, mountain-climbing) that appear to offer minimal extrinsic rewards (Csikszentmihalyi, 1975). Briefly, he argued that they do so because of the *intrinsic* feeling of satisfaction that arises whenever there is a perfect match between the challenge of the task at hand and the skill-level of the performer. Since the 1980s, sport psychologists have explored the nature and characteristics of flow states in athletes. Given the mercurial quality of these states of mind, however, it is not surprising that research on this topic has encountered conceptual and methodological difficulties. For example, Jackson (1996) found that some of Csikszentmihalyi's (1990) alleged correlates of flow states were absent from the experiences of her sample of elite athletes. This finding raises the possibility that flow experiences may be more task-specific than was believed previously. Turning to methodological problems, there is evidence that people are not always reliable judges of their own mental processes. To illustrate, Brewer, Van Raalte, Linder, and Van Raalte (1991) discovered that when people were given spurious feedback concerning their performance on certain tasks, they unwittingly distorted their subsequent recall of the way in which they had performed these tasks. In other words, their recollections of task performance were easily contaminated by "leading" information. Is there a danger of similar contamination of athletes' retrospective accounts of flow states?

Critical thinking questions

Why is it so difficult to predict when flow states are likely to occur? Why, in your view, are these states so rare in sport? Do you think that athletes could experience flow states in practice – or do they happen only in competition? Is it possible to study flow states without disrupting them? Can you think of one advantage and one disadvantage of using questionnaires to assess athletes' peak performance experiences (see Jackson and Eklund, 2002)? What other methods could be used to study flow states? See Jackson (1996) for some ideas in this regard. Do you think that a flow state comes *before* or *after* an outstanding athletic performance? Give reasons for your answer. Finally, do you think that athletes can be trained to experience flow states more regularly?

One of the critical thinking questions in Box 4.1 concerned the apparent rarity of peak experiences in sport. One possible reason why flow states are not more common in sport is that our concentration system is too fragile to maintain the type of absorption that is necessary for them. To explain, psychologists believe that concentration is controlled mainly by the "central executive" component of our working memory system (whose main objective is to keep a small amount of information active in our minds while we make a decision about whether or not to process it further: see Logie, 1999). This component of the memory system regulates what we consciously attend to, such as holding a telephone number in our heads before we write it down. Unfortunately, the working memory system is very limited in its capacity and duration. This limitation helps to explain why people are easily distracted. Put simply, we find it very difficult to focus on our intentions when there is a lot of activity going on around us. Other causes of distractibility will be examined briefly later in the chapter. In any case, as soon as we begin to pay attention to task-*irrelevant* information – something other than the job at hand – our mental energy is diverted and we lose our concentration temporarily. Despite the issues raised in Box 4.1, there is little doubt that athletes who perform at their peak tend to report focusing only on *task-relevant* information – which is a sign of effective concentration.

The third source of evidence on the importance of concentration in sport comes from experimental research on the consequences of manipulating athletes' attentional focus in competitive situations. For example, Mallett and Hanrahan (1997) found that sprinters who had been trained to use race plans that involved deliberately focusing on task-relevant cues ran faster than those in baseline (control) conditions. Similarly, the use of "associative" concentration techniques in which athletes are trained to focus on bodily signals such as heart beat, respiratory signals and kinaesthetic sensations has been linked with faster performance in running (Masters and Ogles, 1998; Morgan, 2000) and swimming (Couture, Jerome and Tihanyi, 1999) in comparison with "dissociative" techniques such as paying attention to thoughts other than those concerned with bodily processes.

To summarise, the preceding strands of evidence converge on the conclusion that concentration is vital for success in sport. This conclusion has been echoed by researchers such as Abernethy (2001) who observed that it is difficult to imagine any skill that could be more important to athletic performance than "paying attention to the task at hand" (p. 53). But how can psychologists measure people's attentional skills?

Measurement of attentional processes in athletes

As concentration is a hypothetical construct, and hence unobservable, it cannot be measured directly. Nevertheless, attentional processes can be assessed *indirectly* using methods drawn from three main paradigms: the psychometric (or individual differences), experimental and neuroscientific traditions in psychology. Due to space restrictions, we can provide only a brief overview of these paradigms here. For a more detailed review of these methodological approaches, see Abernethy (2001), Abernethy, Summers and Ford (1998) and Boutcher (2002).

Psychometric approach

Some sport psychologists have attempted to measure individual differences in attentional processes in athletes through the use of specially designed paper-and-pencil tests. For example, the "Test of Attentional and Interpersonal Style" (TAIS;

Nideffer, 1976) is one of the most popular inventories in this field and is used as a screening device in many applied sport psychology settings, such as in the Australian Institute for Sport (Bond and Sargent, 1995; Nideffer, Sagal, Lowry and Bond, 2001). It contains 144 items, broken down into 17 sub-scales, which purport to measure people's attentional processes in everyday situations (e.g., "When I read, it is easy to block out everything but the book"). Although the original version of this test was not intended for use with athletic populations, several sport-specific versions of the TAIS have emerged in recent years. The TAIS is based on Nideffer's model of attention which can be outlined briefly as follows. According to Nideffer, people's attentional focus varies simultaneously along two independent dimensions – namely, "width" and "direction". With regard to width, attention is believed to range along a continuum from a broad focus (where one is aware of many stimulus features at the same time) to a narrow one (where irrelevant information is excluded effectively). Attentional "direction" refers to the target of one's focus: whether it is external or internal. These dimensions of width and direction may be combined factorially to yield four hypothetical attentional styles. To illustrate, a narrow external attentional focus in sport is implicated when a golfer looks at the hole before putting. By contrast, a narrow internal focus is required when a gymnast mentally rehearses a skill such as back-flip while waiting to compete. Despite its plausibility and popularity, however, this test has several flaws which are discussed in Box 4.2.

Box 4.2 Thinking critically about . . . the Test of Attentional and Interpersonal Style (TAIS)

The Test of Attentional and Interpersonal Style (TAIS; Nideffer, 1976) is a popular and plausible test of attentional processes. Nevertheless, its validity and utility have been questioned. So, what are the strengths and weaknesses of the TAIS?

On the positive side, the TAIS has face validity because it seems to make "intuitive sense to coaches and athletes" (Bond and Sargent, 1995, p. 394). Also, there is some empirical support for its construct validity. For example, Nideffer (1976) reported that unsuccessful swimmers were attentionally "overloaded" when compared to successful counterparts. Similarly, Wilson, Ainsworth and Bird (1985) discovered that volleyball players who had been rated by their coaches as "good concentrators" under competitive stress scored significantly lower on the "broad external" focus (BET) and "broad internal" focus (BIT) sub-scales than did "poor concentrators". Unfortunately, such strengths must be weighed against the following weaknesses of this test. First, it is questionable whether athletes are capable of evaluating their own attentional processes using self-report instruments (Boutcher, 2002). Second, the TAIS assesses *perceived*, rather than actual, attentional skills. Accordingly, we cannot be sure that athletes who complete it are differentiating between what they *actually* do and what they would like us to believe that they do in everyday situations requiring attentional processes. Third, the TAIS fails to differentiate between athletes of different skill levels in sports in which selective attention is known to be important (Summers and Ford, 1990). Fourth, Nideffer's theory is conceptually flawed because it does not distinguish between task-relevant and task-irrelevant information in sport situations. In view of these difficulties, Cratty (1983) concluded that the TAIS was only "marginally useful, and the data it produces are not much better than the information a coach might obtain from simply questioning athletes or observing their performance" (p. 100).

Critical thinking questions
From the evidence above, what conclusions would you draw about the validity of the TAIS? If you were re-designing this test, what changes would you make to its content and format? Can a psychological test be useful in applied settings even if its construct validity is questionable? More generally, do you think that paper-and-pencil tests of attention should be augmented by other measurement paradigms? If so, which ones would you suggest and why?

As you can see, the psychometric paradigm, as epitomised by the TAIS, is a popular if somewhat flawed approach to the measurement of attentional processes in athletes. Nevertheless, this approach has yielded several promising new instruments which claim to measure concentration skills. For example, Hatzigeorgiadis and Biddle (2000) developed a seventeen-item test called the "Thought Occurrence Questionnaire for Sport" (TOQS) which purports to assess the degree to which athletes experience distracting thoughts (e.g., about previous mistakes that they have made) during competition. Although this measure lacks validation data at present, it is a promising tool because of its explicit theoretical origins.

Neuroscientific approach

The second measurement paradigm in this field involves the search for reliable psychophysiological correlates and/or neural substrates of attentional processes in athletes. Within this paradigm, three main waves of measurement development may be identified.

To begin with, indices of attention such as heart rate (HR) have been monitored in athletes as they perform self-paced skills in target sports like archery, pistol-shooting and rifle-shooting (see review by Hatfield and Hillman, 2001). A reliable finding that has emerged from this line of research is that cardiac deceleration (or a slowing of the heart rate) tends to occur among elite rifle-shooters in the seconds before they pull the trigger of their guns (see review by Boutcher, 2002). This finding is interesting in the light of Garry Sobers's comments at the beginning of this chapter because it suggests that expert target sport performers can indeed "switch on" their concentration processes at will. Interestingly, a recent study by Radlo, Steinberg, Singer, Barba and Melnikov (2002) reported that dart-throwers' heart rates may vary in accordance with the type of attentional focus that they adopted. For example, when they used an external attentional strategy, their heart rates tended to decline just before they threw the darts. As yet, however, the psychophysiological significance of this heart rate change is unknown.

The next methodological innovation in this paradigm occurred with the development of equipment designed to measure continuous patterns of electrical activity in the brain. This "brain wave" technology included electroencephalographic (EEG) methods and those based on "event-related potentials" (or ERPs). In a typical EEG experiment, an electrode is attached to a person's scalp in order to detect the electrical activity of neurons in the underlying brain region. Another electrode is then attached to the person's earlobe, where there is no electrical activity to detect. Then the EEG is recorded to indicate the difference in electrical potentials detected by the electrodes (Kolb and Whishaw, 2003). In recent years, a considerable amount of research has been conducted on EEG activity in athletes (Hatfield and Hillman, 2001). From such research, certain cerebral asymmetry effects are evident. For example, in keeping with previous findings from heart rate studies, research suggests that just before expert archers and pistol performers execute their shots, their EEG records tend to display a distinctive shift from left-hemisphere to right-hemisphere activation (*ibid.*). This shift is believed to reflect a change in executive control from the verbally based left hemisphere to the visuo-spatially specialised right hemisphere. Put differently, target-shooters display a marked reduction in the extent of their verbal-analytical processes (including self-talk) prior to shot execution. In the light of this finding, perhaps the snooker player Mark Williams's strategy of covert singing (see earlier in chapter) was not so daft after all because it may have helped him to avoid thinking too much prior to shot execution. More generally, EEG research findings suggest that top-class athletes know how to regulate their physiological processes as they prepare for the performance of key skills (see also Chapter 6 for a discussion of expertise in sport). Unfortunately, this theory has not been tested systematically to date as the EEG is a relatively blunt instrument because its data are confounded with the brain's *global* level of electrical activity. Nevertheless, EEG research in sport has had at least one practical implication. Specifically, it has led to the use of biofeedback techniques designed to help athletes to become more effective at controlling their cortical activity (Boutcher, 2002). Staying with brain wave measurement in sport, event-related potentials (ERPs) are brief changes in EEG signals that are synchronised with or "time locked" to some eliciting event or stimulus. Unlike the EEG, which is a measure of continuous electrical activity in the brain, ERPs reflect transient cortical changes that are evoked by certain information-processing events. Typically, ERPs display characteristic peaks of electrical activity that begin a few milliseconds after the onset of a given stimulus (e.g., a loud noise) and continue for up to a second afterwards (see Kolb and Whishaw, 2003, for more details).

The most recent methodological wave in neuroscientific research on attention concerns the use of functional brain imaging techniques. With these procedures (e.g., positron emission tomography and functional magnetic resonance imaging; see also Chapter 5), researchers can obtain clear and dynamic insights into the specific brain regions that are activated when people perform specific cognitive tasks. Unfortunately, little research has been conducted to date on brain imaging in athletes. In summary, the major advantage of neuroscientific techniques over their psychometric counterparts is that they yield *objective* data on biological processes which can be recorded *while* the athlete is performing his or her skills. Unfortunately, the major drawbacks associated with the neuroscientific paradigm are cost and practicality.

Experimental approach

The third approach to the measurement of attentional processes in athletes comes from capacity theory in experimental psychology (see review by Abernethy, 2001). Briefly, capacity theory (Kahneman, 1973) suggests that attention may be defined operationally in terms of the interference between two tasks (a primary task and a secondary task) that are performed simultaneously. To explain this "dual-task paradigm", if the two tasks can be performed as well simultaneously as individually, then it may be concluded that at least one of them was automatic (i.e., demanding minimal attentional resources). However, if the primary task is performed less well when it is combined with the secondary task, then both tasks are believed to require attentional resources. Adopting this experimental approach, the dual-task method of measuring attention requires participants to perform two tasks over three conditions. In condition one, the person has to perform the primary task on its own. Likewise, in condition two, s/he must perform the secondary task on its own. In condition three, however, s/he is required to perform both tasks concurrently.

When the dual-task paradigm is used in sport psychology, the primary task usually consists of a self-paced or "closed" skill (i.e., one that can be performed without interference from others such as target-shooting in archery) whereas the secondary task typically requires the subject to respond to a predetermined probe signal (e.g., an auditory tone). Following comparison of performance between these three conditions, conclusions may be drawn about the attentional demands of the primary and secondary tasks. Using this method, sport psychologists are usually interested in people's performance in condition three – the concurrent task situation. In this condition, participants are required to perform a primary task which is interrupted periodically by the presentation of the probe stimulus. When this probe is presented, the person has to respond to it as rapidly as possible. It is assumed that the speed of responding to the probe is related inversely to the momentary attention devoted to the primary task. Therefore, if a primary task is cognitively demanding, then a decrement should be evident in secondary task performance. However, if the performance of the secondary task in the dual-task condition does not differ significantly from that evident in the relevant control condition, then it may be assumed that the primary task is relatively effortless (or automatic).

In summary, the dual-task paradigm is an attempt to measure the spare mental capacity of a person while s/he is engaged in performing some task or mental activity. To illustrate an early application of this approach, consider a study by Landers, Qi and Courtet (1985) on rifle-shooting. Briefly, these authors tested the hypothesis that under conditions of increased arousal, performance on a primary task would improve or be maintained whereas performance of a secondary task would deteriorate. Here, it is assumed that when people show deficits in performance of the secondary task, some attentional narrowing has occurred. Therefore, performance on this secondary task may serve as an index of an athlete's peripheral awareness. Based on this logic,

Landers *et al.* (1985) compared rifle-shooters' performance on a primary target-shooting task with that on a secondary auditory task, while they competed under low-stress and high-stress conditions. Results showed that when the difficulty of the primary task was increased (e.g., by increasing time demands), performers in the high-stress condition took longer to react to the auditory stimuli (i.e., secondary task) than they did when performing in the low-stress condition. This result suggests that as their level of arousal increased, the shooters had less spare attentional capacity available to monitor the peripheral auditory task. More recently, Beilock, Carr, MacMahon and Starkes (2002) investigated the attentional demands of dribbling skills in soccer for players of different skill levels. In this study, expert and novice soccer players were required to dribble a ball through a series of pylons (the primary task) while simultaneously listening to a series of words for the occurrence of a specified target (the secondary task). Results showed that the secondary task impaired the performance of the primary task for the less skilled players regardless of which foot they dribbled with – but had no effect on experts' dominant foot-dribbling performance. But Beilock *et al.* (2002) also discovered that the experts' dribbling performance deteriorated in the presence of the secondary task when they had to use their non-dominant foot for dribbling. These findings corroborate the view that the skills of expert athletes in any sport require minimal attentional scrutiny.

Unfortunately, despite its ingenuity, the dual-task paradigm has not been used widely to measure attentional processes in athletes – although it may offer researchers a way of validating athletes' reports of their imagery experiences (see Chapter 5). A comprehensive review of this paradigm in research on attention in athletes is provided by Abernethy (2001).

To summarise this section of the chapter, the self-report approach to the measurement of concentration processes is favoured by most sport psychologists for reasons of brevity, convenience and economy. Given the issues raised in Box 4.2, however, the results yielded by psychological tests of concentration must be interpreted cautiously. Also, few if any of the available measures of attention deal explicitly with *concentration* skills. Moreover, no consensus has emerged about the best combination of these methods to use when assessing athletes' attentional processes in applied settings. Now that we have explained the nature, importance and measurement of concentration in sport, let us consider some psychological principles which govern an optimal focus in athletes.

Principles of effective concentration

Based on general reviews of the relationship between attention and athletic performance (Abernethy, 2001; Moran, 1996), at least five theoretical principles of effective concentration in sport may be identified (see Figure 4.2). As you will see, three of them concern the establishment of an optimal focus whereas the other two describe how it may be disrupted or lost.

The first principle of effective concentration is that a focused state of mind requires deliberate mental effort and intentionality on the part of the athlete concerned. In short, one must *prepare* to concentrate rather than hope that it will occur by chance. This principle was endorsed by Oliver Kahn, the German international

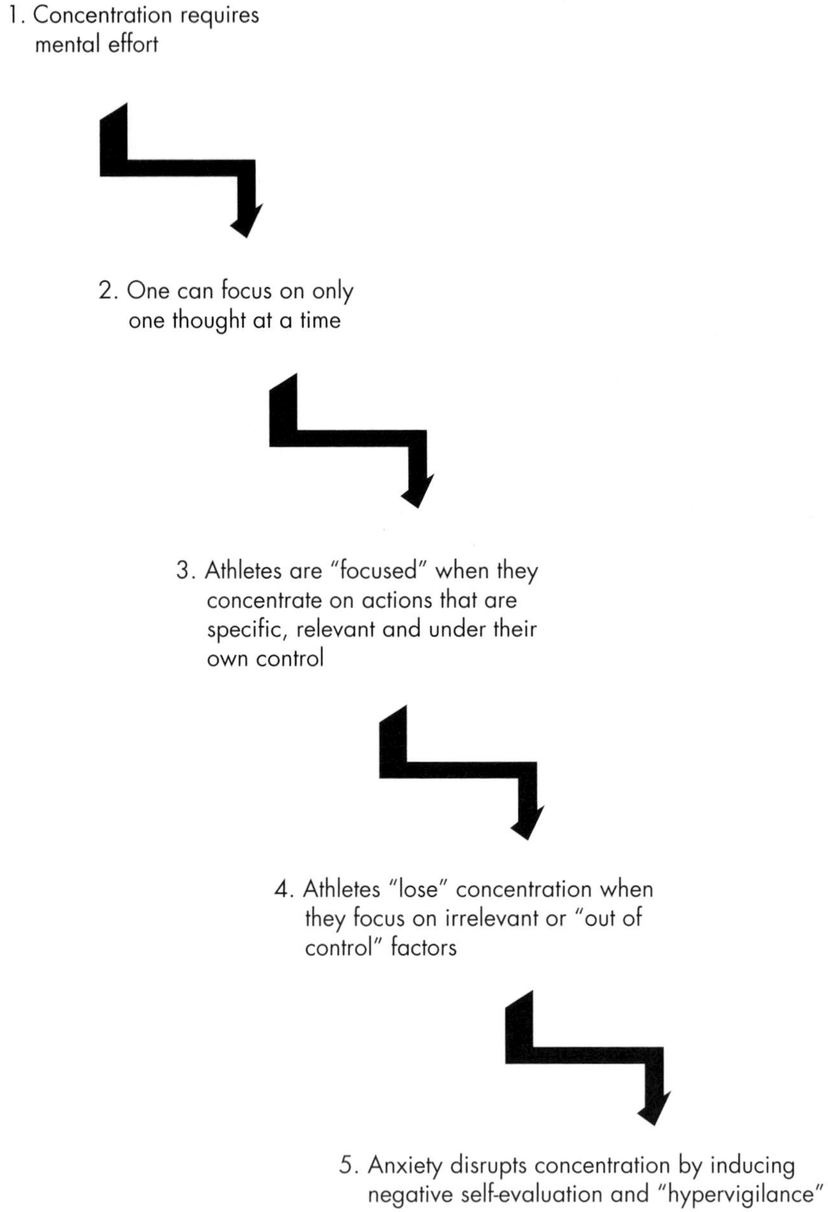

1. Concentration requires
   mental effort

2. One can focus on only
   one thought at a time

3. Athletes are "focused" when they
   concentrate on actions that are
   specific, relevant and under their
   own control

4. Athletes "lose" concentration when
   they focus on irrelevant or "out of
   control" factors

5. Anxiety disrupts concentration by inducing
   negative self-evaluation and "hypervigilance"

Figure 4.2 Concentration principles
Source: based on Moran, 1996

and Bayern Munich goalkeeper, who remarked that "if you don't prepare yourself mentally it's impossible to maintain consistently high standards" (cited in Brodkin, 2001, p. 34). Second, although skilled athletes can divide their attention between two or more concurrent actions (see earlier discussion), they can focus consciously on only *one thought* at a time. Indeed, this "one thought" principle may be hard-wired into our brains because research shows that the working memory system which regulates conscious awareness (see Logie, 1999) is fragile and limited in duration (unless extensive practice occurs; see also Chapter 6). Third, as we indicated earlier in the chapter, research on the phenomenology of peak performance states (e.g., Jackson, 1995) indicates that athletes' minds are focused optimally when there is no difference between what they are thinking about and what they are doing. By implication, sport performers tend to concentrate most effectively when they direct their mental spotlight (recall our earlier discussion of various metaphors of attention) at actions that are specific, relevant and, above all, under their own control. Fourth, research shows that athletes tend to lose their concentration when they pay attention to events and experiences that are in the future, out of their control, or otherwise irrelevant to the task at hand (Moran, 1996). We shall return to this issue in the next section. The final principle of effective concentration acknowledges the potentially disruptive influence of emotions such as anxiety. In particular, anxiety impairs concentration systems in several distinctive ways. For example, it overloads working memory with worries (or cognitive anxiety; see Chapter 3). In addition, it tends to restrict the beam of one's mental spotlight and also shifts its focus onto self-referential stimuli. Interestingly, Baumeister (1984) invoked this principle in attempting to explain the psychological mechanisms underlying the phenomenon of choking under pressure (see Chapter 3). Briefly, he postulated that anxiety causes people to monitor their own skills excessively, thereby leading to a sudden deterioration of performance. Anxiety also precipitates task-irrelevant information processing. Thus Janelle, Singer and Williams (1999) discovered that anxious drivers who participated in a motor-racing simulation were especially likely to attend to irrelevant cues. Another way in which anxiety affects sport performance is by its influence on the *direction* of athletes' attentional focus. In particular, anxiety may encourage them to dwell on real or imagined personal weaknesses (self-focused attention) and on potential threats in the environment, thereby inducing a state of "hypervigilance". Interestingly, Liao and Masters (2002) suggested that anxiety hampers performance paradoxically by inducing performers to rely too much on explicit conscious control of their skills. It is clear, therefore, that anxiety affects the content, direction and width of athletes' concentration beam (see also Janelle, 2002; Moran, Byrne and McGlade, 2002).

In summary, at least five principles govern either the maintenance or loss of an optimal focus for athletes. But why do sport performers lose their concentration in the first place?

Why do athletes lose their concentration?

As we learned from Figure 4.2, when people focus on factors that are either irrelevant to the job at hand or beyond their control, they lose concentration and their performance deteriorates. However, psychologists believe that concentration is never really "lost" – but merely *re-directed* at some target that is irrelevant to the task at hand. For example, have you ever had the experience of realising suddenly that you have been reading the same sentence in a book over and over again without any understanding simply because your mind was "miles away"? If so, then you have distracted yourself by allowing a thought, daydream or feeling to become the target of your attention. By the way, this problem can be overcome by writing down two or three specific study questions before you approach a textbook or notes (see advice in Moran, 2000b). Let us now consider the question of why athletes lose their concentration.

In general, psychologists distinguish between external and internal sources of distraction (see review by Moran, 1996). Whereas the former term refers to objective stimuli which divert our attentional spotlight away from its intended target, internal distractions include a vast array of thoughts, feelings and/or bodily sensations (e.g., pain, fatigue) which impede our efforts to concentrate on the job at hand.

Typical external distractions include such factors as sudden changes in ambient noise levels (e.g., the click of a camera), gamesmanship by opponents (e.g., at corner-kicks in football opposing forwards often stand in front of the goalkeeper to prevent him/her from tracking the incoming ball; see Moran, 2003a) and unpredictable playing surface or weather (e.g., a golfer may become distracted by windy conditions). Often, these distractions lead to impaired performance at the worst possible moment for the athlete concerned. For example, consider what happened to Tiger Woods in the 2002 American Express World Championship in Mount Juliet, Ireland. He was leading the field, playing the final hole and well on the way to becoming only the second golfer ever to win a tournament without registering a single bogey when he was distracted by the click of a camera as he prepared to play his second shot to the green. This distraction cost him a bogey and a place in the record-books – although he still won the tournament! Nevertheless, he was very angry afterwards: "It was the most important shot of the week. Of all the times to take a photo . . . I didn't want to end the tournament with a shot like the one I hit" (cited in Mair, 2002, p. S9). By contrast, internal distractions are self-generated concerns which arise from our own thoughts and feelings.

Typical distractions in this category include wondering what might happen in the future, regretting what has happened in the past, worrying about what other people might say or do and/or feeling tired, bored or otherwise emotionally upset (see Figure 4.3).

A graphic example of a *very* costly internal distraction occurred in the case of the golfer Doug Sanders who missed a putt of less than three feet which would have earned him victory at the 1970 British Open championship in St Andrews, Scotland. This error not only prevented him from winning his first major tournament – but also deprived him of millions of pounds in prize-money, tournament invitations and advertising endorsements. Remarkably, Sanders's attentional lapse was precipitated by thinking too far ahead – making a victory speech before the putt had been taken. Years later, he revealed what had happened: "I made the mistake about thinking which section of the crowd I was going to bow to"! (cited in Gilleece, 1999, p. 23). Clearly, Sanders had inadvertently distracted *himself* by allowing his mental spotlight to shine into the future instead of at the task in hand.

Figure 4.3 Internal distractions can upset athletes' concentration in competitive situations

Unfortunately, few studies have been conducted by psychologists on the phenomenology of distraction in athletes. This neglect of distractibility is attributable to two main problems: one theoretical and the other methodological. First, for many years (e.g., dating back to the multi-store model of memory; see Matlin, 2002, for details) cognitive researchers assumed falsely that information flows into the mind in only one direction – from the outside world inwards. In so doing, they ignored the possibility that information (and hence distractions) could travel in the opposite direction – from our long-term memory into our working memory system or current awareness. A second reason for the neglect of internal distractions in psychology stems from a methodological bias. Specifically, researchers focused on external distractions simply because they were easier to measure than were self-generated distractions. As a result of this bias, the theoretical mechanisms by which internal distractions disrupt concentration were largely unknown until recently. Fortunately, Wegner (1994) developed a model which rectifies this oversight by attempting to explain why people tend to lose their concentration ironically or precisely at the most *inopportune* moment.

Briefly, Wegner's (1994) theory proposed that the mind wanders *because* we try to control it. In other words, when we are anxious or tired, trying *not* to think about something may paradoxically increase its prominence in our consciousness. For example, if you try to focus on falling asleep, you will probably achieve only a prolonged state of wakefulness! Similarly, if you attempt to block a certain thought from entering your mind, you may end up becoming more preoccupied with it. This tendency for a suppressed thought to come to mind more readily than a thought that is the focus of intentional concentration is called "hyperaccessibility" and is especially likely to occur under conditions of mental load. Clearly, there are many situations in sport in which such ironic self-regulation failures occur. For example, issuing a negative command to your doubles partner in tennis (such as "whatever you do, don't double-fault") may produce counter-intentional results. What theoretical mechanisms could account for this phenomenon?

According to Wegner (1994), when people try to suppress a thought, they engage in a controlled (conscious) search for thoughts that are different from the unwanted thought. At the same time, however, our minds conduct an automatic (unconscious) search for any signs of the unwanted thought. In other words, the intention to suppress a thought activates an automatic search for that very thought in an effort to monitor whether or not the act of suppression has been successful. Normally, the conscious intentional system dominates the unconscious monitoring system. But under certain circumstances (e.g., when our working memories are overloaded or when our attentional resources are depleted by fatigue or stress), the ironic system prevails and an ironic intrusion of the unwanted thought occurs. Wegner attributes this rebound effect to cognitive load. But although this load is believed to disrupt the conscious mechanism of thought control, it does not interfere with the automatic (and ironic) monitoring system. Thus Wegner (1994) proposed that "the intention to concentrate creates conditions under which mental load enhances monitoring of irrelevancies" (p. 7). To summarise, Wegner's (1994) research helps us to understand why athletes may find it difficult to suppress unwanted or irrelevant thoughts when they are tired or anxious.

Perhaps not surprisingly, Wegner (2002) has investigated ironies of *action* as well as those of thought. For example, consider what happens when people who are asked *not* to overshoot the hole in a golf putt are given tasks which impose a heavy mental load on them. In such situations, the unwanted action (overshooting the hole) is exactly what happens.

Interestingly, the ironic theory of mental control has begun to attract attention within sport psychology (e.g., see a review paper by Janelle, 1999). Furthermore, it has also received empirical support from research within this field. For example, Dugdale and Eklund (2002) asked participants to watch a series of videotapes of Australian Rules footballers, coaches and umpires. In one experiment, results revealed that participants became *more* aware of the umpires when instructed *not* to pay attention to them. Clearly, this finding raises doubts about the validity of asking anxious athletes *not* to worry about an important forthcoming athletic event or outcome.

At this stage, it might be helpful to do some research on distractions. So, if you are interested in exploring the factors that cause athletes to lose their focus, try the exercise in Box 4.3.

Box 4.3 Exploring distractions in sport

The purpose of this exercise is two-fold. First, you will find out what the term "concentration" means to athletes. In addition, you will try to classify the distractions which they perceive to have affected their performance.

To begin with, find three athletes who compete regularly in different sports (e.g., golf, soccer, swimming). Request their permission to tape your interview with them on either an audio-cassette recorder or a mini-disc recorder. Then, ask them the following questions:

1   What does the term "concentration" mean to you?
2   On a scale of 0 (meaning "not at all important") to 5 (meaning "extremely important"), how important do you think that the skill of concentration is for successful performance in your sport?
3   What sort of distractions tend to upset your concentration *before* a game/match? Describe the situation and the distraction which results from it.
4   What distractions bother you *during* the event itself? Describe the situation and the distraction which results from it.
5   Please give me a specific example of how a distraction changed your focus and/or affected your performance. Tell me what the distraction was, how it occurred and how you reacted to it.
6   What techniques do you use, if any, to cope with distractions?

Analysis
Compare and contrast the athletes' answers to your questions. The word "focus" will probably feature in responses to Q 1. Try to establish exactly what athletes mean by this word. You should also find that athletes regard concentration as being very important for successful performance in their sport (Q 2). After you have compiled a list of distractions (Qs 3 and 4), you will probably find that they fall into two main categories: external and internal. Is there any connection between the type of sport which the athletes perform and the distractions that they reported?

Having explored what concentration is, how to measure it and why we often lose it, we should now examine the various strategies recommended by sport psychologists for improving focusing skills.

Concentration training exercises and techniques

Applied sport psychology is replete with strategies which claim to improve concentration skills in athletes (see Greenlees and Moran, 2003, for a recent review). In general, the purpose of these strategies is to help an athlete to achieve a focused state of mind in which there is no difference between what s/he is thinking about and what s/he is doing (see Figure 4.2). If this happens, the athlete's mind is "cleared of irrelevant thoughts, the body is cleared of irrelevant tensions, and the focus is centred only on what is important at that moment for executing the skill to perfection" (Orlick, 1990, p. 18). But what concentration strategies do sport psychologists recommend to athletes and what do we know about their efficacy?

In general, two types of psychological activities have been alleged to enhance focusing skills in sport performers: concentration training exercises and concentration techniques (Moran, 1996; Moran, 2003b). The difference between these activities is that whereas the former ones are intended for use mainly in athletes' training sessions, the latter are designed primarily for competitive situations.

Among the plethora of concentration exercises recommended by sport psychologists are such activities as the "concentration grid" (a visual search task endorsed by Schmid and Peper, 1998, in which the participant is required to scan as many digits as possible within a given time limit), watching the oscillation of a pendulum (which is alleged to show how "mental concentration influences your muscle reactions", Weinberg, 1988, p. 87) and looking at a clock "and saying 'Now' to yourself every alternate 5 and 10 seconds" (Hardy and Fazey, 1990, p. 9). Unfortunately, few of these activities are supported by either a coherent theoretical rationale or adequate evidence of empirical validity. For example, take the case of the ubiquitous concentration grid. Surprisingly, no references were cited by Weinberg and Gould (1999) to support their claim that it was used "extensively in Eastern Europe as a pre-competition screening device" (p. 347) or that "this exercise will help you learn to focus your attention and scan the environment for relevant cues" (*ibid.*). Despite the absence of such evidence, the grid is recommended unreservedly by Schmid and Peper (1998) as a "training exercise for practising focusing ability" (p. 324). Similar criticisms apply to the idea of watching a pendulum in an effort to enhance one's concentration. Interestingly, this exercise has a long and controversial history. Thus according to Spitz (1997), it was a precursor of the Ouija board and has been used in the past for water divining, diagnosing physical illness and even for "receiving messages from the great beyond" (p. 56)! In summary, there appears to be little empirical justification for the use of generic visual search and/or vigilance tasks in an effort to improve athletes' concentration skills. Indeed, research suggests that visual skills training programmes are not effective in enhancing athletes' performance in sports such as soccer (Starkes, Helsen and Jack, 2001) – a finding which challenges the validity of using visual search tasks like the concentration grid as a training tool.

In contrast to the previous concentration exercises, "simulation training" (Orlick, 1990) may have a satisfactory theoretical rationale. This exercise, which is also known as "dress rehearsal" (Schmid and Peper, 1998), "simulated practice" (Hodge and McKenzie, 1999) and "distraction training" (Maynard, 1998), proposes that athletes can learn to concentrate more effectively in real-life pressure situations by simulating them in practice conditions. Interestingly, a number of anecdotal testimonials to the value of this practice have emerged in recent years. To illustrate, Earl Woods, the father and initial coach of Tiger Woods, used such methods on him when he was a boy. Indeed, Woods Senior claimed that "all the strategies and tactics of distraction I'd learned I threw at that kid and he would just grit his teeth and play ... and if anyone tries pulling a trick on him these days he just smiles and says 'my dad used to do that years ago'" (cited in *Evening Herald*, 2001, p. 61). Similarly, Javier Aguirre, the coach of the Mexican national soccer team, instructed his players to practise penalty-taking after every friendly match in the year leading up to the 2002 World Cup in an effort to prepare for the possibility of penalty-shootouts in that competition. As he explained: "there will always be noise and that is the best way to practise" (cited in Smith, 2002b, p. S3). Interestingly, Sven-Göran Eriksson is reported to have required his penalty-takers to practise walking from the centre-circle to the penalty-area in an effort to simulate match conditions (Winter, 2002a). Some additional suggestions for the simulation of distractions in team-sports may be found in Moran (2003a).

Unfortunately, despite its intuitive appeal, simulation training has received little or no empirical scrutiny as a concentration strategy. Nevertheless, some support for its theoretical rationale may be found in cognitive psychology. For example, research on the "encoding specificity" principle of learning shows that people's recall of information is facilitated by conditions which resemble those in which the original encoding occurred (Matlin, 2002). Based on this principle, the simulation of competitive situations in practice should lead to positive transfer effects to the competition itself. In addition, adversity training may counteract the tendency for novel or unexpected stimuli to distract athletes in competition. The simulation of these factors in training should reduce their attention-capturing qualities subsequently. To summarise, there is some theoretical justification for the belief that simulation training could enhance athletes' concentration skills. Nevertheless, this conclusion is tentative for one important reason. Specifically, even the most ingenious simulations cannot replicate completely the *actual* arousal experienced by athletes in competitive situations. For example, Ronan O'Gara, the Ireland and Lions rugby out-half, admitted that although he can practise taking penalty-kicks in training, "it's completely different in a match where my heartbeat is probably 115 beats a minute whereas in training it's about 90–100" (cited in Fanning, 2002, p. 6). Clearly, it is difficult to simulate accurately the emotional aspects of competitive action.

Having reviewed some popular concentration exercises, we should now turn to the second type of attentional skills intervention used in sport psychology – namely, concentration techniques listed in Figure 4.4.

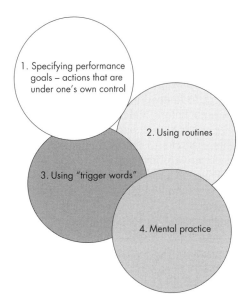

Figure 4.4 Concentration techniques
Source: based on Moran, 1996, 2003a; b

Specifying performance goals

In Chapter 2, we explained the theory and practice of goal-setting. As you may recall, sport psychologists (e.g., Weinberg, 2002) distinguish between result goals (e.g., the outcomes of sporting contests) and performance goals (or specific actions lying within the athlete's control). Using this distinction, some researchers (e.g., Winter and Martin, 1991) have proposed that specifying performance goals can improve athletes' concentration skills. According to this theory, tennis players could improve their concentration on court by focusing solely on such performance goals as seeking 100 per cent accuracy on their first serves. This suggestion seems plausible theoretically because performance goals encourage athletes to focus on task-relevant information and on controllable actions. Additional support for this idea springs from studies on the correlates of people's best and worst athletic performances. Thus Jackson and Roberts (1992) found that collegiate athletes performed worst when they were preoccupied by result goals. Conversely, their best displays coincided with an explicit focus on performance goals. Similarly, Kingston and Hardy (1997) discovered that golfers who focused on specific action goals improved both their performance and their concentration. In summary, there seems to be some support for the idea that performance goals can facilitate concentration skills in athletes.

Using pre-performance routines

Most top-class athletes display characteristic sequences of preparatory actions before they perform key skills. For example, tennis players tend to bounce the ball a preferred number of times before serving. Similarly, rugby place-kickers like to go through a systematic series of steps before striking the ball (see Figure 4.5).

These preferred action sequences and/or repetitive behaviours are called "pre-performance routines" and are typically conducted prior to the execution of self-paced skills (i.e., actions that are carried out largely at one's own speed and without interference from other people). According to Harle and Vickers (2001), such routines are used to improve concentration and performance.

At least three types of routines are common in sport. First, pre-event routines are preferred sequences of actions in the run up to competitive events. Included here are stable preferences for what to do on the night before, and on the morning of, the competition itself. Second, pre-performance routines are characteristic sequences of thoughts and actions which athletes adhere to prior to skill-execution – as in the case of tennis players bouncing the ball before serving. Finally, post-mistake routines are action sequences which may help performers to leave their errors in the past so that they can re-focus on the task at hand. For example, a golfer may "shadow" the correct swing of a shot that had led to an error.

Support for the value of pre-performance routines as concentration techniques comes from both theoretical and empirical sources. Theoretically, pre-performance routines may improve concentration for several reasons. First, they are intended to encourage athletes to develop an appropriate mental set for skill-execution by helping them to focus on task-relevant information. For example, many soccer goal-

Figure 4.5 Pre-performance routines help players to concentrate
Source: courtesy of Sportsfile and UCD Department of Sport

keepers follow pre-kick routines in an effort to block out any jeering that is directed at them by supporters of opposing teams. Second, such routines may enable athletes to concentrate on the present moment rather than on past events or on possible future outcomes. Finally, pre-performance routines may prevent athletes from devoting too much attention to the mechanics of their well-learned skills – a habit which can unravel automaticity (see Beilock and Carr, 2001; see also Chapter 3). Thus routines may help to suppress the type of inappropriate conscious control that often occurs in pressure situations. A useful five-step pre-performance routine for self-paced skills is described by Singer (2002) and Lidor and Singer (2003).

Augmenting the preceding arguments is empirical evidence derived from case studies which show that routines can improve athletes' concentration skills and performance. For example, Crews and Boutcher (1986) compared the performances of two groups of golfers – those who had been given an eight-week training programme of only swing practice and those who had participated in a "practice-plus-routine" programme for the same duration. Results revealed that the more proficient golfers benefited more from using routines than did the less skilled players. However, recent research suggests that the routines of expert athletes may actually be far more variable than had been anticipated. Thus Jackson and Baker (2001) analysed the pre-strike routine of the prolific former Welsh international and Lions rugby kicker, Neil Jenkins, who scored 1,049 points in 87 games for his country. As expected, he reported using a variety of concentration techniques (such as thought-stopping and mental imagery) as part of his pre-kick routine. But surprisingly, these researchers discovered that Jenkins varied the timing of his pre-kick behaviour as a function of the difficulty of the kick he faced. This finding shows that routines are not as rigid or stereotyped as was originally believed. More recently, in another case study, Shaw (2002) reported that a professional golfer had experienced some attentional benefits arising from the use of a pre-shot routine. Specifically, the golfer reported that "the new routine had made him more focused for each shot and therefore less distracted by irrelevancies" (p. 117). In the absence of objective data, however, caution is warranted about the validity of this conclusion.

Apart from their apparent variability in different situations, pre-performance routines give rise to two other practical issues that need to be addressed here. First, they may lead to superstitious rituals on the part of the performer. For example, consider the mixture of routines and rituals used by the Yugoslavian tennis player Jelena Dokic. Apparently, she never steps on white lines, she always blows on her right hand while waiting for her opponent to serve and she bounces the ball five times before her own first serve and twice before her second serve (Edworthy, 2002). Furthermore, she insists that "the ball boys and girls always have to pass me the ball with an underarm throw which is luckier than an overarm throw" (cited in *ibid.*, p. S4). Clearly, this example highlights the fuzzy boundaries between pre-performance routines and superstitious rituals in the minds of some athletes.

At this stage, it may occur to you that routines are merely superstitions in disguise. To explore this issue further, read Box 4.4.

Box 4.4 Thinking critically about . . . routines and superstitions in sport

Pre-performance routines are consistent sequences of thoughts and behaviour displayed by athletes as they prepare to execute key skills. Given the apparently compulsive quality of this behaviour, however, it may be argued that routines are not really concentration techniques but merely *superstitions*. Is this allegation valid?

Superstition may be defined as the belief that, despite scientific evidence to the contrary, certain actions are causally related to certain outcomes. Further-more, we know that athletes are notoriously superstitious – largely because of the capricious nature of sport (Vyse, 1997). Thus the South African golfer Ernie Els never plays with a ball marked with the number two because he associates it with bad luck. Similarly, the former tennis player Martina Hingis refused to step on the lines on the tennis court for fear of misfortune (Laurence, 1998, p. 23). In general, sport psychologists distinguish between routines and super-stitious behaviour on two criteria: control and purpose. First, consider the issue of control. The essence of superstitious behaviour is the belief that one's fate is governed by factors that lie *outside* one's control. But the virtue of a routine is that it allows the player to exert complete control over his or her preparation.

Indeed, players often shorten their pre-performance routines in adverse circumstances (e.g., under unfavourable weather conditions). Unfortunately, the converse is true for superstitions. Thus they tend to grow *longer* over time as performers "chain together" more and more illogical links between behaviour and outcome. A second criterion which may be used to distinguish between routines and rituals concerns the technical role of each behavioural step followed. To explain, whereas each part of a routine should have a rational basis, the components of a superstitious ritual may not be justifiable objectively. Despite these neat conceptual distinctions, the pre-shot routines of many athletes are often invested with magical thinking and superstitious qualities.

Critical thinking questions
Do you think that athletes really understand the difference between routines and rituals? What do you think of the idea that it does not really matter that athletes are superstitious – as long as it makes them feel mentally prepared for competition?

A second problem with routines is that they need to be reviewed and revised regularly in order to avoid the danger of automation. To explain, if athletes maintain the same pre-performance routines indefinitely, their minds may begin to wander as a consequence of tuning out. Clearly, an important challenge for applied sport psychologists is to help athletes to attain an appropriate level of conscious control over their actions before skill-execution.

"Trigger words" as cues to concentrate

During the 2002 Wimbledon ladies' singles tennis final between the Williams sisters, Serena Williams (who defeated Venus 7–6, 6–3) was observed by millions of viewers to be reading something as she sat down during the change-overs between games. Afterwards, she explained that she had been reading notes that she had written to herself as trigger words or instructional cues to remind her to "hit in front" or "stay low" (R. Williams, 2002b, p. 6) (see Figure 4.6).

For similar reasons, many sport performers talk to themselves either silently or out loud when they compete – usually in an effort to motivate themselves. This covert self-talk may involve praise (e.g., "Well done! That's good"), criticism ("You idiot – that's a stupid mistake") and/or instruction ("Swing slowly"). Accordingly, self-talk may be positive, negative or neutral. As a cognitive self-regulatory strategy, self-talk may enhance concentration skills (Williams and Leffingwell, 2002). In particular, Landin and Herbert (1999) discovered that tennis players who had been trained to use instructional cues or trigger words (such as "split, turn") attributed their improved performance to enhanced concentration on court. More recently, a survey of the nature and uses of self-talk in athletes was conducted by Hardy, Gammage and Hall (2001). One of the findings reported in this study was that athletes used it for such mastery reasons as staying "focused" (p. 315).

Figure 4.6 Serena Williams uses trigger words to help her to concentrate effectively
Source: courtesy of Inpho Photography

Can self-talk improve athletes' concentration? Unfortunately, no published research on this question could be located. However, it is possible that positive and/or instructional self-statements could enhance attentional skills by reminding athletes about what to focus on in a given situation. For example, novice golfers may miss the ball completely on the fairway in the early stages of learning to swing the club properly. In an effort to overcome this problem, golf instructors may advise learners to concentrate on sweeping the grass rather than hitting the ball. This trigger phrase ensures that learners stay "down" on the ball instead of looking up to see where it went. In general, trigger words must be short, vivid and positively phrased to yield maximum benefits. They should also emphasise positive targets (what to aim for) rather than negative ones (what to avoid).

Mental practice

As we shall explain in Chapter 5, the term mental practice (MP) or "visualisation" refers to the systematic use of mental imagery in order to rehearse physical actions. It involves "seeing" and "feeling" a skill in one's imagination before actually executing it (Moran, 2002a). Although there is considerable empirical evidence that MP facilitates skill-learning and performance (see Chapter 5), its status as a concentration technique remains uncertain. Anecdotally, however, mental imagery is used widely by athletes for the purpose of focusing. Thus Mike Atherton, the former England cricket captain, used to prepare mentally for test matches by actually going to the match venue and visualising "who's going to bowl, how they are going to bowl . . . so that nothing can come as a surprise" (cited in Selvey, 1998, p. 2). From this quote, it seems that imagery helps performers to prepare for various hypothetical scenarios, thereby ensuring that they will not be distracted by unexpected events. However, this hypothesis has not been tested empirically to date. Therefore, despite the fact that mental imagery is known to improve athletic performance, its status as a concentration technique is uncertain.

In summary, we have reviewed four psychological techniques that are used regularly in an effort to improve athletes' concentration skills. Unfortunately, few studies have evaluated the efficacy of these techniques in enhancing concentration skills. Despite the absence of such evidence, these four concentration techniques appear to be both plausible and useful in sport settings.

Old problems and new directions in research on concentration in athletes

Despite a considerable amount of research on attentional processes in athletes, some old problems remain. The purpose of this section of the chapter is to identify these unresolved issues and to sketch some potentially fruitful new directions for research in this field.

To begin with, as is evident from the insights of Garry Sobers, Darren Clarke and Stephen Hendry earlier in this chapter, further research is required on the "meta-attentional" processes of athletes or their intuitive theories about how their own concentration systems work. Interestingly, it could be argued that concentration skills enhancement in applied sport psychology is really an exercise in meta-attentional training whereby athletes learn to understand, and gain some control over, their apparently capricious concentration system. As yet, however, we know very little about the nature, accuracy and/or malleability of athletes' theories of how their own mental processes operate. Next, we need to address the question of why athletes lose their concentration so easily in competitive situations. Unfortunately, until recently, few studies addressed this topic. Therefore, little or nothing was known about the influence of internal distractions – those which arise from athletes' own thoughts and feelings – on performance (but see review by Moran, 1996). However, with the advent of Wegner's (1994, 2002) ironic processes model and the development of novel ways of assessing athletes' susceptibility to cognitive interference (e.g., see the test developed by Hatzigeorgiadis and Biddle, 2000), a greater understanding has emerged of the mechanisms underlying athletes' internal distractions. Third, Simons (1999) raised the old question of whether or not sport performers actually know precisely what they should be concentrating *on* in different sport situations. This question is often neglected by sport psychologists in their enthusiasm to provide practical assistance to athletes. As a solution, Simons (1999) recommended that instead of exhorting players to "watch the ball", sport psychology consultants should ask such questions as "What way was the ball spinning as it came to you?" or "Did you guess correctly where it would land"? Fourth, what is the best way to measure concentration skills in athletes? Although three different approaches to this question have been proposed in sport psychology (i.e., the psychometric, neuroscientific and experimental; see earlier in chapter), there is a dearth of validation data on tests of concentration in sport. This situation is disappointing because unless concentration skills can be measured adequately, it is impossible to evaluate whether or not they have been improved by the exercises and techniques discussed earlier. A related problem is that few tests have been devised explicitly to assess concentration skills in athletes. This situation is puzzling given the importance of this construct for successful performance in sport. Fifth, additional research is required on the relationship between the *structure* of various athletic activities and their attentional demands (see also Chapter 1 for a discussion of this issue). For example, do untimed games such as golf place different cognitive demands on athletes' concentration systems as compared with those imposed by timed activities (e.g., soccer)? If so, what theoretical mechanisms could account for such differences? A related issue concerns the *type* of concentration required for success in various sports. Intuitively, it seems reasonable to expect that sports such as weight-lifting may require short periods of intense concentration while others (e.g., cycling) may demand sustained alertness for a longer duration. If this idea is supported by empirical research, is it reasonable to expect that the same concentration intervention packages should work equally well in all sports? Unfortunately, at present, many applied sport psychologists seem to endorse a "one-size-fits-all" approach in advocating the same toolbox of psychological strategies (e.g., goal-setting, self-talk) for a variety of different athletic problems. Finally, additional research is needed to establish the precise mechanisms by which emotions (such as anxiety) affect athletes' concentration processes. One way to address this question is to explore the visual search behaviour of anxious athletes as they tackle laboratory simulations of sport-relevant tasks (see Moran *et al.*, 2002).

Ideas for research projects on concentration in athletes

Here are six ideas for possible research projects on attentional processes in athletes.

1   It would be interesting to investigate precisely what athletes of different levels of ability, and also from different sports, understand by the term "focusing". Unfortunately, many studies in this field assume that athletes interpret this term in the same way as researchers. Is this assumption valid?

2   You could fill a gap in the field by exploring the nature and extent of expert–novice differences in athletes' "meta-attentional awareness" (i.e., their understanding of, and control over, how their concentration system works). Little is known about this topic so far.

3   You could address some of the unresolved questions in research on flow states in athletes. For example, do athletes ever experience such states when practising or training? Or do they occur only in competitive situations?

4   It would be a good idea to evaluate the reliability and validity of Nideffer's (1976) "Test of Attentional and Interpersonal Style" (TAIS) using a large sample of athletes.

5   It would be helpful to test Wegner's (1994) theory of ironic control in a sport setting. For example, using the methodology developed by Dugdale and Eklund (2002), can ironic rebound effects be reduced by manipulating athletes' attentional focus?

6   Do concentration techniques such as pre-performance routines and cue-words increase athletes' performance of self-paced skills such as golf putting, tennis serving or rugby place-kicking in actual sport settings? Surprisingly few field studies have been conducted in this area.

Summary

I began this chapter by explaining that the term "concentration" refers to the ability to focus mental effort on what is most important in any situation while ignoring distractions. As we discovered, this ability is a crucial prerequisite of successful performance in sport. For example, research suggests that the ability to focus effectively is associated with peak performances in athletes. Unfortunately, despite a century of empirical studies on attentional processes, there is still a great deal of confusion about what concentration is and how it can be measured and improved in athletes. Therefore, the purpose of this chapter was to alert you to the progress and prospects of research in this field.

*   We began by examining the nature, dimensions and importance of the construct of concentration in sport.
*   In the next section, we outlined briefly three approaches to the measurement of attentional processes (including concentration) in athletes.
*   The third section of the chapter explained the main principles of effective concentration that have emerged from research on the ideal performance states of athletes.

- In the fourth section of the chapter, we explored the question of why athletes lose their concentration so easily.
- The fifth section reviewed various practical exercises and psychological techniques that are purported to enhance concentration skills in athletes.
- The sixth section outlined some unresolved issues concerning attentional processes in sport performers and also indicated some potentially fruitful new directions for research in this field.

Chapter 5

Using imagination in sport: mental imagery and mental practice in athletes

You have to see the shots and feel them through your hands. (Tiger Woods, quoted in Pitt, 1998a, p. 5)

I work with a psychologist on imagery training. Sometimes when I am driving to the ground and am sitting in traffic, I will do a couple of crosses in my mind. (David James, West Ham and England goalkeeper, quoted in Winter, 2002a, p. S3)

The image is the ice-man. You walk like an ice-man and think like an ice-man. (Richard Faulds, 2000 Olympic gold medal-winning trap-shooter, quoted in Nichols, 2000, p. 7)

Introduction

As the above quotations show, athletes such as golfers (e.g., Tiger Woods), footballers (e.g., the goalkeeper David James) and Olympic champions (e.g., Richard Faulds) believe that "mental imagery", or the ability to simulate in the mind information that is not currently being perceived by the sense organs, is helpful for the learning and performance of sport skills. Similar testimonials to the value of "visualisation" abound in other fields of skilled performance such as dance. For example, Highfield (2002) described brain imaging research which showed that Deborah Bull, the British former ballet star, used imagery extensively when watching others dance. The imagery strategies used by dancers have also been investigated by Hanrahan and Vergeer (2000–2001). Perhaps not surprisingly, mental imagery techniques are widely recommended by sport psychologists (e.g., Vealey and Greenleaf, 1998) as intervention procedures to enhance various mental processes (e.g., self-confidence) as well as motor skills. To illustrate, Callow, Hardy and Hall (1998) reported that an imagery-based training programme had facilitated enhanced confidence in elite badminton players. Therefore, as imagery has become a common component of sport psychological interventions (Holmes and Collins, 2002), it has been acclaimed as a "central pillar of applied sport psychology" (Perry and Morris, 1995, p. 339). Nevertheless, athletes who practise imagery may be regarded as rather eccentric. For example, when the England goalkeeper David James rehearses his skills imaginatively during traffic delays, he often receives puzzled glances from other drivers. As he says, "I have had a few strange looks when people see my head nodding from side to side but I firmly believe that it is part of the repetitive process that every sportsman requires" (D. James, 2003, p. 36). In summary, athletes, dancers and sport psychologists endorse the value of imagery as a cognitive tool for giving performers a winning edge in their chosen field. But is this belief in the power of imagery supported by empirical evidence in psychology? Or does it merely reflect some "New Age", pseudo-scientific mysticism?

In attempting to answer these challenging questions, the present chapter will explore a variety of intriguing issues at three different levels: practical, methodological and theoretical. For example, if mental imagery *does* improve athletic performance, is it possible that athletes could practise their skills in their heads without leaving their armchairs? Or are the alleged benefits of systematic mental rehearsal too small to be of any practical significance to sport performers? Turning to methodological issues, how can we measure people's mental images? After all, they are among the most private and ephemeral of all our psychological experiences. At a theoretical level, many fascinating questions have emerged in this field. For example, what happens in our brains when we imagine something? Also, what psychological mechanisms could account for the effects of mental rehearsal on skilled performance? More generally, can research on imagery processes in athletes provide us with any valuable insights into how the mind works? For example, could it be that imagery is not something that we "have" in our minds but something that we "do" with our brains? Perhaps the best way to address these questions is to explore the main psychological theories, findings and issues in research on mental imagery in sport performers. In order to achieve this objective, the present chapter is organised as follows.

In the first section, I shall investigate the nature and types of mental imagery and also explain what the term "mental practice" means in sport psychology. The next section will review the main findings, theories and issues arising from research on mental practice in sport. The third part of the chapter will consider briefly the measurement of mental imagery skills in sport. After that, I shall describe what researchers have learned about the ways in which athletes use mental imagery in various athletic situations. Next, I shall sketch some new directions for research on imagery in athletes. Finally, a few ideas for possible research projects in this field will be provided.

What is mental imagery?

Historically, the term "mental imagery" has been used in two ways (Wraga and Kosslyn, 2002). On the one hand, it designates the content of one's imagination – namely, the subjective experience of "seeing with the mind's eye", for example. On the other hand, imagery refers to "an internal representation that gives rise to the experience of perception in the absence of the appropriate sensory input" (p. 466). It is this latter understanding of the term that guides the present chapter.

One of the most remarkable features of the mind is its capacity to mimic or simulate experiences. Psychologists use the term mental imagery to describe this cognitive (or knowledge-seeking) process which we use every day in order to represent things (e.g., people, places, experiences, situations) in working memory in the absence of appropriate sensory input (Moran, 2002a). For example, if you close your eyes, you should be able to imagine a set of traffic lights changing from green to red (a visual image), the sound of an ambulance siren (an auditory image) or maybe even the muscular feelings evoked by running up steep stairs (a kinaesthetic image). Theoretically, imagery involves perception without sensation. Specifically, whereas perception occurs when we interpret sensory input, imagery arises from our interpretation of stored, memory-based information. Thus the process of generating a mental image may be understood crudely as running perception backwards (Behrmann, 2000). As we shall see later, the term "mental practice" (MP) refers to a particular application of mental imagery in which performers "practise" in their heads, or rehearse their skills symbolically, before actually executing them. MP is also known as motor imagery (Slade, Landers and Martin, 2002).

If imagery resembles perception, then there should be similarities between the measurable cortical activity involved in these psychological processes. Put simply, similar parts of the brain should "light up" when we imagine things as when we actually perceive them. For example, visual imagery should be associated with neural activity in the cortical areas that are specialised for visual perception. Until relatively recently, this hypothesis remained untested simply because no technology was available to allow researchers to peer into the brain in order to measure the neural substrates of "real time" or ongoing cognitive activities. Over the past decade, however, a variety of neuroimaging techniques have been developed to allow brain activation to be measured objectively. What are these dynamic brain techniques and how do they work?

According to Kolb and Whishaw (2003), the modern era of brain imaging began in the early 1970s with the development of an X-ray procedure called "computerised tomography" (derived from the word "tomo" meaning "cut") or the CT scan. The logic of this approach is that a computer may be used to draw a three-dimensional map of the brain from information yielded by multiple X-rays directed through it. With the advent of more sophisticated computational strategies to reconstruct images, three other brain imaging procedures emerged: positron-emission tomography (PET scans), magnetic resonance imaging (fMRI) and transcranial magnetic stimulation (TMS). These procedures are designed to detect changes in metabolism or blood flow in the brain as people are engaged in cognitive tasks. Such changes are correlated with neural activity. Briefly, in the PET scan, people are given radioactively labelled compounds such as glucose which are metabolised by the brain. This radioactivity is subsequently recorded by special detectors. For reasons of convenience, however, PET scan measurement of metabolism was replaced by the measurement of blood flow. Magnetic resonance imaging is a less invasive technique and is based on two key principles. First, blood oxygenation levels tend to change as a result of neural activity. Second, oxygenated blood differs from non-oxygenated blood in its magnetic properties. When combined, these principles allow researchers to detect changes in brain activity using special magnets. TMS is a procedure in which a magnetic coil is placed over the skull either to stimulate or to inhibit selectively certain areas of the cortical surface.

Using these neuroimaging techniques, research shows that the occipital cortex or visual centre of the brain (which is located at the back of our heads) is activated when people are asked to imagine things (Kosslyn, Ganis and Thompson, 2001). In addition, these brain-imaging studies have also shown that, contrary to what most people believe, mental imagery is *not* a single undifferentiated ability but, instead, a collection of different cognitive capacities localised in different brain regions. To illustrate, brain imaging studies show that when we "rotate" images in our mind (as happens, for example, when we try to imagine what an object would look like if it were turned upside down), neural activity is detected in the parietal lobes (which are located behind the frontal lobe and above the temporal lobe). By contrast, visualising previously memorised patterns tends to elicit neural activity in the occipital lobes at the back of our heads where vision is co-ordinated (*ibid.*). Similarly, research on brain-damaged patients shows that if the ventral pathways from the occipital lobes are impaired, people often lose their ability to recognise and/or imagine shapes. But if damage occurs in the dorsal system, the person may suffer deficits in his or her ability to visualise the locations of objects. Further details of recent developments in the neuropsychology of imagery are available in Behrmann (2000) and Kosslyn *et al.* (2001). Before concluding this section, it is important to mention a conceptual issue that has been debated vigorously by imagery researchers over the past thirty years. Briefly, this debate concerns the question of whether images are visuo-spatial depictions ("pictures in the head") or abstract descriptions (propositions) describing what they represent. The main proponent of the depictive position is Kosslyn (1994) whereas the principal advocate of the propositional account is Pylyshyn (1973). For an account of the background to this debate, see Mellet, Petit, Mazoyer, Denis and Tzourio (1998). For a contemporary flavour of the exchanges which it has generated, see Kosslyn, Ganis and Thompson (2003) and Pylyshyn (2003).

Types and dimensions of mental imagery

At the outset, at least three general points can be made about mental imagery processes. To begin with, research suggests that imagery is a multi-sensory experience. In other words, we have the capacity to imagine "seeing", "hearing", "tasting", "smelling" and "feeling" various stimuli and/or sensations. Second, the greater the number of sensory modalities that we use to create our mental representation of the non-present information, the more *vivid* is the resulting mental imagery experience. Third, images differ from each other not only in vividness but also in controllability (Richardson, 1995). Let us now explore each of these points briefly.

Of the various senses contributing to imagery experiences in daily life, vision is the most popular. Thus diary studies (Kosslyn, Seger, Pani and Hillger, 1990) showed that about two-thirds of people's mental images in everyday life are visual in nature. For example, have you ever had the experience of trying to remember where you parked your car as you wandered around a large, congested carpark? If so, then the chances are that you tried to form a mental map of the location of your vehicle. Interestingly, recent neuroscientific research corroborates the primacy of the visual modality over other types of imagery. To explain, Kosslyn *et al.* (2001) reported that visual images rely on about two-thirds of the same brain areas that are used in visual perception. Specifically, the areas that appear to be most active during visual imagery lie in the occipital lobe (especially areas 17 and 18 or "V1" and "V2"). Evidence to support this conclusion comes from the fact that when people visualise things with their eyes closed, the "V1" and "V2" areas of the brain become active. Also, if these areas are temporarily impaired by the effects of strong magnetic pulses, the person's visual imagery abilities are disrupted (Kosslyn *et al.*, 2001). Despite this phenomenological and neurological evidence that most of our images are visual in nature, our imagination is not confined solely to the visual sense. To illustrate, if you pause for a moment and close your eyes, you should also be able to imagine the sensations evoked by feeling the fur of a cat (a tactile image), hearing the sound of your favourite band or song (an auditory image) or experiencing the unpleasant grating sensation of a nail being scraped across a blackboard (a combination of tactile and auditory images).

Although visual and auditory sensations are easily imagined in sport (e.g., can you "see" yourself taking a penalty and then "hear" the crowd roar as your shot hits the net?), the type of feeling-oriented imagery that Tiger Woods referred to earlier in the chapter is more difficult both to conceptualise and to investigate empirically (see Figure 5.1).

Although few studies have been conducted on feeling-oriented imagery in sport, Moran and MacIntyre (1998) investigated kinaesthetic imagery processes in elite canoe-slalom performers (see Box 5.1).

To summarise, we have learned that although mental imagery is a multi-sensory construct, most studies of imagery processes in athletes have been confined to the visual sensory modality.

Turning to the second and third points – how images differ from each other – it is clear that images vary in controllability as well as vividness. "Controllability" refers to the ease with which mental images can be manipulated by the person who creates them. To illustrate, can you imagine a feather falling down from the ceiling of your room, slowly wafting this way and that before gently landing on your desk? Now, see if you can imagine this feather reversing its path – floating back up towards the ceiling like a balloon, as if carried higher by a sudden current of air. If you found these mental pictures easy to create, then you probably have reasonably good control over your imagery. As another example of this skill, try to imagine yourself standing in front of your house. How many windows can you see? Count them. Now, using your imagination as a camera with a zoom lens, try to get a close-up picture of one of the windows. What material are the frames made of? What colour are the

Figure 5.1 Tiger Woods uses kinaesthetic imagery to "feel" his shots before he plays them
Source: courtesy of Inpho Photography

Box 5.1 Exploring "feel" in athletes? A study of kinaesthetic imagery

Research on mental imagery in athletes has focused almost exclusively on the visual sensory modality. This trend is unfortunate because elite performers in sports such as golf (e.g., Tiger Woods) rely greatly on "touch" and tend to use their imagination to "feel" shots or movements before they actually execute them. Such kinaesthetic imagery involves feelings of force and motion or the mental simulation of sensations associated with bodily movements. Using a combination of qualitative and quantitative methods, Moran and MacIntyre (1998) studied kinaesthetic imagery processes in a sample (n = 12) of elite canoe-slalom athletes participating in World Cup competitions. These athletes were first interviewed about their understanding and use of feeling-oriented imagery in their sport. Then they were assessed using a battery of measures which included specially devised Likert rating scales and the "Movement Imagery Questionnaire-Revised" (Hall and Martin, 1997). Next, in an effort to validate their subjective reports on their imagery experiences (see later in the chapter for a discussion of this problem), the canoe-slalom competitors were timed as they engaged in a "mental travel" procedure during which they had to visualise a recent race in their imagination and execute it as if they were paddling physically. The time taken to complete these mental races was then compared with actual race times. As expected, there was a significant positive correlation between mental and physical race times (r = 0.78, p < .05). Finally, a content analysis of the canoeists' accounts of their kinaesthetic imagery experiences revealed the importance which these performers attached to sensations of force and effort.

frames? Can you see them in a different colour? If you can "see" these details of your windows accurately, then you have good imagery control skills.

Clearly, imagery representations have three important characteristics. First, they are multi-sensory constructs which enable us to bring to mind experiences of absent objects, events and/or experiences. Second, they are believed to be functionally equivalent to percepts in the sense that they share a great deal of the same brain machinery or neural substrates with perception. Finally, mental images vary in their vividness and controllability – two dimensions which facilitate their measurement (see the third part of this chapter). Having explained the nature and types of imagery, let us now consider the topic of mental practice (MP).

Mental practice

As I explained earlier, MP refers to a systematic form of covert rehearsal in which people imagine themselves performing an action without engaging in the actual physical movements involved (Driskell, Copper and Moran, 1994). Because it relies on simulated movements (see Decety and Ingvar, 1990), MP is sometimes known as "visuo-motor behavioural rehearsal" (VMBR; Suinn, 1994). It has also been called:

"symbolic rehearsal"; "imaginary practice"; "implicit practice"; "mental rehearsal"; "covert rehearsal"; "mental training"; and "cognitive practice" (see Murphy and Jowdy, 1992) as well as "motor imagery" (Decety and Michel, 1989).

Psychological interest in mental practice is as old as the discipline of psychology itself. For example, W. James (1890) suggested rather counter-intuitively that by anticipating experiences imaginatively, people actually learn to skate in the *summer* and to swim in the *winter*! Interestingly, the 1890s witnessed various expressions of an idea called the "ideo-motor principle" which suggested that all thoughts have muscular concomitants. For example, in 1899 Beaunis (cited in Washburn, 1916) proposed that "it is well known that the idea of a movement suffices to produce the movement or make it tend to be produced" (p. 138). Similarly, Carpenter (1894) claimed that low-level neural impulses are produced during imagined movement. Furthermore, he argued that these impulses are similar in nature, but lower in amplitude, to those emitted during actual movement. I shall return to this ideo-motor hypothesis later in the chapter when evaluating theories of mental practice.

Although research on MP was vibrant in the wake of Galton's (1883) research on imagery vividness, it declined in popularity shortly afterwards as a result of the Behaviourist manifesto (Watson, 1913) which attacked "mentalistic" constructs such as imagery because they were too subjective to be amenable to empirical investigation. Fortunately, a resurgence of research on mental practice occurred in the 1930s with the work of Jacobson (1932), Perry (1939) and Sackett (1934). These studies continued in a rather sporadic, atheoretical manner until the 1960s, when the first comprehensive reviews of mental practice were published by Richardson (1967a, 1967b). Unfortunately, despite (or maybe, because of!) more than a century of research on imagery, criticisms have been levelled at both the definition of MP and at the typical research designs used to study it. For example, Murphy and Martin (2002) identified a contradiction at the heart of this construct. Specifically, the term mental practice conveys an implicit, dualistic distinction between physical and mental practice that is at variance with current neuroscientific understanding of how the brain works. Thus the fact that visualising something in the mind's eye usually elicits measurable brain activity in the visual cortical areas (Kosslyn *et al.*, 2001) suggests that mind and body are not really separate processes but function as an integrated unit. In addition, Murphy and Martin (2002) criticised research in this field for assuming that mental practice is a standardised, homogeneous intervention. But it is not. To illustrate, visualising a perfect tennis serve could mean either seeing *yourself* playing this stroke or perhaps seeing someone else (e.g., Lleyton Hewitt) perform this action. It seems likely that there will be many differences between these two types of MP. Further criticism of MP research will be considered in the next section of the chapter. But now that we have examined the nature of mental imagery and mental practice, let us explore research methods and findings on MP. Research on athletes' use of mental imagery will be examined in the fourth section of the chapter.

Research on mental practice in sport

For over a century, the effects of MP on skilled performance have attracted research attention from psychologists. Reviews of this large research literature (amounting to several hundred studies) have been conducted, in chronological order, by Richardson (1967a, 1967b), Feltz and Landers (1983), Grouios (1992), Murphy and Jowdy (1992), Driskell *et al.* (1994) and Murphy and Martin (2002). Before I summarise the general findings of these reviews, here is a brief explanation of the typical research paradigm used in studies of MP.

Typical research design and findings

In general, the experimental paradigm in MP research involves a comparison of the pre- and post-intervention performance of the following groups of participants: those who have been engaged only in physical practice of the skill in question (the physical practice group, PP); those who have mentally practised it (the mental practice group, MP); those who have alternated between physical and mental practice (PP/MP); and, finally, people who have been involved in a control condition. Historically, the target skills investigated in MP research have largely been relatively simple laboratory tasks (e.g., dart-throwing or maze-learning) rather than complex sports skills. After a pre-treatment baseline test has been conducted on the specific skill involved, participants are randomly assigned to one of these conditions (PP, MP, PP/MP, or control). Normally, the cognitive rehearsal in the MP treatment condition involves a scripted sequence of relaxing physically, closing one's eyes, and then trying to see and feel oneself repeatedly performing a target skill (e.g., a golf putt) successfully in one's imagination. After this MP intervention has been applied, the participants' performance on this skill is tested again. Then, if the performance of the MP group exceeds that of the control group, a positive effect of mental practice is reported.

Based on this experimental paradigm, a number of general conclusions about mental practice have emerged. First, relative to not practising at all, MP appears to improve skilled performance. However, MP is less effective than is physical practice. More precisely, a meta-analytic review by Driskell *et al.* (1994) showed that physical practice (PP) treatment conditions produced greater statistical effect sizes than was evident in mental rehearsal conditions (recall from Chapter 2 that "meta-analysis" is a statistical technique which combines the results of a large number of studies in order to determine the overall size of a statistical effect). Statistically, the relative effect sizes of physical practice and mental practice were estimated by these researchers as 0.382 and 0.261 (both Fisher's Z), respectively. These figures can be interpreted with reference to Cohen's (1992) suggestion that values of 0.20, 0.50 and 0.80 represent effect sizes that are small, medium and large, respectively. The second general finding from the research literature is that MP, when combined and alternated with physical practice, seems to produce superior skill-learning to that resulting from either mental or physical practice conducted alone. Third, research suggests that mental practice improves the performance of cognitive skills (i.e., those that involve sequential processing activities; e.g., mirror drawing tasks) more than it does for motor skills (e.g., as balancing on a stabilometer). Next, there seems to be an interaction between the level of expertise of the performer and the type of task which yields the best improvement from mental rehearsal (Driskell *et al.*, 1994). Specifically, expert athletes tend to benefit more from MP than do novices, regardless of the type of skill being practised (either cognitive or physical). Fifth, the positive effects of MP on task performance tend to decline sharply over time. Indeed, according to Driskell *et al.* (1994), the beneficial effects of visualisation are reduced to *half* of their original value after approximately two weeks of time has elapsed. A practical implication of this finding is that in order to gain optimal benefits from mental practice, "refresher" training should be implemented after this critical two-week period. Finally, there is evidence that imagery ability mediates the relationship between MP and motor skill performance. More precisely, athletes who display special skills in generating and controlling vivid images tend to benefit more from visualisation than do counterparts who lack such abilities. In summary, there is now considerable evidence (much of it experimental) to support the efficacy of mental practice as a technique for improving the performance of a variety of sport skills. These skills include not only "closed" actions (i.e., ones which are self-paced and performed in a relatively static environment) such as golf putting or place-kicking in rugby but also "open" or reactive skills. For example, the rugby tackle (McKenzie and Howe, 1991) and the counter-attacking forehand in table-tennis (Lejeune, Decker and Sanchez, 1994) have shown improvements under mental rehearsal training.

Critical evaluation of research on mental practice

At first glance, the preceding evidence on the efficacy of mental practice conveys the impression of a vibrant and well-established research field in cognitive sport psychology. But closer inspection reveals a less satisfactory picture. Specifically, as I mentioned in the previous section, MP research has encountered many conceptual and methodological criticisms over its century-long history (see Moran, 1996; Murphy and Martin, 2002). Of these criticisms, perhaps the two most persistent concerns have been the "validation" problem and an issue stemming from a lack of field research in the area. The validation problem can be conveyed by a simple question. How do we know that people who claim to be visualising a target skill are actually using mental imagery? In other words, how can we validate people's subjective reports about their imagery processes? The problem stemming from the neglect of field research concerns the fact that few published studies of MP have been conducted on athletes engaged in learning and performing sport skills in real-life settings. Let us now sketch these problems in more detail.

The validation problem: how do we know that athletes are actually using imagery?

At the beginning of this chapter, we encountered some quotations from athletes (e.g., Tiger Woods) which provided compelling anecdotal testimonials to the value of mental imagery. As critical psychologists, however, should we accept at face value what these performers tell us about their imagery experiences? After all, cognitive researchers (e.g., Nisbett and Wilson, 1977) and sport psychologists (e.g., Brewer *et al.*, 1991) have warned us that people's retrospective reports on their own mental processes are susceptible to a variety of memory biases and other distortions (e.g., "response sets" whereby people may wish to convey the impression that they have a good or vivid imagination). Unfortunately, few researchers over the past century have attempted either to keep precise records of the imagery scripts used by participants in MP studies or otherwise validate athletes' reports of their alleged imagery experiences. This neglect is probably attributable to the fact that in order to validate these latter reports, sport psychology researchers require either objective methods (e.g., functional brain imaging techniques to find out if the imagery centres in the brain are activated when the person claims to be visualising; see Kosslyn *et al.*, 2001) or experimental procedures (e.g., manipulation checks such as asking people detailed questions about their images; Murphy and Martin, 2002).

Although the use of brain imaging technology with athletes is prohibited by cost and inconvenience at present, progress has been made in devising theoretically based procedures to check if athletes are really using imagery when they claim to be doing so. For example, Moran and MacIntyre (1998) (see Box 5.1) checked the veracity of canoe-slalomists' imagery reports by using a theoretical principle derived from Decety, Jeannerod and Prablanc (1989) and MacIntyre (1996). Specifically, this proposition suggests that the greater the congruence between the imagined time and "real" time to complete a mental journey, the more likely it is that imagery is involved. This mental chronometry paradigm offers an intriguing way to check whether or not athletes are actually using imagery when claiming to do so. To explore what can be learned from comparing the time it takes to complete actual and imaginary tasks, try the exercise in Box 5.2.

Box 5.2 Timing your action: experiencing your imagination at work

In a fascinating book on mental imagery, Robertson (2002) suggests the following exercise for learning more about the timing of real and imaginary skills. Imagine that you are about to write down your name, address and phone number on a sheet of paper. Before you begin this mental task, make sure the second hand of your watch is at the zero position. Then, make a note of how long it took you to write the three pieces of information in your mind's eye. Next, find another piece of paper and repeat the writing exercise. Now, compare the two times that you recorded. If you were to repeat this exercise several times, you would find that the time it takes to write down your name, address and phone number is about the same as it takes to complete this task mentally. Robertson (2002) also suggests that if you were to repeat this experiment using your non-dominant hand, the "mental" and "physical" task times would also be similar – even if both times would probably be slower than when performed with your dominant hand.

Perhaps not surprisingly, the temporal congruence between actual and imagined movements seems to be affected by intervening variables such as the nature of the skill being performed and the level of expertise of the performers. For example, Reed (2002) compared physical execution times for springboard dives with the time taken to execute this skill mentally. Three groups of divers were used: experts, intermediate performers and novices. Results revealed that, in general, visualisation time increased with the complexity of the dives. Also, by contrast with the experts and novices, visualised dive execution time was slower than physical dive execution time. A further complication within this field of mental chronometry emerged from a study by Orliaguet and Coello (1998). Briefly, these researchers found little or no similarity between the timing of actual and imagined putting movements in golfers. Until recently, most research on the congruence between actual and imagined movement execution used skilled tasks (e.g., canoe-slalom, diving) in which there were no environmental constraints imposed on the motor system of the performer. However, Papaxanthis, Pozzo, Kasprinski and Berthoz (2003) conducted a remarkable study in which cosmonauts were tested on actual and imagined motor skills (e.g., climbing stairs, jumping and walking) before and after a six-month space flight. The specific issue of interest to these researchers was the degree to which a long exposure to microgravity conditions could affect the duration of actual and imagined movements. Results showed that, in general, the cosmonauts performed the actual and imagined movements with similar durations before and after the space flight. Papaxanthis *et al.* (2003) interpreted this finding to indicate that motor imagery and actual movement execution are affected by similar adaptation processes and share common neural pathways. In summary, the fact that the timing of mentally simulated lengthy actions tends to resemble closely the actual movement times involved suggests that motor imagery is functionally equivalent to motor production. Let us now return to the issue of how to assess the veracity of athletes' imagery reports. Another possibility in this regard is to validate such experiences through "functional equivalence" theory (Kosslyn, 1994). Briefly, according to this theory, mental imagery and perception are functionally equivalent in the sense that they are mediated by similar neuropsychological pathways in the brain. As Kosslyn *et al.* (2001) concluded, current cognitive neuroscientists believe that "most of the neural processes that underlie like-modality perception are also used in imagery; and imagery, in many ways, can stand in for (re-present, if you will) a perceptual stimulus or situation" (p. 641). If this theory is valid, then interference should occur when athletes are required to activate perceptual and imagery processes concurrently in the same sensory modality. This interference should manifest itself in errors and longer response times when athletes face this dual-task situation. Interestingly, as Figure 5.2 shows, interference can also occur between mental imagery and perception in other situations in everyday life such as driving a car while listening to the radio.

Why is it so difficult to use perception and imagination in the same sensory modality? See Box 5.3.

The idea of using cognitive interference to validate imagery reports has certain obvious limitations, however. For example, apart from being modality-specific, it is rather unwieldy if not impractical as it depends on finding a suitable pair of perceptual and imagery tasks. Let us now turn to the second problem afflicting MP research. Why have there been so few imagery studies conducted on elite athletes who have to learn and perform sport skills in field settings?

Figure 5.2 It is dangerous to listen to a football match while driving a car

Box 5.3 Why you should not listen to football commentaries while driving: interference between imagery and action

It has long been known that people have great difficulty in perceiving and imagining information presented in the same sensory modality. For example, try to form a mental image of your friend's face while reading this page. If you are like most people, you should find this task rather difficult because the cognitive activities of forming a visual image and reading text on a page draw upon the same neural pathways. Another example of this "like-modality" interference problem occurs if you try to imagine your favourite song in your "mind's ear" while listening to music on the radio. Just as before, auditory perception and auditory imagery interfere with each other because both tasks compete for the same processing pathways on the brain. An interesting practical implication of this interference phenomenon is that you should not listen to football matches while driving your car because both tasks require visual processing. This time, unfortunately, cognitive interference could result in a nasty accident (see Figure 5.2)! Similar interference could occur if you try to visualise an action while driving. Are you listening, David James?

Lack of field research problem in MP research

Earlier in this chapter, I indicated that most research on mental practice has been carried out in laboratories rather than in real-life settings. Unfortunately, this trend has led to a situation in which few studies on MP have used "subjects who learned actual sport skills, under the same conditions and time periods in which sport activities are typically taught" (Isaac, 1992, p. 192). This neglect of field research is probably attributable to the fact that studies of this type are very time-consuming to conduct – which is a major drawback for elite athletes whose training and travel schedules are usually very busy. In addition, laboratory studies offer a combination of convenience and experimental control which is not easily rivalled in research methodology (see Chapter 1 for a brief summary of research methods in sport and exercise psychology). Interestingly, recent years have seen an upsurge of interest in "single-case" multiple-baseline research designs. In this paradigm, all participants receive the treatment but also act as their own controls because they are required to spend some time earlier in a baseline condition. A major advantage of these research designs is that they cater for individual differences because the intervention in question is administered at different times for each of the different participants in the study. As yet, however, only a handful of imagery studies in sport (e.g., Casby and Moran, 1998) have used single-case research designs.

Despite the conceptual and methodological criticisms discussed above, few researchers deny that MP is effective in improving certain sport skills in certain situations. So, what theoretical mechanisms could account for this MP effect?

Theories of mental practice: overview

Although many theories have been proposed since the 1930s to explain MP effects (see review by Moran, 1996), the precise psychological mechanisms underlying symbolic rehearsal remain unclear. One reason for this equivocal state of affairs is that most MP studies are "one-shot" variations of a standard experimental paradigm (described in the previous section) rather than explicit hypothesis-testing investigations. In spite of this problem, three main conceptual approaches have been postulated to explain MP effects: the "neuromuscular" model (e.g., Jacobson, 1932), the cognitive or symbolic account (e.g., Denis, 1985) and the "bio-informational" theory (e.g., Lang, 1979). As we shall see, the neuromuscular perspective proposes that mental practice effects are mediated mainly by faint activity in the peripheral musculature whereas the cognitive model attributes causal mechanisms to a centrally stored representation in the brain. The "bio-informational" theory postulates that MP effects reflect an interaction of three different factors: the environment in which the movement in question is performed ("stimulus" information), what is felt as the movement occurs ("response" information) and the perceived importance of this skill to the performer ("meaning" information). Let us now outline and evaluate each of these theories briefly (but see Murphy and Martin, 2002, for a more detailed review) before proposing a possible compromise between these rival models of mental practice.

Neuromuscular theories of mental practice

The earliest theories of mental rehearsal (e.g., Carpenter's, 1894, ideo-motor principle; Washburn, 1916) contained two key propositions. First, they suggested that imagination of any physical action tends to elicit a pattern of faint and localised muscle movements. Second, they claimed that such muscular activity can provide kinaesthetic feedback to the performer which enables him or her to make adjustments to this skill in future trials. This version of neuromuscular theory was supported by Jacobson (1932) who suggested that visualisation causes tiny "innervations" to occur in the muscles that are actually used in the physical performance of the skill being rehearsed covertly. Such minute subliminal muscular activity was held to be similar to, but of a lower magnitude than, that produced by actual physical execution of the movements involved. A more recent term for this theory is the "inflow explanation" approach (Kohl and Roenker, 1983) whereby the covert efferent activity patterns elicited by imagery are held to "facilitate appropriate conceptualizing for future imagery trials" (p. 180).

In order to corroborate neuromuscular theories of MP, evidence would have to be found which shows that there is a strong positive relationship between the muscular activity elicited by imagery of a given skill and that detected during the actual performance of this skill. Unfortunately, there is very little empirical support for neuromuscular theories of mental practice. For example, there is no convincing evidence that the faint muscular activity which occurs during imagery of a given skill is similar to that recorded during its overt performance. Thus Shaw (1938) found that increased electromyographic (EMG) activity during motor imagery was distributed across a variety of muscle groups in the body – including some which were not directly related to the imagined action. In other words, the muscular innervations elicited by imagery may merely reflect *generalised* arousal processes. Furthermore, doubts have surfaced about the type of muscular activity elicited by imagery. Thus despite using nuclear magnetic resonance (NMR) spectroscopy to monitor what happens in people's muscles during imaginary performance of a specific skill, Decety, Jeannerod, Durozard, and Baverel (1993) could not detect any change in relevant muscular metabolic indices. Finally, in a recent test of some predictions from neuromuscular theory, Slade *et al.* (2002) reported that the EMG pattern of activation in biceps and triceps for two types of imagined movements (namely, dumbbell and "manipulandum" curls) did not match the EMG pattern detected during actual movement. The authors of this study concluded that it added to "the mounting research evidence against the psychoneuromuscular theory" (p. 164). On the basis of the preceding evidence, Murphy and Martin (2002) concluded that there is little or no empirical support for a relationship between the muscular activity elicited by MP and subsequent performance of sport skills. This conclusion was supported in recent research by Lutz (2003). Briefly, this investigator used a sample of novice darts players to test the relationship between covert muscle excitation elicited during motor imagery and subsequent performance in dart-throwing. Results showed that although motor imagery led to elevations in covert muscle excitation (as predicted by neuromuscular theory), the *pattern* of activation did not match that shown by the participants during actual dart-throwing. Also, this covert muscle excitation did not predict motor skill acquisition or retention errors.

Therefore, Lutz (2003) concluded that covert muscle excitation is an outflow from the central generation of motor imagery rather than an inflow from peripheral structures.

Cognitive theories of mental practice

Cognitive (or symbolic) accounts of visualisation propose that mental practice facilitates both the coding and rehearsal of key elements of the task. One of the earliest proponents of this approach was Sackett (1934) who discovered that people's performance on a finger-maze task improved following mental rehearsal of the movement patterns involved. This finding was held to indicate that mental imagery facilitates the symbolic coding of the "ideational representation of the movements involved" (p. 113). For example, if you are a keen tennis player you could use imagery to practise a top-spin serve in your mind. This might involve seeing yourself in your mind's eye standing at the service line, feeling yourself bouncing the ball a few times before tossing it upwards and then feeling the strings of your racket brushing up behind it as you hit the ball and move onto the court.

By contrast with neuromuscular accounts of MP, cognitive models attach little importance to what happens in the peripheral musculature of the performer. Instead, they focus on the possibility that mental rehearsal strengthens the brain's central representation or cognitive blueprint of the skill or movement being visualised. In general, two types of evidence have been cited in support of cognitive theories of MP (Murphy and Martin, 2002). To begin with, central representation theories may explain why visualisation is especially suitable for mastering tasks (e.g., mirror drawing) which contain many cognitive or symbolic elements such as planning sequential movements (see research findings on MP discussed previously). Interestingly, some anecdotal evidence complementing this finding comes from athletes who use mental imagery to anticipate what might happen in a forthcoming competitive situation (see the quote from the former batsman Mike Atherton in Chapter 4). In addition, a cognitive explanation of MP is corroborated by certain research findings on the transfer of learned skills. Specifically, Kohl and Roenker (1980) investigated the role of mental imagery in the bilateral transfer of rotary pursuit skill from participants' right hands to their left hands. Results showed that such transfer of learning occurred even when the training task (involving the contralateral limb) was imagined.

Despite receiving some empirical support, symbolic theories of mental practice have been criticised on several grounds. For example, they cannot easily explain why MP sometimes enhances motor or strength tasks (see Budney, Murphy, and Woolfolk, 1994) which, by definition, contain few cognitive components. Remarkably, over the past decade, evidence has emerged that imagery training can lead to enhanced muscular strength. Thus Yue and Cole (1992) used a variation of the mental practice research design to show that imagery training could increase finger strength. More recently, Yue and his colleagues extended this paradigm to other types of strength training. Thus Uhlig (2001) reported that Yue and his research team required ten volunteers to take part in an imagery-training exercise involving a mental work-out five times a week. This "mental gym" exercise, which consisted of the imaginary lifting of heavy weights with their arms, increased the bicep strength of the participants by 13.5 per cent! Control participants, who missed such mental work-outs, did not show any significant gains in muscle strength. In contrast to these studies, however, Herbert, Dean and Gandevia (1998) discovered that imagined training produces increases in the strength of the elbow flexor muscles which did not differ significantly from those attained by a control group. Nevertheless, another problem for symbolic theories is that they find it difficult to explain how MP enhances the performance of experienced athletes who, presumably, already possess well-established blueprints or motor schemata for the movements involved. Finally, and perhaps most worryingly, most cognitive theories of MP are surprisingly vague about the theoretical mechanisms which are alleged to underlie imagery effects.

Bio-informational theory of mental practice

The bio-informational theory of imagery grew out of Lang's (1979) attempt to understand how people respond emotionally and psychophysiologically to feared objects. It was subsequently applied to research on MP in motor skills by Bakker, Boschker and Chung (1996).

Influenced by the ideas of Pylyshyn (1973), Lang (1979) began with the claim that mental images are not "pictures in the head" but propositional representations in long-term memory. These propositional representations are abstract, language-like cognitive codes that do not physically resemble the stimuli to which they refer. Three types of information about the imagined object or situation are coded in these propositional representations. First, stimulus propositions are statements that describe the content of the scene or situation being imagined. For example, if one were to visualise a penalty-kick in football, stimulus information might include the sight of the opposing goalkeeper, the sound of the crowd, and the feel of the ball in one's hands as one places it on the penalty-spot. Next, response propositions are statements that describe how and what the person feels as s/he responds to the scenario imagined. For example, stepping up to take a penalty-kick is likely to cause some degree of tension and physiological arousal in the player. Images that are composed of response propositions tend to be more vivid than those containing only stimulus propositions (Bakker *et al.*, 1996). Finally, meaning propositions refer to the perceived importance to the person of the skill being imagined. For example, if there were only a few seconds left in the match, and one's team is a goal down, then the hypothetical penalty-kick is imbued with great significance. Lang's (1979) theory postulates that information from these three types of propositions is organised in an associative network in the mind.

Within this network, the response propositions are of special interest to imagery researchers. This is so because these propositions are believed to be coded as bodily responses which are primed by efferent outputs to the muscles of the body. In other words, the propositions regulating imagined responses reflect how a person would actually react in the real-life situation being imagined. Interestingly, Lang (1977, 1979) suggested that response propositions are modifiable. Therefore, based on this theory, it should be possible to influence athletes' mental practice by using imagery scripts that are heavily laden with response propositions. Unfortunately, with the exception of studies by researchers such as Bakker *et al.* (1996) and Hecker and Kaczor (1988), this hypothesis has not been tested systematically in sport psychology. Nevertheless, there is some evidence that imagery scripts emphasising response propositions elicit greater physiological activation than do those containing stimulus propositions predominantly (Lang, Kozak, Miller, Levin and McLean, 1980). This conclusion was supported by Cremades (2002) who recorded the EEG activity of golfers during imagery of a putting task using different types of visualisation scripts. Analysis of alpha activity in these participants revealed that greater arousal and effort were needed during the golfers' imagery emphasising response propositions as compared with that apparent during imagery emphasising stimulus propositions.

In summary, according to bio-informational theory, imagery not only allows people to rehearse what they would do in certain hypothetical situations but also leads to measurable psychophysiological changes associated with the response and meaning propositions triggered by the situation being imagined. Although this theory has not been widely tested in sport and exercise psychology, it has at least three interesting implications for MP research. First, it encourages researchers to regard imagery as more than just a "picture in the head". To explain, Lang's (1977, 1979) theories postulate that for MP to be effective, both stimulus and response propositions must be activated by the imagery script used (Gould, Damarjian and Greenleaf, 2002). Second, it highlights the value of "individualising" imagery scripts so that they take account of the personal meaning which people attribute to the skills or movements that they wish to rehearse (see also Holmes and Collins, 2002). Finally, bio-informational theory emphasises the need to consider emotional factors when designing imagery scripts – an issue which has been largely neglected by advocates of neuromuscular and cognitive theories of mental practice. Interestingly, there is now compelling evidence that visualising a stimulus has an effect on the body similar to that when actually seeing it. Thus Lang, Greenwald, Bradley and Hamm (1993) discovered that people who imagine threatening objects experience the same signs of emotional arousal (e.g., increased heart rate, shallow breathing) as they do when actually looking at them.

An integrated model of mental practice: functional equivalence theory

Having considered the strengths and limitations of three traditional theories of mental practice (namely, the neuromuscular, cognitive and bio-informational models), it may be helpful to propose an integrated, compromise position which takes account of recent neuropsychological research on mental imagery. Briefly, two key propositions underlying this integrated position may be expressed as follows. First, neuroimaging studies suggest that imagery is functionally equivalent to perception because these two types of cognitive activity share similar neural pathways in the brain (Kosslyn *et al.*, 2001). Second, research indicates that mental practice is functionally equivalent to physical practice in the sense that imagery is guided by the same kinds of central mental representations as are motor movements (Hall, 2001). Evidence to support this proposition comes from Decety and Ingvar (1990) who discovered that certain brain structures (e.g., the prefrontal areas, supplementary motor areas and cerebellum) show a pattern of neural activity during imagery that resembles the activity elicited by actual motor performance (see also Holmes and Collins, 2002). Taken together, these propositions suggest that mental practice (MP) is best understood, at present, as a centrally mediated cognitive activity that mimics perceptual, motor and certain emotional experiences in the brain. This view integrates the strengths of all three theories of mental practice – the neuromuscular account (because MP has neural substrates even though these are regulated neither centrally nor peripherally), the cognitive model (because MP is believed to be mediated by a central mental representation) and the bio-informational approach (because MP elicits emotional reactions as well as cognitive and neural activity).

Conclusions about research on mental practice in athletes

In summary, research on MP has shown that the systematic covert rehearsal of motor movements and sport skills has a small but significant positive effect on their actual performance. But this conclusion must be tempered by at least three cautionary notes.

First, as Box 5.4 shows, mental practice effects are influenced by a number of intervening variables.

Box 5.4 Thinking critically about . . . the effects of mental practice on sport performance

Despite an abundance of research on mental practice over the past fifty years, relatively few studies have been conducted on visualisation in athletes. Therefore, any conclusions about the effects of MP on sporting performance must be regarded as tentative because they reflect extrapolations from a body of research literature that has a rather different focus. In addition, traditional studies of visualisation have adopted a "between groups" experimental design rather than field experiments or single case studies. Also, for reasons of convenience and control, the criterion tasks employed by most MP researchers have tended to be laboratory tasks (e.g., dart-throwing) rather than complex sport skills (e.g., the golf drive). Finally, a host of intervening variables affect the relationship between MP and performance. These factors include such key variables as the nature of the task or skill to be performed, the content of the imagery instructions provided, the duration of the imagery intervention employed, the extent of the performer's previous experience with the task, his/her imagery abilities, the level of expertise of the performer, the type of imagery perspective adopted (i.e., internal or external), the imagery outcome (i.e., success or failure) visualised and whether or not a relaxation treatment was provided before the mental practice intervention was applied.

In addition, research on imagery processes in athletes is hampered by inadequate theoretical explanation of the psychological mechanisms underlying MP effects. In this regard, however, the weight of evidence at present tends to favour the functional equivalence model of mental rehearsal. The third cautionary note arises from the possibility that MP research may constrain our understanding of imagery use in athletes. To explain, as Murphy and Martin (2002) observed, research on the symbolic rehearsal of movements and skills may blind us to the many other ways in which athletes use imagery in sport. Put differently, MP research "offers little guidance regarding the many uses of imagery by athletes beyond simple performance rehearsal" (p. 417). I shall return to this last point in the fourth section of this chapter.

Measuring mental imagery skills in sport

Research on the measurement of mental imagery has a long and controversial history in psychology. It may be traced back to the earliest days of experimental psychology when Galton (1883) asked people to describe their images and to rate them for vividness. Not surprisingly, this introspective, self-report strategy proved contentious. In particular, as we explained earlier in the chapter, Behaviourists like Watson (1913) attacked it on the grounds that people's imagery experiences could neither be verified independently nor linked directly with observable behaviour. Fortunately, theoretical advances in cognitive psychology (see Kosslyn, 1994) and the advent of brain imaging techniques in neuroscience (discussed earlier in this chapter) overcame these methodological objections and led to a resurgence of interest in imagery research. Thus imagery is now measured via a combination of techniques that include experimental tasks (e.g., asking people to make decisions and solve problems using imagery processes), timing of behaviour (e.g., comparing imagined with actual time taken to execute an action), neuroscientific procedures (e.g., recording what happens in brain areas activated by imagery tasks) and psychometric tools (e.g., for the assessment of imagery abilities and imagery use in athletes). Arising from these empirical strategies, two questions are especially relevant to the present chapter. First, how can psychologists measure people's private experience of mental imagery? Second, what progress has been made in assessing imagery processes in athletes? In order to answer these questions, a brief theoretical introduction is necessary.

Earlier in this chapter, we learned that although mental images are ephemeral constructs, they differ from each other along at least two psychological dimensions: vividness and controllability. Over the past century, these two dimensions of imagery have been targeted by psychologists in their attempt to measure this construct. Throughout this period, two different strategies have been used to assess these imagery dimensions. Whereas the subjective approach is based on the idea of asking people about the nature of their images, the objective approach requires people to complete visualisation tasks that have right or wrong answers. The logic here is that the better people perform on these tasks, the more imagery skills they are alleged to possess.

These approaches to imagery measurement can be illustrated as follows. To begin with, the vividness of an image (which refers to its clarity or sharpness) can be assessed using self-report scales in which people are asked to comment on certain aspects of their mental representation. For example, close your eyes and form an image of a friend's face. On a scale of 1 (meaning "no image at all") to 5 (meaning "as clear as in normal vision"), how vivid is your mental image of this face? Similarly, the clarity of an auditory image might be evaluated by asking people such questions as: "If you close your eyes, how well can you hear the imaginary sound of an ambulance siren?" Unfortunately, subjective self-report scales of imagery have certain limitations (see Moran, 1993). For example, they are subject to contamination from response sets such as social desirability. Put simply, most people are eager to portray themselves as having a good or vivid imagination regardless of their true skills in that area. For this reason, objective tests of imagery have been developed. Thus the controllability dimension of a visual mental image (which refers to the ease and accuracy with which it can be transformed symbolically) can be measured objectively by requesting people to complete tasks which are known to require visualisation abilities. For example, in the "Group Mental Rotations Test" (GMRT; Vandenberg and Kuse, 1978), people have to make judgements about whether or not the spatial orientation of certain three-dimensional target figures matches (i.e., is congruent with) or does not match (i.e., is incompatible with) various alternative shapes. The higher people's score is on this test, the stronger are their image control skills. For a more comprehensive account of the history of imagery measurement, as well as of the conceptual and methodological issues surrounding it, see A. Richardson (1995) and J. T. E. Richardson (1999).

Let us now turn to the second question guiding this section. What progress has been made in measuring imagery processes in athletes? In general, two types of instruments have been developed in this field: tests of athletes' imagery *abilities* and tests of their imagery *use* (see reviews by Hall, 1998, and Moran, 1993). Although an exhaustive review of these measures lies beyond the scope of this chapter, some general trends and issues in imagery measurement may be summarised as follows.

First, perhaps the two most popular and psychometrically impressive tests of imagery skills in athletes are the "Vividness of Movement Imagery Questionnaire" (VMIQ; Isaac, Marks and Russell, 1986) and the revised version of the "Movement Imagery Questionnaire" (MIQ-R; Hall and Martin, 1997). The VMIQ is a twenty-four-item measure of "visual imagery of movement itself and imagery of kinaesthetic sensations" (Isaac *et al.*, 1986, p. 24). Each of the items presents a different movement or action to be imagined (e.g., riding a bicycle). Respondents are required to rate these items in two ways: "watching somebody else" and "doing it yourself". The ratings are given on a five-point scale where 1 = "perfectly clear and as vivid as normal vision" and 5 = "no image at all". Although not extensive, available evidence suggests that the VMIQ satisfies conventional standards of psychometric adequacy (Hall, 1998). For example, Eton, Gilner and Munz (1998) reported that it had high internal consistency coefficients (e.g., 0.97 for the total scale) and a test-retest reliability score of 0.64 (for the "other" sub-scale) to 0.80 (for the "self" score) over a two-week interval. Turning to the MIQ-R, this test is especially interesting for sport researchers because it was designed to assess individual differences in *kinaesthetic* as well as visual imagery of movement. Briefly, this test contains eight items which assess people's ease of imaging specific movements either visually or kinaesthetically. In order to complete an item, respondents must execute a movement and rate it on a scale ranging from "1" (meaning "very hard to see/feel") to 7 (meaning "very easy to see/feel"). Imagery scores are calculated as separate sums of the two sub-scales of visual and kinaesthetic imagery skills. Available evidence indicates that the MIQ-R displays adequate reliability and validity (see review by Hall, 1998).

The second point to note about imagery assessment in sport is that the "Sport Imagery Questionnaire" (SIQ; Hall, Mack, Paivio and Hausenblas, 1998) is an increasingly popular and reliable tool for measuring imagery use in athletes. The SIQ is a thirty-item self-report scale which asks people to rate on a seven-point scale (where 1 = "rarely" and 7 = "often") how often they use five specific categories of imagery. These categories include "motivation general – mastery" (e.g., imagining appearing confident in front of others), "motivation general – arousal" (e.g., imagining the stress and/or excitement associated with competition), "motivation specific" (e.g., imagining winning a medal), "cognitive general" (e.g., imagining various strategies for a competitive event) and "cognitive specific" (e.g., mentally practising a skill). The six items that comprise each sub-scale are averaged to yield a score that indicates to what extent respondents use each of the five functions of imagery. According to Hall (1998), this test has acceptable psychometric characteristics. This claim is supported by Cumming and Ste-Marie (2001) who reported internal consistency values of 0.75 to 0.91 for the various sub-scales. Similarly, Beauchamp, Bray and Albinson (2002) reported internal consistency values ranging from 0.72 (for a scale measuring motivational general-arousal) to 0.94 (for a scale assessing motivational general-mastery) for a modified version of the SIQ. Interestingly, a recent addition to measures in this field is a scale developed by Hausenblas, Hall, Rodgers and Munroe (1999) designed to measure exercise-related motivational and cognitive imagery. Initial psychometric analysis indicates that this test is a promising tool for the study of imagery processes in aerobics exercisers.

Unfortunately, despite the preceding progress in imagery measurement, a number of conceptual and methodological issues remain in this field. For example, even though evidence has accumulated from neuroimaging techniques that imagery is a multidimensional construct, most imagery tests in sport and exercise psychology rely on a single imagery scale score. Also, few of these tests have an explicit theoretical rationale despite the availability of sophisticated models of imagery (e.g., see Kosslyn, 1994). Finally, much of the psychometric evidence cited in support of imagery tests in sport psychology comes from the research teams that developed the tests. A brief summary of other issues in the field is contained in Box 5.5.

Box 5.5 Thinking critically about . . . imagery tests in sport psychology

Many tests of imagery abilities and imagery use are available in sport psychology (see Hall, 1998; Moran, 1993). Which one should you use? Although the answer to this question depends partly on the degree to which the test matches your specific research requirements (e.g., are you studying visual or kinaesthetic imagery or both?), it also depends on psychometric issues. These issues are expressed below as critical thinking questions.

- If the psychometric adequacy of the imagery test is unknown, how would you assess its reliability? What value of a reliability coefficient is conventionally accepted as satisfactory by psychometric researchers?
- How would you establish the construct validity of an imagery test in sport? Specifically, what other measures of this construct would you use to establish the "convergent validity" of the test? Also, how would you establish the "discriminant validity" of the test (i.e., what measures should your test be unrelated to statistically)?
- If you were designing an imagery test for athletes from scratch, what precautions would you take to control for response sets (e.g., social desirability) or acquiescence (i.e., the tendency to apply the same rating to all items regardless of the content involved)?

Having analysed how mental imagery processes have been measured in sport performers, we should now consider how they are used by athletes.

Athletes' use of mental imagery

People use mental imagery for many purposes in everyday life. To illustrate, Kosslyn, Seger, Pani, and Hillger (1990) asked a sample of university undergraduates to keep a diary or log of their imagery experiences over the course of a week. Results revealed that imagery was used for such functions as problem solving (e.g., trying to work out in advance whether or not a large suitcase would fit into the boot of a car), giving and receiving directions (e.g., using mental maps to navigate through the physical environment), recall (e.g., trying to remember where they had left a lost object), mental practice (e.g., rehearsing what to say in an important interview on the way to work) and motivation (e.g., using images of desirable scenes for mood enhancement purposes). This type of research raises several interesting questions. How widespread is imagery use among athletes (see review by Munroe, Giaccobi, Hall and Weinberg, 2000)? Do elite athletes use it more frequently than less proficient counterparts? For what specific purposes do athletes employ imagery?

Before we explore empirical data on these questions, let us consider briefly some anecdotal reports and textbook accounts of reports on imagery use in sport. In this regard, many testimonials to the value of imagery have emerged from interviews with, and profiles on, athletes in different sports. For example, current and former world-class performers such as Michael Jordan (basketball), Tiger Woods and Jack Nicklaus (golf), John McEnroe and Andre Agassi (tennis), George Best and David James (football) all claim to have seen and felt themselves performing key actions successfully in their imagination before or during competition (Begley, 2000). As critical thinkers, however, we should be careful not to be too easily influenced by anecdotal testimonials. After all, as a critic once remarked acerbically about another psychologist's work which was heavily based on colourful examples, the plural of anecdote is not data! In other words, examples do not constitute empirical evidence. As I explained in Chapter 1, psychologists are wary of attaching too much importance to people's accounts of their own mental processes simply because such insights are often tainted by biases in memory and distortions in reporting. For example, athletes may recall more cases of positive experiences with imagery (i.e., occasions on which their visualisation coincided with enhanced performance) than negative experiences with it (where visualisation appeared to have no effect).

Turning to the textbooks, many applied sport psychologists have compiled lists of alleged uses of imagery in sport (see Box 5.6).

Box 5.6 Thinking critically about . . . athletes' use of mental imagery

Many applied sport psychologists provide lists of assumed applications of mental imagery by athletes. For example, Vealey and Greenleaf (1998) suggested that athletes use imagery to enhance three types of skills: physical (e.g., a golf putt), perceptual (e.g., to develop a strategic game-plan) and psychological (e.g., to control arousal levels). Within these three categories, imagery is alleged to be used for the following purposes:

- Learning and practising sport skills (e.g., rehearsing a tennis serve mentally before going out to practise it on court);
- Learning strategy (e.g., formulating a game-plan before a match);
- Arousal control (e.g., visualising oneself behaving calmly in an anticipated stressful situation);
- Self-confidence (e.g., "seeing" oneself as confident and successful);
- Attentional focusing/re-focusing (e.g., focusing on the "feel" of a gymnastics routine);
- Error correction (e.g., replaying a golf swing slowly in one's mind in order to rectify any flaws in it);
- Interpersonal skills (e.g., imagining the best way to confront the coach about some issue);
- Recovery from injury/managing pain (e.g., visualising healing processes).

Critical thinking issues
Sometimes, speculation goes beyond the evidence in sport psychology. To explain, there is a big difference between speculating about what athletes *could* use imagery for and checking on what they *actually* use it for in sport situations. For example, few studies have found any evidence that athletes use imagery to enhance either interpersonal skills or recovery from injury. Therefore, despite the unqualified enthusiasm which it commonly receives in applied sport psychology, mental imagery is not a panacea for all ills in sport. Clearly, it is advisable to adopt a sceptical stance when confronted by claims about the alleged use of mental imagery by athletes.

How can we test the claims made in Box 5.6? To answer this question, two main research strategies have been used by sport psychologists: descriptive and theoretical. Whereas the descriptive approach has tried to establish the *incidence* of general imagery use in athletes, the theoretical approach has examined specific *categories* of imagery use (e.g., imagery as an aid to motivation and cognition) in these performers. These two approaches to imagery use can be summarised as follows.

Using the descriptive approach, special survey instruments have been designed to assess imagery use in various athletic populations. This approach has led to some interesting findings. For example, successful athletes appear to use imagery more frequently than do less successful athletes (Durand-Bush, Salmela and Green-Demers, 2001). We should not be surprised at this discovery because Murphy (1994) reported that 90 per cent of a sample of athletes at the US Olympic Training Centre claimed to use imagery regularly. Also, Ungerleider and Golding (1991) found that 85 per cent of more than 600 prospective Olympic athletes employed imagery techniques while training for competition. Clearly, imagery is used extensively by expert athletes. By contrast, Cumming and Hall (2002b) found that recreational sport performers used imagery less than did more proficient counterparts (namely, provincial and international athletes) and also rated it as being less valuable than did the latter group. This trend was apparent even out of season (Cumming and Hall, 2002a). Moreover, as one might expect, visual and kinaesthetic imagery are more popular than other kinds of imagery in athletes (Hall, 2001).

Although this type of descriptive research provides valuable baseline data on imagery use among athletes, it does not elucidate the precise tasks or functions for which athletes employ their visualisation skills. To fill this gap, a theoretically derived conceptual model of imagery use in athletes was required. In this regard, Hall *et al.* (1998) postulated a taxonomy of imagery use in athletes based on Paivio's (1985) theory that imagery affects both motivational and cognitive processes. As indicated in the previous section of the chapter, this taxonomy of Hall *et al.* (1998) proposed five categories of imagery use. First, "motivation general-mastery" involved the imagination of being mentally tough and focused in a forthcoming competitive situation. Second, "motivation general-arousal" involved imagining the feelings of excitement that accompany an impending competitive performance. Third, "motivation-specific" was implicated in visualising the achievement of a goal such as winning a race. Fourth, "cognitive general" imagery occurred when athletes imagined a specific strategy or game-plan before or during a match. Finally, "cognitive specific" imagery involved mentally rehearsing a skill such as a golf putt or a penalty-kick in football.

At first glance, this taxonomy is helpful not only because it distinguishes between imagery *function* and imagery *content* but also because it allows researchers to explore the relationship between these variables and subsequent athletic performance. For example, Short, Bruggerman, Engel, Marback, Wang, Willadsen and Short (2002) discovered that both imagery direction (i.e., whether imagery was positive or negative) and imagery function ("motivation – general mastery" and "cognitive specific") can affect people's self-efficacy and performance in golf putting. Despite its heuristic value, however, Hall *et al.*'s (1998) classification system has been criticised for conceptual vagueness. To illustrate, Abma, Fry, Li and Relyea

(2002) pointed out that athletes who use "cognitive specific" imagery regularly (e.g., in rehearsing a particular skill) may be classified as using "motivation general-mastery" if they believe that mental practice is the best way to boost their confidence. Another limitation of this taxonomy is that it offers no explanation of the cognitive mechanisms underlying imagery processes. Despite such criticisms, the theoretically driven taxonomies developed by Hall *et al.* (1998) and Martin, Moritz and Hall (1999) offer greater scope for research on imagery use by athletes than do the intuitive classifications promulgated by applied sport psychologists (e.g., Vealey and Greenleaf, 1998).

Let us now summarise some general findings on imagery use in athletes. According to Hall (2001), three general trends may be detected in this field. To begin with, athletes tend to use imagery more in pre-competitive than in practice situations – a fact which suggests that they tend to visualise more frequently for the purpose of mental preparation or performance enhancement in competition than for skill acquisition. Second, available evidence suggests that, as predicted by Paivio (1985), imagery is used by athletes for both motivational and cognitive purposes. Although the former category is rather "fuzzy" and ill-defined, it includes applications like seeing oneself achieving specific goals and feeling oneself being relaxed in competitive situations. Interestingly, it is precisely this latter application that Richard Faulds pursued in creating the image of an "ice-man" prior to winning the 2000 Olympic gold medal for trap-shooting (see early in chapter). With regard to cognitive uses of imagery by athletes, two main applications have been discovered by researchers. On the one hand, as is evident from anecdotal and survey evidence, imagery is widely used as a tool for mental rehearsal (a "cognitive specific" application). On the other hand, imagery is often used as a concentration technique. Thus as we learned in Chapter 4, the former England cricket batsman Mike Atherton used to practise in his "mind's eye" in an effort to counteract anticipated distractions on the big day. A third general research finding in this field concerns the *content* of athletes' imagery. In this regard, Hall (2001) claims that athletes tend to use positive imagery (e.g., seeing themselves winning competitive events) and "seldom imagine themselves losing" (p. 536). But is this really true? After all, everyday experience would suggest that many club-level golfers are plagued by negative mental images such as hitting bunkers or striking the ball out of bounds. Nevertheless, Hall (2001) concluded that athletes' imagery is generally accurate, vivid and positive in content.

New directions for research on imagery in athletes

Two questions dominate this section of the chapter. First, what new directions can be identified in research on imagery processes in athletes? Second, does this research shed any light on how the mind works?

At least six new directions may be identified for imagery research on athletes (Moran, 2002a; Murphy and Martin, 2002). First, despite its obvious importance to many athletes (e.g., see the quote from Tiger Woods at the beginning of the chapter), kinaesthetic or feeling-oriented imagery has not been addressed adequately by researchers in this field. Perhaps the main reason for this neglect is that there are no theoretical models of this construct available in cognitive psychology. Second, very little is known about athletes' "meta-imagery" processes – or their beliefs about the nature and regulation of their own imagery skills (see Moran, 1996). Within this topic, it would be interesting to discover if expert athletes have greater insight into, or control over, their imagery processes than do relative novices. Third, additional research is required to establish the extent to which athletes use mental imagery in the period immediately prior to competition (Beauchamp *et al.*, 2002). Fourth, we need to tackle the old issue of how to validate athletes' reports of their imagery experiences. As I mentioned early in this chapter, however, we may be approaching this task with the wrong theory in mind. Put simply, what if imagery were not so much a characteristic that people "have" but something – a cognitive process – that they "do"? If, as Kosslyn *et al.* (2001) propose, imagery and perception are function- ally equivalent, then interference should occur when athletes are required to use these processes concurrently in the same modality. As I indicated earlier, this possibility of creating experimental analogues of this type of interference could help to discover whether athletes are really using imagery when they claim to be mentally practising their skills. Psychophysiological indices may also be helpful in "tracking" athletes' imagery experiences. Fifth, Cumming and Hall (2002b) raise the intriguing proposition that the theory of deliberate practice (see Chapter 6) can be explored in athletes using research on imagery processes. This idea, which is based on Hall's (2001) speculation that mental and physical practice are equivalent in certain ways, could be a profitable avenue for future research. Finally, not enough studies have been conducted on the issue of how top-level athletes use mental imagery in learning and performing complex sport skills.

Let us now turn to the issue of whether or not imagery research has any implications for the pursuit, in mainstream cognitive psychology, of how the mind works. In a recent paper, Moran (2002a) considered several ways in which research on mental imagery in athletes can enrich mainstream cognitive psychology. Up to now, however, cognitive psychology has devoted little attention to the world of athletic performance (although Frederick Bartlett used tennis and cricket examples when explaining his theory of schemata in the early 1930s). Nevertheless, imagery research in sport may help to enrich cognitive theory in several ways. First, it can provide a natural laboratory for the study of neglected topics such as kinaesthetic and meta-imagery processes. Second, it offers a sample of expert participants (top- class athletes) and a range of imagery tests (Hall, 1998) which may help researchers to make progress in understanding individual differences in cognitive processes. Interestingly, Kosslyn *et al.* (2001) observed that the issue of why people differ so much in imagery abilities remains largely unresolved. Finally, research on athletes could facilitate our understanding of the neural substrates of imagery. To explain, recent studies (Behrmann, 2000; Kosslyn *et al.*, 2001) show that people with vivid imagery show significantly increased blood flow in the occipital region when visual- ising. Does this pattern also emerge when functional brain-mapping techniques are applied to athletes skilled in the use of imagery? What neural activation is elicited by kinaesthetic imagery processes in sport performers? These are just some of the cognitive issues raised by research on imagery processes in athletes.

Ideas for research projects on imagery in athletes

Here are six suggestions for possible research projects on the topic of mental imagery in sport and exercise psychology.

1   It would be interesting to explore the relationship between imagery perspective (i.e., the viewpoint that a person takes during imagery – namely, either a first-person or a third-person perspective) and the performance of a closed skill such as a tennis serve. To illustrate the difference between these rival perspectives, consider two different ways of visualising the serve. For this skill, an "external" imagery would involve watching oneself serving from the perspective of an outside observer (e.g., as if one were looking at someone else performing this skill on television). Conversely, an internal perspective would entail the simulation of what one would *actually* experience if one were physically serving the ball. According to Mahoney and Avener (1977), task performance should improve when participants adopt an internal (or first-person) rather than an external (or third-person) imagery perspective. On the other hand, Hardy and Callow (1999) found that the adoption of an external visual imagery perspective was superior to that of an internal perspective when learning skills in which correct "form" is important (e.g., karate, gymnastics). It would be useful to design a study that could arbitrate empirically between these rival theoretical predictions using the skill of tennis serving. In conducting such a study, however, it is essential to match participants for kinaesthetic imagery ability as measured by a scale such as the Movement Imagery Questionnaire-Revised (MIQ-R; Hall and Martin, 1997).

2   Using the mental chronometry paradigm, you could investigate the extent to which the level of expertise of the performer affects the congruence between his or her imagined and actual time taken to execute a series of golf putts (see Orliaguet and Coello, 1998).

3   It would be interesting to conduct a field study with athletes such as rugby or basketball players on the efficacy of mental practice in enhancing skills such as place-kicking or free-throwing, respectively.

4   You could evaluate the psychometric adequacy of a popular test of mental imagery (e.g., the MIQ-R) for a sample of athletes over a three-month interval.

5   You might be interested in establishing the degree to which people who engage in regular physical activity use exercise imagery as part of their training routine (see Hausenblas *et al.*, 1999; Gammage, Hall and Rodgers, 2000).

6   It would be interesting to conduct a replication and extension of the study by Abma et al (2002) on the imagery content of athletes who differ in their level of self-confidence.

Summary

- Mental imagery is a cognitive process which enables us to represent in our minds experiences of things which are not physically present. Although this ability is valuable in many everyday situations (e.g., in reminding you to perform a certain task), it is especially useful for the planning of future actions. So, the term mental practice (MP) or visualisation refers to a form of symbolic rehearsal in which people "see" and "feel" themselves executing a skilled action in their imagination, without overt performance of the physical movements involved.
- Having outlined the nature and characteristics of mental imagery, I explored research on mental practice in athletes.
- Within this section, special attention was devoted to the imagery validation problem (namely, how do we know that athletes are really using imagery when they purport to be engaged in mental rehearsal?) as well as to the relative dearth of field studies on MP in athletes.
- Also, this section featured a review of three main theories of mental practice – the neuromuscular, cognitive and bio-informational models.
- The next section of the chapter examined the measurement of mental imagery skills in athletes.
- After that, the main research findings on athletes' imagery use were assessed.
- Next, an evaluation was provided of some old problems and new directions in research on imagery processes in athletes.
- The chapter concluded with six ideas for possible research projects on imagery processes in sport and exercise psychology.

Chapter 6

What lies beneath the surface? Investigating expertise in sport

Expert performance is similar to an iceberg . . . only one tenth of the iceberg is visible above the surface of the water and the other nine tenths are hidden below it. (Ericsson, 2001b, p. 2)

Introduction

Whether out of envy or admiration, we have long been fascinated by the exploits of expert performers in any field – those who display exceptional talent, knowledge and/or outstanding skills in a particular area of human achieve-ment. For example, most of us would love to be able to score a goal like Ronaldo, drive a golf ball with the power of Tiger Woods or serve a tennis ball with the skill of Venus Williams – yet all we can do is sit and watch as these experts perform remarkable athletic feats. But an important question arises when we marvel at the gifts of such performers. Specifically, what is the relationship between talent, expertise and success in sport? At first glance, the answer to this question seems obvious. If someone has sufficient innate talent and is lucky enough to have received instruction from an excellent coach, then s/he will develop expertise and become successful. As in most areas of psychology, however, research findings paint a different picture of the facts. More precisely, there are at least three flaws in the "pure talent" explanation of athletic excellence. First, just like the rest of us, sports stars are unreliable judges of the factors which influenced their career success. For example, in seeking to explain how they reached the top of the athletic ladder, they may inadvertently overestimate the influence of natural ability and underestimate the influence of other factors such as physical training regimes and/or the time they spent practising their skills. Second, as coaches and psychologists have discovered, *quality* is better than quantity when it comes to practice. For example, there is a big difference between mindless drills (where athletes repeat basic skills without any specific purpose in mind) and *mindful* practice (also known as "deliberate practice" – where athletes strive to achieve specific and challenging goals in a deliberate attempt to improve their skills; discussed later in the chapter). Third, success in sport is determined as much by psychological factors (e.g., motivation) and by strategic planning (e.g., anticipating one's opponent's actions, having a "game-plan" for a competition) as by innate technical skill. When combined, these three points highlight the importance of experience and practice in determining athletic expertise (see also Durand-Bush and Salmela, 2002, for the views of Olympic and world champions on these issues). This combination of experience and practice lies beneath the surface in Ericsson's (2001b) iceberg metaphor of athletic expertise. Thus when we observe a moment of spontaneous genius by Ronaldo, Tiger Woods or Venus Williams, we should not overlook the fact that this action is a consequence of at least 10,000 or more hours of practice in the sport in question. Similar sentiments were expressed by the former golf champion Gary Player who quipped paradoxically, "you must work very hard to become a natural golfer!" (cited in MacRury, 1997, p. 95). Of course, this remark is not intended to dismiss the influence of innate skills in sport. Nonetheless, it challenges us to understand the complex interplay that occurs between talent, motivation, practice habits, quality of coaching and family support (see Durand-Bush and Salmela, 2002) in shaping athletic expertise. Controversially, as we shall see later in this chapter, some researchers (e.g., Ericsson, 2001a, 2001b) have gone so far as to proclaim that practice is the *foremost* cause of expert performance in any field.

Against this background of claims and controversies, the present chapter investigates the nature and determinants of athletic expertise. Therefore, it will address a number of intriguing questions. For example, what makes someone an expert in a given field? Is athletic expertise simply a matter of being endowed with the right genetic "hardware" (e.g., visual acuity skills above the average) or do "software" characteristics such as practice habits and psychological skills play an important role? If sporting excellence lies partly in the mind, then how do the knowledge and skills of expert athletes differ from those of less successful counterparts? What stages of learning and development do novice athletes pass through on their journey to expertise? Finally, can research on expertise illuminate any significant principles that might help us to understand how the mind works?

In order to answer these questions, the chapter is organised as follows. To begin with, I shall explain what "expertise" means and indicate why it has become such an important topic in psychology. The second section will address the general question of whether athletic success is determined more by hardware or by software characteristics of sport performers. In the third part of the chapter, I shall outline and evaluate research methods and findings on expert–novice differences in the domain of sport. Interestingly, one of the issues that we shall raise in this section is the degree to which athletic expertise transfers effectively from one domain to another within a given sport. Specifically, do former top-class football players make expert managers? The fourth section will explore the development of expertise in sport performers. Included in this section is an explanation and critique of Ericsson's (1996, 2001b) theory that expertise is due mainly to a phenomenon called "deliberate practice". In the fifth part of the chapter, I shall examine the significance of, and some problems and new directions in, research on expertise in athletes. Finally, some suggestions will be provided for possible research projects in this field.

The nature and study of expertise in sport

"Expertise", or the growth of specialist knowledge and skills through experience, is currently a hot topic in cognitive science (Lehmann and Ericsson, 2002) as well as in sport psychology (Starkes and Ericsson, 2003; Starkes, Helsen and Jack, 2001). Before we consider the reasons for its popularity among researchers in these disciplines, however, we need to explain precisely what the term expert actually means.

In everyday life, the term "expert" is used in a variety of different ways. For example, at a humorous level, it could refer to someone who is wearing a suit, carrying a laptop computer and who is more than 50 km from home! More seriously, this term is often used to refer to the possession of specialist knowledge in a designated field (e.g., medical pathology). For example, an "expert witness" may be summoned to appear in court in order to offer an informed opinion about some legally contentious issue. On other occasions, the term is ascribed to someone who is deemed to be exceptionally skilful in performing a specific task such as tuning a piano or repairing a watch. What these two definitions have in common is the idea that expertise depends on some combination of experience and specialist training in a given field. But how much experience and what duration of training qualifies one as an expert?

In an attempt to answer this question, cognitive psychologists tend to invoke Hayes' (1985) "ten-year rule" when defining expertise. Briefly, Hayes discovered from his study of geniuses in different fields (e.g., musicians, chess players) that nobody had reached expert levels of performance without investing approximately ten years of sustained practice in the field in question. Using this criterion, we can define an expert as someone who has displayed consistent evidence of a high level of proficiency in a specific field of knowledge as a result of at least *ten years* of sustained training and experience in it (Ericsson and Charness, 1997). By convention, this criterion is deemed equivalent to about 10,000 hours of practice in the field in question (Starkes *et al.*, 2001). Interestingly, by contrast with many other definitions in psychology, this ten-year rule (or its "10,000 hours of practice" equivalent) appears to be remarkably consistent across a range of different activities within the domains of music and sport. For example, Ericsson, Krampe and Tesch-Romer (1993) found that expert pianists and violinists had conducted over 10,000 hours of practice between the ages of 8 and 20 years. Similar corroboration of this rule has emerged from research in sport with evidence that elite soccer players (Helsen, Starkes and Hodges, 1998), figure skaters (Starkes, Deakin, Allard, Hodges and Hayes, 1996) and wrestlers (Hodges and Starkes, 1996) satisfied the stated criterion. In summary, Starkes (2001) concluded that the best athletes in these three sports have accumulated about 10,000 hours of practice within 10–12 years of specialisation in their chosen sport. Additional support for this rule comes from Ericsson (2001a) who claimed that the typical age at which most sport stars reach their peak is between the mid- and late-twenties – which is approximately ten years after most young athletes have begun to practise seriously for their sport.

Despite the canonical status of the ten-year rule, some sport psychology researchers (e.g., Starkes *et al.*, 2001) have identified certain problems with it and some exceptions to it. First, as we mentioned earlier, the quality of practice undertaken to become an expert is at least as important as the quantity of practice. As Starkes *et al.* (2001) concluded, it is more important to understand "*what* practice is best and *how* practice should be carried out" (p. 175) than simply to count the duration of such practice in hours or years. Second, most people develop expertise in certain complex skills (e.g., learning to cycle) in less than the requisite ten years. Again, this point has not been adequately addressed by proponents of the rule. Third, there are exceptions to the ten-year rule in certain games and/or sports. For example, the legendary Bobby Fischer had attained the status of an international chess master by the age of 15 years – a remarkable feat which suggests less than the stipulated amount of experience. Regardless of these caveats, however, most researchers agree that the ten-year rule is a robust and useful criterion for distinguishing between expertise and average levels of performance in any given domain of inquiry. In summary, expertise in sport refers to consistently superior performance in athletic activities that takes at least ten years to develop.

Although the ten-year rule has been accepted uncritically in cognitive science, it has received some criticism in sport psychology. This criticism has led to alternative ways of defining athletic expertise. For example, Starkes (2001) suggested that an expert athlete was someone who competed at an international level and whose performance is generally at least two standard deviations above average. However, she acknowledged an obvious limitation of this approach – namely, the fact that this status is easier to achieve in sports where the level of participation (and hence competition) is relatively low. For example, it is easier to be acknowledged as an expert in a little-known sport such as curling as compared with one which is truly global in popularity (such as football). For this reason, it is unlikely that this alternative approach to defining expertise in sport will supplant the ten-year rule. Having considered the nature of expertise from a theoretical perspective, we should now explore the human face of an expert sport performer – the multiple world champion darts player, Phil "The Power" Taylor (see Figure 6.1).

What is so special about this man? For a brief profile of Phil Taylor, see Box 6.1.

Why does the topic of expertise in sport appeal equally to the popular media (e.g., see Gordon's, 2001, analysis of Tiger Woods' dominance in golf) as to researchers (e.g., see Starkes *et al.*, 2001)? Three main reasons are apparent.

First, the existence of athletic expertise gives us a tantalising glimpse of the benefits which people attained through dedicated practice and self-development. By implication, our admiration of other people's expertise beguiles us into believing that *we too* could have untapped potential which could be turned to our advantage.

Figure 6.1 Phil "The Power" Taylor – the greatest darts player of all time?
Source: courtesy of Inpho Photography

Box 6.1 Profile of an expert sport performer: Phil "The Power" Taylor

Despite its stereotypical association with beer-swilling, overweight men in smoke-filled pubs (and they are just the performers!), darts is a popular and skilful game. Briefly, the objective of this game, which probably dates back to the Middle Ages, is to throw a set of projectiles (darts) at a board which is placed about eight feet away (approximately 237 cm). Different locations on the board yield different points for the dart thrower. Success in darts requires a high degree of concentration, eye–hand co-ordination and fine motor control skills. These characteristics are epitomised in abundance in the career of Phil "The Power" Taylor – who is widely regarded as the most skilful darts player of all time. Indeed, in January 2002, after he had won his eighth consecutive world championship title and his tenth overall, he was described by darts commentator Sid Waddell as "the greatest arrows-thrower who ever drew breath" (cited in Hughes, 2002, p. S7). So, who is this star player and what makes him so successful?

Born in Stoke, Phil Taylor was working as a tool machinist when his wife gave him a birthday present of a set of darts in 1986. He began to play once a week and showed enough skill at this sport to represent his county after a mere two years. One day, Eric Bristow (the most famous darts player of his generation) saw him practising and offered to advise him about the game. This advice soon paid off because in 1990, Taylor entered the world darts championship – and won it. Ironically, he defeated his mentor, Bristow, in the final! This victory was the first of a series of stunning performances that saw him demolish opponent after opponent with remarkable displays of accurate dart-throwing under intense competitive pressure. Famed for his dedication to physical and mental fitness (e.g., he practises for six hours a day; Hughes 2002), and for his ruthless ability to finish matches when he gets the chance, he deliberately refuses to socialise with his fellow competitors in case he loses his competitive edge. For him, darts is a battle and "familiarity breeds contempt . . . I can see when people play me that they're worried. I can see the fear in their eyes and I know I've got them then . . . As soon as he (the opponent) shows weakness, I'm in there, humiliating him. It's like boxing. You need to get your guy on the ropes" (cited in Kervin, 2001, p. S6).

In capturing this idea, an adage from the study of attentional skills comes to mind: there is no such thing as a difficult task only an unpractised task. Second, the study of expert athletic performance is appealing because it enables researchers to examine how skills are acquired and perfected over time in real-life rather than artificial contexts. This distinction is an important point because traditional laboratory studies of human skill-learning were confined mainly to short-term activities (e.g., maze-learning) that had little relevance to everyday life. By contrast, contemporary researchers are striving to understand how people become proficient at complex everyday skills such as swimming or playing tennis. Of course, there is also a methodological explanation for the upsurge of research interest in athletic expertise. Specifically, the scientific study of skill-learning in sport is facilitated by the profusion of ranking and rating systems available to researchers – a fact which enables investigators to define and measure "success" in this field with some degree of objectivity. The same point holds true for chess which may explain why it is so popular among problem-solving researchers in cognitive psychology. Third, expert athletes are admired not only for their speed, economy of movement, and timing but also because they appear to transcend the limits of what is humanly possible. For example, the Spanish rider Miguel Indurain, who won five *successive* Tour de France cycling titles between 1991 and 1995, is famous for having a resting heart rate of only 28 beats per minute (Shontz, 1999). To put this figure in perspective, the average resting heart rate is about 70 beats per minute (bpm) – whereas that of an experienced endurance athlete is between 35 and 40 bpm. Other extraordinary sporting champions include Tiger Woods, who won four consecutive major golf championships in the 2000–2001 season and Carl Lewis, who won four Olympic long-jump titles in succession between 1984 and 1996. The existence of such outstanding competitors suggests that the horizons of human physical achievements are expanding. This impression is supported by historical analyses of sporting records. To illustrate, top amateur swimmers and marathon runners at present can routinely beat the records set by Olympic gold-medallists in the early 1900s – even though the times recorded by the latter athletes were regarded in that era as being close to the impermeable boundaries of human performance (Ericsson, 2001a).

Interestingly, analysis of the horizons of human performance in sport can help cognitive scientists to understand how the mind achieves some of its remarkable feats. For example, how do skilled athletes such as Andre Agassi (who is widely regarded as the player with the best return of serve in the world today) manage to hit winning returns off tennis balls that travel towards him at about 120 miles per hour – faster than the eye can see? Ostensibly, this feat should be theoretically impossible because there is about a 200 millisecond time-lag between noticing a stimulus and responding to it. To explain this delay, it takes about 100 milliseconds for a nerve impulse to travel from the eye to the brain and about another 100 milliseconds for a motor message to be sent from the brain back to the muscles. Remarkably, therefore, expert athletes in fast-ball, reactive sports like tennis, hurling (a type of aerial hockey that is played in Ireland and regarded as being one of the fastest games in the world) and cricket manage to overcome the severe time-constraints imposed by this "hard-wired" delay in the human information-processing system. In short, they effortlessly achieve the impossible feat of responding to fast-flying balls *before* they have any conscious knowledge of them! But this feat may not be as paradoxical as it seems. After all, some neuroscientists claim that our conscious awareness of *any* neural event is delayed by several hundred milliseconds although we do not normally notice this time-lag because we refer this awareness back in time – so that we convince ourselves that we were aware of the stimulus from its onset (Gazzaniga, Ivry and Mangun, 2002).

In any case, the conclusion that fast reactions in sport lie in the unconscious mind of the athlete has at least one surprising implication. Specifically, it suggests that contrary to coaching wisdom, top players in fast-ball sports do *not* actually watch the ball in flight. Instead, they use early signals or "advance cues" from their opponents' body position and/or limb movements to anticipate the type of delivery, trajectory and likely destination of the speeding ball (Radford, 2000). Perhaps not surprisingly, this capacity to extrapolate accurately from the information yielded by advance cues appears to be a distinctive characteristic of expert athletes. For example, Abernethy and Russell (1987) found that top-class squash players based their predictions about ball-flight on early signals from opponents' movements (e.g., from both the position of the racquet and the racquet arm) when watching film simulations of squash matches. However, squash beginners tended to adopt a more constrained visual search process – looking only at those cues that were yielded by the racquet itself. The significance of this finding is clear. Expert athletes have a *knowledge-based* rather than an innate speed advantage over less proficient rivals. In general, therefore, speed of reaction in sport depends as much on the mind (because it depends on game-specific knowledge and anticipation skills) as on the body. Put differently, research on anticipatory cue usage suggests that expert athletes have a *cognitive* rather than a physical advantage over less successful counterparts. This finding raises the contentious question of whether hardware or software explanations of athletic expertise are more plausible scientifically.

What makes an expert in sport? Hardware or software characteristics?

Are sport stars born or made? Unfortunately, it is not possible to answer this general question scientifically because genetic and environmental factors are inextricably intertwined. Nevertheless, some progress has been made in identifying the relative contributions of physical (or hardware) and mental (or software) processes to expertise in sport (Andersen, Schjerling and Saltin, 2000).

To start with, let us consider the popular idea that athletic expertise is largely a matter of being born with the right physical hardware such as a muscular physique, fast reactions, acute vision and exceptional sensitivity to peripheral visual information. According to this intuitively appealing theory, success in sport is attributable to the possession of some fixed and prototypical constellation of physiological attributes (namely, a "superior" nervous system) as well as to exceptional perceptual-motor skills (e.g., rapid reflexes, dynamic visual acuity). Furthermore, it is assumed that by using these advantages, top athletes can run faster, see more clearly and display sharper reactions than average performers. At first glance, this approach is persuasive because it is easily exemplified in sport. To illustrate, Jonah Lomu, the brilliant All-Black rugby winger, is not only 6 feet 5 inches in height (1.96 m) and 260 lb (118 kg) in weight – but is also capable of running 100 metres in little more than 10 seconds (*The Economist*, 1999). Similarly, Venus Williams, who won four Grand Slam events in one season, stands at an impressive height of 6 feet 1 inch (1.85 m) and can hit tennis serves that travel at over 120 miles per hour (193 kph) (*ibid.*). Clearly, the hardware possessed by Lomu and Williams is as impressive as their athletic achievements. By contrast, the appearance and actions of most sporting novices seem ungainly, poorly co-ordinated and badly timed – even to an untutored eye. But this physical theory of athletic expertise is flawed by several problems. First, even at an anecdotal level, "bigger" does not always mean "better" in sport (see Box 6.2).

Box 6.2 Does size really matter? Bigger is not always better in sport!

In the 1999 World Cup in rugby, Jonah Lomu, New Zealand's giant winger, scored a remarkable try against England when he surged through *four* tackles before crossing the line. Clearly, his impressive athletic hardware equipped him with prodigious strength and speed for this task. But is bigger always better in sport? An article in *The Economist* (1999) questions this assumption.

At first glance, few could argue against the claim that size matters in competitive sport. After all, it seems that today's athletes are generally taller, stronger and fitter than their predecessors at the beginning of the last century. Perhaps it is this fact that explains why so many of the athletic records set in the early 1900s have been smashed a century later. For example, whereas the men's world record for throwing the hammer in 1900 was 51.10 metres (set by an Irish athlete called John Flanagan), it was 86.74 metres in 2000 (set by a Russian performer named Yuri Sedykh) – a figure which represents an increase of almost 70 per cent in the distance involved! Further anecdotal evidence to support the "bigger is better" theory comes from the sport of baseball. For example, the legendary Mark McGwire, who set a record for hitting home runs, is about the same height as Jonah Lomu (1.96 m) and is only marginally lighter (weighing 250 lb or 113 kg) than the rugby star. But despite these two examples – Lomu and McGwire – bigger is certainly *not* always better in sport. First, big athletes may be clumsier than their smaller counterparts. For example, in sports like tennis and squash, tall players may have trouble in playing shots aimed at their feet. In addition, tall or strong players may tend to neglect other parts of their game. So, in modern tennis, despite the increasing prevalence of tall (over 6 feet) stars, short players like Andre Agassi and Lleyton Hewitt have won as many, if not more, Grand Slam titles than their taller counterparts. Of course, there are distinct advantages to being tall and strong in sport. For example, big athletes tend to have large lungs and powerful hearts – physical assets which increase their cardiovascular efficiency in pumping oxygenated blood around the body. In addition, larger limbs are advantageous in certain sports. For example, in swimming, long arms can give an athlete leverage for speedy passage through the water. Similarly, long legs are essential for high-jumpers. Of course, there are also sports in which a small stature and a wiry physique are mandatory. Accordingly, marathon runners tend to be slight, if not scrawny, in build and they usually have "slow twitch" muscles. Likewise, successful jockeys are usually small, light, wiry and strong.

Second, there is little or no empirical evidence that top-class sports performers possess hardware characteristics, such as unusually fast reflexes or extreme visual acuity, that differentiate them significantly from less successful counterparts (A. M. Williams and Davids, 1998). For example, elite adult athletes do not perform consistently better than novices on tests of visual abilities (A. M. Williams, 2002b). The same principle seems to apply also to younger athletes. Thus Ward and Williams (2003) found that elite and sub-elite soccer players were "not meaningfully discriminated on nonspecific tests of visual function throughout late childhood, adolescence or early adulthood" (p. 108). More generally, there is little reliable evidence of expert–novice differences in simple reaction time. In fact, as explained earlier, it takes about 200 milliseconds for *anyone* to react to a given stimulus – regardless of whether that person is an expert athlete or an unfit "couch potato"! Remarkably, this finding suggests that there is little or no difference between the average reaction time of Andre Agassi and that of a spectator picked randomly from a courtside seat. The implication of this point is clear. The rapid reactions exhibited by top athletes in sport situations do *not* reflect "hard-wired", innate talents but are probably due instead to acquired skills (such as the ability to read and anticipate what an opponent is likely to do next). In short, expert athletes have a distinct *anticipatory* advantage over everyone else, which makes it *seem* as if their reaction times are exceptionally fast.

The third problem for hardware theories of sporting expertise comes from research findings on the age at which athletes tend to reach their peak level of performance (see Ericsson, 2001b). Briefly, if expertise were limited mainly by biological factors, such as the functional capacity of the brain and body, then we would expect that the age at which athletes reach their peak would be around the time that they reach physical maturation – namely, in their late teens. However, research shows that the age at which most athletes attain peak levels of performance occurs many years later – usually, in the mid- to late-twenties. This latter finding has challenged the validity of hardware theories of athletic expertise.

In the light of the preceding evidence, expertise in sport appears to be "dependent on perceptual and cognitive skills as well as on physical and motor capabilties" (A. M. Williams, 2002b, p. 416). Put differently, knowledge-driven factors (software processes) can account significantly for differences between expert and novice athletes in a variety of sports (Starkes and Ericsson, 2003; Williams, Davids and Williams, 1999; A. M. Williams, 2002b). To illustrate the extent to which exceptional athletic performance is cognitively driven, consider how an expert tennis player and a relative novice might respond to the same situation in a match. Briefly, if a short, mid-court ball is played to an expert performer, s/he will probably respond to it with an attacking drive "down the line" followed by an approach to the net in order to volley the anticipated return shot from the opponent. In similar circumstances, however, a novice player is likely to be so preoccupied with the task of returning the ball anywhere back over the net that s/he will fail to take advantage of this attacking opportunity. In other words, the weaker player is handicapped *cognitively* (i.e., by an inability to recognise and respond to certain patterns of play) as well as technically. We shall return to this point in the next section of the chapter.

Despite its flaws, the hardware theory of sporting expertise has some merit. For example, there is evidence that people's performance in certain athletic events is facilitated by the type of musculature that they possess (Andersen *et al.*, 2000). Thus top-class sprinters tend to possess an abundance of "fast twitch" muscles which provide the explosive power which they need for their event. Conversely, "slow" muscle fibres have been shown to be helpful for endurance sports such as long-distance running and cycling. Intriguingly, the field of hardware research in sport may serve in future as a natural laboratory for testing the effects of genetic engineering. Indeed, Walsh (2000) suggested that scientists may soon be able to modify existing hardware characteristics of athletes in order to enhance their chances of achieving success in sport. For example, in an effort to boost their chances of success, sprinters could be equipped genetically with more "fast twitch" muscles, long-distance runners could be given the genes that create the blood-enhancing hormone erythropoietin, and basketball players may seek artificial height increases! Fortunately for legislators and sports associations, this type of genetic therapy for athletes is not a feasible proposition at present.

In summary, despite its intuitive plausibility, the hardware approach is inadequate for the task of explaining the theoretical mechanisms which underlie athletic expertise. But what about the software approach? Can research on expert–novice differences in cognitive processes help us to understand the nature of athletic expertise?

Expert–novice differences in sport: research methods and findings

Since the pioneering research of de Groot (1965) and Chase and Simon (1973) on the cognitive characteristics of chess grand-masters, cognitive psychology researchers have used laboratory simulations of various real-life tasks in order to determine how expert performers differ from novices. Initially, the main fields of expertise investigated were formal knowledge domains such as chess and physics where problem-solving processes and outcomes can be measured objectively. The archetypal research in this regard was a set of studies conducted by de Groot (1965) on chess expertise.

In one of these experiments, de Groot, who was a chess master player, explored how performers of different abilities planned their moves. Briefly, he found that the grand-masters made *better* moves than less skilled experts – even though they did not appear to consider more moves than the latter players. Some years later, Chase and Simon (1973) discovered that although chess experts were superior to novices in recalling the positions of chess pieces from real or meaningful games, they did not differ from this group in their memory for chess pieces that had been randomly scattered around the board. The evidence for this conclusion came from two key findings. First, whereas chess masters could recall, on average, about sixteen of the twenty-four chess pieces displayed on the board in their correct positions after a single five-second glance, novices could recall only about four such pieces correctly. Second, when the chess pieces were presented in random or meaningless configurations on the board, the experts were no better than the novices at recalling their positions correctly. Indeed, neither group could recall more than two or three chess pieces in their correct location. This classic study shows that expert chess players do not have superior memories to those of novices – but that they use their more extensive knowledge base to "chunk" or code the chess configurations in meaningful ways. Another conclusion from this study is that the cognitive superiority of expert chess players over novices is knowledge-based and context-specific – not indicative of some general intellectual advantage. In the light of this finding, research on expertise since the 1990s has shifted away from formal knowledge domains (such as chess) towards informal, everyday skills such as sport, music and dance (Starkes *et al.*, 2001).

Research methods in the study of expertise

Within the domain of sport, a variety of research methods have been used to study expert–novice differences. These methods include both qualitative techniques (such as in-depth interviews and "think aloud" verbal protocols) and quantitative procedures (e.g., pattern recall and recognition tasks, the "temporal occlusion" paradigm and eye-tracking technology). Although we shall describe each of these techniques briefly below, additional information on their strengths and weaknesses is available in Lavallee, Kremer, Moran and Williams (2004), A. M. Williams *et al.* (1999) and A. M. Williams (2002b).

In-depth interviews

Intensive interviews are widely used by researchers in an effort to elicit experts' knowledge and opinions about different aspects of their sports. The advantages and disadvantages of the interview method were mentioned briefly in Box 1.4 in Chapter 1. Recently, Eccles, Walsh and Ingledew (2002) interviewed the British orienteering squad ($n = 17$) in an attempt to develop a "grounded theory" of how expert performers in this sport manage to divide their attention successfully between three key sources of information: the map, the environment and the travel path. Grounded theory is a qualitative approach in psychology in which researchers build a conceptual model inductively from the data yielded by participants rather than deductively from the researcher's assumptions about the phenomenon in question.

"Think aloud" verbal protocols and "thought sampling" techniques

As we learned in Chapter 1, interviews are limited as research tools because of their reliance on people's retrospective reconstructions of their past experiences – a procedure which is known to be flawed (Brewer, Van Raalte, Linder and Van Ralte, 1991). An alternative to this approach is the "think aloud" verbal protocol method whereby people are required to talk about and/or give a running commentary on their thoughts and actions as they tackle real or simulated problems in their specialist domain. This technique was pioneered by de Groot (1965) in an effort to explore the cognitive processes of chess masters as they contemplated their next move in a simulated game. It is a valuable tool as it helps researchers to represent not only what people know (declarative knowledge) but also how they perform skilled behaviour (procedural knowledge). Of course, there are certain limitations associated with the collection and analysis of verbal protocols. First, an editing problem arises from the sheer volume of data collected. Second, protocols are limited to consciously accessible processes on the part of the person studied. Finally, a difficulty arises from the fact that recording what people say as they solve a problem may inadvertently distort the quality of the data obtained. Put simply, people may become more self-conscious, guarded and/or spuriously rational if they know that their every utterance is being analysed by a researcher. In spite of these limitations, verbal protocols are useful because they are not vulnerable to the retrospective recall biases that afflict interviews.

"Thought sampling" or "experience sampling" methods (based on Csikszentmihalyi, 1990; Nakamura and Csikszentmihalyi, 2002) involve equipping athletes with electronic beepers during training or competitive encounters and cueing them randomly to pay attention to their thoughts and experiences at the precise moment in question. Thus athletes are prompted electronically to respond to such questions as "What were you thinking of just now?" Using this technique, researchers can keep track of athletes' thoughts, feelings and focus of attention in real-life situations. For example, in a variation of this procedure, McPherson (2000) asked expert and novice tennis players questions such as "What were you thinking about while playing that point?" and "What are you thinking about now?" during the period between points in competitive tennis matches. Unfortunately, despite its ingenuity, certain flaws in this method are apparent. For example, there are obvious practical and ethical constraints surrounding athletes' willingness to be "thought sampled" during competitive situations. In addition, little or no data have been gathered to evaluate the reliability of this procedure.

Pattern recall and recognition tasks

Pattern recall recognition tasks are based largely on the classic studies of de Groot (1965) and Chase and Simon (1973) on chess experts' memories for briefly presented chess patterns. When these tasks are adapted for use in sport situations, athletes and/or coaches are tested on their ability to remember precise details of rapidly presented, game-relevant information such as the exact positions of players depicted briefly in a filmed sport sequence. In the Chase and Simon (1973) study, expert and novice chess players were asked to study chessboards with pieces on them for 5 seconds. Then, they had to reconstruct the positions of these pieces on another board. As I indicated previously, results showed that the chess masters were superior to the novices in recalling the pieces – but only if these pieces came from structured game situations. No differences between the groups were evident when the pieces were randomly presented initially. In a typical sport psychological modification of this paradigm, participants may be shown a slide or a video sequence of action from a game-specific situation for a brief duration. Then, they are asked to recall as accurately as possible the relative position of each player in the slide or sequence. Interestingly, the ability to recall and recognise evolving patterns of play seems to be an excellent predictor of athletes' anticipatory skills in team sports (A. M. Williams, 2002b).

As a practical illustration of this pattern recall paradigm applied to the sport of rugby, consider the configurations of players displayed in Figure 6.2a and Figure 6.2b. In both cases, the aim of the diagrams is to depict a "three-man defence" tactical strategy. But only one of these patterns is meaningful. Can you identify which of them makes sense and which of them is random or meaningless? Take a moment to examine the diagrams carefully.

If you are not knowledgeable about rugby, you should find this task very difficult, if not impossible! But if you were an expert rugby coach, you would quickly realise that Figure 6.2b is the meaningless pattern. To explain, Figure 6.2a portrays an orthodox three-man defence in which the number 10 player covers the opposing number 10, the number 12 takes the opposing number 12, the number 13 covers the opposing number 13 with the winger taking the last person. By contrast, in Figure 6.2b there is no obvious pattern to the defensive alignment. In fact, the only defensive player who is in the correct position is the number 10.

Extrapolating from Chase and Simon's (1973) study, we would expect that expert rugby players or coaches would be able to memorise the pattern of players depicted in the orthodox three-man defence (Figure 6.2a) much better than the meaningless pattern depicted in Figure 6.2b.

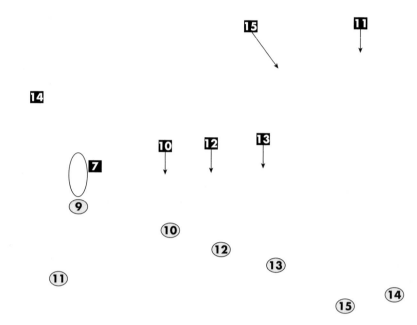

Figure 6.2a   A meaningful "three-man defence" pattern in rugby

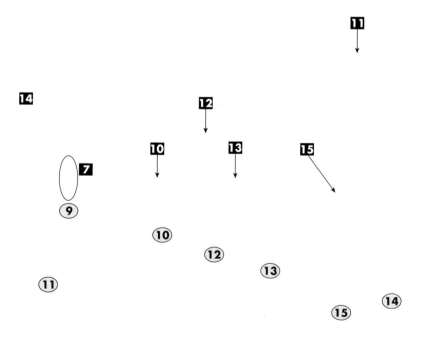

Figure 6.2b A meaningless "three-man defence" pattern in rugby

Temporal occlusion paradigm

The temporal occlusion paradigm is a method which requires participants to guess "what happens next" when asked to view video or film sequences in which key sport-related information has been occluded deliberately (e.g., by disguising the ball flight-path). In an ecological variation of this method, liquid crystal occlusion glasses may be used to replicate film occlusion procedures in actual sport settings. For example, a tennis player may be asked to wear such glasses while receiving a serve on court. Both variations of this paradigm are especially useful for assessing expert–novice differences in advance cue usage (A. M. Williams, 2002b). For example, a top-class tennis player can guess which side of the court his or her opponent is likely to serve to by making predictions from the direction of the server's ball-toss. Thus a right-handed server tossing the ball to his or her right will probably swing the serve to the right of the receiver. The occlusion paradigm has also been used to study how soccer goalkeepers anticipate the direction of penalty-kicks against them in the actual pitch environment. Early anticipation of the direction of a penalty-kick is vital as goalkeepers have less than half a second to decide which way to dive in an effort to save the shot. Thus researchers at the Australian Institute of Sport in Canberra have used occlusion goggles with goalkeepers in an effort to vary the amount and type of pre-contact cue information available to them. In this way, the goalkeeper's use of early visual cues from the penalty-taker (e.g., his or her posture, foot angle and arm swing) can be analysed (M. Smith, 2003). From such research, it should be possible to develop anticipatory training programmes for goalkeepers. Unfortunately, little is known as yet about the efficacy of instructional programmes designed to improve athletes' knowledge of situational probabilities in specific sports (A. M. Williams, 2003). Before concluding this brief discussion of the laboratory version of the occlusion paradigm, we need to acknowledge that its fidelity or realism is open to question. For example, to what extent is watching a video sequence of a tennis serve on a large screen equivalent to being on the receiving end of it on court during windy conditions? A detailed discussion of the advantages and disadvantages of this technique may be found in A. M. Williams *et al.* (1999).

Eye-tracking technology

If the eyes serve as windows to the mind, then the study of eye movements can provide insights into the relationship between "looking" (or visual fixation) and "seeing" (or paying attention). Two main types of eye movements have been identified (Kowler, 1999). On the one hand, saccadic movements are conjugate, high-speed jumps of the eyes which shift people's gaze from one location to another (e.g., notice how your gaze is moving from one word to the next while you read this sentence). On the other hand, smooth pursuit eye movements help people to focus on a given target (e.g., a ball) during the intervals between the saccades. These smooth pursuit movements are important because they enable perceivers to compensate for any displacements on the retina that may be caused by variations in either head or object position.

A variety of eye-movement registration techniques have been developed for use in sport settings (see A. M. Williams, 2002a). One of the most popular of these approaches is the Applied Science Laboratories' (ASL) 5000 SU eye-tracking system (see Figure 6.3).

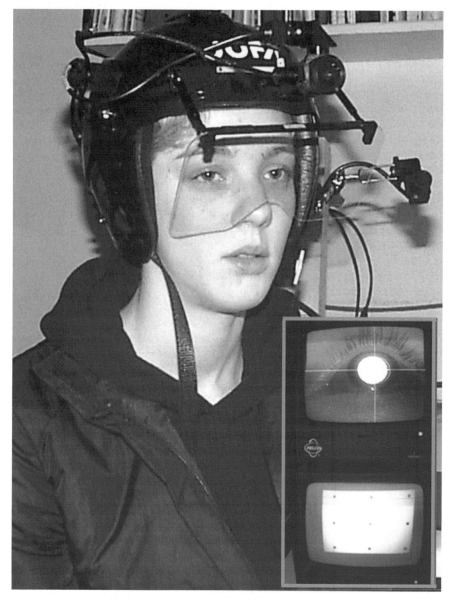

Figure 6.3 Eye-tracking technology allows psychologists to study visual search behaviour in expert athletes
Source: Courtesy of Andrew Flood, Department of Psychology, University College, Dublin

The ASL system is a video-based monocular corneal-reflection system that measures the perceiver's point of gaze with respect to video images recorded by an infra-red eye camera and a scene camera (which is usually floor-mounted). This system works by detecting two features, namely, the position of the pupil and the corneal reflex, in a video image of the eye. The relative position of these features is used to compute the visual point of gaze. The infra-red eye camera records displacement data from the left or right pupil and cornea.

Using such eye-tracking systems, a considerable amount of research has been conducted on the eye movements of athletes in recent years. Typical stimuli used in these studies include static slides depicting schematic sport situations as well as dynamic video presentations of similar material (see review by A. M. Williams *et al.*, 1999). Certain inferences are drawn from the location and duration of the perceiver's visual fixations. For example, the location of a fixation is usually regarded as an index of the relative importance of a given cue within a stimulus display. In addition, the number and duration of fixations recorded (which define "search rate") are believed to reflect the information-processing demands placed on the perceiver. Using such variables, expert–novice differences in visual search strategies have been discovered in such sports as soccer (Helsen and Starkes, 1999), tennis (Singer, Cauragh, Chen, Steinberg and Frehlich, 1996), boxing (Ripoll, Kerlirzin, Stein and Reine, 1993), golf (Vickers, 1992) and basketball (Vickers, 1996).

A prediction that is frequently tested in this field is that expert athletes will display a more efficient visual search strategy than relatively less skilled counterparts when inspecting sport-specific displays. This means that they will show fewer visual fixations of longer length – and focus more on "information rich" areas of the display than will relative novices. To find out if this prediction is supported in cricket, see Box 6.3.

Box 6.3 Expert–novice differences in the eye movements of cricket batsmen

Cricket is an exciting and skilful sport in which batsmen face the task of striking balls bowled to them at fast speeds with uncertain spins and bounces. This task is made all the more difficult by the fact that cricket balls travel in an arc, change speed when they bounce and rarely arrive at the eye-level of the batsman. Despite such difficulties, expert batsmen can judge the arrival time of the ball surprisingly precisely. How is this remarkable perceptual feat achieved? Recent research by Land and McLeod (2000) tried to answer this question using eye-tracking technology. Briefly, these authors measured the eye movements of three expert batsmen as they faced balls bowled at them at speeds of 25 metres per second. Results showed that in accordance with previous studies, the cricketers did not keep their eyes continuously on the ball throughout its flight. Instead, they fixated on its initial delivery, made predictive saccades to the place where they expected it to bounce, waited for it to hit the ground and then tracked its trajectory for up to 200 milliseconds after the bounce. In other words, they used their cricket knowledge and experience to make predictions about the likely destination of the ball before preparing to execute an attacking or defensive stroke. Interestingly, the expert batsmen were distinguished from their less competent players by the speed and accuracy of anticipatory saccades. In other words, they saw the ball early. To summarise, the skill of batting in cricket seems to lie as much in the head as in the hands.

Using a combination of the four preceding methods, a number of expert–novice differences in sport have been identified in recent years (see review by Starkes *et al.*, 2001). These findings may be summarised as follows.

Research findings on expert–novice differences in athletes

The following research findings summarise what is known about the differences between expert and novice athletes at present. For a more detailed discussion of these five research trends, see Lavallee, Kremer, Moran and Williams (2004), Starkes and Ericsson (2003), Starkes, Helsen and Jack (2001), A. M. Williams *et al.* (1999) and A. M. Williams (2002b).

Experts have a more extensive knowledge-base of sport-specific information

To begin with, expert athletes and coaches *know more* about their specialist domain than do relative novices but as we shall see later, this knowledge tends to be "domain specific" or restricted to one specific field. In the case of chess masters, the size of this chess database or "vocabulary" has been estimated at approximately 50,000 "chunks" of information (Simon and Gilmartin, 1973), where a chunk is defined as a meaningful grouping of chess piece positions.

This quantitative advantage associated with expertise means that experienced athletes and coaches possess a larger and better cross-referenced knowledge-base about their chosen sport than do relative novices. Typically, this cognitive superiority is evident in three different areas: declarative knowledge (i.e., factual knowledge about the sport in question such as knowing its rules), procedural knowledge (i.e., the ability to perform basic technical skills in this sport accurately and efficiently) and strategic knowledge (i.e., the ability to recognise and respond optimally to various patterns of play in the sport). Thus Morris, Tweedy and Gruneberg (1985) found that people who knew a lot about soccer displayed significantly greater recall of match results than did less knowledgeable participants. Also, Hyllegard (1991) discovered that expert batters were better than novices in predicting the type of pitch they were about to receive in a simulated baseball situation. Finally, Abernethy, Neal and Koning (1994) found that expert snooker players were more adept than novices at planning future shots.

*Experts use their knowledge more efficiently to identify,
remember and manipulate relevant information*

Apart from knowing more about their specialist sport than novices, expert athletes can *do more* with information deemed relevant. For example, Chase and Simon (1973) discovered that top chess players were better than novices at encoding and recalling meaningful (but not random) patterns from actual game situations. This cognitive advantage of experts over novices has been replicated extensively in sport situations. Thus top athletes and coaches are adept at recognising and memorising patterns of play in their sport. For example, Bedon and Howard (1992) found that expert karate practitioners were significantly superior to beginners in memorising various strategic techniques which had been presented to them. There is also evidence that experts tend to represent problems at a deeper level than novices because they search for principles and rules rather than superficial features of the tasks in question (Woll, 2002).

One explanation of the cognitive superiority of experts over novices comes from "skilled memory" theory (Chase and Ericsson, 1981). This theory proposes that experts use their long-term memory advantages to enrich the coding of new information. In other words, their rich database of knowledge appears to guide their chunking of new information. This proposition is significant for two reasons. First, it highlights a paradox of expertise (Smith, Adams and Schorr, 1978). Put simply, this paradox concerns the fact that although experts have more knowledge to search through in their database than have novices, they can retrieve information in their specialist domain more quickly. Perhaps the reason for this difference in speed of search and retrieval is that experts' knowledge tends to be extensively cross-referenced whereas that of novices is usually compartmentalised. The second reason that skilled memory theory is significant psychologically is that it challenges a common misconception about the way in which our memory system is designed. Briefly, many people believe that our minds resemble containers which fill up with the knowledge we acquire but which may overflow if we are exposed to too much information. Research on experts, however, shows that our memory system is not passive but expands to accommodate new information. Put simply, the more we know about a given field, the *more* we can remember in it (Moran, 2000b). In summary, the study of expert–novice differences in memory yields several interesting findings about the way in which our minds work.

*Experts are faster, more consistent and have better
anticipation skills than novices*

Classical studies on expertise showed that elite performers are usually faster at solving problems in their specialist field than are novices (Woll, 2002). Furthermore, experts tend to be more consistent than novices in performing their skills accurately. For example, top golfers are able to perform basic skills like driving or putting several times more consistently than are average players (Ericsson, 2001b). Finally, as indicated earlier, a number of laboratory studies of ball sports have shown that expert athletes are superior to novices in using advance cues from opponents to predict accurately shot placement and destination ("what will happen next?") in simulated sport-specific situations. Typically, in these studies, participants are presented with specially prepared video sequences in which key ball-flight information has been occluded selectively. The task is to predict the likely destination or flight-path of the ball in the film. For example, A. M. Williams and Burwitz (1993) reported that expert soccer players were better able to predict the destination of filmed penalty-kicks than novices – but only during conditions of minimal exposure (40 milliseconds after impact). Arising from these findings on expert–novice differences in advance cue utilisation, a practical question arises. Do anticipatory abilities in athletes develop over time? This issue is examined in Box 6.4.

Box 6.4 Do anticipatory abilities develop over time?

In sport, the term "anticipation" refers to an athlete's ability to predict task-relevant events accurately. Although it is well known that top performers are adept at this skill, little research has been conducted on whether or not this skill develops over time. Therefore, in an effort to fill this gap in the literature, Tenenbaum, Sar-El and Bar-Eli (2000) explored how visual anticipatory abilities developed in young tennis players of different skill levels over time. Using a temporal occlusion paradigm (described earlier in the chapter), high- and low-skilled tennis players from the Israeli Academy of Tennis watched specially prepared video segments and had to predict the final ball location after various tennis strokes (e.g., a backhand down the line, a serve) had been executed by model players. Results showed that, as expected, the more skilful players anticipated ball location more accurately than did less proficient performers. However, contrary to the theory of Ericsson *et al.* (1993) (see later in the chapter) some differences in visual anticipatory abilities were found to exist between the players of different skill levels from the earliest stages of their development. These latter differences suggest that deliberate practice alone cannot account for differences in anticipation skills in young tennis players. Therefore, Tenenbaum *et al.* (2000) concluded that "extensive practice is a necessary but not a sufficient condition for developing highly skilled performance" (p. 126).

Expertise in sport is domain-specific

Research suggests, as mentioned earlier in this section, that the skills of expert athletes tend to be "domain-specific" or confined to one area. In other words, few of the specialist skills acquired by expert athletes transfer to other sporting fields. At first glance, this finding is surprising as it challenges the existence of sporting "all rounders" or athletes who appear to be capable of achieving expert-level performance in several different sports simultaneously. On closer scrutiny, however, the domain-specificity of athletic skills is not completely surprising. After all, consider the case of Michael Jordan who was one of the greatest basketballers of all time. In the late 1990s, he retired from basketball and tried to become a professional baseball player. Unfortunately, his involvement with this new sport was not a success by his standards and he failed to attain his desired level of expertise in it. Anecdotally, similar experiences are evident in the case of several world-class athletes who tried to become successful golfers on the professional tour (see Capostagno, 2002). Among these former athletes are Nigel Mansell (former Formula One world champion), Ivan Lendl (a former world number one tennis player in the 1980s) and Julian Dicks (a former West Ham soccer star). Of course, we must be cautious about extrapolating from anecdotal examples. Also, we must be careful to point out that some sports stars do indeed become skilled exponents of another game. For example, Mats Wilander, the former tennis star, is an excellent golfer. Nevertheless, research suggests that top athletes rarely achieve equivalent levels of expertise in sports outsider their own specialist domain – unless there is a substantial level of overlap between the skills required by the sports in question. An interesting test-case of the "transferability" of athletic skills concerns the question of whether or not expert football players also make expert coaches or managers (see Box 6.5).

Box 6.5 Thinking critically about . . . whether or not expert soccer players make successful managers?

Does expertise transfer from one specialist role to another within a given sport? This question comes to mind when we explore whether or not expert footballers become successful managers (Marcotti, 2001; Moore, 2000). At the outset, we need a definition of expertise in playing. An obvious possibility in this regard is to use the ten-year rule explained earlier in the chapter. The difficulty with this criterion, however, is that it does not distinguish between players who excel consistently over a period of time and those whose performance is more variable and/or short-lived. In view of this problem, another definition of success could be postulated – namely, whether or not one is selected to represent one's country. This latter criterion is promising because research suggests that less than one per cent of professional players will be selected for their countries' national teams (Marcotti, 2001). As regards a definition for "success" in management, coaching one's team to win a league championship or cup competition may suffice. Initially, it is easy to think of some excellent football players who subsequently became successful managers. For example, Kenny Dalglish was a star for Liverpool and subsequently managed that club to league championship honours. Similarly, on the international stage, Jack Charlton, who won a World Cup medal with England in 1966, managed the little known Republic of Ireland team to a quarter-final place in the World Cup finals in Italy in 1990. Also, legendary stars like Franz Beckenbauer won World Cup medals both as a player and as a manager. From these examples, it is clear that one advantage of possessing playing experience at an elite level is that it adds credibility to one's views on coaching. But on the other hand, Moore (2000) calculated that of the twenty-six managers who had coached winning teams in the Premier League championship in England between 1945 and 2000, only *five* had won more than six caps for their countries. Surprisingly, even acknowledged expert managers like Bob Paisley and Bill Shankley (both of Liverpool) and Sir Alex Ferguson (manager of Manchester United – perhaps the most successful club manager in England over the past fifty years) – were *never* capped by their native country, Scotland. In addition, statistics reveal that only one (Jack Charlton) of the eight English World Cup-winning team of 1966 who went into management was subsequently successful in this role. Additional support for the idea that one does not have to be a great player to become a great manager comes from the fact that top managers such as Arsène Wenger (Arsenal) and Gerard Houllier (Liverpool) were never capped for their countries either. But let us leave the last word on this issue to Arigo Sacchi who won the Italian league and two European Cups with AC Milan even though he had never even played professional soccer! He said, "What's the problem here? So I never played. I was never good enough. But so what? If you want to be a good jockey, it's not necessary to have been a horse earlier in your career. In fact, sometimes it's a hindrance" (cited in Marcotti, 2001, p. 9).

Critical thinking questions
Do you agree with the definitions of success that were used above? How could you analyse scientifically whether or not great players become great managers? Is it enough merely to stack up examples on both sides of the question – or is there another way to proceed? One possibility is to elicit the views of a large sample of expert coaches on this question. An alternative method is to devise a checklist of managerial skills and to survey the views of players and managers on the relative importance of each of these factors. Why do you think that expertise in playing may not transfer to expertise in coaching or management? Remember that coaching largely involves teaching – and it is often quite difficult to teach a skill that one learned intuitively.

Experts have more insight into, and control over, their own mental processes

The term "metacognition" refers to people's insight into, and control over, their own mental processes (Matlin, 2002). It has long been assumed that experts are superior to novices in this area. If this principle holds true in sport, then expert athletes and coaches should have greater insight into, and more control over, their minds than do novices. Although few studies have tested this hypothesis, there is some evidence to support it with regard to planning behaviour. For example, McPherson (2000) found that expert collegiate tennis players generated *three times* as many planning concepts as novices during "between point" periods in tennis matches. Similarly, Cleary and Zimmerman (2001) discovered significant differences between expert, non-expert and novice basketball players in self-regulatory processes exhibited during practice sessions. Specifically, the expert players planned their practice sessions better than did other groups by choosing specific, technique-oriented processes (e.g., "to bend my knees").

In summary, research shows that expert adult athletes differ consistently from relative novices with regard to a variety of perceptual, cognitive and strategic aspects of behaviour. This conclusion appears to apply equally to young athletes. Thus Ward and Williams (2003) discovered that perceptual and cognitive skills discriminated between elite and sub-elite soccer players between the ages of 9 and 17 years. These general findings are consistent with those derived from more formal domains like chess and physics where experts have been shown to display both quantitative and qualitative knowledge advantages over novices. Thus experts' knowledge is better organised and largely domain-specific and is probably represented differently from that of novices. But how do people become athletic experts in the first place? In order to answer this question, we need to consider the role of practice in the acquisition of expertise.

Becoming an expert athlete: Ericsson's theory of "deliberate practice"

Earlier in this chapter, we mentioned the joy of watching expert athletes such as Tiger Woods or Venus Williams. Why do we find it impossible to emulate the skills of these players? Of course, the "hardware" answer to this question is that we are not born with sufficient athletic talent to do so. But there is another possibility. Perhaps we simply do not practise hard enough, long enough or well enough to fulfil our potential. This controversial "nurturist" possibility raises an intriguing issue. How important is practice in the development of expertise in any field?

Surprisingly, it is only in the past decade that this question has begun to receive sustained empirical attention in psychology. Nevertheless, several stage theories have been developed to account for the development of expertise in young performers in different fields (e.g., see Bloom, 1985; Dreyfus, 1997). Of these approaches, the work of Ericsson has generated the greatest volume of research in recent years.

According to Ericsson and his colleagues (Ericsson et al., 1993; Ericsson and Lehman, 1996), innate talent is a necessary but not sufficient condition for the development of expertise in a given domain. Instead, top-level performance is believed to be an acquired skill which is attributable largely to the quantity and quality of the performer's practice schedule (where "practice" is understood as any exercise that is designed to fulfil the goal of improving the person's performance). This claim about the primacy of practice is based on two main sources of evidence – first, research which highlights the "plasticity" or amenability of many cognitive characteristics to practice effects, and second, studies on the practice habits of elite musicians. Let us now consider each of these two strands of evidence in more detail.

For a long time, it was assumed that many of our mental limitations (e.g., the fact that our short-term memory is very brief and fragile) were caused by flaws in the design of our brain. For example, early cognitive research (see details in Matlin, 2002) showed that the average person's short-term memory span is restricted to between seven and nine units of information – which probably explains why we find it difficult to remember people's mobile phone numbers. However, this structural limitation principle was challenged by Chase and Ericsson (1981) who showed that with between 200 and 400 hours of practice, a person could be trained to remember up to *80* randomly presented digits. Details of this remarkable case study are presented in Box 6.6.

Box 6.6 How practice can improve your memory

One of the oldest tasks in experimental psychology is the memory-span test. This test requires people to remember a number of digits (e.g., 1, 9, 6, 6, 2, 0, 0, 1) in the precise sequence in which they were presented. Early research (e.g., see details in Matlin, 2002) showed that most people can remember between seven and nine such digits – hence the estimation of the apparent limit on our short-term memory span. But what if one were trained to group or chunk these digits together so that they could be transformed into meaningful units? For example, the previous digit sequence could be segmented into two composite units rather than eight separate digits (e.g., "1966" or the year that England won the World Cup and "2001" or the title of a famous science-fiction film directed by Stanley Kubrick). Using this chunking approach, Chase and Ericsson (1981) trained a volunteer (whose original memory-span was about the average of seven units) over 200 practice sessions spanning several months to achieve a remarkable memory-span whereby he could recall accurately over 80 digits presented randomly! How was this feat accomplished? What chunking strategies were exploited? Interestingly, the volunteer in question ("S.F.") was a keen varsity track-athlete who used his knowledge of running times to chunk the digits to be remembered into familiar units of 3–4 digits. For example, he might break up six digits such as 2 2 0 4 1 6 into two chunks using the time taken to run a marathon (2 hours and 20 minutes) followed by that to run a mile (4 minutes and 16 seconds). Remarkably, in keeping with the domain specificity principle explained earlier, SF's extraordinary memory skill was confined to numbers only. Thus he was no better than average in his ability to recall long strings of *letters*. The clear implication of this study is that people's memory-span can be increased if they practise chunking techniques based on specialist knowledge or personal interest. To illustrate, SF managed to increase his short-term memory-span for digits *ten-fold* by practising extensively.

Box 6.6 shows us that practice can circumvent certain information-processing limitations of the mind. Put differently, Chase and Ericsson's (1981) study showed that remarkable changes in performance (albeit in one field only) could be produced in otherwise unexceptional performers simply by practising rigorously over time. Augmenting this line of evidence was other research which showed that practice could induce actual *anatomical* changes in athletes. For example, evidence indicates that years of intensive practice can increase the size and endurance of athletes' hearts as well as the size of their bone structure (Ericsson, 2001a). Thus the playing arm of a professional tennis player is often more heavily muscled and larger boned than his or her non-dominant arm. In summary, a recurring theme of research in modern neuroscience is the malleability or plasticity of anatomical and physiological mechanisms.

The second important influence on Ericsson's work emerged from studies which his research team conducted on the practice habits of eminent musicians. Specifically, Ericsson *et al.* (1993) interviewed violinists of different levels of ability at the Berlin music academy in order to analyse the nature, type and frequency of their practice sessions. These interviews were supplemented by diary studies. Results showed that not only did the expert group practise longer than their less successful counterparts (e.g., by the age of 20, they had spent over 10,000 hours in practice compared with about 2,000 hours accumulated by amateur pianists at the same age) but they also practised differently – spending more time on perfecting their skills (4–5 hours a day on average) than in mindlessly repeating elementary drills. From this evidence, Ericsson *et al.* (1993) concluded that "across many domains of expertise, a remarkably consistent pattern emerges: The best individuals start practice at earlier ages and maintain a higher level of daily practice" (*ibid.*, p. 392). Furthermore, these researchers proposed that *practice*, rather than innate talent, was the main cause of expertise or achievement level – not a correlate of it. More precisely, Ericsson suggested that expertise is a direct function of the total amount of "deliberate practice" (or "individualised training on tasks selected by a qualified teacher"; Ericsson and Charness, 1994, p. 738) that has been undertaken by performers. This proposition is the cornerstone of his theory. But what exactly is "deliberate practice" and how does it change over time?

"Deliberate practice"

According to Ericsson *et al.* (1993), "deliberate practice" is a highly structured, purposeful form of practice that is particularly relevant to the improvement of performance in any domain. It involves individualised training on tasks that are highly structured by skilled instructors in order to provide "optimal opportunities for learning and skill acquisition" (Ericsson and Charness, 1994, p. 739). The goal of such practice is to challenge the learner to go beyond his or her current level of performance. It may be contrasted with mechanical practice which is characterised solely by mindless repetition of basic drills. Recall that we raised this distinction between "mindful" (or deliberate) and "mindless" practice at the beginning of this chapter.

What are the characteristics of deliberate practice? To begin with, Ericsson *et al.* (1993) suggested that deliberate practice activities are "very high on relevance for performance, high on effort, and comparatively low on inherent enjoyment" (p. 373). More precisely, four criteria of such practice may be specified as follows. First, deliberate practice targets specific skills that can improve performance. Second, it requires hard work and intense concentration on the part of the learner. A practical implication of this feature is that the duration of deliberate practice is determined mainly by the ability of the performer to sustain his or her concentration during the training session. Third, Ericsson believes that deliberate practice activities are not intrinsically rewarding. For example, in sport, a top tennis player may have to spend an hour working repetitively on the ball-toss for his or her serve rather than engaging in the more pleasant task of rallying with a partner. A fourth criterion of deliberate practice is that it requires feedback from a specialist coach or instructor. This feedback helps the performer to monitor discrepancies between his or her current level of performance and some designated target standard. In summary, deliberate practice consists of activities that require effort and attention but are not play, not enjoyable intrinsically and not part of one's paid employment. Let us now turn to the issue of how expertise is held to develop from sustained engagement in deliberate practice.

Stages in the development of expertise

People are not born experts in anything – they become that way as a function of practice and instruction. Based on this assumption, several stage theories of expertise have been postulated. For example, Dreyfus (1997) proposed a five-stage model of the transition from novice to expert. These stages are novice (stage 1), advanced beginner (stage 2), competent (stage 3), proficient (stage 4) and expert (stage 5). An alternative approach was proposed by Ericsson and his colleagues. This model can be explained as follows.

Inspired by the theories of Bloom (1985), Ericsson and his colleagues postulated three stages in the development of expertise. These stages are distinguished from each other largely on the basis of the type of practice engaged in at each phase of development. They may be described in relation to athletic expertise as follows. In stage 1, a child is introduced to a given sport and may display some athletic talent which is recognised by his or her parents. At this stage, practice usually takes the form of "play", which may be defined as an unstructured and intrinsically enjoyable activity. During this era, the child's parents may facilitate skill development by encouraging him or her to take some lessons in the activity in question. Stage 2 can extend over a long period. It is here that a protracted period of preparation occurs during which the young learners are taught to perform their skills better. Therefore, "deliberate practice" begins in earnest in Stage 2. As explained previously, this form of practice stems from having a well-defined task with an appropriate level of difficulty for the individual concerned, informative feedback, and opportunities for the correction of errors. During this stage, the young athlete's performance usually improves significantly. Usually, the stage ends with some commitment from the performer to pursue activities in the domain on a full-time basis. Finally, in stage 3, the average amount of daily deliberate practice increases and specialist or advanced coaches are sought by the parents to assist the young performer. Indeed, on occasion, parents of some performers may move home in order to live closer to specialist coaches or advanced training facilities. Stage 3 usually ends either when the performer becomes a full-time competitor in the sport in question or when s/he abandons the sport completely. A fourth stage has been recognised by Ericsson and his colleagues. Here, certain outstanding performers may go beyond the competence (skills and knowledge) of their coaches to achieve exceptional levels of success in their chosen sport. One interesting implication of Ericsson's stage theory is that it suggests that mere exposure to a given sport will not make someone an expert performer in it. Research shows that the ability to perform to an expert standard in sport does not come from merely watching it but requires instead active interaction with its structure (Starkes *et al.*, 2001).

Testing the theory of deliberate practice in sport

As we learned above, Ericsson (2001a, 2001b; Ericsson *et al.*, 1993) proposed that expertise in any field is directly related to the amount of deliberate practice undertaken by the performer in question. How valid is this theory when applied to the domain of sport?

Although only a small number of studies have been conducted on this issue so far, research reviews by Starkes (2001) and Starkes *et al.* (2001) lend qualified support to Ericsson's crucial emphasis on the importance of deliberate practice. Thus as Starkes (2001) concluded: "In every sport we have examined to date, we have found that level of skill has a positive linear relationship with amount of accumulated practice throughout one's sports career. The best athletes . . . have put in significantly more practice than their lesser skill [*sic*] counterparts" (p. 198). But some caution is necessary when interpreting this conclusion. To explain, research suggests that there are at least two key differences between the deliberate practice schedules of musicians and athletes. First, whereas most musicians tend to practise on their own, athletes tend to train with team-mates or practice partners (Summers, 1999). Second, the concept of deliberate practice in sport may differ from that in the domain of music. To illustrate, recall that one of the criteria of such practice stipulated by Ericsson is that the activity in question should be relatively unenjoy-able. In sport, however, there is evidence that many athletes (e.g., wrestlers; Hodges and Starkes, 1996) seem to *enjoy* engaging in deliberate practice activities. This finding was confirmed by Helsen *et al.* (1998) who analysed the practice habits of soccer and hockey players of various levels of ability. The results of this study revealed two key findings and an anomaly. To begin with, the ten-year rule was confirmed. Specifically, results showed that after this period of time, both the soccer and hockey players realised that a significantly greater investment of training time would be required to enable them to achieve further success. Second, as expected, there was a direct linear relationship between the amount of deliberate practice undertaken by these athletes and the level of proficiency that they attained. But an anomaly also emerged from this study. In particular, these researchers found that contrary to Ericsson's model, those practised activities which were deemed to be *most relevant* to skill development were also seen by the soccer and hockey players as being *most enjoyable*. Again, this finding contradicts Ericsson's assertion that deliberate practice of basic skills is not inherently enjoyable. Influenced by such findings, Young and Salmela (2002) assessed middle-distance runners' perceptions of Ericsson's definition of deliberate practice. Briefly, these researchers asked the runners to rate various practice and training activities on the amount of effort and concentration required to perform them and the degree of enjoyment to which they gave rise. Contrary to what Ericsson's theory predicted, Young and Salmela (2002) found that these runners rated the most relevant and most effortful of these training activities as also being the most inherently enjoyable. This finding led these authors to conclude that the construct of deliberate practice in sport should be redefined to refer to activities that are highly relevant for performance improvement, highly demanding of effort and concentration – and highly enjoyable to perform. In summary, there is evidence that top athletes differ from expert musicians by appearing to *enjoy* the routine practice of basic skills in their domain.

To summarise, we have learned that the work of Hodges and Starkes is generally supportive of Ericsson's claim that deliberate practice is crucial to athletic success. Nevertheless, doubts remain about at least one of the criteria specified for this form of practice – namely, the alleged lack of enjoyment shown by experts when engaging in basic training drills. In order to explore this anomaly further, however, additional research on the "micro-structure" of athletic practice is required.

Implications of Ericsson's research

At least six interesting implications arise from Ericsson's research on deliberate practice. First, his stage theory of expertise suggests that practice *by itself* is not sufficient to achieve excellence. Specialist advice and corrective feedback from a skilled instructor are essential for the development of expertise (Ericsson *et al.*, 1993). Second, Ericsson's research raises the intriguing possibility that continuous improvement is possible in skill-learning – even among people who have achieved the proficiency level of experts. This proposition challenges conventional accounts of skill-learning in at least one significant way. In the past, automaticity, or fluent, effortless and unconscious performance, was regarded as the end point of all skill-learning. In other words, it was believed that once this state has been achieved, no further progress is possible. This assumption is challenged by Ericsson who suggests that experts' performance "*continues* to improve as a function of increased experience and deliberate practice" (2001b, p. 18). In this regard, Ericsson's theory is controversial because it suggests that "expert performance is not fully automated" (*ibid.*, p. 39) because most experts prepare consciously, deliberately and strategically for impending competitive encounters. The fact that experts can also remember their performances in great detail also challenges the idea that expertise is completely automated (Ericsson, 2001b). As yet, however, little research has been conducted to test the proposition that experts can continue to improve their performance beyond automaticity. Nevertheless, Ericsson's theory purports to explain why most recreational golfers and tennis players do not improve beyond a certain level in spite of practising regularly: "The key challenge for aspiring expert performers is to avoid the arrested development associated with automaticity that is seen with everyday activities and, in addition, to acquire cognitive skills to support continued learning and improvement of their performance" (Ericsson, 2001b, p. 12). Third, Ericsson's theories offer suggestions as to why continuous practice is so important to experts. Briefly, if elite performers fail to practise continuously, they will lose the "feel" or kinaesthetic control that guides their skills (see Ericsson, 2001b, p. 42). Fourth, Ericsson's research on expertise highlights the role of *acquired knowledge* rather than innate talent in shaping top-level performance. Put simply, if someone can master the knowledge and skills required for expertise, then expert performance should occur. On the other hand, Ericsson concedes that there may well be individual differences in the degree to which people are motivated to engage in deliberate practice. Nevertheless, a key theme of Ericsson's research is that expertise is inextricably linked to knowledge compilation. Fifth, research on deliberate practice shows us that concentration is essential for optimal learning (Ericsson, 2001b; see also Young and Salmela, 2002). Finally, the theory of deliberate practice has some interesting implications for talent identification programmes (Summers, 1999). For example, it suggests that instead of attempting to identify precociously talented young performers, sports organisations may be better advised to concentrate instead on searching for youngsters who display the types of psychological qualities (e.g., dedication to practice, determination to improve) which are likely to facilitate and sustain requisite regimes of deliberate practice.

Some criticisms of Ericsson's theories

As one might expect of such an environmentalist approach, Ericsson's theory of expertise has aroused as much controversy as enthusiasm within sport psychology. The main problem is that many coaches baulk at the claim that practice is more important than innate talent in determining athletic success. Against this background, what are the principal criticisms directed at Ericsson's research on deliberate practice (see also Starkes *et al.*, 2001)?

At least six criticisms of Ericsson's theories and research may be identified in sport psychology. To begin with, the theory of deliberate practice has been criticised on the grounds of invalid extrapolation from the field of music to that of sport. The argument here is that there are important differences between these fields which Ericsson and his colleagues may have neglected. For example, as we mentioned earlier, deliberate practice is usually undertaken alone by musicians but in pairs or collectively in sport. As a result of this contextual difference, the nature of the practice activities undertaken may differ significantly. For example, the camaraderie generated among team-mates training together may explain why athletes differ from musicians in their tendency to enjoy performing basic practice drills in their specialist domain (see earlier discussion of this issue). A second criticism of Ericsson's theory is that it is based on evidence that is correlational rather than experimental in nature. According to this argument, these data may merely indicate that people who are highly motivated in a given field will spend more time practising in it and hence are more likely to become experts. Unfortunately, correlational research designs cannot control adequately for possible intervening variables such as motivation. As Starkes *et al.* (2001) concluded: "what is not determined by this model, but is absolutely crucial, is the role that motivation plays in determining who will put in the necessarily huge amounts of practice to become an expert" (p. 186). Third, like many theories in psychology, Ericsson's stage theory of expertise may be criticised for ignoring important contextual and socioeconomic variables. In particular, this theory lacks a precise analysis of the effects of different resource constraints (e.g., access to suitable training facilities or specialist instructors) on people's progress through the three postulated stages of expertise. In a similar vein, Ericsson has not addressed adequately the impact of socioeconomic variables on the maintenance of deliberate practice schedules. A fourth criticism is that Ericsson's claims are difficult to falsify or disprove empirically because it is hard to find a performance domain in which people have managed to attain expertise without engaging in extensive practice (*ibid.*). Another methodological issue in this regard is that Ericsson's theory relies heavily on people's retrospective accounts of their practice schedules. As we have indicated in this and earlier chapters, data obtained retrospectively are potentially contaminated by exaggerations, memory biases and response sets. Finally, Ericsson has been criticised for his failure to include control groups in his studies (Sternberg, 1999). Despite these criticisms, the theory of deliberate practice has proved to be rich and insightful in helping researchers to understand the nature and development of expertise in sport.

Evaluating research on expertise in sport: significance, problems and new directions

Research on expertise in athletes is important both for theoretical and practical reasons. Theoretically, expertise is one of the few topics that bridge the gap between sport psychology and mainstream cognitive psychology. Indeed, until the advent of research on everyday cognition (see Woll, 2002), research on athletic expertise was seen as falling between two stools in the sense that it was perceived as being too "physical" for cognitive psychology and too "cognitive" for sport psychology (Starkes *et al.*, 2001). However, over the past decade, largely as a result of Ericsson's research programme on the relationship between practice and exceptional performance, athletic skills have begun to attract the interest of researchers from cognitive psychology. Meanwhile, at a practical level, research on athletic expertise is valuable because it has highlighted the need for greater understanding of the practice habits of sport performers of different levels of ability (Starkes, 2001). In addition, it has raised the intriguing practical question of whether or not perceptual training programmes can accelerate the skills of novices so that they can "hasten the journey" to expertise (*ibid.*). With regard to this issue, research suggests that cognitive interventions designed to develop the knowledge-base underlying expertise are probably more effective in facilitating elite performance than are perceptual skills training programmes (see A. M. Williams, 2002b, 2003).

Despite its theoretical and practical significance, however, research on athletic expertise is hampered by at least three conceptual and methodological problems (see Starkes *et al.*, 2001). First, a great deal of confusion surrounds the use of the term "expert" at present. To illustrate, this term has been applied in a rather cavalier fashion to such heterogeneous groups as inter-varsity level athletes, provincial team members, professional performers and members of national squads – without any obvious recourse to the ten-year rule criterion. Therefore, greater precision and consistency are required in the operational definitions of the term expert. Second, little is known at present about the retention of expertise in sport skills over time. In other words, how long does expertise in a given sport last? The paucity of evidence on this question is a consequence of the fact that most research on athletic expertise uses retrospective recall paradigms rather than longitudinal research designs. Third, the methods used to study expertise in sport (reviewed in the third part of this chapter) have been challenged on the grounds that they are often borrowed uncritically and without modification from mainstream psychology.

For example, as A. M. Williams *et al.* (1999) pointed out, it is questionable whether researchers can extrapolate validly from research methods in which two-dimensional static slides are used to present dynamic three-dimensional sporting information. In recognition of these problems, Starkes *et al.* (2001) recommended that future researchers in this field should use stricter and more consistent operational definitions of the term expert, more longitudinal research designs and more field studies than have been employed to date.

Ideas for research projects on expertise in sport

Here are four suggestions for possible research projects on expertise in sport performers.

1   It is implicitly in sport psychology that the term "expert" applies equally to athletes and coaches. But as yet, nobody has examined the similarities and differences between these two types of experts (namely, performers and instructors, respectively) on recall of information presented to them. Therefore, it would be interesting to explore "expert versus expert" differences between athletes and coaches from a particular sport using the pattern recognition paradigm explained earlier in this chapter.

2   It would be valuable to seek the views of expert athletes and coaches on the main tenets of Ericsson's theory of the stages of expertise and the nature of deliberate practice (see Ericsson *et al.*, 1993; Ericsson, 2001a, 2001b). A special questionnaire could be designed for this purpose. So far, no published research is available on this issue.

3   Additional research is required on the application of thought-sampling techniques to explore expertise in sport situations. For example, it would be interesting to equip snooker players with "beepers" in order to investigate possible expert–novice differences in thinking as players are forced to sit in their chairs while their opponents are competing at the table (see earlier discussion of this phenomenon in Chapter 1).

4   In the light of the discovery by Young and Salmela (2002) that Ericsson's criteria of deliberate practice may not apply completely to athletes, it would be interesting to investigate systematically the degree to which athletes enjoy the basic practice drills required by their sport. In particular, no studies have yet been conducted in which the "enjoyability" of practice activities has been compared using an expert–novice paradigm across different sports.

Summary

We have long been fascinated by the exploits of expert performers in any field – those who display exceptional talent, knowledge and/or outstanding skills in a particular domain such as sport. Until relatively recently, however, little was known about the psychological differences between expert and novice athletes. Therefore, the purpose of this chapter was to investigate the nature and significance of research on athletic expertise in sport psychology.

- We began by explaining the meaning of the term "expertise" and indicating some reasons for its current popularity as a research topic.
- The second part of the chapter explored the general question of whether athletic success is determined more by hardware (i.e., physical) or by software (i.e., psychological) characteristics of sport performers. As we learned, available evidence largely supports the latter approach.
- In the third part of the chapter, we reviewed a variety of research methods and findings on expert–novice differences in sport.
- The next section examined the question of how athletic expertise develops over time. A special feature of this section was an explanation and critique of Ericsson's theory that expertise is largely due to the amount of deliberate practice accumulated by the performer.
- In the fifth part of the chapter, we evaluated the significance of, as well as some problems and new directions in, research on expertise in athletes.
- Finally, some ideas were provided for research projects in this field.

Part three

TEAM COHESION

Overview

So far in this book, we have introduced the discipline and profession of sport and exercise psychology (Chapter 1) and the various psychological processes (e.g., motivation, anxiety, concentration, imagery) that affect individual athletes in their pursuit of excellence (see Chapters 2 to 6). But at this stage, it is important to acknowledge that group processes (e.g., team cohesion) are equally important in sport. Indeed, Widmeyer, Brawley and Carron (2002) claimed recently that "ignoring this influence may be a major conceptual and methodological error" (p. 302). Therefore, the next chapter will explore the main theories, findings and issues arising from research on team cohesion in sport.

Chapter 7

Exploring team cohesion in sport: a critical perspective

Lions tours are about bonding together. As a touring side you are always up against it. Success depends on whether you come together or you split into factions . . . There were times with this Lions squad when we felt invincible – that we could take on the whole world and beat them. (Former British and Irish Lions rugby player, Jeremy Guscott, cited in Guscott, 1997, p. 153)

In previous squads we would see players sitting down to meals and staying within their club groups. A Munich table here, a Cologne table there. This year, it has been different. Everyone mixes in and it makes for a better team. (Franz Beckenbauer, coach of the West German soccer team that won the World Cup in 1990, cited in Miller, 1997, p. 107)

The importance of team spirit is a hobby-horse of mine . . . it is probably in team-sports like football that the advantages of the right group dynamics or chemistry may be seen most clearly. (Alan Hansen, former Liverpool and Scotland soccer player, 1999, pp. 135–136)

The creation of team spirit and the building of "the good team" is therefore one of the coach's most important jobs. (England soccer manager, Sven-Göran Eriksson, 2002, p. 116)

I am only there to finish the job of the team. (Thierry Henry, Arsenal and French international footballer, quoted in Winter, 2002b, p. 21)

Introduction

Few athletes compete alone in their sports. Instead, most of them interact either *with* or *against* other athletes collectively. Indeed, even in individual sports such as golf or tennis, competitive action is often assessed or aggregated as a team-game (e.g., the Ryder Cup in golf or the Davis Cup in tennis). But what exactly is a "team"? Are Jeremy Guscott, Sven-Göran Eriksson and Thierry Henry correct in believing that "team spirit" or unity is essential for the achievement of sporting excellence? If so, do team-building exercises really work? More generally, is it true that young people's involvement in school sports builds their "character" and imbues them with a sense of team spirit? In this regard, the Duke of Wellington is alleged to have remarked that the battle of Waterloo "was won on the playing fields of Eton" (Knowles, 1999, p. 810). In order to answer the preceding questions, the present chapter is organised as follows.

To begin with, I shall explore how psychologists define "groups", "teams" and "group dynamics". In the next section, I shall introduce the concept of team spirit which has been defined operationally by sport psychologists as "cohesion" (also known as "cohesiveness") – or the extent to which a group of athletes or players is united by a common purpose and bonds together in pursuit of that objective. This section will also examine the measurement of cohesion and its relationship to athletic performance. Given the assumption that cohesion can be enhanced, the third part of the chapter will investigate the nature and efficacy of team-building activities in sport psychology. Next, I shall evaluate briefly the commonly held belief that team sports foster desirable psychological qualities in participants. The fifth section of the chapter will outline some new directions for research on team cohesion in sport. Finally, suggestions will be provided for possible research projects in this field.

Unfortunately, due to space restrictions, this chapter will not be able to deal with other questions concerning the impact of groups on individual athletic performance. For example, the issue of how the presence of other people such as spectators and/or fellow competitors affects athletes' performance lies beyond the scope of this chapter. This latter topic, which was mentioned briefly in Chapter 1, is called social facilitation, and was first studied empirically by Triplett (1898). A comprehensive review of research on social facilitation in athletic performance was conducted by Strauss (2002). Similarly, the converse phenomenon of "social loafing" in sport, whereby individual athletes may sometimes exert less effort when performing a group task (e.g., working as a defensive unit with others) than when performing the same task on their own (Cashmore, 2002), also lies beyond the boundary of this chapter.

"Groups", "teams" and "group dynamics" in sport

In everyday life, we tend to see any collection of people as a group. However, social psychologists use this term more precisely. In particular, they define a group as two or more people who interact with, and exert mutual influences on, each other (Aronson, Wilson and Akert, 2002). It is this sense of mutual interaction or interdependence for a common purpose which distinguishes the members of a group from a mere aggregation of individuals. For example, as Hodge (1995) observed, a collection of people who happen to go for a swim after work on the same day each week does not, strictly speaking, constitute a group because these swimmers do not interact with each other in a structured manner. By contrast, a squad of young competitive swimmers who train every morning before going to school *is* a group because they not only share a common objective (training for competition) but also interact with each other in formal ways (e.g., by warming up together before-hand). It is this sense of people coming together to achieve a common objective that defines a "team".

According to Carron and Hausenblas (1998), a sports team is a special type of group. In particular, apart from having the defining properties of mutual interaction and task interdependence, teams have four key characteristics. First, they have a collective sense of identity – a "we-ness" rather than a collection of "I-ness". This collective consciousness emerges when individual team-members and non-team-members agree that the group is distinguishable from other groups ("us" versus "them"). For example, the leaders of the successful Wimbledon soccer team of the late 1980s called themselves the "crazy gang" and their manager Dave Bassett used this self-styled identity as a cohesive force when preparing his team to compete against more established football clubs. Often, this type of social bonding led to enhanced team performance. Thus the former Liverpool player Alan Hansen was amazed at the intimidatory tactics and "all-for-one" spirit which the Wimbledon players showed in the tunnel before they defeated his team in the 1988 FA Cup Final (Hansen, 1999). Second, sports teams are characterised by a set of distinctive roles. For example, soccer and rugby teams have creative players as well as tough-tackling "enforcers". The third feature of sports teams is their use of structured modes of communication within the group. This type of communication tends to involve nicknames and shorthand instructions. Finally, teams develop "norms" or social rules that prescribe what group members should or should not do in certain circumstances. For example, individual performers learn to ignore the idiosyncratic routines of their team-mates as they prepare for important competitive events.

In view of the preceding characteristics, teams are regarded as dynamic entities by sport psychologists. Thus certain aspects of team behaviour change over time. In this regard, Tuckman (1965) has identified four hypothetical stages in the development of any team. In the first stage ("forming"), the team's members come together and engage in an informal assessment of each other's strengths and weak-nesses. Next, a "storming" stage is postulated in which interpersonal conflict is common as the players compete for the coach's attention and strive to establish their rank in the pecking order of the team. The third stage is called "norming" and occurs when group members begin to see themselves as a team united by a common task and by interpersonal bonds. Finally, the "performing" stage occurs when the members of the team resolve to channel their energies as a cohesive unit into the pursuit of agreed goals. A similar account of the way in which teams change over time has been offered by Whitaker (1999) who identified three stages of evolution: "inclusion" (where new members are preoccupied with how to become a part of the team), "assertion" (where members struggle to establish their position within the hierarchy of the team) and "co-operation" (where members strive to work together to fulfil team goals). Unfortunately, although both of these hypothetical stage models of team development seem plausible intuitively, they have not been validated adequately by empirical evidence.

Having discussed briefly the fact that teams change over time, it is important to clarify what psychologists mean by the term "group dynamics". In general, sport psychologists use this term in at least three different ways (Carron and Hausenblas, 1998; Widmeyer, Brawley and Carron, 2002). First, it denotes the scientific study of how athletes behave in groups, especially in face-to-face situations (e.g., when coaches address players in team talks). Secondly, "group dynamics" refers broadly to a host of factors (e.g., confidence) that are believed to play a role in determining team performance. Finally, this term designates the processes that generate *change* in groups (Cashmore, 2002). It is mainly the second and third of these meanings that we shall explore in this chapter – especially, the question of how team spirit or cohesion is related to team performance. Let us now explore this idea of team spirit in more detail.

Team spirit or social cohesion: from popular understanding to psychological analysis

It has long been believed that successful sports teams have a unique spirit or sense of unity that transcends the simple aggregation of their individual components. This idea is captured by an old Irish proverb which states "ní neart go cur le chéile" or "there is no strength without unity". An example of this unity was the extra-ordinary cohesion of the victorious European team during its 2002 Ryder Cup golf match against the USA. Thus according to one of the European players, Darren Clarke, "we played as a team, we dined as a team, we talked as a team and we won as a team . . . The team spirit this week has been the best that I have experienced in this my third Ryder Cup" (cited in O'Sullivan, 2002b, p. 4).

Before we analyse what team spirit means in sport, however, let us pause for a moment to consider the benefits of teamwork in a rather unusual domain – the animal kingdom. Have you ever wondered why birds fly in a peculiar "V"-like formation? Well, according to Mears and Voehl (1994), this pattern is adaptive because as each bird in the "V" flaps its wings, it creates an "uplift" current for the bird behind it. This uplift enables the entire flock of birds to fly significantly farther than any of the individual birds could fly alone. But how can this idea of synergy among flocks of bird apply to sports behaviour? In order to answer this question, we need to analyse what team spirit or cohesion means to athletes, coaches and sport psychologists.

Athletes' and coaches' views on cohesion

As the quotations at the beginning of this chapter indicate, cohesion is valued highly by coaches and sports performers. More significantly, many team managers believe that it can be enhanced. For example, Sam Torrance, the manager of the European Ryder Cup golf team in 2002, sought advice from two successful soccer managers –

Figure 7.1 Team spirit helped the European team to victory over the USA in the 2002 Ryder Cup
Source: courtesy of Inpho Photography

Sir Alex Ferguson (manager of Manchester United) and Sven-Göran Eriksson (coach of England) (R. Williams, 2002a) – in an effort to enrich the task and social cohesion of his players before the match. Apparently, the key message delivered by these managers was to treat all the golfers in the team in the same way (R. Williams, 2002c). This principle was appreciated greatly by the players. For example, in commenting on Torrance's captaincy, Pádraig Harrington said, "everybody got the same treatment, there were no stars in the team . . . he kept the spirits up all the way" (cited in Reid, 2002, p. 22). By contrast with this egalitarian approach, Curtis Strange, the captain of the US team, showed evidence of preferential treatment for certain players. For example, he allowed Tiger Woods to engage in his customary early morning practice round on his own before the match whereas he insisted that the other players had to practise together. Interestingly, recent research on university athletes suggests that perceived inequity, or favouritism on the part of coaches towards certain individuals, decreased team cohesion (Turman, 2003).

In addition to believing that team cohesion can be developed (see later in the chapter for some practical techniques in this regard), many athletes and coaches claim that individual performers must learn to subordinate their skills and efforts to the goals of the team. For example, Thierry Henry, the Arsenal soccer star and Professional Footballers' Association player of the year in 2003, proclaimed that "you can't have the individual ahead of the collective. Never" (cited in Winter, 2002b, p. 21). This view supports the old coaching adage that "there is no I in team". But what happens when the *captain* of a team challenges the authority of its manager?

An interesting case study of this problem occurred in May 2002 shortly before the World Cup soccer finals in Japan and Korea when Roy Keane, who was then the captain of the Republic of Ireland team, was sent home after a heated argument with his manager, Mick McCarthy. This incident happened in Saipan, the location of the team's training camp for the finals.

By way of background, the relationship between Keane and Mick McCarthy was never cordial. For example, look at Figure 7.2 and consider the body language between these men.

Figure 7.2 Strained relations between captain and manager . . . Roy Keane and Mick McCarthy shake hands but avoid eye-contact
Source: courtesy of Inpho Photography

Despite this coolness between the captain and the manager, the team had played very well in qualifying for the World Cup finals. But the relationship between these men changed dramatically in Saipan when Roy Keane gave a controversial interview to a journalist in which he criticised both the training facilities and preparation methods of the Irish squad.

Following this interview, he was summoned to attend a "clear the air" meeting with McCarthy and the rest of the players. At this meeting, Keane not only questioned the adequacy of the Irish team's facilities (citing a lack of training gear and footballs as well as deficient medical support) but also publicly rebuked his manager in a vitriolic speech. Not surprisingly, this speech and its consequences attracted media coverage around the world. More significantly, it raised a debate about an important psychological issue – namely, whether or not one player's striving for perfection can impede the progress of the team. For the manager (and some of the team's senior players), Keane's speech was inexcusable and had to be punished by instant dismissal from the rest of the tournament. This is precisely what happened. Unfortunately, as no physical injury had been involved in prompting Keane's departure, the dismissal left the Ireland squad one player short of the quota permitted by the World Cup organisers. It also left the players emotionally drained by the shock of losing their captain in such highly controversial circumstances.

Although there are two sides to this incident (e.g., why did the manager not try to resolve his differences with his captain privately or through an agreed intermediary before summoning him to a specially convened squad meeting?), McCarthy's decision to dismiss Roy Keane reflects a popular coaching belief that any potential threat to team harmony must be removed instantly. For example, Weinberg and Gould (1999) urge players and coaches "to respond to the problem quickly so that negative feelings don't build up" (p. 185). Similarly Sven-Göran Eriksson, the manager of England, warned about the danger of negative thinking within a squad: "A bad atmosphere can spread quickly, particularly if one of the 'leaders of opinion' in the team represents the negative thinking – the captain, for instance" (Eriksson, 2002, p. 116). Curiously, the Irish team performed exceptionally well during this competition in spite of losing its most influential player and was defeated in the "knockout" stages by Spain only after a penalty shootout. In summary, we have seen that team spirit or "cohesion" is important to athletes and coaches. But what progress have psychologists made in understanding and measuring the construct of team cohesion? Also, what does research reveal about the relationship between the cohesion and performance of a team? The remainder of this section of the chapter will address these questions.

Cohesion in psychology

Until now, I have used the term "cohesion" to refer to a form of social bonding between individuals in order to achieve a common purpose. Let us now analyse this term in more depth. According to the *New Penguin English Dictionary*, the word "cohesion" comes from the Latin word "*cohaerere*", meaning "to stick together" (Allen, 2000). Therefore, in everyday life, cohesion refers to acting or working together as a unit. In physics, however, the term has a slightly different meaning. Specifically, it designates the molecular attraction by which the particles of a body are united together (*ibid.*). Psychologists have combined the common sense and physicists' approach to cohesion when describing it as "the total field of forces which act on members to remain in the group" (Festinger, Schacter and Back, 1950, p. 164). Historically, this definition emerged from psychological research on group integration processes evident in accommodation units for returned US veterans of the Second World War. Apart from Festinger and his colleagues, another seminal figure in research on cohesion was the social psychologist Kurt Lewin, a refugee from German Nazi oppression, who was fascinated by the powerful ways in which groups affect people's behaviour. Adopting a "field of forces" model of human behaviour, Lewin (1935) regarded cohesion as a set of ties that bind members of a group together. He also proposed that the main objectives of any group were to maintain cohesion and to enhance performance – two recurrent themes throughout the team cohesion literature.

This idea of cohesion as the "glue" that integrates members of a group was echoed subsequently by sport psychologists but with one important modification – namely, the idea that cohesion is multidimensional rather than unidimensional. In particular, Carron (1982) proposed that this construct designates "a tendency for a group to stick together and remain united in the pursuit of its instrumental objectives and/or for the satisfaction of member affective needs" (Carron, Brawley and Widmeyer, 1998, p. 213). This definition of cohesion has two implications (Dion, 2000). First, it suggests that this construct emerges from two kinds of perceptions: those arising from members' perceptions of the group as a totality ("group integration") and those generated by members' perceptions of the personal attractiveness of the group ("individual attractions to group"). Put simply, these dimensions reflect a bifurcation between "task" and "social" components of any group. Second, Carron's analysis of cohesion implies that it is a desirable state. In other words, if cohesion reflects people's tendency to stick together in order to pursue common goals, then it should be associated with team success. But is this hypothesis supported by empirical evidence? We shall address this question later in the chapter. Before that, let us quickly sketch four key features of cohesiveness in sport psychology.

To begin with, cohesion is a multidimensional construct. In particular, as Carron and his colleagues have suggested, two dimensions of this construct are important – a desire of group members to complete a given task ("task cohesion") as well as a need by team-members to form and maintain interpersonal bonds ("social cohesion"). Based on this proposition, Carron (1982) and Carron *et al.* (1998) developed a conceptual model of group cohesion that is similar to that displayed in Figure 7.3.

As this diagram shows, Carron *et al.* (1998) distinguished between two overarching strands of cohesion: "group integration" and "individual attractions to the group". Group integration represents each team-member's perception of the closeness, bonding and degree of unity in the group as a totality. On the other hand, individual attraction to the group refers to each team-member's perception of what encourages him or her to remain in the group. Figure 7.3 also shows that both types of perceptions may be divided into "task" and "social" orientations. Combining these various aspects, four dimensions of cohesion were proposed by Carron *et al.* (1998). These four dimensions of cohesion are group integration-task (GI-T), group integration-social (GI-S), individual attractions to the group-task (ATG-T), and individual attractions to the group-social (ATG-S). Applying this model to sport, Hodge (1995) and Hodge and McKenzie (1999) suggested that "task" and "social" cohesion are synonymous with "teamwork" and "team spirit", respectively. The second characteristic of group cohesion is that it is a *dynamic* process. In other words, cohesion is not a fixed property of a group but changes over time as a function of a number of variables such as the degree of success or failure experienced by the team. For example, a soccer team could score highly on cohesion if it has won a considerable number of games in succession. But this cohesion might diminish if the team were to lose one or two important matches. Unfortunately, despite acknowledging the dynamic nature of this construct, few researchers in sport psychology

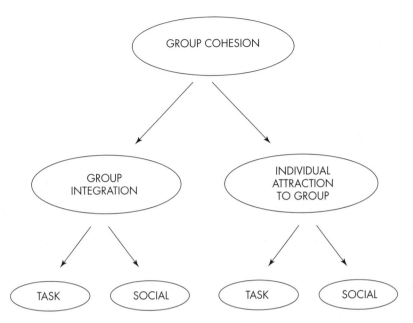

Figure 7.3 Carron's model of group cohesion (adapted, by kind permission, from A. V. Carron, M. N. Widmeyer, and L. R. Brawley, 1985, "The development of an instrument to assess cohesion in sport teams: The Group Environment Questionnaire" *Source: Journal of Sport Psychology, 7*(3): 248

have monitored changes in team cohesion over the course of a competitive season. One exception to this trend, however, is a study by Holt and Sparkes (2001) who followed a university soccer squad throughout a season and found that when the team was eliminated from a tournament, the players revised their goals for the remainder of the period. This result is not surprising because when a team competes in two tournaments simultaneously, some confusion is likely about which of these tournaments is more important. The third property of cohesion is that it is characterised by "instrumentality". In other words, people join or become a team for utilitarian reasons – to achieve a common purpose. Finally, Carron *et al.* (1998) proposed that the construct of cohesion has an emotional dimension which is derived from social relationships and feelings of togetherness among the players. In summary, cohesion is a multidimensional construct whose practical importance for team performance can be gauged from the variety of contexts in which it has been studied, such as in military settings (Siebold, 1999), in the industrial/organisational sphere (Bernthal and Insko, 1993) and, of course, in the world of sport (Heuzé and Fontayne, 2002).

Despite the apparent clarity of the preceding theoretical analysis, the construct of cohesion has been criticised on both conceptual and methodological grounds. For example, Mudrack (1989a) noted a dilemma at the heart of this construct – the fact that although cohesion is a property of groups, the group itself "as a distinct entity is beyond the grasp of our understanding and measurement" (p. 38). Put differently, the problem is the "field of forces" approach to cohesion is difficult to operationalise and the "attractions to the group" approach is conceptually inadequate because "it focuses exclusively on individuals at the expense of the group, and therefore may not entirely capture the concept of group cohesiveness" (*ibid.*, p. 42). Later in the chapter, we shall return to this thorny issue of how to select the most appropriate unit of analysis (group or individual) when studying cohesion in teams. Another conceptual criticism of research on cohesion comes from Dion (2000) who complained that studies in this field have been plagued by "confusion, inconsistency, and almost inexcusable sloppiness" (p. 45). To illustrate this allegation, he listed a variety of meanings spawned by the term cohesion. These include interpersonal attraction, group resistance to break-up, a desire to remain in the group, feelings of group membership, and the value that people place on group membership. As these referents do not share many common features, the meaning of the term "cohesion" is rather ambiguous. A similar problem was noted by Widmeyer, Brawley and Carron (2002) who concluded recently that "there is no conceptual or theoretical model that can be used as the basis for defining and measuring cohesion" (p. 298). As an illustration of this difficulty, Mudrack (1989b) reported that of twenty-three investigations conducted between 1975 and 1985, no two studies used the same operational indices of cohesiveness. This latter observation raises the issue of how best to measure team cohesion in sport.

Measuring team cohesion

Although the perceived cohesion of a group can be assessed using "sociograms" (in which members are asked confidentially to name other group members whom they either like or dislike), specially developed self-reports scales are more popular among researchers in this field. One of the earliest of these scales was a measure developed by Martens, Landers and Loy (1972) called the "Sport Cohesiveness Questionnaire" (SCQ). This seven-item test requires respondents to rate perceived cohesion in terms of friendship (interpersonal attraction), personal power or influence, enjoyment, closeness, teamwork, sense of belonging, and perceived value of membership. Unfortunately, despite its superficial plausibility or face validity, this test has never been validated adequately for use with athletes. Also, it is limited to the extent that it focused more on social cohesion (or the closeness between players) than on task cohesion (or the degree of common purpose between players). To overcome such limitations, two other measures of team cohesion were developed – the "Team Cohesion Questionnaire" (TCQ; Gruber and Gray, 1982) and the "Multidimensional Sport Cohesion Instrument" (MSCI; Yukelson, Weinberg and Jackson, 1984). The TCQ contains thirteen items which provide measures of six different factors: satisfaction with team performance, satisfaction with one's own performance, task cohesion, affiliation cohesion, desire for recognition, and value of group membership. Unfortunately, as with its predecessor, little evidence is available on the psychometric adequacy of this test. The MSCI is a twenty-two-item self-report scale which asks people to rate perceived cohesion in terms of such factors as attraction to the group, unity of purpose, quality of teamwork and valued roles (which is alleged to reflect identification with group membership). As with its predecessor, however, the validity of the Multidimensional Sport Cohesion Instrument is unknown. Furthermore, it is hampered by the fact that its items relate only to basketball. Apart from their psychometric shortcomings, the TCQ and MSCI suffer from another problem – namely, a flimsy theoretical basis. This problem arose from the fact that many of their items were borrowed from other instruments without adequate theoretical justification (Widmeyer *et al.*, 2002).

By contrast with the preceding measures, the "Group Environment Question-naire" (GEQ; Carron, Widmeyer and Brawley, 1985) has become the most widely used instrument in research on team cohesion. The dominance of this test is attrib-utable mainly to the fact that it is based on an explicit conceptual model of cohesion (see Carron, 1982; also Figure 7.3). The GEQ is an eighteen-item self-report ques-tionnaire scale which purports to measure the four key dimensions of cohesion described in the previous section. In this test, "group integration-task" (GI-T: five items) refers to an individual member's perceptions of the similarity, closeness, and bonding within the group as a whole with regard to the task it faces. It is measured by items such as "our team is united in trying to reach its goals for performance" or "we all take responsibility for any loss or poor performance by our team". Next, "group integration-social" (GI-S: four items) refers to an individual member's feel-ings about the similarity and unification of the group as a social unit. A sample item here is that "members of our team would rather go out on their own than get together as a team" (reverse scored) or "our team would like to spend time together in the off-season". Third, "individual attractions to the group-task" (ATG-T: four items) designates a team-member's feelings about his or her personal involvement with the group's task. It is typically assessed using items like "I'm not happy with the amount of playing time I get" (reverse scored) or "I do not like this team's style of play" (reverse scored). Finally, "individual attractions to the group-social" (ATG-S: five items) describes an individual team-member's feelings about his or her personal social interactions with the group. A sample item to assess this component of cohesion is "I am not going to miss the members of this team when the season ends" (reverse scored) or "some of my best friends are on this team".

Responses to these items are indicated by choosing the appropriate answer on a nine-point Likert scale ranging from "strongly disagree" (1) to "strongly agree" (9). Negative items are reverse scored to ensure that relatively higher scores on the GEQ reflect stronger perceptions of team cohesiveness. This test is very popular in sport psychology and has recently been translated into French (Heuzé and Fontayne, 2002). It has also been used in exercise settings. For example, Estabrooks and Carron (1999) investigated the relationship between exercise intentions, atti-tudes and behaviour among a sample of elderly adults in an exercise group. Results showed that as expected, both types of cohesion (social- and task-) were associated positively with the participants' attitudes to, and frequency of attendance at, the exercise classes (see Chapter 8 for a discussion of exercise psychology).

In general, the psychometric characteristics of the Group Environment Questionnaire are quite impressive (Dion, 2000). Specifically, with regard to test reliability, the internal consistency coefficients of the four cohesion sub-scales range from 0.64 (in the case of "individual attractions to the group-social") to 0.75 (for "individual attractions to the group-task"). Perhaps more importantly, Carron *et al.* (1998) supported the construct validity of the GEQ on the basis of evidence that the four dimensions of cohesion were significantly positively associated with such variables as role clarity in teams and adherence to exercise programmes. They were also and significantly negatively correlated with variables like social loafing – which we defined earlier in this chapter as a tendency for some people within a group to "slacken off" when working towards a common goal. Unfortunately, Dion (2000) noted that the factorial structure of the test remains unclear due to equivocal research findings. For example, whereas Li and Harmer (1996) replicated Carron's four-factor model in their analysis of cohesion processes in baseball and softball players, Dyce and Cornell's (1996) factor analysis of cohesion data from musicians yielded different results. Specifically, these latter investigators concluded "the results support social-task distinctions . . . but not the group integration-individual attractions to the group distinctions" (p. 264). Similar doubts about the factorial validity of the GEQ were raised by Schutz, Eom, Smoll and Smith (1994) who discovered that different factor structures emerged depending on the gender of the participants. Taken together, these results indicate that the construct validity of the Group Environment Questionnaire remains inconclusive.

Before we conclude this section, we should consider the issue of the most appropriate level of analysis to adopt in studying team cohesion (see also Dion, 2000). Put simply, is cohesion investigated best as a property of a group, as a characteristic of its individual members, or perhaps as some combination of these different units of analysis? Depending on how this question is answered, different interpretations of the cohesion-performance relationship may emerge. For example, in their meta-analysis of the relationship between cohesion and performance, Gully, Devine and Whitney (1995) discovered that the correlations between these variables was stronger for studies that had used the *group* rather than the individual as the unit of analysis. In response to this issue, Carron, Bray and Eys (2002a) suggested that the choice of a particular unit of analysis should be determined by the type of research question under investigation. To illustrate, if researchers are interested in exploring the relationship between cohesion and individual adherence behaviour in an exercise group, then the individual's perception of group cohesion is crucial. By contrast, if a researcher wishes to explore the relationship between perceived cohesion and team performance in a sport setting, then the average level of cohesion in the group is the variable of most interest. In summary, Carron *et al.* (2002a) advised researchers to be aware that individual athletes' perceptions of cohesion offer little insight into the relationship between composite team cohesion and team success. But what exactly is the relationship between cohesion and performance?

Team cohesion and performance

For many years, sport psychologists have assumed that team cohesion is positively associated with desirable outcomes such as improved communication between athletes/players, increased expenditure of effort and enhanced team success (Carron and Spink, 1993). But is this assumption supported by empirical evidence? Do cohesive teams really achieve more success than teams in which disharmony reigns? Unfortunately, there is no easy answer to this question because the relationship between team cohesion and success is complex. For example, there are many anecdotal accounts of sports teams that were highly successful *in spite* of enmity and disharmony between team-mates. For example, the former basketball star Dennis Rodman was frequently at odds with his fellow players in the Chicago Bulls team of the late 1990s and yet he managed to contribute significantly to this team's extraordinary success in that era (Weinberg and Gould, 1999). Also, Syer (1986) suggested that the existence of friendship-based cliques in a team may impede rather than facilitate its success. As before, however, this speculation has received little or no empirical scrutiny. However, Klein and Christiansen (1969) reported that basketball players who were close friends tended to pass the ball disproportionately often to each other – often to the relative neglect of team efficacy. But in general, what conclusions have emerged from studies of the link between team cohesion and performance?

Before we review the literature on this issue, it is important to comment briefly on the research paradigms used in cohesion research. In general, studies of the relationship between cohesion and success have adopted either a correlational or an experimental paradigm. The former approach is more popular and consists of studies in which perceived levels of team cohesion are elicited from individual members and subsequently correlated with team performance or success. For example, Carron *et al.* (2002a) investigated the relationship between the perceived cohesiveness of elite basketball and soccer teams and their winning percentages in competitive games. Results revealed quite a strong relationship between team cohesion and success, with correlation values ranging between 0.55 and 0.67. The experimental research paradigm, by contrast, involves evaluation of the effect on team performance of some intervention designed to manipulate the level of cohesion in the group. Few studies in the field have used this paradigm, however. A possible explanation for this neglect is that sport researchers tend to be reluctant to use the artificial and *ad-hoc* groups that are required by the experimental approach. Instead, they prefer to use actual sports teams.

Using the correlational approach, some evidence emerged to indicate that teams could achieve success in spite of enmity between their members. For example, Lenk (1969) suggested that cohesion was not necessary for team success in rowing. Briefly, he investigated the cohesiveness of two teams of German rowers – the 1960 Olympic gold medal-winning eight and the 1962 world champions. Although he did not measure team cohesion explicitly, Lenk assessed group unity by participant observation of social relationships among team-members. The results were counter-intuitive because they showed that team success occurred in spite of considerable disharmony among the rowers. Accordingly, this study refuted the traditional view that cohesion is an essential prerequisite of team success. Put differently, Lenk's results challenged "a thesis that seems to have been taken for granted . . . (namely that) only small groups, which are low in conflict, or highly integrated can produce especially high performances" (p. 393). Subsequently, he concluded that "sports crews can, therefore, perform top athletic achievements in spite of strong internal conflicts" (Lenk, 1977, p. 38). Of course, as critical consumers of research, we should be cautious about extrapolating too boldly from the results of this study for at least two reasons. First, it is possible that these results are attributable partly to the nature of the sport of rowing. To explain, Syer (1986) noted that it is not too damaging for members of a rowing eight to dislike each other because each one of them has a specific task to perform and is focused on the cox rather than on each other. Thus no matter how much bickering the rowers engaged in with each other, the nature of their sport prevented them from forming cliques that might impede collective performance of the task. Second, Carron *et al.* (1998) reinterpreted Lenk's results on the grounds that although the rowers in the study had not been socially cohesive, they had been *task* cohesive. So, Lenk's research findings are ambiguous as they have different meanings depending on which aspect of cohesion one examines.

Despite its flaws, Lenk's (1969) study was pivotal in challenging the assumption that cohesion is crucial to team success. Thus some subsequent studies (e.g., Melnick and Chemers, 1974) found no relationship between cohesiveness and team success whereas others discovered negative relationships between these two variables (e.g., see Landers and Luschen, 1974). Nevertheless, research by Carron and Ball (1977) and J. M. Williams and Hacker (1982) found that team cohesion was associated positively with athletic performance. Indeed, a review by Widmeyer, Carron and Brawley (1993) claimed that 83 per cent of studies in this field corroborated a positive relationship between team cohesion and performance. Furthermore, most of these studies found that athletes in successful teams tend to perceive their team as scoring highly in cohesion whereas the converse is true among athletes of unsuccessful teams. But a note of caution regarding this relationship was expressed by Aronson *et al.* (2002). Briefly, these researchers observed that team cohesion facilitates success *only* if the task facing the team requires close co-operation between members. Furthermore, they warned that team cohesion can impair performance if members of a group are so close emotionally that they allow their social bonds to obscure their critical awareness.

Overall, sport psychologists have shown that the relationship between team cohesion and performance is neither simple nor predictable. Let us consider each of these two points separately. To begin with, as the work of Aronson *et al.* (2002) indicates, the cohesion–performance relationship is mediated by a host of intervening variables. For example, consider how the type of sport played may moderate the cohesion–performance relationship. Specifically, Carron and Chelladurai (1981) speculated that in interactive sports (e.g., basketball, soccer), where team-members have to rely on each other, cohesion is likely to be associated with enhanced team success. By contrast, in co-active sports, where athletes play for a team but where individual performance does not depend on teamwork (e.g., golf, rifle-shooting), team cohesiveness should either have either no effect or be associated with less team success. This theory was challenged by Matheson, Mathes and Murray (1995) who failed to discover any significant interaction between team cohesion and sport type (a finding supported by Mullen and Copper, 1994). Nevertheless, a subsequent review of the literature by Carron and Hausenblas (1998) concluded that in general, team cohesion is positively associated with performance. Similarly, as indicated earlier in the chapter, Carron *et al.* (2002a) reported that in a large sample of athletes (n = 294) from twenty-seven different basketball and soccer teams, cohesion was correlated positively with team success (with r values ranging from 0.55 to 0.67). Nevertheless, other variables that are believed to mediate the cohesion–performance relationship include such factors as goal clarity and acceptance (Brawley, Carron and Widmeyer, 1987) and "collective efficacy" or group members' shared beliefs in their conjoint capacity to organise and execute actions to produce a desired goal (Bandura, 1997). Indeed, according to Feltz and Lirgg (2001), teams with a relatively high degree of team self-efficacy beliefs should perform better, and persist longer when behind, than teams with lower levels of such beliefs. But a team's collective efficacy is thought to be more than the simple aggregate of individual levels of self-efficacy (Spink, 1990). Not surprisingly, therefore, the relationship between team cohesion and performance may be moderated by this intervening variable of collective self-efficacy.

The second counter-intuitive conclusion from the research literature is that team cohesion may be a *consequence* rather than a cause of team success. In other words, the relationship between cohesion and performance may be *circular* rather than linear. This possibility is supported by Mullen and Copper (1994) who concluded that "although cohesiveness may indeed lead the group to perform better, the tendency for the group to experience greater cohesiveness *after* successful performance may be even stronger" (p. 222, italics mine). If this is so, then perhaps there is some truth to the old idea that "team spirit" is what a team gains *after* it achieves success! A critical perspective on the issue of distinguishing between cause and effect is presented in Box 7.1.

Box 7.1 Thinking critically about . . . the direction of causality in cohesion–performance research

Every psychology student is taught that "correlation does not imply causality". In other words, just because two variables are related to each other does not mean that one *caused* the other. After all, there could be a third, confounding factor which is the real cause of the correlation in question. Nevertheless, certain correlational research designs allow investigators to draw conclusions about causal relationships between variables in the absence of experimental manipulations or controls. To illustrate, a "cross-lagged panel correlation" research design (Rozelle and Campbell, 1969) can provide useful clues to the question of causality. Briefly, this design is based on the assumption that analysis of the pattern of correlations between variables at different times (note that the term "lagged" means that there is a time-lag between the collection of some of the correlations) allows certain inferences to be drawn about possible causal links between these variables. In particular, if one variable causes another, then it seems likely that it should be more strongly related to the second variable *later* in time – because it is assumed that causes take time to produce effects. Using this cross-lagged research design, Bakeman and Helmreich (1975) measured cohesion and performance in water-sports teams on two separate occasions. Results showed that "first-segment" cohesiveness was highly associated with "second-segment" cohesiveness but not with second-segment performance. Accordingly, these authors concluded that team cohesion was not a good predictor of team performance but that successful performance may have contributed to the development of strong cohesiveness.

Some critical questions
Why is it important for researchers to indicate the precise time at which team cohesiveness and performance data were collected? Can you think of any flaws in the logic underlying cross-lagged panel research designs? If performance influences cohesion more than cohesion influences performance, what mechanisms could explain this finding? What are the practical implications of this idea that performance affects team cohesion?

Apart from the preceding conclusions, what other findings have emerged from the research literature on cohesion and performance? One way of answering this question is by augmenting narrative reviews (i.e., those in which researchers draw informal conclusions from reviewing relevant evidence) with meta-analytic reviews of available research. As we indicated in Chapter 2, a meta-analysis is literally an analysis of analyses, or a quantitative synthesis of published research on a particular question (e.g., "does team cohesion affect athletic performance?") in order to determine the effect of one variable on another variable across many different studies and samples (see Hunt, 1997, for a good introduction to this technique). The extent of this effect is indicated by the effect size statistic – a number which represents the average strength of the effect in standard score units, independent of sample size. Using this statistical technique, Mullen and Copper (1994) examined forty-nine studies of groups derived from a broad cross-section of settings including industrial, military, social and sport psychology. A number of conclusions emerged. First, the authors concluded that the cohesion–performance relationship was small but positive and significant. Interestingly, this relationship was stronger for sports teams than for any other groups (e.g., *ad hoc*, artificial groups) in the sample. The authors attributed this trend to the fact that sports groups tend to have a unique sense of collective identity. In addition, they differ from other groups by virtue of being formally organised according to explicit rules of competition. Second, Mullen and Copper (1994) found that stronger cohesion–performance relationships existed among "real" (i.e., naturally formed) groups than among "artificial" groups. In addition, they concluded that performance was more strongly related to cohesion than was cohesion to performance (see also Box 7.1). Fourth, the type of athletic activity (e.g., interactive versus co-active sports) did not seem to mediate the relationship between cohesion and performance in sports teams. Finally, Mullen and Copper (1994) claimed that commitment to the *task* was the primary component of cohesiveness in the cohesion–performance relationship. This conclusion suggests that team-building techniques aimed at enhancing the other components of cohesion (see Figure 7.3) may not be effective. In other words, Mullen and Copper (1994) were sceptical of the merit of fostering interpersonal attraction among members and/or attempting to "pump up" the group in an effort to enhance team performance. Incidentally, the next section examines the nature and efficacy of some popular team-building techniques in sport.

Recently, Carron, Colman, Wheeler and Stevens (2002b) updated the preceding meta-analytic review by focusing on studies conducted only in the domain of sport. Using a database of forty-six published papers, they discovered that there was a "significant moderate to large" effect size of 0. 655 for cohesion on performance – indicating that cohesiveness was significantly associated with team performance in sport. In contrast to the findings of Mullen and Copper (1994), however, Carron *et al.* (2002b) found that both task *and* social cohesion were significantly related to athletic performance. Another notable finding emerging from this study was that cohesiveness in female teams was more strongly related to performance than was cohesiveness in male teams.

So far, we have examined the relationship between cohesion and performance only in relation to the variable of objective team success. But as Kremer and Scully (2002) observed, this focus on only one type of outcome is too narrow as it neglects other ways in which cohesion may affect team dynamics. For example, the cohesion of a group may affect subjective variables such as team satisfaction, team identity and the perceived self-efficacy of a team. Clearly, these variables could be included fruitfully in future research in this field, although it should be pointed out that "satisfaction" may be either a cause or a consequence of team cohesion. In this regard, we should note a recent longitudinal field study of cohesion by Holt and Sparkes (2001). Briefly, these researchers explored the factors that contributed to the cohesion of a university soccer team over an eight-month season. Using a variety of ethnographic methods (such as participant observation and interviews), Holt and Sparkes (2001) identified four main factors that shaped team cohesiveness. These factors were clear and meaningful roles (e.g., in mid-season, some of the teams' midfield players wanted to play a more attacking game to the relative neglect of their defensive duties), team goals (in late-season, the fact that the team was eliminated from one competition helped to re-focus the team for the league campaign), personal sacrifices (e.g., the team captain made a three-hour train journey in order to play in the final match of the league) and communication (especially, "on-field" communication among the players).

Before we conclude this section of the chapter, it may be interesting to explore what *coaches* think about the question of what makes a successful team. In this regard, Box 7.2 presents Sven-Göran Eriksson's views on the ingredients of a successful team.

Box 7.2 Thinking critically about . . . a coach's view of successful teams

According to the England soccer manager Sven-Göran Eriksson (2002), who has coached championship winning teams in three countries (Sweden, Portugal and Italy; Every, 2002), there are eight key characteristics of a successful team in sport.

First, the members of the team must have a common vision. Second, they should have a clear understanding of the team's goals. Third, they must have a good understanding of team strategy and tactics. Fourth, they must have "inner discipline" – which involves both knowing and adhering to the rules of the team (e.g., with regard to time-keeping). Fifth, successful teams must have players who complement each other. For example, Eriksson claims that more than one Ronaldo in a team could cause problems because of the unpredictability of his skills. Sixth, effective teams require a division of roles – but the coach must respect each of them equally. Seventh, players in a successful team must learn to put the common good before their own interests. Finally, the members of a successful team must accept collective responsibility and think of "we" instead of "me".

Critical thinking questions
Notice that Eriksson did not specify "social cohesion" as one of his criteria of successful teams. Do you agree with this decision? If not, why not? Do you think that all of Eriksson's eight team characteristics can be developed psychologically in players? Which ones are the most difficult to develop?

Now that we have learned about the nature, measurement and correlates of team cohesion, let us now consider the issue of how it can be developed in athletes.

Team building in sport

Having established the nature and importance of team cohesion in sport, let us now consider the main methods by which coaches, managers and psychologists have attempted to increase it. Unfortunately, little empirical research has been conducted on the nature and efficacy of team-building techniques in sport psychology – apart from the studies reported in the March 1997 special issue of the *Journal of Applied Sport Psychology* (Hardy and Crace, 1997). From the research literature available, however, it is possible to identify the following principles and findings in this field.

To begin with, a definition of team building is required. Several possibilities are available. For example, Newman (1984) defined this term as an attempt to "promote an increased sense of unity and cohesiveness and enable the team to function together more smoothly and effectively" (p. 27). More precisely, Bettenhausen (1991) described team building as an attempt "to improve group performance by improving communication, reducing conflict, and generating commitment among work group members" (p. 369). In a similar vein, Hardy and Crace (1997) suggested that team building involves interventions that purport to enhance team performance by positively affecting team processes or team synergy. Echoing this view, Brawley and Paskevich (1997) defined team building as "a method of helping the group to (a) increase effectiveness, (b) satisfy the needs of its members, or (c) improve work conditions" (p. 13). In summary, the process of team building is designed explicitly to enhance team cohesion.

Although the goal of team building is clear, three caveats must be noted when evaluating research and practice in this field (Crace and Hardy, 1997; McLean, 1995). First, team building should not be regarded as a type of "quick fix, pep talk" which ensures team harmony through the cursory application of some arcane psychological strategies. Instead, it involves a long-term commitment to the development of task-related and interpersonal dynamics of a team in the interests of enhancing its performance. Emphasising this point, McLean (1995) claimed that team building "is not a set of exercises that get wheeled out from time to time, but it is a way of thinking which pervades every interpersonal interaction within that group" (p. 424). Second, team building is not designed to increase similarity or agreement between group members but to enhance mutual respect among team-mates. As Yukelson (1997) suggested, sports teams resemble families in the sense that although team-mates may not always like or agree with each other, they know that they belong to the same "household". Finally, we should acknowledge that most of the principles and strategies of team building in sport are derived from research on organisational development in business settings. Although this cross-fertilisation of ideas between business and sport has been valuable in certain areas of sport psychology (most notably, perhaps, in goal-setting; see Chapter 2), it has also generated activities (e.g., participation in outdoor adventure weekends) whose appeal is based more on intuition than on empirical evidence. Put simply, the fact that a team-building technique is popular in business does not make it either valid or effective in sport settings. Bearing these caveats in mind, let us now consider the theory and practice of team-building interventions in sport psychology.

Developing team cohesion: from theory to practice

As we learned in the previous section, the main objective of team-building interventions is to increase the effectiveness of a group by enhancing the cohesiveness of its members (Carron, Spink and Prapavessis, 1997). But as cohesion is a multidimensional construct (see earlier in chapter), what aspects of it should team builders focus on in designing interventions? More generally, what team-building exercises are most effective in strengthening cohesion? Let us now consider each of these two questions.

　　According to Mullen and Copper (1994), the three most important dimensions of cohesion are interpersonal attraction, commitment to a common task and pride in the group itself. Most cohesion theorists have explored the first and second of these aspects of cohesion but have tended to neglect the "group pride" aspect. Naturally, these different aspects of cohesion have different implications for team-building initiatives. For example, if one wishes to strengthen the interpersonal determinants of cohesion, then team-building techniques should focus on increasing mutual liking and affiliation among team-members. Alternatively, if one wishes to increase group members' commitment to a given task, then team-building exercises should be directed at helping them to increase the intrinsic enjoyment of tackling this task. Finally, if group pride is seen as the most important dimension of cohesion, then activities that "psych up" the group may be appropriate (see also Chapter 3).

　　In general, two types of team-building interventions may be distinguished in sport and exercise psychology – direct and indirect interventions (Carron and Hausenblas, 1998). In the direct interventions paradigm, the coach, manager or sport psychology consultant works directly with the athletes in the team in an effort to increase cohesion among them and to foster a communal vision and sense of identity.

Conversely, in the indirect paradigm, the consultant instructs coaches and managers in the skills of team-building rather than working directly with the athletes or players concerned.

Usually, team-building in sport is conducted through the *indirect* intervention paradigm for three main reasons (Carron and Hausenblas, 1998; Estabrooks and Dennis, 2003). First, most coaches/managers like to be involved in mediating the interventions of consultants to their team-members because they tend to know the individual athletes well. Second, many coaches are reluctant to relinquish their control over the team to an outside consultant. Finally, some coaches may be wary of the possibility that the consultant in question may use his or her work with the team for personal promotional purposes. Let us now consider some examples of direct and indirect team-building interventions.

Direct team-building interventions

Based on his experience as a sport psychology consultant to a variety of university athletes, Yukelson (1997) delineated four stages of direct team-building work with athletes: assessment, education, brainstorming, and goal-setting. First, he suggested that the consultant must assess the current team situation as accurately as possible. This step requires his or her meeting relevant coaching staff and listening to and observing the athletes/players in order to determine the goals, expectations and concerns of the entire team. Next, in the education stage, the consultant should provide the team with some elementary information about how groups develop over time. In the third stage, Yukelson proposed that the consultant should use brainstorming techniques to help the team to generate and prioritise its current needs. In the final stage, these needs should be analysed to determine the goals of the team-building intervention.

Across these four stages, a number of practical team-building techniques are recommended. These techniques are evaluated in Box 7.3.

Box 7.3 Thinking critically about . . . direct team-building interventions

Yukelson (1997) recommended a number of practical techniques for direct team-building activities in sport psychology. Among these techniques are:

- Getting to know the players as unique individuals;
- Developing players' pride in their team and fostering a sense of team identity;
- Establishing team goals and strengthening the players' commitment to them;
- Providing regular evaluations of the team's progress towards goals;
- Clarifying the roles and expectations of each member of the team.

Critical thinking questions

Imagine that you are a sport psychologist hired to engage in direct team-building work with a squad of athletes. Do you think that there may be any conflict between getting to know these players as individuals and trying to mould them into a cohesive team? How would you handle a situation in which some of the players rejected the manager's goals for the team? Can you see any contradiction between teaching team-members to be self-reliant and yet encouraging them to depend on each other? How would you like to be introduced to the team – as a sport psychologist or as a team-building consultant? Give reasons for your answer.

Apart from the suggestions contained in Box 7.3, a variety of other team-building exercises have been used by coaches and managers in sport. Some of the more unusual ones are described in Box 7.4.

Box 7.4 Team-building exercises in soccer: bingo, bathing and drinking!

Soccer coaches and managers have used many unusual strategies in an effort to foster team spirit among their players. For example, Don Revie, who managed the highly successful Leeds United team of the 1960s and 1970s, used to organise games of bingo for his players. In addition, former players claim that he often used to personally "soap" and massage them in baths after training and matches! Apart from such "hands on" techniques, other favourite bonding strategies include playing practical jokes on team-mates and engaging in drinking games. For example, the "crazy gang" members of the Wimbledon team of the 1980s used to cut each other's suits, set their clothes on fire and pack talcum powder into team-mates' motor-cycle helmets as initiation rites. More recently, Taylor (2003) reported that when Neil Warnock was manager of Bury, he used to encourage his players to drink cocktails made of raw eggs and sherry after training every Friday. According to Dean Kiely, Bury's goalkeeper at the time, this technique was Warnock's way of saying "we stand and fall together" (p. 2).

Incidentally, the late Don Revie was ahead of his time in extolling the psychological value of bingo because recent research by Winstone (cited in Horwood, 2002) revealed that this activity can yield measurable cognitive benefits. Specifically, she reported that people who played bingo regularly tended to perform faster and more accurately on visual search tasks than those who did not.

Direct team-building techniques are increasingly evident in sport – even in games which are regarded as quintessentially individual activities such as golf. To illustrate, Sam Torrance used a variety of practical strategies to foster team spirit when preparing the European Ryder Cup golf team for its match against the USA in 2002. In particular, during the thirteen months between the date on which the European team was selected and the match itself (recall that the long delay was caused by the cancellation of the 2001 Ryder Cup match in the wake of the "September 11" terrorist attack), Torrance tried to boost the confidence of his players through the use of catchy inspirational statements such as "out of the shadows come heroes" and "Curtis has one Tiger – but I've got 12 lions". These motivational phrases were delivered regularly at team meetings and were accompanied by video screenings in which the players were encouraged to view themselves holing putts, hitting wonderful shots and winning tournaments (Reid, 2002). He also appealed to his players emotionally. Thus just before the match itself, Torrance apparently addressed the team with the words, "this is going to be the best day of your life. You were born to do this. This is what we practise for. This is what we live for" (cited in *ibid.*, p. 22).

Before we conclude this section, we should note that a great deal of caution is necessary when evaluating the impact of direct team-building interventions. Specifically, when comparing the preparation techniques used by the European and US teams we must be careful not to fall into the trap of assuming that team success means that team preparation must have been ideal. In other words, we should be wary of *post hoc* reasoning when attempting to determine the possible causes of a given sporting outcome. This problem is also called the "glow of success" bias and reflects the invalid reasoning procedure by which people think "we won – so we must have been cohesive" (Gill, 2000).

Indirect team-building interventions

As explained previously, indirect team-building involves the sport psychologist working with the coaching staff rather than the team-members. Within this paradigm, an influential theoretical model was developed by Carron *et al.* (1997). In this model, a four-step intervention process is proposed as follows. In the introductory stage (which typically lasts for less than twenty minutes), the consultant outlines for the team coach/manager both the nature and benefits of team-building. Next, in the "conceptual stage", which takes about the same length of time, the goal of enhanced team cohesion is explained as being the result of three main factors: the team's environment (e.g., the distinctiveness of the team), the team's structure (e.g., norms) and its communication processes. The third step of the intervention (called the "practical stage") takes place in collaboration with the team coach/manager and involves the practical work of generating as many team-building strategies as possible. Finally, in the "intervention stage", the team-building methods are implemented by the coach/manager with the assistance of trained assistants, if necessary. Box 7.5 presents examples of the various team-building exercises advocated by Carron *et al.* (1997).

Box 7.5 Theory and practice of team-building (based on Carron *et al.*, 1997)

Team-building objective	*Strategy*
Enhance team distinctiveness	Design special team t-shirt or sportswear
Increase team togetherness	Organise social outings for team-mates Design team drills in the lead-up to matches
Clarify team goals and norms	Set goals in consultation with team-members Encourage "goals for the day" exercise
Facilitate team communication	Arrange regular meetings for team-members Alternate "social organiser" role within team

Evaluating team-building interventions

How effective are the direct and indirect team-building interventions described above? Unfortunately, only a few studies have been conducted in this area and they have produced inconclusive results. For example, Prapavessis, Carron and Spink (1996) assigned soccer teams to one of three conditions: a team-building intervention condition, an attention-placebo condition, or a control condition. The attention-placebo condition consisted of an intervention strategy which involved soccer-specific information (e.g., nutrition) rather than team-building information. The soccer players' perceptions of team cohesion were evaluated before the beginning of the season and also after an eight-week intervention period. Surprisingly, results indicated no significant difference in cohesiveness between the players in the various conditions. In other words, the team-building intervention was not effective in this study. By contrast, similar team-building interventions have been shown to be moderately effective in exercise settings (Carron and Hausenblas, 1998). One possible reason for this discrepancy between team-building effects in sports teams and exercise groups is that a "ceiling effect" may be at work. To explain, the cohesiveness among sport team-members is probably greater than that among exercise group members and so interventions designed to enhance cohesion may produce less change in the former than in the latter participants. Thus, as Carron and Hausenblas (1998) speculated, the "opportunities for increased cohesiveness through team building are greater in exercise groups" (p. 342).

How do athletes themselves react to team-building interventions? Although little or no research data exist on this issue, some relevant insights can be gleaned from athletes' autobiographical accounts of their experiences of team-building. For example, Jeremy Guscott, the former England international rugby player who travelled on a seven-week tour of South Africa with the British and Irish Lions in 1997, was very wary of the management consultants who were hired to engage in team-building exercises with the squad prior to its departure. In particular, he revealed that "rugby players are not the most receptive audiences to new-fangled ideas . . . I shared the scepticism. I'm a bit old-fashioned about these things and, as far as I'm concerned, a quick drink down the pub would have been enough for me to get to know everyone" (Guscott, 1997, pp. 19–20). One of the exercises which was the target of his derision involved the attempt by a sub-group of players to balance a long bamboo cane on the edges of their fingertips before lowering it to the floor. Canoeing and crate-stacking exercises were also used in an effort to develop team spirit among the Lions squad members. As we indicated previously, however, such techniques lack both a coherent theoretical rationale and evidence of empirical validity.

Implication of team-building techniques for coaches

A number of practical implications for coaches may be identified from theories of effective team-building (Weinberg and Gould, 1999). First, coaches should try to create a team environment in which open channels of communication exist among team-mates and between team-members and the coaching/management staff. The assumption here is that clear communication processes foster mutual trust among team-members. Practical ways of improving communication in teams include arranging regular team meetings to discuss issues that can be filled into sentences such as "It would be better if . . .". Second, although many coaches proclaim that "there is no "I" in team", it is essential that they recognise the importance of individual roles within groups of athletes. At the very least, all players should be told exactly how they can contribute to the success of the team. Also, if individual players know what skills they have to work on, they are likely to work harder for team objectives. Third, coaches must learn to set challenging group goals for their teams. Fourth, a collective sense of team identity can be strengthened by encouraging team-mates to wear similar team clothing. Finally, successful coaches tend to spend a lot of time in getting to know their players as well as possible (see also Estabrooks and Dennis, 2003, for some practical advice on team-building techniques).

School sports: helpful or harmful?

School sports are among the earliest and most powerful ways in which young people are introduced to athletic activities. But what are the psychological benefits and hazards associated with playing competitive sports in school? Let us now consider this question briefly.

One the one hand, many people have fond memories of their youthful days on the playing field. For example, Samuel Beckett, a Nobel Prize-winner for literature, wrote fondly of the time he spent playing cricket for Portora Royal School in Enniskillen, Northern Ireland. Similarly, the sheer delight of scoring a try is captured in the faces of the junior rugby players in Figure 7.4.

Figure 7.4 The joy of schools' rugby – celebrating a try
Source: courtesy of Inpho Photography

On the other hand, we must remember that for every winner in competitive sport, there has to be a loser. Therefore, cheers can quickly turn to tears for young athletes – especially if excessive emphasis is placed by parents and coaches on winning (Murphy, 1999). Psychologically, there are two main problems with winning as a primary goal for sports performers of any age. Apart from being outside one's control, it suggests that victory can come only at someone else's expense. But as we learned in Chapter 2, many of the world's top athletes are motivated not by a desire to defeat others but by the goal of improving upon their own performance. Not surprisingly, however, research suggests that many young people drop out of competitive sports because of the anxiety and distress generated by a "win at all costs" mentality among their coaches (R. H. Cox, 2002). But what do we know about the psychological consequences of participation in youth sports?

Unfortunately, the long-term effects of competitive athletic activity in young people have attracted relatively little research attention from psychologists.

Therefore, it is difficult to evaluate the widely held assumption that school sports develop "character", team spirit and/or the moral virtues of sportspersonship. Nevertheless, in a recent review of the meagre literature in this field, Shields and Bredemeier (2001) proposed that sport does not *automatically* build character. Furthermore, they concluded that "the longer one stays in sport, and the higher the competitive level reached, the more winning becomes the dominant value" (p. 599). This conclusion is echoed by Murphy (1999) who suggested that the longer athletes remain in sport, the less sportspersonship they display and the more likely they are to condone cheating and violent behaviour on the field of play! In a similar vein, Miracle and Rees (1994) found no support for the claim that sport builds character in school or anywhere else. Although these conclusions are controversial, they have played a valuable role in stimulating popular and scientific debate about the advantages and disadvantages of youth sport involvement. Fortunately, advances have been made in the development of coaching programmes that are designed to enhance enjoyment and to promote moral and ethical development in young athletes (see R. E. Smith and Smoll, 1996, 2002). In addition, progress is evident in the measurement of the construct of sportspersonship. Thus Vallerand, Brière, Blanchard and Provencher (1997) reported the development and validation of a psychometric scale to assess this construct – which may be defined broadly as a general commitment to fair play in sport as well as a respect for the rules, officials, social conventions and opponents encountered in the specific game in question.

Although the link between sport and character development is tenuous, what of the claim that athletic involvement can forge a sense of identity and cohesion among competitors? As before, little or no research exists on this issue. Nevertheless, there is some historical evidence to corroborate the idea that sport fosters cohesion. For example, in Ireland, S. Moran (2001) showed how Gaelic games in the nineteenth century played a significant role in strengthening people's sense of identity in their struggle to establish independent political rule. Unfortunately, problems can arise when this sense of identity becomes rigid or entrenched. For example, in Northern Ireland, allegiance to various sports and teams has a distinctive sectarian dimension (McGinley, Kremer, Trew and Ogle, 1998). Indeed, a graphic example of the depth of this sectarianism occurred in August 2002 when Neil Lennon, the Northern Ireland player, was forced to retire from international soccer after he had received death threats from "supporters" of his own national team (McIntosh, 2002). These death threats were believed to have been prompted by Lennon's affiliation with the predominantly Catholic team for which he played at the time – Glasgow Celtic.

To summarise, it may be argued that school sports offer potential health, social and psychological benefits to young people. For example, they can help them to discover the benefits of systematic practice (A. P. Moran, 2001). But to achieve these benefits fully, young sports performers need to be exposed to an enlightened coaching philosophy rather than a "win at all costs" mentality that causes stress to athletes of all ages and levels of ability.

New directions for research on team cohesion

From recent reviews of the empirical literature (e.g., Widmeyer *et al.*, 2002), at least five new directions can be suggested for research on team cohesion in sport. To begin with, in view of formidable definitional problems in this field, there is an urgent need for conceptual clarification of such key terms as "group", "team", "social cohesion" and "task-cohesion". Second, there is a need for empirical studies designed to test explicit hypotheses about, and/or possible explanations for, group processes in athletes. This type of hypothesis-testing research is preferable to descriptive, atheoretical studies. Third, there is a paucity of knowledge at present about possible *changes* in group dynamics within sports teams over time. Therefore, longitudinal research is required in which such key variables as athletes' social and task cohesion could be measured at various stages over a competitive season. This type of research would rectify the danger of over-reliance on data obtained from "snapshot" studies in this field. Fourth, in examining the relationship between team cohesion and athletic performance, it is important either to measure or to control for the moderating influence of such variables as sport type, group structure and intra-group relationships. Finally, just as in many other areas of sport and exercise psychology, there has been a dearth of field studies using top-level athletes.

Ideas for research projects on team cohesion in sport

Here are six ideas for research projects on group processes in athletes.

1   Given the need for additional longitudinal and field research in this field, it would be interesting to explore possible changes in social- and task-cohesion in a team of sports performers over the course of a season. The hypotheses to be tested in this study should be derived from a current, influential model of team cohesion (e.g., see Widmeyer *et al.*, 2002).

2   A comprehensive psychometric evaluation of the "Group Environment Questionnaire" (GEQ; Carron *et al.*, 1985), both for sports teams and for people engaged in exercise classes, could provide some valuable evidence on the construct validity of this instrument.

3   It would be interesting to examine the relationship between team cohesion and cognitive processes such as decision making in sport situations. As yet, little or nothing is known about this topic.

4   Few studies have been conducted on the relationship between a coach's leadership style and the cohesion of his or her team (but see Turman, 2003, for a case study approach to this topic).

5   It would be interesting to examine the similarities and differences between the team-building strategies advocated by experienced and novice coaches.

6   Additional research is required on the nature and development of sports-personship in athletes from different sports (see Vallerand *et al.*, 1997). In particular, what are the similarities and differences between athletes from different sports in their understanding of, and attitudes to, the topic of cheating in sport?

Summary

Despite the importance of group processes in athletic performance, less research has been conducted on team-related processes in sport than on the individual characteristics of the performers. To rectify this trend, the present chapter examined the nature, measurement and correlates of one of the most popular constructs in this field: "team spirit/cohesion" (or the degree of closeness and collaboration between team-mates).

- It began by explaining the meaning of such terms as "group", "team" and "group dynamics".
- Next, a review was provided of psychological research on the measurement and correlates of "team cohesiveness" (or the degree to which team-members stick together) and "teamwork" (or the productive co-operation between group members) in sport.
- The third part of the chapter examined the nature and efficacy of "team-building" activities in sport psychology.
- This section concluded with a summary of the practical implications of these activities for coaches.
- Next, a short account was provided of the advantages and disadvantages of young people's participation in school sports.
- After that, I sketched some potentially fruitful new directions for future research on team dynamics in athletes.
- Finally, I outlined six ideas for possible research projects in this field.

EXPLORING HEALTH, EXERCISE AND INJURY

Overview

Part one of the book examined the nature of the discipline and profession of sport and exercise psychology. In Parts two and three, we examined individual and collective components of athletic performance. In Part four, however, we return to the "exercise" aspect of "sport and exercise psychology". More precisely, we shall investigate the positive and negative health consequences of engaging in regular physical activity (Chapter 8) as well as some psychological aspects of physical injury (Chapter 9).

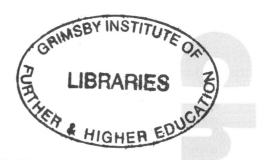

GRIMSBY INSTITUTE OF FURTHER & HIGHER EDUCATION LIBRARIES

Does a healthy body always lead to a healthy mind? Exploring exercise psychology

(with the assistance of Tadhg MacIntyre)

I can only meditate when I am walking. When I stop, I cease to think; my mind only works with my legs. (Jean-Jacques Rousseau, 1953/1781, p. 382)

Our muscular vigour will . . . always be needed to furnish the background of sanity, serenity, and cheerfulness to life . . . and make us good-humoured. (William James, 1899, pp. 205–207)

Exercise is bunk. If you are healthy, you don't need it. And if you are sick, then you shouldn't take it! (attributed to Henry Ford)

Whenever I get the urge to exercise, I lie down until it passes. (Actor Al Pacino, cited in *The Sunday Times*, 2002, p. 12)

Throughout most of human history and outside the first world nowadays, food has been relatively scarce and physical exercise abundant; only when the status of these two things is reversed does "exercise" make sense. (Solnit, 2001, p. 261)

Introduction

In recent years, a great deal of research evidence has accumulated to show that regular physical activity is associated with a range of physical and mental health benefits (e.g., see Biddle and Mutrie, 2001; Mutrie, 2002). Sadly, despite the compelling nature of this evidence, many people are reluctant to take up leisure-time physical activity (the exercise initiation problem) and/or are easily dissuaded from continuing with it (the exercise adherence or maintenance problem). To illustrate, surveys show that only about 25 per cent of the adult population of most industrialised countries are regularly active and that only 10 per cent of such populations exercise either sufficiently vigorously (e.g., by jogging, running) or often to obtain significant benefits in fitness (Dishman, 2001). These statistics suggest not only that physical inactivity is a growing concern for many communities but also that intervention campaigns are required to promote exercise initiation and adherence (Marcus and Forsyth, 2003). Unfortunately, such interventions face formidable barriers. For example, despite the fact that most people report feeling refreshed or invigorated after they have exercised (Gauvin and Rejeski, 1993), about half of those who commence a supervised physical activity programme drop out of it within six months (Dishman, 2001). Although these twin difficulties of exercise initiation and exercise adherence have been acknowledged by scholars for several decades, little agreement exists about their causes, consequences or solution (Morgan and Dishman, 2001). The main reason for this state of affairs is that historically, research on physical activity has been descriptive in nature rather than theory-driven. As a consequence, it is only recently that formal conceptual models of physical activity (e.g., see Spence and Lee, 2003) have begun to replace intuitive models. Compounding this difficulty, critics such as Solnit (2001) have even questioned the degree to which our modern preoccupation with exercise makes sense from an evolutionary perspective (see her quotation at the beginning of this chapter).

Against this background of controversy, the purpose of the present chapter is two-fold. On the one hand, it will review psychological research findings on the benefits and hazards of engaging in regular physical activity. On the other hand, it will summarise some key discoveries and unresolved issues in the study of people's exercise behaviour. As we shall see, these two themes are linked by the paradox to which we referred earlier. Specifically, although most people realise that physical activity is good for them, they appear to be reluctant to engage in it habitually. Unfortunately, this problem has a long history. Thus for every advocate of exercise, such as the eighteenth-century French philosopher Jean-Jacques Rousseau (who celebrated the relationship between walking and thinking) or the nineteenth-century psychologist William James (who cherished the emotional effects of physical activity), there are mischievous sceptics like Henry Ford and Al Pacino who extol the merits of indolence and a sedentary lifestyle. Although these latter sentiments are usually intended to be humorous, they remind us that certain kinds of exercise are potentially hazardous. For example, if people's involvement in physical activity becomes excessive, they may develop a maladaptive pattern of compulsive behaviour known as "exercise dependence" (see later in the chapter). Indeed, given the physical and psychological distress which this syndrome can cause the afflicted person, it is important to learn about its aetiology and treatment. In summary, the main objective of the present chapter is to investigate the "exercise" part of the discipline of sport and exercise psychology. This task involves analysis of the benefits, costs and psychological issues arising from people's involvement in physical activity.

I shall proceed as follows. To begin with, I shall explain the nature and goals of the discipline of exercise psychology. This section will include an analysis of the meaning of key terms such as "exercise", "physical activity" and "physical fitness". Then, in the second part of the chapter, I shall provide a summary and critical appraisal of research on the main health benefits associated with regular physical activity. To balance this discussion, two potential problems linked to habitual exercise (namely, "overtraining" and "exercise dependence") will also be examined. In the third section, I shall outline the main theories and research findings on the issues of exercise initiation (the "take up" problem) and exercise adherence (the "keeping it up" problem). This section will include a brief analysis of why people drop out from physical activity programmes as well as some practical advice on how to build up an effective habit of exercise. Finally, a number of ideas for possible research projects in this field will be sketched.

What is "exercise psychology"? Exploring physical activity, exercise and fitness

Exercise psychology emerged as a distinct field of academic study in the1980s (Fox, 2001). According to Buckworth and Dishman (2002), this discipline explores "the brain and behaviour in physical activity and exercise settings" (p. 17). Although research on the correlates of physical activity has a long if chequered history, it is only since the late 1980s that exercise psychology became an accepted sub-discipline of sport psychology. More precisely, in 1988 the *Journal of Sport Psychology* was renamed the *Journal of Sport* and Exercise *Psychology* (Gill, 1987; my emphasis) in recognition of the emergence of a distinct field of research pertaining to physical activity, exercise and fitness. Not surprisingly, this change heralded the official arrival of "exercise" as a scientifically respectable construct for research psychologists. More importantly, it showed that the traditional goal of the discipline of sport psychology – namely, performance enhancement in athletes (see also Chapter 1) – had expanded to include a concern for the promotion of exercise behaviour in the general population. In summary, whereas the traditional focus of sport and exercise psychology was on performance enhancement, there has been an upsurge of interest since the late 1980s in the relationship between people's participation in exercise and their health and well-being (Singer and Burke, 2002).

Although exercise psychology is a relatively new field, it has a venerable ancestry. To illustrate, one of the progenitors of this field was Hippocrates, the Greek physician, who emphasised the health benefits associated with regular physical activity. Influenced by such ancient ideas as well as by subsequent developments in sport psychology, physical education and sports medicine, exercise psychology is concerned broadly with two main research questions. First, what are the psychological effects of exercise? Second, what factors are associated with people's participation in physical activity? This latter question involves the study of the adoption, maintenance and consequences of exercise behaviour. According to Fox (2001), the origin of these two seminal questions can be traced as follows. The first of them arose mainly from curiosity about the scientific basis of the "feel good" phenomenon whereby people who exercise regularly tend to experience positive mood changes and an enhanced sense of well-being which they usually attribute to the physical activity in question. The second objective of exercise psychology emerged largely from a concern with certain health-related benefits of regular exercise. Specifically, if exercise is associated with a reduced susceptibility to coronary heart disease, obesity and high blood pressure, then how can people be persuaded to take up and maintain the habit of taking exercise regularly? These twin aims of exercise psychology will be addressed later in the chapter. Before doing so, however, some conceptual clarification is necessary.

So far in this chapter, we have used the terms "physical activity" and "exercise" synonymously. But there are important differences between these terms which need to be elucidated. Perhaps most significantly, although exercise is a type of physical activity, not all physical activity may be classified as exercise. In short, the construct of "physical activity" is broader than that of "exercise". Thus Caspersen (1985) defined physical activity as any bodily movement that is produced by the skeletal muscles and which results in the expenditure of energy. Of course, for any significant health benefits to be derived from such energy expenditure, the activity would have to be well above resting levels. Thus physical activity may be divided informally into such categories as "moderate" (e.g., walking briskly) and "vigorous" (e.g., jogging, running). Another popular distinction within this construct is that between "leisure time" physical activity (where people choose to expend energy in the service of some hobby or interest) and "occupational" physical activity (which is undertaken in the context of one's job or domestic setting). "Exercise" is usually regarded as being a sub-category of physical activity. In other words, it is understood as a leisure-time physical activity that people engage in for the purpose of developing physical fitness (which can be defined broadly as "the ability to perform work satisfactorily"; Gauvin and Spence, 1995, p. 435). More precisely, exercise is the "planned, structured, repetitive bodily movements that someone engages in for the purpose of improving or maintaining" (Buckworth and Dishman, 2002, p. 28) physical fitness or health. Of course, there is considerable overlap between the terms "physical activity" and "exercise". So, in keeping with the recommendation of Biddle and Mutrie (2001), this chapter will use the term "exercise" to designate such structured, leisure-time types of physical activity as walking, running, "keep fit" activities and participation in recreational sports. By the way, psychologists distinguish between two types of exercise behaviour: "acute" and "chronic" activity. Whereas acute exercise refers to a single, relatively short bout of exercise, the criterion for chronic exercise is that it is conducted several times a week for relatively long periods of time. They also distinguish between the intensity with which the exercise is conducted. Interestingly, recent research by Westerterp (2001) suggests that short bursts of high-intensity exercise (e.g., "working out" in the gym) may not be as beneficial to health as is engaging in low-intensity physical activities such as walking. Apparently, strenuous exercisers tend to compensate for bouts of energy expenditure by doing less activity for the remainder of the day!

In general, psychology researchers regard exercise as a multifaceted construct. For example, it can include various types of physical behaviour which people perform alone (e.g., a set of fitness exercises that one engages in before going to work) or in groups (e.g., dance classes). It also includes activities that are categorised as being either competitive (e.g., sport) or non-competitive (e.g., leisure pursuits) and "aerobic" (e.g., vigorous actions such as jogging which stimulate pulmonary and cardiovascular systems) or "anaerobic" (e.g., less intense activities such as golf). In summary, despite its wide variety of referents, the term "exercise" always involves the idea of exertion. This exertion can be undertaken either as a means to an end (e.g., when climbing the stairs to one's office because the elevator is broken) or as an end in itself (e.g., going for a long walk for the intrinsic pleasure of the activity itself; see also Chapter 2). Interestingly, we shall see later in the chapter that the question of whether or not exercise has a *purpose and context* has important implications for people's willingness to adhere to it. Thus Morgan (2001) argued that "Factor P" – a sense of purpose – is missing from many exercise regimes that people adopt at present. In particular, he criticised much of the exercise behaviour that people undertake in gymnasia as being "non-purposeful" because it involves a great deal of "walking or running on a treadmill to nowhere, climbing stairs to nowhere, cycling and rowing . . . to nowhere" (p. 372). It is not surprising, he suggested, that such exercise soon becomes boring for many people. By contrast, he exhorted people to rediscover the joy of "purposeful" physical activity such as walking one's dog or commuting actively (e.g., cycling) to work. Interestingly, some of these ideas are echoed in Solnit's (2001) analysis of the significance of modern gymnasia, drawn from her remarkable book *Wanderlust: A History of Walking* (see Box 8.1).

Box 8.1 On treadmills, gymnasia and the myth of Sisyphus . . . thinking about the modern meaning of exercise

In *Wanderlust: A History of Walking*, Rebecca Solnit (2001) meditated on the question of what it means to go for a walk. As this is no longer possible in many urban areas due to road design and traffic congestion, gymnasia have arisen as places of exercise. But what happens symbolically in such places? In a chapter entitled "Aerobic Sisyphus", Solnit draws an analogy between people's exercise behaviour in gymnasia (especially their use of treadmills) and the psychological experience of repetitive labour captured in the ancient Greek myth of Sisyphus. Briefly, according to this myth, the Gods punished Sisyphus, who had robbed and murdered people, by condemning him to push a boulder up a hill for eternity. Extending this analogy, Solnit (2001) argued that just as the suntan became fashionable when poor people moved from outdoor work to the factories, muscular development has now become a status symbol simply because most jobs no longer require bodily strength. In other words, muscles, like tans, are "an aesthetic of the obsolete" (p. 261). Based on this assumption, the gymnasium becomes something more than a convenient location in which to engage in exercise behaviour. Instead, it is a " factory for the production of muscles, or of fitness" (p. 262). Viewed from this perspective, the treadmill becomes "a Sisyphean contraption" that prevents people from walking anywhere – a device which celebrates people's alienation because it allows them "to go nowhere in places where there is now nowhere to go" (p. 264). In summary, the treadmill has replaced the outdoor environment that people used to walk in naturally: "space – as landscape, terrain, spectacle, experience – has vanished" (p. 266).

Questions
Do you agree with Solnit's controversial conclusions about the gymnasia as shrines to narcissism or "factories" concerned with the production of fashionable body shapes? Is she correct when she attacks the mindless glorification of exercise in gyms? What are the advantages and disadvantages of exercising indoors? Do you think that the myth of Sisyphus is a valid analogy for certain kinds of exercise? After all, in the original version of the myth, Sisyphus varied the absurd and repetitive task of pushing the boulder up the hill by changing the *pace* of the activity. In other words, he trained himself to change the way in which he tackled the task so that it would never be boring (Ravizza, 2002).

An important theme emerging from the criticisms of Morgan (2001) and Solnit (2001) is that in order to yield optimal benefits, physical activity requires both a sense of purpose and a natural context. It is not surprising, therefore, that the potential advantages of exercising *outdoors* are attracting increasing interest from the scientific community. For example, Dr William Bird (2001, cited in Murphy, 2001) has established "The Green Gym"– a conservation project that combines the idea of ecological work with purposeful physical activity. Specifically, this project requires people to "work out" by undertaking tasks such as building stiles, cutting trees and repairing fences in natural surroundings. As yet, however, the health and fitness impacts of this programme have not been evaluated adequately. More recently, however, Bodin and Hartig (2003) investigated the relative effects of different environmental contexts on the benefits yielded by a bout of vigorous exercise. In particular, they conducted a field experiment in which twelve regular runners exercised alternately in park and urban environments. These environments differed with regard to such factors as the extent of greenery encountered, proximity to water and amount of motor traffic apparent. The hypothesis was that the psychological benefits of running would be stronger for the runners in the park than in the urban condition. Results showed that although the runners preferred the park to the urban environment, and perceived it as being more psychologically "restorative", no significant effect of exercise environment was evident on psychometric indices of emotional and attentional variables.

Having raised some questions about the symbolic meaning of exercise in modern life, let us consider what the term "physical fitness" means. According to Buckworth and Dishman (2002), this concept of fitness refers to people's "capacity to meet successfully the present and potential physical challenges of life" (p. 29). In a similar vein, the President's Council on Physical Fitness (Fitness Fundamentals,

2003) defined it as "the ability to perform daily tasks vigorously and alertly, with energy left over for enjoying leisure-time activities and meeting emergency demands. It is the ability to endure, to bear up, to withstand stress . . . and it is a major basis for good health and well-being" (p. 1). According to this council, there are four main components of fitness. First, "cardio-respiratory endurance" (or aerobic fitness) refers to the ability of the circulatory and respiratory systems to supply oxygen and nutrients to body tissues during sustained physical activity. In other words, it is an index of the efficiency with which one's heart, lungs and cardiovascular system work. It is assessed in the laboratory using the "VO_2 max" test (which measures the body's maximal oxygen uptake or its aerobic capacity for endurance exercise) and in field settings by tests like the "one mile run" or the "one mile walk". The second component of fitness is "muscular strength" or the ability of the muscles to exert force for brief periods of time. It is assessed commonly by the "handgrip" test. Third, "muscular endurance" refers to the ability of the muscles to sustain repeated contractions and to exert force against a fixed object, without fatigue. It is usually measured using isokinetic machines. Finally, fitness is also indicated by muscular "flexibility", understood as the range of motion available to a joint without discomfort or pain. It may be measured in the lab using apparatus like the "goniometer" and in field contexts using various "sit-and-reach" exercises. Another putative index of fitness is "body composition" as assessed by the ratio of fat to lean body mass (LeUnes and Nation, 2002). In summary, the health-related components of physical fitness include cardiovascular fitness, muscular strength, endurance and flexibility, and body composition.

Given the importance of regular physical activity for a healthy lifestyle, how does health psychology fit into the picture? According to Buckworth and Dishman (2002), this latter discipline is concerned with "the scientific understanding of how behavioural principles relate to health and illness" (p. 10). It differs from exercise psychology in at least one significant way. To explain, whereas the latter field is concerned mainly with the study of physical activity, exercise behaviour and/or physical fitness as *dependent* variables (typically indicated by measures such as VO_2 max), health psychology has traditionally explored these processes as *independent* variables (Rejeski and Thompson, 1993).

Exploring the benefits and hazards of physical activity

The idea that physical exercise confers a number of health benefits on people dates back at least as far as BC fourth or fifth centuries (Buckworth and Dishman, 2002). Thus the Greek physicians Herodicus (*c.* 480 BC), Hippocrates (*c.* 460–377 BC) and Galen (*c.* 199–129 BC) advocated the importance of exercise in treating various forms of illness. This "gymnastic medicine" approach continues to the present day – but with one important difference. Specifically, contemporary physicians do not just recommend exercise as a form of treatment for illness but as a *preventive* measure in an effort to counteract the health risks posed by people's increasingly sedentary lifestyles. By the way, a person is usually deemed as being "sedentary" if s/he engages in little or no physical activity. The health risks associated with such a lifestyle include coronary artery disease, colon cancer, depression, hypertension, osteoporosis and strokes (President's Council on Physical Fitness and Sport, 2002). Indeed, so worried are many health scientists about these problems that the insidious effects of an inactive lifestyle have been called "the silent enemy" or "sedentary death syndrome" (*ibid.*). The prevalence of this problem can be gauged from certain epidemiological trends. For example, Caspersen and Merritt (1995) discovered that less than 10 per cent of a sample of almost 35,000 adults in the US exercised enough to obtain significant fitness benefits from their efforts. More generally, the problem of physical inactivity has been reported to be more common among women than men, among older than younger adults and among less affluent than more affluent people in most developed countries (United States Department of Health and Human Services, 1996). As a consequence of such data, a picture is emerging of a lifestyle in the twenty-first century whereby people have to *plan* to exercise simply because they no longer expend enough physical energy to achieve health benefits through manual work or even as result of walking or cycling to work on a daily basis. But as we shall see later in this chapter, planning or having an intention to exercise is no guarantee of actually doing it. In addition, another problem that we shall encounter concerns the fact that exercise prescription should not be undertaken naïvely. To explain, Sime (2002) warned that, for this practice to be effective, the physician in question must set realistic goals and provide regular supervision or guidance to the patient. Otherwise, this patient may not achieve his or her exercise targets and hence end up feeling more depressed and guilty than beforehand.

Before reviewing the research literature on the effects of regular physical activity, it is important to point out that there have been far more studies on the *positive* effects (i.e., the benefits) of exercise on physical and psychological processes than on its negative consequences – a trend which I hope to rectify in this chapter. Let us now summarise the principal research findings on the benefits of exercise for both physical and mental health processes. After that, a brief evaluation of some important conceptual and methodological issues in this field will be provided.

Physical benefits of regular activity

Sedentary people can increase their level of physical activity in two main ways. On the one hand, they can take up exercise classes or engage in such traditional fitness pursuits as walking briskly, cycling, running or swimming. On the other hand, they can increase their level of physical activity by adopting a lifestyle approach whereby they make active choices to engage in exercise in everyday situations. For example, they might decide to walk or cycle to work and/or to take the stairs to their office rather than using the elevator. Regardless of the mode of physical activity chosen, a considerable volume of research has accumulated on the health benefits of regular physical activity (see reviews by Biddle and Mutrie, 2001; Berger and Motl, 2001; Landers and Arent, 2001).

Much of this research was summarised in the 1996 Surgeon General's report (United States Department of Health and Human Services, 1996). At least three key conclusions emerged from this report concerning the physical health benefits of regular exercise. First, people of all ages can derive significant health benefits from cumulative amounts of moderately intense physical activity (e.g., thirty minutes of brisk walking or fifteen minutes of running) undertaken on several days per week. This finding is important because it shows that physical activity does not have to be strenuous in order to be advantageous – a point to which I shall return later in the chapter. So, it looks as though the popular phrase "no pain, no gain" is seriously mistaken. Interestingly, Mutrie, Carney, Blamey, Crawford, Aitchison and Whitelaw (2002) demonstrated recently that a self-help, active commuting intervention called the "walk in to work out" programme was successful in increasing people's walking behaviour (but not cycling) in travelling to work. Research cited by the Surgeon General's report also indicates that additional health benefits can be achieved by taking part in physical activity that is of a longer duration or of a more vigorous intensity than the minimal "thirty minutes a day" criterion. Second, physical activity reduces the risk of premature mortality, coronary heart disease, high blood pressure, colon cancer, obesity and non-insulin dependent diabetes mellitus. It is also important for maintaining the health of people's bones, muscles and joints – and is a useful aid in the prevention of osteoarthritis. Thirdly, activities which develop muscular strength ("resistance training") should be performed at least twice per week in order to yield significant fitness benefits. Ideally, at least eight to ten such exercises should be performed at each session, with at least ten repetitions of the relevant exercise required each time. In summary, physical activity is associated with a reduction in a number of risk-factors for health. The magnitude of this relationship is quite strong and can be gauged from the fact that the Surgeon General's report (United States Department of Health and Human Services, 1996) claims that the link between physical inactivity and cardiovascular illness is approximately equivalent to that between smoking and coronary heart disease.

What physiological mechanisms underlie these positive effects of physical activity on health? Not surprisingly, the answer to this question depends on the type of medical condition involved (see Ogden, 2000). For example, regular activity seems to reduce coronary heart disease either by stimulating the muscles that support the heart or by increasing the electrical activity of the heart itself. Also, it lowers blood pressure, thereby decreasing the chances of a stroke. Furthermore, because exercise improves glucose metabolism, it is associated with a reduction in people's susceptibility to diabetes (a medical condition in which one's body either fails to produce enough insulin to power the muscles or else uses prevailing insulin inefficiently). Put differently, physical exercise can act like insulin for people who suffer from diabetes (Weston, 2002). Finally, regular exercise strengthens the skeletomuscular system by improving joint and muscle flexibility. On account of these benefits, people who exercise regularly are "functionally younger in these various physical capacities and aerobic power than their sedentary age-mates" (Bandura, 1997, p. 407). By contrast, sedentary adults age twice as fast as nature intended (O'Brien Cousins, 2003).

Psychological health benefits of regular physical activity

In accordance with the intuitive insights of William James (see beginning of chapter), regular activity appears to produce a number of mental as well as physical health benefits for people of all ages. The purpose of this section is to summarise some of these psychological (affective and cognitive) benefits (but see Buckworth and Dishman, 2002 for a more extensive review). Before doing so, however, an important caution must be expressed. Briefly, due to their ephemeral nature, the affective aspects of people's exercise behaviour – namely, their feelings, moods and emotions – are difficult to conceptualise and measure. As a result of this problem, research in this area is bedevilled by semantic confusion. For example, consider the phenomenology of "feelings". Is a feeling *of* something (e.g., fatigue after a run) the same as a feeling *about* something (e.g., apprehension before a race)? Clearly, many definitional issues need to be clarified in this field (see Gauvin and Spence, 1998). Therefore, for the purpose of the present chapter, I shall use the term "mood" to refer to an emotional state that is characterised by the experience or anticipation of either pleasure or pain (Buckworth and Dishman, 2002). Accordingly, one can be in a "positive" mood (when anticipating pleasure) or a "negative" mood (when anticipating pain).

To begin with, research suggests that people who perform moderate amounts of physical activity regularly (e.g., at least three times a week for approximately thirty minutes each time) tend to experience significantly improved mood states (as measured by such self-report instruments as the Profile of Mood States, POMS; McNair, Lorr and Droppleman, 1992) and/or reductions in anxiety (e.g., Berger and Motl, 2000; Folkins and Sime, 1981). In a meta-analysis of forty studies on this topic, Long and van Stavel (1995) reported that exercise had a significant effect on anxiety levels – with an effect size of 0.36 standard deviations relative to control conditions. Other research shows that, in practical terms, self-rated levels of state anxiety (see Chapter 3) are lowered by about one-quarter of a standard deviation within twenty minutes of participation in acute bouts of continuous exercise such as cycling, swimming or running (O'Connor, Raglin and Martinsen, 2000). More generally, Berger and Motl (2000) recommend that in order to maximise exercise-induced mood enhancement, the physical activity undertaken should be enjoyable, aerobic, non-competitive and performed at moderate intensity for at least twenty to thirty minutes. This relationship between exercise and mood is complex, however, because it is mediated by several factors. For example, consider the intensity with which the physical activity is conducted. In this regard, Mutrie (2001) reported that moderate levels of such activity (e.g., taking a brisk walk) tend to produce more positive effects on people's sense of well-being than do more vigorous activities such as jogging or running.

A second finding in this field is that frequent exercise is associated with a reduction in reported symptoms of depression (e.g., Martinsen and Morgan, 1997). To evaluate this relationship more rigorously, Lawlor and Hopker (2001) conducted a meta-analysis of studies in this field. Adopting strict inclusion criteria, these authors focused solely on studies which had used randomised controlled trials in their research design. By combining relevant results from fourteen such studies, these authors discovered that physical activity had a relatively large effect on depression scores when compared with data yielded by control conditions. Interestingly, the results also showed that the effects of such activity on depression were similar to those of cognitive therapy – a finding which raises the intriguing possibility that exercise can be prescribed as a form of therapy for people who are depressed (see also Sime, 2002). Incidentally, among the putative mechanisms for this effect is the neurobiological possibility that exercise triggers the release of "morphine-like", pain-reducing neurotransmitters in the brain. Alternatively, exercise may give people a "time out" from their daily stresses and/or boost their self-esteem. Box 8.2 explores these rival explanations of the psychological effects of exercise behaviour.

Box 8.2 Explaining the beneficial effects of physical activity: is it all in the mind?

It is widely agreed that people who are physically active tend to report significantly lower rates of anxiety and depression than do their more sedentary counterparts. What theoretical mechanisms could account for this finding?

Exercise psychologists have proposed at least three possible explanations for this relationship. These three explanations – the neurobiological, cognitive and "self-efficacy" theories – may be summarised as follows. First, advocates of the neurobiological approach argue that both acute and chronic physical activity triggers the release of neurotransmitters such as norepinephrine or serotonin in the brain (e.g., Hoffmann, 1997; Chauloff, 1997). This release is alleged to reduce the painful effects of exercise while enhancing concomitant pleasurable sensations. Unfortunately, although the "endorphin hypothesis" has great popular appeal, it is poorly supported scientifically. Thus few studies have reported any evidence of empirical associations between exercisers' mood changes and their release of endorphins (Buckworth and Dishman, 2002). Next, proponents of cognitive explanations of exercise effects (e.g., Morgan, 1985) tend to emphasise a "distraction" or "time out" effect. Briefly, the idea here is that exercise offers participants a period of respite from the stresses and worries of everyday life. One implication of this theory is that it is not the exercise itself but the change in context in which it occurs that enhances people's sense of psychological well-being. Unfortunately, as the evidence bearing upon this theory is somewhat equivocal (e.g., see Bodin and Hartig, 2003), its explanatory value is questionable. The third explanation of beneficial exercise effects comes from research on "self-efficacy" or people's beliefs in their "capabilities to organise and execute the courses of action required to produce given attainments" (Bandura, 1997, p. 3). According to this theory, exercise is beneficial because it helps people in a practical way to increase their sense of mastery over their behaviour. Some support has been reported for the theory that self-efficacy mediates the relationship between exercise and health (see Bozoian, Rejeski and McAuley, 1994).

Questions for discussion
Which of these explanations do you think is most plausible? Why do you think the "endorphin" explanation of exercise benefits is so popular given its shaky scientific foundations? Can you think of any other ways (besides that of Bodin and Hartig, 2003) of testing the theory that physical activity offers people some respite from the stress and tedium of everyday life?

A third finding from relevant research is that regular physical activity seems to enhance people's sense of self-esteem. In evaluating research on this topic, Fox (2000) reviewed thirty-six randomised controlled studies on the relationship between physical activity and self-esteem. Of these thirty-six studies, twenty-eight (78 per cent) reported evidence of positive changes in self-perception or self-esteem – especially with regard to body image. Also, greater benefits were apparent among those who were initially relatively low in self-esteem. Overall, these data led Fox (2002) to conclude that the relationship between exercise and self-esteem is a "robust and significant finding" (p. 95). Unfortunately, the psychological mechanisms underlying this beneficial effect remain largely unknown.

The fourth documented benefit of habitual exercise on mental processes concerns apparent improvements in cognitive functioning – especially in the elderly. This conclusion emerged from narrative (e.g., Boutcher, 2000) and meta-analytic reviews of relevant research (Etnier, Salazar, Landers, Petruzzello, Han and Nowell, 1997). In the latter review of 134 relevant studies, Etnier et al. (1997) discovered that exercise had a small but significant positive impact (overall adjusted mean effect size of 0.29) on such cognitive variables as memory, mathematical ability, verbal ability, reasoning skills, reaction time and creativity. This beneficial effect was larger for chronic exercise (effect size of 0.33) than for acute exercise (effect size of 0.16). More recently, Harada, Okagawa and Kubota (2001) discovered a link between regular jogging and improved performance on certain working memory tasks. Briefly, seven healthy students jogged for thirty minutes a day (a recommended "dose" of exercise for health benefits – see previous section), three times a week for twelve weeks. The joggers took a series of cognitive tests at three different stages during the study: at the start, after six weeks, and again after twelve weeks. For comparison purposes, seven sedentary participants also took these cognitive tests. Results showed that after the study, the joggers scored significantly higher than their sedentary counterparts on the cognitive tests. These results were interpreted by Harada et al. (2001) as indicating that jogging somehow stimulates the prefrontal areas of the brain. In summary, on the basis of the research findings reviewed above, there seems to be strong evidence to support the age-old maxim "*mens sana in corpore sano*" or "a healthy mind in a healthy body"(a motto which is attributed to Juvenal). But lest we accept this conclusion prematurely, it is important to evaluate the quality of the evidence on which it is based.

Evaluation of research on the benefits of physical activity

Now that we have identified the main research findings on the health benefits of regular physical activity, we need to take a step back in order to evaluate the quality of research evidence in this field. This critical appraisal is necessary because it goes to the heart of any claim that habitual exercise is good for us. In a nutshell, researchers and practitioners in the field of exercise psychology must be satisfied that the alleged health benefits described above are caused solely by physical activity rather than by other factors. These factors could include intervening variables such as people's expectations about the likely effects of exercise interventions, contextual factors like the environment in which the physical activity occurs (see Bodin and Hartig, 2003) and a host of methodological flaws such as researchers' failure to use non-exercise control groups or to match people for their fitness histories. To prevent inaccurate interpretation of research in this field, therefore, at least five conceptual and methodological issues concerning the benefits of physical activity can be specified as follows.

To begin with, consider the familiar direction of causality issue. In simple terms, are such experiences as "feeling well" and "thinking clearly" the cause or the consequence of people's involvement in regular exercise? As with all causal issues in psychology, this is a complex issue which can be addressed only by the use of controlled experimental research designs. Ideally, such designs would involve a chronic exercise programme in which sedentary participants are assigned randomly to physical activity or control conditions. Unfortunately, the prevalence of corre-lational research designs in this field makes it difficult to test causal hypotheses about the relationship between exercise and mental processes. In any case, there is a vast array of intervening variables in this relationship. For example, research indicates that the motives of exercisers and the behaviour of their instructors may affect health experiences. Thus Grant (2000) suggested that the physical activity tends to have its strongest effect on people's mood and sense of well-being when exercisers have a task orientation (see Chapter 2), in which they focus on master-ing the exercise activity for its own sake rather than in an effort to exercise better or faster than others in the group (thereby reflecting an ego orientation). In structured exercise situations, the behaviour of the instructor could modify the health benefits yielded by the activity undertaken. For example, Turner, Rejeski and Brawley (1997) explored the effect of an exercise teacher's leadership style on the affective states of exercise participants. Briefly, these authors asked a sample of female university students to complete a scale designed to measure "exercise-induced" feeling states (see Gauvin and Rejeski, 1993). Then, the women were assigned randomly either to an "enriched" or to a "bland" exercise instruction con-dition. Finally, they were tested on the inventory once again. Results revealed that participants in the enriched condition scored significantly higher than did those in the bland condition on the affective dimensions of "revitalisation" and "positive engagement". This finding was interpreted as showing that the social environment created by an activity instructor may influence the benefits produced by the exercise activity itself. Unfortunately, many exercise psychology researchers have failed either to eliminate or to measure the effects of such intervening variables. To illustrate, few studies have controlled for the expectations of participants about the efficacy of exercise interventions. This is a pity because Desharnis, Jobin, Côte, Lévesque and Godin (1993) found that when people were led to believe that they were receiving exercise which had been designed to improve their well-being, their self-esteem levels actually increased as much as those who had been involved in "real" exercise interventions. In other words, there was a self-fulfilling prophecy among people who had volunteered to take part in an exercise programme. For this reason, experimental controls for placebo effects are mandatory in this field.

A second conceptual issue in this field stems from terminological confusion. For example, researchers do not always treat physical fitness as a multidimen-sional construct and may not distinguish between its different forms – aerobic and anaerobic fitness. In a similar vein, the construct of "subjective well-being" is a semantic minefield. To illustrate, it is sometimes defined by positive characteristics (e.g., the presence of feelings of happiness or satisfaction) but on other occasions by the absence of "negative" emotions such as depression or mood disturbance (see Berger and Motl, 2001). Clearly, such conceptual vacillation leads to problems of measurement. Thus several reviewers (e.g., see *ibid.*) have lamented the usage of idiosyncratic, unstandardised measures of key variables (e.g., psychological well-being) in exercise psychology. This criticism also applies to measures of affective constructs like anxiety and depression. Thus it is debatable whether available psychometric measures of these constructs are sufficiently sensitive to detect actual changes in these variables as a result of exercise interventions (Buckworth and Dishman, 2002).

A third flaw affecting research on the effects of physical activity is that many researchers in this field have combined results obtained from different participant populations. This cavalier attitude is unfortunate because there are significant differences between elite athletes, non-athletic university students, patients in psychiatric settings and people being treated for coronary heart disease. The fourth problem encountered in this field concerns the fact that few researchers have bothered to conduct "follow-up" studies on their participants in an effort to assess the long-term effects of exercise activity. A final difficulty is the relative neglect by researchers of possible negative consequences of exercise. It is to this issue that we now turn.

Exploring some adverse effects of exercise on health

So far in this chapter, we have argued that physical exercise is a healthy habit. But research suggests that occasionally this habit can have adverse consequences. For example, injury is a significant risk for people who exercise vigorously or who participate in competitive sports (see Chapter 9). In addition, for certain vulnerable people (especially young women), exercise is associated with specific psychopathologies arising from eating disorders and distortions of body image (Buckworth and Dishman, 2002). Furthermore, a variety of physiological health hazards have been found to be associated with habitual physical activity and/or sport. These hazards include metabolic abnormalities (e.g., hypothermia in swimmers or dehydration in marathon runners), blood disorders (e.g., anaemia in endurance athletes) and cardiac problems (e.g., arryhthmia as a result of prolonged vigorous activity). Unfortunately, as these conditions fall largely within the realm of sports medicine, they lie outside the scope of this book. Instead, this section is concerned with the issue of what happens when people's exercise habits become excessive, compulsive or otherwise maladaptive. Therefore, we shall now consider briefly two health hazards that are associated with exercise behaviour – namely, "overtraining" and "exercise dependence". Although the symptoms of these problems are similar, there is one important difference between the conditions. Briefly, whereas the former difficulty is largely confined to sports performers, exercise dependence can also occur in non-athlete populations (Buckworth and Dishman, 2002).

It has long been known that intensive training regimes do not always enhance athletic performance. More precisely, when the nature, intensity and/or frequency of athletic training exceed the body's adaptive capacity and lead to a deterioration in sport performance, then "overtraining" has occurred (Cashmore, 2002). Commonly regarded as a generalised stress response of the body to an extended period of over-load, overtraining may be defined as "an abnormal extension of the training process culminating in a state of staleness" (Weinberg and Gould, 1999, pp. 434–435). Other terms for this syndrome include "staleness", "burnout" and "failing adaptation" (Hooper, Traeger Mackinnon, Gordon and Bachman, 1993). A theoretical model of this state was proposed recently by Tenenbaum, Jones, Kitsantas, Sacks and Berwick (2003).

In general, overtraining has been attributed to a combination of excessive levels of high-intensity training and inadequate rest or recovery time. Although no single, universally agreed diagnostic index of this problem exists, a host of typical physiological and psychological symptoms have been identified. For example, physiological signs of overtraining include suppressed immune function (with an increased incidence of upper respiratory tract infection), increases in resting heart rate, decreases in testosterone and increases in cortisol concentration and decreases in maximal blood lactate concentration. Similarly, apart from a deterioration in athletic performance, common psychological symptoms of this disorder include mood disturbances, feelings of chronic fatigue, loss of appetite, repetitive loading injuries (e.g., shin-splints) and sometimes insomnia (Cashmore, 2002; Morgan, Brown, Raglin, O'Connor and Ellickson, 1987). The prevalence of this syndrome can be gauged from the claim by Morgan (2000) that over 50 per cent of all elite male and female marathon runners have overtrained in their careers.

Paradoxically, overtrained athletes tend to perform progressively worse as they try harder. We encountered this phenomenon of diminishing returns in sport performance earlier in this book in the section on "choking" (Chapter 3). But overtraining differs from choking because it appears to be caused by factors other than excessive anxiety. In particular, these factors include inadequate recovery time between bouts of training, prolonged or over-intense training regimes, personal problems and inadequate coping resources (Weinberg and Gould, 1999). Unfortunately, although overtraining has been recognised by sports scientists for decades, little research has been conducted on the putative psychological mecha-nisms underlying this problem. Nevertheless, one mechanism that has been proposed in this regard is mood state. Thus Morgan (2000) claimed that mood disturbance in athletes (as measured by the Profile of Mood States, POMS; McNair et al., 1992) may be causally related to overtraining. Unfortunately, this speculation has received only limited empirical scrutiny. As a result, little theoretical progress has been made in understanding either the precise causes of this problem or the best way to overcome it. Despite the fact that this state is poorly understood, its very existence highlights the need to be sceptical of the adage that "more is better" when it comes to training regimes in sport and exercise.

Let us now consider the second psychological hazard associated with habitual physical activity: the problem of "exercise dependence". According to Hausenblas and Downs (2002), such dependence refers to "a craving for leisure-time physical activity, resulting in uncontrollable excessive exercise, that manifests in physiological (e.g., tolerance/withdrawal) and/or psychological (e.g., anxiety/depression) symp-toms" (p. 90). Other terms for this compulsive behavioural syndrome, which has been studied mainly in runners, include "obligatory exercise", "excessive exercise" and "exercise addiction" (see detailed review by Hausenblas and Downs, 2002). The last-mentioned of these terms is proposed on the basis that the obligatory exerciser may experience withdrawal symptoms if s/he is deprived of the required physical activity. Despite such withdrawal symptoms, exercise dependence has not yet been classified as an addiction by clinicians.

In general, people who exercise excessively tend to report such symptoms as mood changes, restlessness, irritability, lack of appetite, insomnia and feelings of guilt if a twenty-four- to thirty-six-hour duration passes by without vigorous physical activity (Sachs, 1981). Support for the addictive nature of this compulsive exercise syndrome in runners was provided by a study by Morgan (1979) who described eight case studies. One index of the strength of this compulsion to exercise came from the fact that the runners in Morgan's (1979) study regarded this activity as being more important than their jobs or than interacting with their spouses, children or friends. Furthermore, these obligatory runners reported that they had sometimes exercised even when in pain and when acting against the advice of their physicians. Despite such case studies of this problem, several questions remain. For example, can people really become addicted to aerobic exercise in the same way as they might become addicted to drugs? If so, what are the symptoms of this problem? Are there any distinctive psychological factors (e.g., personality characteristics) that make exercisers vulnerable to this problem? In order to answer these questions, we need to examine the research literature on exercise dependence (which amounts to almost eighty published studies; Hausenblas and Downs, 2002).

To begin with, let us consider the nature and criteria of exercise dependence. According to Hausenblas and Downs (2002), this construct refers to a multidimensional, maladaptive pattern of physical activity which leads to clinically significant impairments or distress in the exerciser. Precise diagnostic criteria include evidence of *three or more* of the following seven features:

1   "tolerance" (i.e., either a need for significantly increased amounts of exercise to achieve the desired effect or diminished effects with the same amount of exercise);
2   "withdrawal" (i.e., evidence of withdrawal symptoms such as anxiety or fatigue when the person is deprived of exercise);
3   "intention effects" (i.e., exercise is often taken in greater amounts or for longer durations than was intended);
4   "loss of control" (whereby unsuccessful efforts are made to reduce the amount of exercise taken);
5   "time" (a large amount of time is taken up by the activity);
6   "conflict" (i.e., important occupational or social activities are given up because of exercise) and
7   "continuance" (i.e., the person continues to exercise even when confronted by physical or psychological impediments, such as injury).

In addition to these diagnostic criteria, another distinction is required when analysing exercise dependence. Briefly, Hausenblas and Downs (2002) indicated that if obligatory exercise is performed as an end in itself, then it is classified as "primary" exercise dependence. On the other hand, if it is undertaken in order to control body composition or shape, as happens in the case of eating disorders (see Blumenthal, O'Toole and Chang, 1984), then it is regarded as "secondary" exercise dependence.

Having explained the nature and types of exercise dependence, we should now return to an important conceptual issue in this field. To what extent is the obligatory exerciser suffering from an addiction? Superficially, the concept of exercise addiction seems plausible for several reasons. First, as we learned earlier in this chapter, chronic exercise is associated with changes in the brain levels of neurotransmitters like norepinephrine and serotonin – substances which are known to influence people's moods. Thus exercise addiction may have a neurobiological basis. In addition, just like people who are addicted to drugs of any kind, exercise addicts may develop a tolerance for their habit. In this case, "tolerance" is indicated when people require longer, more intense and more frequent physical "work-outs" in order to maintain the same levels of satisfaction with their exercise. However, as Aidman and Woollard (2003) pointed out, this tolerance criterion may apply only to the *later* stages of exercise dependence, which makes it unsuitable as a diagnostic indicator. However, this objection does not apply to the third criterion of exercise addiction – namely, the existence of post-deprivation withdrawal symptoms such as increased fatigue, depression, anger and irritability (Sachs, 1981). Remarkably, recent research suggests that these symptoms can be detected in athletes after only *one day* without exercise. Thus Aidman and Woollard (2003) discovered that club runners who abstained from their daily training run experienced significantly more withdrawal symptoms than did runners who maintained their normal training regime. This finding is somewhat counter-intuitive because it suggests that committed runners who have an extra "rest day" may end up feeling more tired than those who exercise every day! This addiction criterion of withdrawal symptoms is by no means clear-cut, however. For example, cocaine dependence does not always yield withdrawal symptoms (*ibid.*). In summary, doubts exist about the validity of classifying compulsive exercise behaviour as an addiction.

In passing, it should be noted that some critics are sceptical of the value of debating the addictive status of exercise dependence. For example, Morgan (2000) suggested that it does not really matter whether a runner is said to be "addicted" to, "dependent" on, or "abusing" exercise. What does matter, he claimed, is that when such runners are prevented from exercising, they usually experience significant distress – a phenomenon which "exercise evangelicals" (*ibid.*, p. 304) have been slow to acknowledge. And so, we come to the question of whether compulsive exercise behaviour is ultimately helpful or harmful. This question is considered in Box 8.3.

Box 8.3 Thinking critically about ... whether compulsive exercise behaviour is helpful or harmful

Is compulsive exercise behaviour helpful or harmful to its practitioners? In the 1970s, at the boom of the "jogging generation", Glasser (1976) referred to obligatory running as a "positive addiction" because it allegedly led to psychological benefits which included increased alertness, an improved sense of well-being and control, and occasional feelings of euphoria. But several years later, Morgan (1979) challenged this optimistic view by describing such behaviour as a "negative addiction" on the grounds that it was not only characterised by punishing schedules of daily physical training but also resulted in withdrawal symptoms (e.g., depression, fatigue and restlessness) when prevented. Which of these theoretical perspectives is more accurate? As usual in psychology, research has shown that there is some truth on both sides of the argument. To explain, Kerr (1997) observed that there are probably two distinct types of exercise-dependent people. On the one hand, some people engage in excessive exercise as a reliable means of achieving a particular state of mind. On the other hand, a small minority of people take exercise to the extremes, perhaps even to the level of an addiction. Unfortunately, the prevalence of this latter problem in the general population is unknown.

Having considered some important conceptual issues surrounding exercise dependence, let us now sketch some research findings in this field.

First, attempts to measure exercise dependence rely mostly on self-reported assessments of the frequency, duration and/or intensity of the physical activity under scrutiny. Whereas earlier scales were unidimensional (e.g., the "Obligatory Running Questionnaire", Blumenthal *et al.*, 1984), more recent measures of exercise dependence are multidimensional. For example, the "Exercise Dependence Questionnaire" (Ogden, Veale and Summers, 1997) measures both neurobiological (e.g., tolerance, withdrawal) and psychosocial symptoms (e.g., interference with social and occupational commitments) of the problem. Unfortunately, many of these self-report scales are inadequate psychometrically. Also, due to a paucity of relevant normative data, most measures of exercise dependence cannot be used validly for diagnostic purposes (Hausenblas and Downs, 2002). A second general finding is that in spite of speculation about the association between compulsive physical activity and such personality characteristics as perfectionism, no distinctive profile of the "exercise addict" has yet emerged. Third, little progress has been made in identifying precisely what exercise-dependent people miss when they are prevented from habitual physical activity. Is it the aerobic activity itself, or the context in which it is undertaken, or some combination of these factors? Unfortunately, until this issue has been resolved, it will be difficult to understand how people's apparent addiction to exercise develops (Aidman and Woollard, 2003). To summarise, given the many gaps in the research literature in this field, it is not surprising that there are no agreed criteria for either diagnosing or treating this problem of compulsive exercise behaviour (Hausenblas and Downs, 2002).

In this section of the chapter, we have explored two health hazards associated with habitual physical activity. Of course, we should not exaggerate these problems as the phenomena of overtraining and exercise dependence affect only a small minority of people. For the majority of the population, two questions are probably far more pressing. First, why do so many people fail to take up the healthy habit of regular physical activity? In addition, why do they find it so difficult to maintain the habit of exercise?

Exploring people's exercise behaviour

At the beginning of this chapter, we learned that most people in industrialised countries do not take enough physical activity to gain significant health benefits. This finding is as perplexing to health promotion campaigners (who have bombarded the public for decades with information about the advantages of regular physical activity) as it is to exercise psychologists. Nevertheless, these groups differ in their approach to the problem of exercise initiation. Specifically, whereas health promotion campaigners rely mainly on descriptive methods (e.g., surveys) to identify demographic correlates of people's propensity to engage in physical activity, exercise psychologists have developed sophisticated theoretical models in an effort to understand why people vary in their levels of physical activity. To illustrate the latter approach, Spence and Lee (2003) pointed out that analysis of "individual" barriers to exercise account for at best 20 per cent to 40 per cent of the variance in physical activity. Accordingly, these researchers suggest that an ecological approach to the problem of exercise initiation may prove fruitful. This approach is based on the assumption that a person's level of physical activity is not just determined by individual intentions but also by environmental factors such as the availability of safe and pleasant spaces in which to engage in exercise behaviour. Until recently, this ecological perspective on physical activity has been neglected.

Although health promotion campaigners and exercise psychologists adopt different theoretical perspectives on the issue of exercise initiation, they have similar views about the desired outcome of any physical activity programme – namely, the inculcation of an active lifestyle (Buckworth and Dishman, 2002). This shift from fitness to health as the optimal goal of physical activity occurred gradually between the 1970s and the 1990s. Thus Blair, Kohl, Gordon and Paffenbarger (1992) distinguished between exercise that improves fitness and that which promotes an active and healthy lifestyle. This latter type of exercise consists mainly of a moderate type of physical activity that can be accumulated over the course of a given day.

Having sketched some background information on the exercise initiation problem, we should now consider what research psychologists have discovered about people's reasons for, and barriers to, an active lifestyle.

Taking up exercise: reasons and barriers

As one might expect, people take up exercise for a wide variety of reasons. According to Biddle and Nigg (2000), among the most popular reasons given by exercisers are that it is enjoyable and challenging, potentially beneficial to health, and that it offers new social outlets and opportunities. Perhaps not surprisingly, these reasons tend to vary with age and gender. In particular, whereas younger adults tend to be motivated by perceived fitness benefits, older adults are more concerned with the apparent *health* advantages arising from physical activity. Also, more women than men tend to emphasise the value of exercise for weight control and improved appearance.

Turning to the barriers which hamper people's exercise behaviour, Dishman (2001) identified a number of demographic and psychological impediments to the initiation of physical activity. These barriers include demographic factors such as habitual smoking, obesity, lower socioeconomic status and poor education as well as personal issues like medical problems, insufficient motivation and an apparent lack of time. Curiously, this "lack of time" explanation for physical inactivity has been challenged by research which shows that even in environments (e.g., prisons) where time-constraints are minimal, people's exercise behaviour is not much different from that in the general population (Morgan, 1977). Although the descriptive approach has been helpful in identifying barriers to exercise initiation and in providing baseline data for public health initiatives, it suffers from the limitation that we referred to in the previous section – its atheoretical nature (Biddle and Nigg, 2000). In other words, it does not explain the psychological processes (e.g., attitudes, intentions) that determine people's level of involvement in habitual physical activity. Fortunately, several theories have emerged in exercise psychology to fill this gap. These theories are borrowed mainly from models of social cognition but have been modified for use in exercise settings. Although they differ from each other in significant ways, these theories share a common assumption that people are rational and goal-directed in their pursuit of physical activity.

Theories of exercise behaviour

Although many theories of exercise behaviour have been developed in recent years (for reviews, see Buckworth and Dishman, 2002; Carron, Hausenblas and Estabrooks, 2003; Culos-Reed, Gyurcsik and Brawley, 2001; and Marcus, Bock, Pinto, Napolitano and Clark, 2002), space limitations prevent us from examining any but the most popular ones in this chapter. Of these theories, three deserve special consideration. These approaches are the theories of "reasoned action" and "planned behaviour" and the "transtheoretical model" of behaviour change.

Although these approaches have certain similarities (e.g., in assuming that people's intentions predict their behaviour; Ogden, 2000), they differ in at least one important respect. Specifically, whereas the theories of reasoned action and planned behaviour are largely static in attempting to predict exercise behaviour, the transtheoretical model of change is a *dynamic* model which assumes that people move in a spiral fashion through a sequence of qualitatively different stages on their journey from inactivity to activity. Furthermore, this latter approach assumes that at any point in this cycle, people can fall back to an earlier stage – as if they were playing an exercise version of the game of "snakes and ladders". Let us now examine these three theories of exercise behaviour in more detail.

Theories of "reasoned action" and "planned behaviour"

The theory of "reasoned action" (TRA) was developed by Ajzen and Fishbein (1974) to explore the degree to which people's voluntary behaviour reflects their intentions. It was subsequently extended by Ajzen (1988) into the theory of "planned behaviour" (TPB). The relationships between the key constructs of these theories are depicted in Figure 8.1.

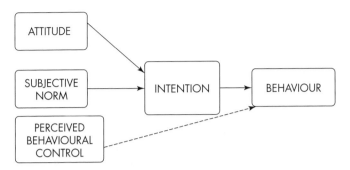

Figure 8.1 Theories of reasoned action and planned behaviour (reprinted, by kind permission, from H. A. Hausenblas, A. V. Carron, and D. E. Mack, 1997, "Application of the theories of reasoned action and planned behaviour to exercise behaviour: A meta-analysis"
Source: Journal of Sport and Exercise Psychology, 19(1): 37

The TRA postulates that people behave in a rational manner by taking into account available information before they act. In particular, it proposes that the best predictor of people's volitional behaviour is their intention to act. This construct of "intention" represents a person's immediate behavioural inclination to engage in a given target behaviour such as physical activity. It is alleged to be determined by two social-cognitive variables – first, the person's attitude to performing the behaviour in question, and second, the subjective norms which surround it. "Attitude" represents the person's beliefs about the target behaviour (exercise) as well as his or her evaluation of the consequences of this behaviour. For example, a student might believe that although exercise is good for her health, it takes away from her study time. "Subjective norms" comprise the person's beliefs about the degree to which significant others want him/her to engage in the target behaviour. In other words, they represent social pressures to behave in a certain way. For example, if John believes that his family thinks he should take more exercise, and he usually follows his family's wishes, then he will experience a positive subjective norm for exercising.

These two variables – attitudes and norms – are held to play a crucial role in determining people's involvement in physical activity. Indeed, the theory of reasoned action suggests that the question of whether or not people take up exercise is influenced more by attitudes and norms than by such demographic variables as their educational level or socioeconomic status (see the barriers to exercise described in the preceding section). An age effect is also evident. Thus a recent research review by Hagger, Chatzisarantis and Biddle (2002) concluded that older people are more likely to implement their intentions than are younger adults. Overall, the TRA has received solid empirical support. Indeed, research suggests that attitudinal factors account for up to 30 per cent of the variance generated by people's intentions to exercise (Buckworth and Dishman, 2002). In addition, a meta-analysis by Hausenblas, Carron and Mack (1997) of relevant research showed that "intention" had a relatively large effect on exercise behaviour (effect size of 1.09) and that "attitude" had a large effect on intention (effect size of 1.22). Unfortunately, a problem for the TRA is the fact that a person's decision about whether or not to engage in exercise behaviour is not always under his or her voluntary control. For example, physical injury or adverse weather conditions may make it difficult to implement one's intention to exercise.

The theory of planned behaviour (TPB) is a modification of the TRA resulting from the addition of a single variable – "perceived behavioural control" – which refers to one's belief about how easy or difficult it is to perform the target behaviour. Azjen and his colleagues suggested that this variable affects people's intentions in any social situation. For example, if people want to exercise but have little opportunity to do so due to certain barriers, then they are unlikely to engage in physical activity – regardless of any positive attitudes to exercise or the existence of favourable social norms.

In summary, reviews of relevant research (e.g., Culos-Reed *et al.*, 2001) indicate that the TRA and TPB models have been quite useful in predicting people's exercise intentions and any subsequent physical activity. When compared, however, the TPB seems to be superior to the TRA in its explanatory scope. Thus the review by Culos-Reed *et al.* (2001) concluded that there are strong positive relationships among the TPB components of attitudes, subjective norms, perceived behavioural control, behavioural intentions and exercise behaviour. This conclusion was supported by the recent meta-analytic review of Hagger *et al.* (2002). Briefly, this review showed that the TPB accounted for more variance in physical activity intentions and behaviour than did the TRA. At least one important practical implication stems from this finding. Specifically, it seems that in order to optimise the likelihood of taking up physical activity, interventions should concentrate on fostering a sense of control and/or self-efficacy in participants. Unfortunately, despite their explicit analysis of the links between intentions, attitudes and behaviour, the TRA and TPB have been criticised on several grounds. For example, because they are unidirectional models, they do not envisage the possibility that engaging in exercise behaviour may cause people to change their attitudes to exercise (Biddle and Nigg, 2000). Also, they are not especially helpful in explaining behavioural *change*. Consideration of this latter problem leads us to an alternative conceptual approach in exercise psychology: the "transtheoretical model".

The Transtheoretical Model of Behaviour Change (TTM)

It has long been known that people can improve their health not only by giving up hazardous activities (e.g., smoking) but also by adopting constructive habits such as exercising regularly. But how can people change from being in a sedentary state to active engagement in a healthy lifestyle? The transtheoretical model of behaviour change (TTM) was developed originally by Prochaska and DiClemente (1983) in an effort to account for the success of "self-changers" in smoking: people who managed to reduce this addictive behaviour without the aid of any professional intervention. The term "transtheoretical" reflects the fact that the concepts and principles of this approach are borrowed from a variety of theories of behaviour change within the fields of psychotherapy and health psychology. The TTM is a dynamic approach because it assumes that intentional behaviour change is not an "all or nothing" phenomenon but reflects a process that unfolds gradually over time. This dynamic approach arose from the observation that people who quit smoking tended to go through a distinctive pattern of behavioural changes as they gradually gave up cigarettes. Not surprisingly, therefore, the TTM is also known as the "stages of change" model. Since the early 1990s, this model has been applied to *preventive health issues,* especially those concerning exercise initiation and maintenance (Marcus and Simkin, 1993).

The TTM has four main components:

1   the idea of stages of change;
2   the hypothetical processes by which such change occurs;
3   the concept of self-efficacy (or one's belief in one's ability to perform the required behaviour; see also Box 8.2); and
4   the theory of "decisional balance" (i.e., an evaluation of the positive and negative aspects of changing one's target behaviour).

Although a detailed analysis of these components is beyond the scope of this chapter, let us now consider the "when" (time-course) and "how" (transformation mechanisms) of the transtheoretical model of behaviour change as it applies to physical activity. To begin with, the TTM postulates that people progress through a series of five stages before they achieve a desired and sustained change in their behaviour. The first stage is "precontemplation" – a sedentary stage in which the person has no intention of becoming physically active in the immediate future (usually measured operationally as within the next six months). The second stage is "contemplation" where the person does not currently exercise but has some intention of becoming more active physically within the next six months. The third stage is "preparation" where the person engages in some physical activity but not on a regular basis (usually understood as less than three times a week). The fourth stage is "action" where the person is physically active regularly but has only been so for less than six months. Finally, the "maintenance" stage occurs when the person is physically active regularly and has been exercising for at least six months. These stages are described in Box 8.4.

Box 8.4 The transtheoretical model of behaviour change as applied to physical activity

Stage	What happens?
Precontemplation	Person is not active physically and has no intention of exercising over the next six months
Contemplation	Person is still inactive but intends to start exercising regularly within next six months

Preparation	Person is active physically but below the criterion level of regularity required for health benefits (i.e., at least three times per week for 20–30 minutes or longer per session)
Action	Person is engaged in regular physical activity but has been doing so at the criterion level for less than six months
Maintenance	Person is engaged in regular physical activity and has been exercising regularly for more than six months

As you can see from Box 8.4, each of these hypothetical stages of change is defined by a unique combination of intentionality and behaviour and can be measured using self-report instruments (see Marcus and Simkin, 1993). Note that the stages are assumed to be cyclical rather than linear because many people do not maintain their intended changes but regress to an earlier stage. These relapses to previous stages of change are common among people who wish to become more physically active and are often caused by injury, illness and by the vicissitudes of travel and personal or business issues. Interestingly, many successful "self-changers" proceed in a spiral fashion several times through the preliminary stages before they achieve the maintenance stage (see Figure 8.2).

Although the above stages describe how people's exercise behaviour changes over time, the *process* by which these changes occur requires a separate explanation. Thus the TTM postulates ten different strategies to account for a person's transformation from a state of inactivity to one of regular physical activity. These strategies are defined as actions that are "initiated or experienced by an individual in modifying affect, behaviour, cognition, or relationships" (Prochaska and DiClemente, 1984, p. 7). Among these strategies are experiential processes like "consciousness raising" (whereby the person tries to learn more about the benefits of regular physical activity) and "dramatic relief" (whereby the person may be moved emotionally by warnings about the dangers of not taking regular exercise). Also, behavioural strategies such as "stimulus control" may be used. Here, the exerciser may try to avoid any situations that promote physical inactivity. Another popular behavioural change mechanism is the use of "helping relationships" in which exercisers seek social support to encourage them to continue with their planned physical activity.

The third component of the TTM is the construct of "self-efficacy" which, as we learned earlier in this chapter, refers to people's confidence in their ability to perform a certain action. Theoretically, people with high levels of self-efficacy are confident of being able to exercise even when they encounter barriers such as bad weather, fatigue or other adverse circumstances. The final component of the TTM is the hypothetical "decisional balance" or cost–benefit analysis in which the person is believed to weigh up the "pros" and "cons" of taking part in regular physical activity. For example, an advantage of exercise could be that "I know I'll meet my friends in the gym tonight" but a disadvantage might arise from apprehension of the fatigue that is likely to follow vigorous physical activity. In general, the TTM predicts that "pros" should increase as people move from the precontemplation to

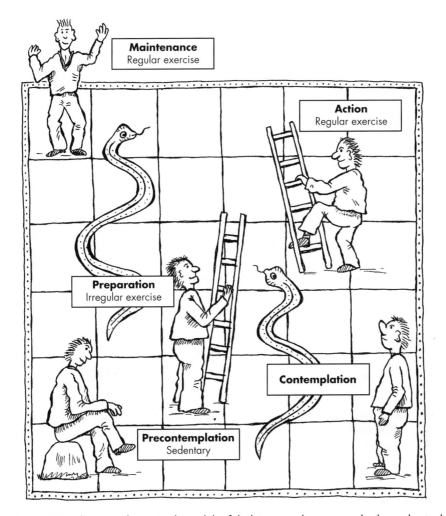

Figure 8.2 The transtheoretical model of behaviour change applied to physical activity
Source: adapted from Buckworth and Dishman, 2002, p. 220

the contemplation stages, whereas the "cons" should diminish as people go from the action to the maintenance stages.

Overall, the TTM appears to offer a plausible and fruitful account of people's exercise behaviour (Culos-Reed *et al.*, 2001). For example, it acknowledges the difficulties that many people experience in attempting to change their exercise habits. In addition, it recognises the fact that people differ from each other in their readiness for becoming more active physically. This idea offers the possibility of matching a particular exercise intervention to a particular state of individual behavioural change. But does available research evidence support the validity of the transtheoretical model? Unfortunately, the data bearing upon this issue are equivocal. Thus although Callaghan, Eves, Norman, Chang and Yuk Lung (2002) summarised a number of predictions from the TTM that have been corroborated by researchers, Culos-Reed *et al.* (2001) identified several flaws and inconsistencies in the research literature in this field. To illustrate these contrasting perspectives on the TTM, consider the following evidence. On the positive side, Peterson and Aldana (1999) reported that a "stage-matched" intervention to increase exercise behaviour (i.e., those in which people are encouraged to use processes of change that correspond to, or match, their current stage of change) was more effective than a generic intervention. On the negative side, the TTM has been criticised for failing to specify the precise psychological mechanisms facilitating successful change from one stage to another. It has also been criticised for its neglect of individual differences that may account for stage relapses (Culos-Reed *et al.*, 2001). A third problem for the TTM is that the instruments designed to test both stages and processes of change have been poorly validated (Buckworth and Dishman, 2002). Finally, in the field of physical activity, TTM research has focused mainly on middle-aged populations rather than on people of a younger age – despite the fact that this latter group is increasingly sedentary (Trost, Pate, Sallis, Freedson, Taylor, Dowda and Sirad, 2002; Woods, Mutrie and Scott, 2002). In view of these limitations, Culos-Reed *et al.* (2001) concluded that the popularity of the TTM "far outweighs its objective research support" (p. 710).

Exercise attrition: why do people drop out of physical activity programmes?

As we learned at the beginning of this chapter, as many as half of the people who join exercise programmes in gyms or elsewhere tend to drop out of them within months. Why are these attrition rates so high? Two ways of answering this question can be identified. On the one hand, the descriptive research approach tries to identify on a range of factors that are associated with dropping out from physical activity programmes. On the other hand, the theoretical approach uses conceptual models of relapse behaviour in an effort to understand people's *reasons* for giving up exercising regularly. Let us now consider each of these approaches briefly.

With regard to the descriptive approach, research suggests that dropping out from exercise activities is associated with variables like low socioeconomic status, habitual smoking, limited coping skills, low motivation and/or the belief that physical activity requires too much effort. By contrast, exercise adherence is associated with intrinsic motivation – enjoying exercise for its own sake (Ogden, 2000). Unfortunately, research in this field is hampered by methodological limitations. For example, few studies on exercise attrition have followed up drop-outs to make sure that they are not continuing to take exercise spontaneously or on their own. As regards the theoretical approach to understanding exercise attrition, Marcus *et al.* (2002) proposed various principles governing effective "relapse prevention" interventions. The first principle emphasises the importance of identifying high-risk situations which are likely to precipitate dropping out. A common example of such situations is a change in work routine or unexpected travel demands. Next, an effective relapse prevention intervention should equip exercisers with psychological strategies designed to cope with the demands of these risky situations. For example, a woman whose travel demands force her to miss her weekly aerobics class may change the location of her next session. Thus she may decide to go for a run while she is away rather than missing her exercise completely. Further details of the causes of, and proposed solutions for, exercise attrition are found in Biddle and Mutrie (2001) and Morgan and Dishman (2001).

Practical tips on becoming more active physically

So far in this chapter, you have learned about the nature and health consequences of exercise as well as the obstacles that can prevent people from engaging in habitual physical activity. After examining relevant theories and findings, it is time to apply what you have learned. So, here are some practical tips on exercising effectively (Baron and Kalsher, 2002; DeAngelis, 2002). See also Chapter 2 for some practical advice on effective goal-setting.

- *Put a "p(ep)" in your step: make your exercise purposeful*
  The gym is not the only place to exercise. Instead, try to include some natural physical activity in your daily list of things to do. For example, go for a walk with your dog, rake the leaves in your garden or cycle down to the shops. Try to accumulate at least thirty minutes of moderate intensity physical activity per day.
- *Think big but start small*
  If the thought of exercising puts you off, then try to take one small step at a time. For example, instead of saying to yourself, "I'm going to walk every day this week for at least an hour", try to say, "I'll build it up in five-minute periods from Sunday to Thursday".
- *Establish an exercise routine*
  Try to develop a habit of physical activity by exercising at the same time every day.
- *Make it sociable and enjoyable*
  It is easy to maintain an exercise regime if you enjoy it and are supported by other people in the same activity. So, if possible, try to make a social occasion of your physical activity so that you and your friends can have fun while exercising.
- *If you start at an older age, take exercise gradually*
  If you are a recent convert to the joy of exercising, begin gradually: slowly but surely is the best advice here.
- *Get on your bike*
  Try to cycle as often as possible. Cycling not only uses all the main muscles of the legs but also tones the buttocks through the repeated "push down" phase of the pedalling action.
- *Develop an active lifestyle*
  You will reap the greatest benefits from exercise if you regard it as just one part of an active lifestyle rather than as an isolated task that you feel compelled to perform a few times per week.

Ideas for research projects on exercise psychology

Here are five suggestions for research projects on aspects of the psychology of exercise behaviour.

1   Although it has long been known that regular exercise can elevate people's moods, relatively few studies have been conducted to find out the nature and extent of these changes over time. Using a standardised test of mood such as the "Profile of Mood States" (POMS; McNair *et al.*, 1992) as well as a diary of people's feelings at different times of the day, can you think of a way of testing the relationship between mood and exercise over a period of several months?

2   Does the environment in which one conducts one's physical activity affect its perceived benefits? It would be interesting to extend the study by Bodin and Hartig (2003) described earlier in the chapter by comparing the relative effects of different types of walking routes (e.g., urban, suburban and rural) on people's mood and well-being.

3   It would be interesting to compare and contrast the views of sports medicine physicians, physiotherapists and expert coaches about the nature, extent and possible causes of the problem of exercise dependence in athletes.

4   Do sports medicine professionals practise what they preach? It would be interesting to explore the attitudes to, and nature of, exercise behaviour displayed by people who work professionally in this discipline.

5   In an effort to understand the reasons why people tend to drop out so frequently from structured physical activity programmes, it would be helpful to compare and contrast the reasons given by gym instructors, exercise adherents and exercise drop-outs (see Lippke, Knäuper and Fuchs, 2003).

Summary

Although many people realise that physical activity is associated with a range of health benefits, they appear to be reluctant either to engage in or to persist with regular exercise. This paradox lies at the heart of exercise psychology – a discipline which is concerned with people's involvement in physical activity in various everyday settings. Given this background, the present chapter set out to investigate the benefits, hazards and psychological issues arising from people's exercise behaviour.

*   It began with an explanation of the nature and goals of exercise psychology.
*   The second part of the chapter provided a critical evaluation of research on the health benefits associated with regular physical activity as well as some potential hazards (e.g., overtraining and exercise dependence).
*   In the third part of the chapter, I examined the main theories and research findings on the issues of exercise initiation (the "take-up" problem) and exercise maintenance (the "keeping it up" problem).
*   The final section presented several ideas for possible research projects on exercise psychology.

Chapter 9

Helping athletes to cope with injury: from theory to practice

It's the power of the mind and being positive. A lot of that had to do with my wife, my family and friends. (Jonah Lomu, New Zealand rugby international player, after he had overcome a chronic kidney illness in 1997, cited in Hodge and McKenzie, 1999, p. 213)

Returning from a major injury is an immense test of a player's physical and mental strength. (Alan Hansen, former Liverpool and Scotland player, 1998, p. 76)

When I injured my shoulder, I couldn't do anything. No work-outs, nothing, I was angry, moody, frustrated. (Steffi Graf, former Wimbledon tennis champion, cited in B. Miller, 1997, p. 124)

A bleak period in my professional life had changed me considerably even if I hadn't been fully aware of what was happening or what it meant. Time spent alone helped me figure myself out. (Roy Keane, captain of Manchester United, 2002, p. 181, on the experience of being injured)

Introduction

In Chapter 8, we explored the health benefits and potential hazards of engaging in regular physical activity. Continuing this theme, the present chapter examines another drawback associated with sport and exercise – namely, injury. Unfortunately, the risk of injury is an inevitable consequence of regular involvement in any form of physical activity (see Figure 9.1).

Figure 9.1 Injury is almost inevitable in sport
Source: courtesy of Inpho Photography

Not surprisingly, sports injuries can be represented on a continuum ranging from minor (e.g., twisting a finger while attempting to catch a ball) to severe (e.g., suffering brain damage in a boxing match – as happened to Michael Watson who was in a coma for forty days after he had been injured in his world super-middle-weight title fight against Chris Eubank in 1991). Regardless of their location on this continuum, however, sports injuries constitute a significant volume of acute admissions to hospitals. For example, in 1994 there were about 24 million sports injuries reported in Britain (Hemmings and Povey, 2002). Similarly, in 1999 about 750,000 people reported to the casualty wards of British hospitals seeking treatment for injuries which they had received while playing sports or engaging in exercise (Hoey, 2002). Indeed, the level of injury risk for professional sports performers is significantly higher than for other occupational groups. To illustrate this disparity, Drawer and Fuller (2002) reported that whereas employees in the UK suffer, on average, 0.36 reportable injuries per 100,000 working hours, professional footballers suffer an average of *710* reportable injuries per 100,000 hours of training and competition. Further evidence on the prevalence of this problem springs from the fact that sports injuries comprise approximately *one third* of all injuries reported to medical agencies in the UK (Uitenbroek, 1996). Not all of these ailments reflect sudden-impact injuries, however. Thus it is increasingly evident that certain types of long-term physical deterioration can occur as a consequence of habitual sporting activity. For example, degenerative joint conditions in rugby players can take up to twenty years to develop (Lee, Garraway, Hepburn and Laidlaw, 2001). In a similar vein, cases of chronic brain damage have been detected in former professional soccer players. Some of this damage has been attributed to repeated heading of the ball. For example, in November 2002, a coroner in England ruled that Jeff Astle, one of the most famous football strikers of his generation, had died at the age of 59 from a degenerative condition that had probably been caused by his prowess in heading. Apparently, the twenty years which Astle had spent in heading rapidly delivered, water-sodden leather balls had damaged his brain irrevocably (McGrory, 2002). But as Box 9.1 shows, we must be careful to avoid uncritical acceptance of the claim that heading in soccer causes brain damage. After all, in Astle's era, leather footballs were more likely to cause head injuries because they became about 20 per cent heavier than normal during wet conditions. By contrast, modern footballs are not only lighter but also waterproof and hence do not absorb rain as a match progresses. Thus it appears that available evidence is not adequate to justify the claim that deliberate heading (as distinct from accidental collisions involving the head) causes brain damage.

Box 9.1 Are footballers heading for injury? Thinking critically about . . . the link between heading and brain damage

The ability to head the ball accurately while standing, running, jumping or diving is a highly valued skill in soccer because it demands excellent technique and precise timing. But can repeated execution of this skill of heading cause brain damage, or traumatically induced alteration in brain function, in footballers? In an attempt to answer this question, Kirkendall and Garrett (2001) and Kirkendall, Jordan and Garrett (2001) reviewed available research evidence from over fifty studies on the nature and causes of head injuries in soccer. At least four key conclusions emerged from these reviews. To begin with, Kirkendall and his colleagues established that head injuries are most likely to occur within the penalty-area when defenders and attackers compete for crosses or corner-kicks or around the half-way line when midfield players challenge each other for aerial clearances from the goalkeeper. Next, they found some evidence that the higher the skill-level of the players involved, the more frequent were the incidents in which concussion occurred. Third, they concluded that although a significant number of retired soccer players show signs of cognitive dysfunctions and various neuropsychological impairments, the causes of these problems are difficult to determine. For example, these maladies may be caused by accidental collisions with other players or with stationary objects (e.g., the goalposts, advertising hoardings) rather than by repeated heading of the ball. Finally, they concluded that the research literature on heading and brain damage is marred by a host of methodological weaknesses. To illustrate, many studies in this field have failed to control for such factors as inconsistencies in the criteria used to define brain damage, unreliable estimates of the frequency of heading engaged in during a match and variations in the age, neurological histories and possible alcohol intake of the players involved. In summary, Kirkendall *et al.* (2001) conclude that "the use of the head for controlling and advancing the ball is not likely to be a significant factor in mild traumatic brain injury" (p. 384) in soccer players. In spite of this conclusion, a recent neuropsychological study by Witol and Webbe (2003) found that cumulative experience (or lifetime frequency) of heading among male soccer players was associated with poor performance on tests of attention/concentration, cognitive flexibility and general intellectual functioning. Therefore, these researchers argued that "players who head the ball frequently may carry a higher risk of neurobehavioural sequelae" (p. 414).

Critical thinking questions
Do you think that the statistics on head injuries in professional soccer are accurate? After all, many players may be unwilling to report symptoms arising from such injuries in order to avoid being dropped from their teams. How many times in a game do you think that defenders, midfielders and attackers head the ball during a competitive match? Check your guess by videotaping a match and then counting the appropriate totals for a random fifteen-minute sequence of play. Given the fact that young soccer players are less skilled technically and have less developed brains, do you think that heading should be banned in children's football?

In summary, the preceding strands of anecdotal and descriptive evidence suggest that sports injuries pose significant national public health concerns. Naturally, such problems have serious economic consequences. For example, it has been estimated that in Britain alone, soccer injuries cost the taxpayer about £1 billion through direct treatment costs and indirect loss of production through the resultant problem of "time off work" (Rahnama, Reilly and Lees, 2002). Leaving aside the medical and economic issues, however, how do athletes react to, and cope with, the injuries that they experience? Is there a psychological dimension to injury rehabilitation as the quotations from Steffi Graf and Roy Keane at the start of this chapter suggest? In addressing these questions, our objectives in this chapter are two-fold. First, we shall try to summarise what is known about current theory and research on the psychological factors involved in athletic injuries. In addition, we shall try to provide some practical insights into the strategies used by sport psychologists to facilitate rapid and effective injury rehabilitation in athletes.

The chapter is organised as follows. To begin with, I shall trace the shift from a physical to a psychological perspective on injuries in sport. Next, a brief analysis of the nature, prevalence and causes of sports injuries will be presented. The third part of the chapter will outline and evaluate two theoretical models which purport to describe how athletes react psychologically to injuries: the "grief stages" theory and the "cognitive appraisal" model. Next, I shall sketch some practical strategies used by sport psychologists in the rehabilitation of injured athletes. After that, some new directions for research on the psychological aspects of injury will be examined. Finally, suggestions will be provided for possible research projects in this field.

The psychological approach to injuries in athletes

Until the 1980s, most sports medicine specialists believed that as injuries had physical causes, they required only physical forms of treatment. Furthermore, it was assumed that athletes who had attained minimal levels of physical rehabilitation were "fully prepared for a safe and successful return to competition" (Williams, Rotella and Heyman, 1998, p. 410). Within a decade, however, at least three strands of evidence combined to challenge this purely physical approach to injury management.

To begin with, interviews with many injured athletes (e.g., see the quote from the former Wimbledon tennis champion Steffi Graf at the beginning of this chapter) revealed the emotional consequences of their physical problems. For example, anger and depression are common reactions to the discovery that one is prevented from pursuing one's hobby or livelihood. Unfortunately, not all coaches or managers are sensitive to the mental repercussions of sports injuries. For example, consider the way in which injured soccer players used to be treated at Liverpool Football Club during the managerial reign of Bill Shankley. Apparently, Shankley believed that the best way to hasten the rehabilitation of such players was to ignore them completely until they had recovered (Bent *et al.* 2000)! This curious practice of scapegoating injured athletes was revealed by the former Liverpool team captain, Tommy Smith, who recalled that his manager used to speak to him via a third party (the club trainer) whenever he was injured. Fortunately, this situation has changed with the advent of specialist medical staff and sophisticated treatment facilities in leading Premiership clubs. A second sign of a psychological approach to injury management comes from surveys of the opinions and experiences of treatment specialists in this field. By way of background, in the mid-1990s several surveys of athletic trainers revealed a growing awareness of the significance of the "mental side" of injuries. For example, 47 per cent of a large (almost 500) sample of trainers in the US recognised that injured athletes tend to suffer significant psychological distress as result of their physical trauma (Larson, Starkey and Zaichkowsky, 1996). In a similar vein, Francis, Andersen and Maley (2000) asked a sample of physiotherapists about the psychological characteristics which facilitated recovery in injured athletes. Among the most important perceived prerequisites of successful rehabilitation were such factors as a willingness to listen to physiotherapists' advice and effective interpersonal communication skills. More recently, Hemmings and Povey (2002) investigated the way in which English chartered physiotherapists perceived psychological aspects of their professional work. Results showed that the physiotherapists reported using a variety of psychological techniques (e.g., creating variety in rehabilitation exercises, setting short-term goals and encouraging positive self-talk) with injured athletes. However, a rather surprising finding was the discovery that few of the physiotherapists in the study had ever referred a patient to an accredited sport psychologist. Clearly, much work remains to be done in promoting the value and image of sport psychology in the medical community. The third boost for a psychological approach to injury management came from recent research in sport science. Specifically, over the past decade there has been a profusion of studies on mental aspects of athletic injuries (e.g., see the special issue of the *Journal of Applied Sport Psychology* on this topic; Brewer, 1998). This body of literature has generated some interesting findings on the interaction between motivation, fatigue and injury in athletes. For example, Rahnama *et al.* (2002) proposed that the increased risk of injury experienced by soccer players near the beginning (first fifteen minutes) or end (last fifteen minutes) of football matches may be due to the effects of initial intensity of tackling combined with subsequent fatigue later in the game. Also, the fusion of athletic accomplishments and personal identity is apparent from evidence that injured runners had significantly lower levels of self-esteem than did fully fit athletes in control groups (Chan and Grossman, 1988). To summarise, several factors have converged to highlight the importance of psychological factors in the causes and treatment of injury in athletes.

Nature, prevalence and causes of injuries in sport

So far, I have introduced the mental side of physical trauma in athletes without actually explaining what the term "sports injury" means. This problem will be rectified below. But as we shall see, there are no universally agreed criteria available to define such injuries. Therefore, any analysis of sports injuries raises certain conceptual and methodological issues that need to be addressed.

What is a sports injury? Nature, types and severity

In sports science, an injury may be defined as any physical or medical condition that prevents a player from participating in a match or training session (Orchard and Seward, 2002). More generally, it may be regarded as any "involuntary, physically disruptive experience" (Cashmore, 2002, p. 141) encountered by an athlete. Unfortunately, despite their apparent clarity, these definitions gloss over several important conceptual issues. For example, as Udry and Andersen (2002) observed, athletes often incur injuries which originate *outside* sporting contexts. For example, what if an athlete suffers a car-crash while driving to the training-ground? Does this disruptive experience constitute a "sports" injury? In an effort to deal with such objections, some sports scientists (e.g., Noyes, Lindenfeld and Marshall,1988) postulated the enforced or unexpected time lost from participation in sport as a key criterion in defining athletic injuries. But once again, this definition was criticised on two grounds. First, some athletes try to play their sport even though they are technically injured (Flint, 1998). One explanation for this phenomenon is that such performers may have higher pain thresholds than others. The second problem with the criterion of time loss is that it neglects the fact that injuries have *medical* as well as temporal consequences for athletes (Kujala, 2002). Thus it may be wise to augment time loss with the requirement that to qualify as an "injury" a given problem should require medical attention. In summary, it is clear that despite several decades of research in this field, there does not seem to be any universally agreed definition of sports injury.

Despite some vagueness about the criteria used to define sports injuries, we know that the tissue damage which characterises them varies considerably in type and severity. For example, there is a clear distinction between "acute" and "chronic" injuries. The former category refers mainly to "direct trauma" or injuries stemming from a known cause such as a sudden impact which may produce a bone fracture, muscle strain or a ligament sprain. By contrast, "chronic" injuries are relatively diffuse conditions that develop slowly and which only gradually lead to tissue break-down. An example of such problems is tendonitis in the wrist of a regular tennis player – an injury which has no single identifiable cause. Given the fact that sports injuries vary along temporal dimensions (acute versus chronic), do they also vary in severity? Although there is no agreed method of measuring objectively the seriousness of an injury, a variety of possible indices of severity have been proposed. For example, the seriousness of an athletic injury has been operationally defined in terms of the amount of time lost from participation in the sport, the degree of pain experienced by the athlete in the injured limb or area, the range of motion available for the injured body part, and the estimated time for recovery (Kerr and Miller, 2001). To illustrate the last of these criteria, Rahnama *et al.* (2002) distinguished between minor, moderate and severe types of injury in soccer players on the basis of the length of time needed for recovery. Nevertheless, no consensus exists about the best way to measure injury severity in sports. Having sketched the nature of sports injuries, we should now consider their prevalence.

Prevalence of injuries in sport

In general, the prevalence of injuries across different sports is difficult to assess because of factors such as variations in the criteria used to define and report physical trauma in athletes as well as inconsistencies in the use of protective equipment in a given sport (Junge and Dvorak, 2000; Walter, Sutton, McIntosh and Connolly, 1985). Despite these methodological problems, some general trends in injury analysis are evident in relation to two popular sports in Britain: cricket (a non-contact sport) and rugby (a contact sport). For example, Hopps (2002) reported that between 2000 and 2002, England's top cricket players were almost *twice* as likely as their Australian counterparts to experience back injuries which had rendered participants unfit to play. This disparity in injury prevalence between cricketers from different countries is difficult to explain but may reflect the arduous, non-stop nature of the modern cricket season in Britain as compared to that in the southern hemisphere. With regard to injury prevalence in rugby, statistics released by the Rugby Football Union in England in 2002 showed that serious injuries (defined operationally as enforced time loss from the sport for a period of more than twenty-one days) had increased significantly from a figure of 1,058 (for the 1992–1993 season, before rugby union became a professional sport) to between 2,120 and 2,461 per year over a five-year period (1997–2002). Again, this apparent increase in injuries in rugby has been attributed to external factors – in this case, the increasing demands of professionalism in this sport (Starmer-Smith, 2002). Unfortunately, little is known about whether or not injuries in soccer have increased to a similar degree. What is known, however, is that at any one time, about 10 per cent of the players in the ninety-two professional football squads in Britain are unable to train because of injury (Woods, Hawkins, Hulse and Hodson, 2002). Also, about 47 per cent of professional footballers are forced to retire from the game as a result of injury (Drawer and Fuller, 2002). These figures highlight the extent of the problem of injury in soccer. In summary, research evidence suggests that injuries are widespread in such popular sports as cricket, rugby and soccer.

The apparent growth of sports injury incidence is attributable mainly to a combination of social and/or professional influences. First, consider the growing emphasis in our society on the pursuit of optimal health and fitness. Put simply, in order to look and feel better, one has to work harder on one's fitness and appearance. Unfortunately, working harder may cause physical injury unless one's training programmes are individually tailored to one's current level of fitness (see also discussion of overtraining in Chapter 8) and one is properly conditioned physically to undertake the exercise in the first place. In relation to this latter point, stretching before exercising has long been regarded as a popular and effective conditioning technique. For example, it is widely believed that runners who stretch their calves and hamstrings before a race not only increase their flexibility but also reduce their chance of incurring injury. But does the research evidence support the validity of stretching exercises? Remarkably, a recent study by Herbert and Gabriel (2002) raised doubts about this matter by questioning the extent to which "warming up" and "warming down" by stretching reduces the risk of muscle injuries (see Box 9.2).

Box 9.2 Thinking critically about . . . the value of stretching before and after exercising

Although certain strategies are useful in preventing sports injuries (e.g., the wearing of helmets is known to protect cyclists from head trauma), others are of doubtful value. For example, although improvements in helmet design in the 1960s led to a reduction in deaths from head injuries in American football players, it was also associated with an *increase* in spine fractures following tackles in the game (Kujala, 2002). Given this uncertainty about the value of certain injury prevention techniques, how useful is a strategy like stretching? At first glance, its value is unquestionable because all athletes are taught that stretching before and after exercise is beneficial in at least three ways. First, it is alleged to reduce muscle soreness. Second, it is held to lessen the likelihood of musculoskeletal injury. Finally, it is reckoned to enhance athletic performance. But where is the empirical evidence to support any of these three claims?

In a recent attempt to answer this question, Herbert and Gabriel (2002) conducted a systematic review of the research literature on stretching. Results revealed that across five relevant studies, there was no significant effect of stretching before or after exercise on delayed-onset muscle soreness. Next, a review of two studies conducted on army recruits indicated that stretching before undertaking exercise does not yield useful reductions in the risk of incurring injury. However, the authors acknowledged that this conclusion applies strictly to the military setting in which the relevant data had been gathered. Unfortunately, little data exist on the effects of stretching on the risk of injury in either recreational or competitive athletes. Indeed, Kujala (2002) claimed that stretching "lacks scientific evidence" (p. 36). Surprisingly, no empirical studies could be located on the issue of whether or not stretching improves athletic performance. In summary, the work of Herbert and Gabriel (2002) highlights the value of evidence-based research in attempting to disentangle the myths of the locker-room from prescriptions based on sound empirical principles. As a consequence of the above studies, sports scientists are beginning to evaluate the optimal time in which to conduct stretching exercises. As a person's body temperature tends to increase *after* exercise, with concomitant enhanced extensibility of ligaments, tendons and muscles, it may make more sense to stretch at this stage (Cottell, 2003). Of course, a key issue that needs to be addressed in this field is the extent to which researchers are really comparing "like with like" when evaluating stretching exercises across different sports. After all, the static stretching displayed by a runner (where each muscle is held to the point of resistance for a given duration) is different from a more dynamic method of stretching that can be found in martial arts (e.g., where short, sharp kicks are practised before combat).

Critical thinking questions
Can you think of any psychological reasons why pre-performance stretching may be helpful to athletes? How could you persuade sports performers to stretch while "warming down" after they have competed?

A second possible explanation for the apparent increase of sports injuries among active people is that at the elite level professional performers are pushing their bodies to the limits of their abilities in pursuit of athletic success. This theory is supported anecdotally by observation of injury trends in tennis and golf. For example, Bill Norris, the principal trainer on the American Tennis Professionals' tennis tour, observed recently that problems of injury and burnout (see also Chapter 2) stem from a combination of the "never-ending pursuit of achievement and the inability of coaches to understand that the human body can only take so much for so long" (cited in Evans, 2002, p. 24). Interestingly, a similar picture has emerged in golf of late. Thus players such as Tiger Woods, David Duval, Ernie Els, Sergio Garcia and Davis Love III all suffered back injuries in the 2001 season which curtailed their involvement in tournament play (Kelly, 2002). Unfortunately, it is difficult to test the claim that athletic injuries are increasing because of the dearth of injury surveillance data from national sports organisations. What *can* be explored, however, is the issue of whether or not sports vary in the injury risks that they pose for participants.

Do sports differ in their levels of "dangerousness"? Intuitively, it seems plausible that one could place sports along a continuum of riskiness with apparently safe activities at one end (e.g., endurance events such as marathon running) and high-risk sports at the other end. Indeed, in motor racing, sixty-nine drivers from Formula One died as a result of "on course" accidents between 1950 and 1994 (Kujala, 2002). Somewhere in the middle of this hypothetical injury risk continuum lie popular sports such as basketball and soccer. Another way of investigating the "danger" of sports is to elicit risk ratings of them from the performers themselves. Using this approach, D. M. Pedersen (1997) asked more than 400 people to assess the risks posed by various sporting activities. Results revealed that motorcycle racing was perceived as the most dangerous sport, followed by cliff-jumping, hang-gliding, sky-diving, bungee-jumping, rock-climbing, scuba-diving, and, last of all, skiing. Perhaps not surprisingly, Pedersen (1997) also found that there was an inverse relationship between the perceived dangerousness of these sports and people's willingness to participate in them. Nevertheless, despite such risks, many people are attracted to dangerous leisure activities (see also Chapter 2 for discussion of people's motivation for participating in dangerous sports). Additional research on the riskiness of sports comes from Grimmer, Jones and Williams (2000) who examined a sample of Australian adolescents in an effort to identify the seven most common sports which were associated with elevated risks of injury. In decreasing order of injury potential, these sports were: martial arts, hockey, Australian Rules Football, roller-blading, netball, soccer and basketball. Most of these activities are team-games in which there is a high degree of bodily contact with opponents and a lot of jumping and landing. In summary, reasonable progress has been made in assessing the riskiness of various sports and in classifying them according to their perceived level of dangerousness. Having analysed the nature, types and prevalence of injuries, we should now consider their causes.

Causes of injuries in sport

Although a detailed analysis of the aetiology of athletic injuries is beyond the scope of this chapter, certain obvious causes can be pinpointed. In this regard, Kirkby (1995) compiled a list of precipitating factors which included inadequate physical conditioning and/or "warm up" procedures (but see Box 9.2), faulty biomechanical techniques used by athletes, deficient sports equipment, poor-quality protective apparel, dangerous sports surfaces and, of course, illegal and aggressive physical contact from opponents. In passing, it is notable that one of these factors – deficient sports equipment – was blamed recently for a spate of injuries among professional footballers in Britain. To illustrate, Woods *et al.* (2002) claimed that modern football boots contribute to the occurrence of injuries due to their "inadequate heel lift, soft and high heel counter, and rigid sole" (p. 439). But apart from these precipitating factors, there are plenty of other ways in which athletes can incur injury. Some of these factors are surprising if not bizarre (see Box 9.3)!

Research on the causes of sports injury has identified two broad classes of risk variables: "extrinsic" and "intrinsic" factors (Kujala, 2002). Among the extrinsic factors are the type of sport played (with high-risk activities like motorcycle racing

Box 9.3 Yes, it really happened! . . . unusual causes of injury in soccer and rugby

Athletic injuries are not always incurred on the sports field. To illustrate this point, here are some unusual causes of injury in soccer and rugby (Hannigan, 2001b; M. Smith, 2002a).

- Kieran Durkan (Rochdale) suffered blisters in his groin area when a team-mate inadvertently spilt a mug of coffee over him.
- Peter Canero (Kilmarnock) received cuts on his arms and legs when he fell through a glass-cased gaming machine in Spain.
- Florentin Petre (Dinamo Bucharest) experienced a nasty electric shock and burns to his head and body when his fishing rod became entangled in a power cable.
- Stefan Hampl, a striker with German third-division team Burghausen, was training with his team-mates in Cyprus when his ring-finger got caught in the nets of a goal-post he was carrying. This finger on his left hand was completely torn off and had to be reattached in hospital!
- Matt Rogers (of rugby union's New South Wales Waratahs) – and a former Australian rugby league star – incurred a freak injury when the massage table on which he was lying collapsed and crushed the middle finger of his right hand.

standing in contrast with safer pursuits like tennis), methods of training undertaken, typical environment in which the sport is played and the nature and amount of protective equipment used. By contrast, the intrinsic factors include personal characteristics of the participants such as age, gender and possible abnormalities of physical maturation. To illustrate this last-mentioned problem, Keith O'Neill, the former Republic of Ireland soccer international player, suffered chronic injuries due to a spurt of rapid growth in adolescence – a problem which caused pelvic and back complications (Fitzmaurice, 2002). Other intrinsic injury determinants include a previous history of physical injury and a vulnerability to stress. Interestingly, the idea that psychosocial factors could serve as antecedents of athletic injury comes from the research of Holmes and Rahe (1967). Briefly, these investigators found that people who had experienced stressful life events were more likely to suffer adverse health subsequently than were those who had experienced less stress in their lives. Evidence to support this theory in sport comes from the fact that injured athletes tend to have experienced higher levels of stress during the year preceding their injury than have athletes who had not been injured (Cryan and Alles, 1983). Such research has been criticised by Petrie and Falkstein (1998), however, for its reliance on subjective reports of injury severity and also for failing to consider the possible influence of intervening variables such as the social support mechanisms available to the injured athletes. Nevertheless, in a review of research in this field, J. M. Williams and Roepke (1993) concluded that eighteen out of twenty studies had found a significant positive relationship between stress and injury in athletes. In the light of such conclusions, let us now explore the psychological significance of athletes' reactions to the injuries that they experience.

How do athletes react to injury? Contrasting theoretical models

Within research on the psychology of injury, two main theories have been postulated to explain the way in which sport performers react to physical setbacks. The first of these approaches is the grief stages model which focuses mainly on the *emotional* consequences of injury for the afflicted athlete. The second approach concentrates on *cognitive* aspects of the injury experience and is influenced by studies of the way in which people perceive and cope with stress. This latter approach is called the "cognitive appraisal" model. One advantage of this approach over the grief stages model is that it tries to take into account personal and situational factors that determine athletes' emotional reactions to injuries. A second advantage is that it addresses the extent and quality of coping resources available to the injured athlete.

"Grief stages" models

Grief stages models (e.g., Rotella, 1985) are based on the assumption that injury is experienced as a form of symbolic *loss* by athletes. As a result of such loss, injured athletes are assumed to go through a predictable sequence of emotional changes on their way to recovery. As Cashmore (2002) put it, "not only do they lose a physical capability, they also lose a salient part of their self" (*sic*, p. 141). But how valid is this assumption of injury as a form of loss? More generally, what are the consequences of this loss for the rehabilitation of the athlete?

"Loss" is a common experience in sport. Thus Lavallee, Grove, Gordon and Ford (1998) analysed the various forms of loss that athletes encounter in sport, ranging from competitive defeat to the loss of self-esteem that is often associated with physical injury. Indeed, according to Ford and Gordon (1999), injured athletes may experience losses affecting factors such as mobility, independence, sense of control, virility, social relationships, income and financial rewards. Among the earliest proponents of the grief response theory of athletes' reactions to injury was P. Pedersen (1986) who suggested that sport performers may display a form of grief similar to that exhibited by people who suffer the loss of a loved one. This theory was based on the seminal work of Kübler-Ross (1969), a Swiss psychiatrist who had witnessed much death and suffering in the Second World War as a young adult and who had subsequently worked as a physician with cancer patients in the Unites States (Gill, 1980). Based on interviews with these patients, and observations of the way in which they dealt with their terminal illness, Kübler-Ross proposed that people go through five hypothetical stages of emotional response after they have been told of their impending death. These stages are denial, anger, bargaining, depression and acceptance. Denial occurs when patients refuse to accept the diagnosis offered to them or deny its implications. Anger results from an attempt to address the apparent unfairness of the situation by asking the question "Why me?" In the third stage of the grief response, "bargaining" happens when patients say prayers or offer to make changes in their lifestyle in an exchange for a postponement of their death. Depression occurs when patients start to grieve deeply. Finally, but not always, acceptance emerges when the patients resign themselves with dignity to their fate. The interpretation of this latter stage is somewhat controversial, however. Thus Hardy, Jones and Gould (1996) pointed out that acceptance does not mean resignation. Indeed in Kübler-Ross's model, the stage of "acceptance" seems to have the connotation of capitulation or giving up. This reaction is rarely the case with injured athletes, however, because the final stage of their reaction involves a readiness to engage in physical activity again.

Although this five-stage theory seems plausible, it has been criticised on the grounds of poor methodology (e.g., Kübler-Ross's recording of data was unsystematic and there are no independent empirical data to validate it) and for unreliable findings (e.g., see Aronoff and Spilka, 1984–1985). In addition, Doka (1995) argues that the alleged reactions of terminally ill patients to bad news are not typical of people facing death in other situations. Despite such criticisms of loss theory, Kübler-Ross's work has exerted a major influence on sport psychologists' understanding of how athletes react to injuries (Brewer, 2001a). Thus according to this grief stages theory, athletes who experience a significant injury or a career-threatening illness tend to go through a predictable sequence of stages as part of their recovery process. At first glance, however, this claim seems fanciful because illness and injury are not the same as death and also because there are many differences between the worlds of terminal illness and sport. Nevertheless, there is no doubt that injury generates doubt and loss in athletes. Thus sports performers who suffer serious injury are not only precluded from engaging in the activity that they love but are also vulnerable to significant losses of income, mobility, independence and social status.

In general, Kübler-Ross's five stages may be translated into the sporting domain as follows. In the first stage, an injured athlete's denial is captured by such statements as "I'll be fine – it can't be very serious". The next stage ("anger") may begin when athletes realise the amount of time they will miss as a result of the injury. After that, some bargaining may occur in which the athlete may offer to make compromises to his or her lifestyle in an attempt to regain lost fitness. Next, depression may arise when the afflicted athlete makes pessimistic predictions about his or her future in sport. This feeling is epitomised by such expressions as "This is hopeless – I'll never be as good as I was in the past". Finally, acceptance should arrive as the athlete comes to terms with the adverse circumstances which s/he has encountered. For example, s/he may say, "It's no use moaning – I'll just have to work myself back to fitness". Interestingly, Heil (1993) proposed a sport-related modification of Kübler-Ross's five-stage model. Briefly, his affective cycle model suggested that athletes go through three broad stages on the way to recovery. First, they are held to experience "distress" (e.g., shock, anger, depression). Then, they are believed to engage in denial and finally, in determined coping (whereby realism sets in and athletes accept their responsibility in the rehabilitation process).

Typically, stage theories of injury reaction have been tested in two ways (Brewer, 2001b). On the one hand, quantitative studies have used questionnaires and standardised psychological tests to assess athletes' emotional responses to injury and to compare them with the normal emotional fluctuations experienced by matched participants in control groups. In this regard, the "Profile of Mood States" (POMS; McNair *et al.*, 1992) has been used extensively to measure six affective states in athletes: tension/anxiety; depression/dejection; anger/hostility; vigour; fatigue; and confusion/bewilderment. In this test, a total mood disturbance score may be calculated by adding the negative mood scale scores (tension, depression, anger, fatigue and confusion) and subtracting the positive mood scale (vigour). An abbreviated, sport-specific version of this instrument has been developed by Grove and Prapavessis (1992). The second approach in this field uses qualitative methodology (see brief account in Chapter 1). Adopting this approach, researchers have used such techniques as "in-depth" interviews and focus groups to examine athletes' emotional reactions to injuries over a given period of time (Hurley, 2003).

What findings have emerged from these parallel lines of inquiry? At least four trends are evident. First, according to Brewer (2001b), higher levels of emotional disturbance (e.g., depression, anger, frustration) have been detected in athletes suffering from injuries than in control groups. To illustrate, Chan and Grossman (1988) discovered that injured runners displayed significantly more depression, anxiety and confusion than did non-injured counterparts. Also, according to Kishi, Robinson and Forrester (1994), patients who had experienced amputations or spinal cord injuries became depressed and even suicidal afterwards. Similarly, using a longitudinal research design, Leddy, Lambert and Ogles (1994) found that injured athletes showed greater depression and anxiety than athletes in control groups immediately after injury occurrence. Perhaps more significantly, these authors discovered that this disparity in distress was still evident as long as two months later. Overall, Brewer (1999) suggested that between 5 and 13 per cent of injured athletes suffer emotional disturbance of clinically significant proportions. A second general finding in the research literature is that physical trauma appears to be associated with elevated levels of emotional distress. Indeed, such distress has been reported in between 5 and 24 per cent of injured athletes who have been tested (*ibid.*). Nevertheless, Brewer (2001b) urges caution as such evidence does not prove that injury actually *causes* emotional disturbance. The third general finding in this field is that, not surprisingly, the emotional reactions of injured athletes tend to change from negative to positive during the course of their rehabilitation. For example, Quinn and Fallon (1999) administered the POMS to 136 elite injured athletes and discovered that a variety of initially negative emotional states (e.g., anger, depression) decreased significantly over time. In a similar vein, Johnston and Carroll (2000) discovered that the degree of emotional confusion precipitated by injury varied directly with athletes' level of involvement in their sport. Following up athletes at different stages of rehabilitation, they found that those performers who had been more involved in sport and exercise before incurring injury reported higher levels of confusion and lower perceptions of recovery during rehabilitation than did colleagues who had been less involved in their sport. The final general trend in the literature is the surprising discovery that occasionally, the experience of injury may *benefit* the athletes afflicted (Udry, 1999). Among the common benefits cited by athletes in this regard are opportunities for personal growth, development of interests outside sport, and increased motivation (Brewer, 2001b). If viewed constructively, recuperation time from a serious injury may not only allow athletes to learn more about themselves and how their bodies work but may also help them to develop interests outside sport. For example, as indicated by the quote at the beginning of this chapter, Roy Keane, the captain of Manchester United and former captain of the Republic of Ireland, derived considerable benefit from the time he spent in solitary reflection as he recovered from the cruciate knee ligament injury which he experienced in 1998. Commonly, this type of injury is career-threatening as it usually requires reconstruction of the knee and precludes the afflicted athlete from active participation in the sport for up to a year afterwards. To illustrate the severity of this injury, athletes who undergo reconstruction of their anterior cruciate ligament may lose up to 1.5 inches of girth size in their quadriceps muscles – a fact which explains why they have to work so hard in rehabilitation (Smith, Hartman and Detling, 2001). During this rehabilitation period, Roy Keane worked on his upper-body strength in the gym, reduced his alcohol intake and planned his life more effectively (Keane, 2002). A similarly constructive use of injury "down-time" was evident in the case of Robert Pires, the Arsenal and French international soccer player. This player experienced a seven-month injury in 2002 which forced him to miss the World Cup finals in Japan and Korea. During this recovery time, Pires claimed that:

> you see things differently after something like that. Compared to people who have really bad accidents, what happened to me was nothing so at a certain point I need to be aware just how lucky I am. I can keep doing what I've always loved doing . . . Life goes on, I still have two legs, and I'll play again. (cited in Fotheringham, 2002a, p. 3)

Of course, another aspect of athletes' emotional reactions to injury concerns the possible "secondary gains" (Heil, 1993) which they may experience. Specifically, sometimes athletes gain sympathy or social support simply as a result of adopting the role of an injured patient. Ironically, this type of secondary benefit could delay the rehabilitation of the athlete concerned because it encourages him or her to become passive and dependent on others.

Critical evaluation of the grief model

Although the "grief reaction" model of injury seems eminently plausible, it has been criticised on a number of grounds (see reviews by Brewer, Andersen and Van Raalte, 2002; Evans and Hardy, 1995).

First, at a conceptual level, there are obvious and significant differences between the type of loss which people tend to experience when bereaved and those that often follow a physical injury. In particular, while the former loss is irrevocable due to death, the latter loss is usually only a temporary phenomenon. Similarly, if the hypothetical emotional reactions of injured athletes are accepted as facts, certain problems may develop in the patient–physician relationship (Brewer, 2001b). For example, sport medicine specialists may perceive injured athletes as being "in denial" when they have got over the initial feelings of distress that accompany any physical trauma. Therefore, we should be cautious in extrapolating from theories based on terminal illness to the world of sport. Second, researchers disagree about the extent to which the alleged sequence of stages in grief reaction models is fixed. Thus some critics claim that these stages are *circular* rather than linear (Evans and Hardy, 1995). If so, then regression to earlier stages in the sequence may occur among certain athletes. Clearly, this possibility makes it difficult to specify testable predictions from grief reaction models of injury. Third, at least one of the hypothetical stages in the grief reaction may be difficult to measure psychometrically (Udry and Andersen, 2002). Specifically, if "denial" is an unconscious process, how can it be assessed validly using self-report scales or interviews that are limited to experiences that are consciously accessible? Fourth, stage models tend to ignore substantial individual differences between athletes in emotional reaction to injuries (Brewer *et al.*, 2002). For example, although some athletes tend to perceive all ailments pessimistically, others (e.g., Roy Keane, Robert Pires) may view the period of enforced rest that follows an injury as being an opportunity for self-discovery. Similarly, stage theories tend to ignore the mediating influence of situational factors (Brewer, 2001b). Thus the degree of emotional upset caused by an athletic injury appears to depend on such factors as the type of ailment (with acute injuries eliciting greater emotional reactions than chronic injuries) and the stage in the sporting season in which the damage occurs. Clearly, the pattern of emotional reactions displayed by injured athletes varies as a function of individual differences and situational factors. Finally, grief stages models lack a clear specification of the possible theoretical mechanisms by which psychological factors influence athletes' reactions to injury. In summary, psychological research has not supported all of the major tenets of grief reaction stage theories. Therefore, Udry and Andersen (2002) concluded that it is "difficult to make firm conclusions regarding the utility" (p. 539) of these models. Not surprisingly, alternative approaches have been postulated to account for the way in which athletes react to injury. Perhaps the most popular and influential of these approaches are the cognitive appraisal models developed by Brewer (1994) and Wiese-Bjornstal, Smith, Shaffer and Morrey (1998). It is to these models that we now turn.

Cognitive appraisal models of injury reaction

Cognitive appraisal models of injury reaction (also known as "stress and coping" approaches; Udry and Andersen, 2002) are based on the idea that people's emotional and behavioural reactions to any type of physical trauma are determined principally by their interpretation (or "appraisal") of it (Lazarus, 1993). But what exactly does the term appraisal mean? For psychologists, it refers to a subjective interpretation of an event or situation. For example, any everyday experience can be appraised either as a threat or as a challenge. Thus some people get annoyed while queueing in a bank whereas others appear to be immune to feelings of frustration in this situation. This happens, according to Lazarus and Folkman (1984), because of individual differences in cognitive appraisal. Specifically, if people perceive every second spent in a queue as a waste of time, then they are likely to feel stressed by the experience. But if they appraise the same situation more constructively (e.g., "waiting in this queue will give me a chance to slow down, catch my breath and plan the rest of my day"), it will not be as stressful to them. So, for cognitive theorists, stress is trans-actional because it involves two processes: the tendency for people to perceive a situation as a threat to their well-being and also the feeling that they will not be able to cope with its demands. Based on this analysis, two types of appraisal processes may be identified. One the one hand, "primary appraisal" occurs when one decides that because a given situation poses a threat, it requires a coping response. On the other hand, "secondary appraisal" occurs when one asks oneself whether or not one has the ability to cope with the situation in question. In any case, when people perceive an event as a challenge to their abilities, and are confident that they have the sufficient mental resources to overcome it, they tend to react positively to the situation in question.

In general, injured athletes' appraisal processes are believed to be determined by a number of factors. These factors include the amount of previous experience the athlete has had of similar injuries, the adequacy of his or her coping resources, the degree of uncertainty in the situation (e.g., is there much consensus among medical specialists about the nature and prognosis of the injury?) and the amount of perceived control the injured athlete can exert over his or her physical setback. Taking these factors into consideration, appraisal theorists propose that athletes with a history of injuries, a way of looking at things pessimistically and a lack of coping resources will be most at risk for slow recovery from whatever injuries they experience. In summary, cognitive appraisal theorists suggest that the way in which athletes interpret their injury determines not only their emotional response to it but also the degree to which they adhere to prescribed rehabilitation programmes.

Theoretically, the psychological variables which determine an athlete's emotional and behavioural reactions to injury fall into three main categories. First, "personal" factors include such variables as whether or not the performer has experienced a similar injury before, his or her motivation and the way in which s/he typically copes with stress in general. Second, "situational" influences include the level at which the athlete competes, the time of the season in which the injury occurred and the amount of social support available to the injured athlete. Finally, cognitive appraisal characteristics include the athlete's ability to perceive the injury experience as manageable and to identify the specific challenges that lie ahead. Interestingly, there is some evidence that cognitive appraisal is affected by situational factors such as the type of injury incurred by the sports performer. For example, athletes are more likely to experience post-traumatic reactive distress when the injuries are acute, severe and relatively uncommon (Brewer, 2001a). A generic cognitive appraisal model of athletes' injury reactions is presented in Figure 9.2.

According to this model, personal and situational factors interact with cognitive and emotional factors to influence the way in which sport performers respond to injuries. In other words, athletes' emotional reactions to physical trauma are influenced by a combination of "pre-injury" variables such as their history of previous injuries, motivation, and coping skills, and various "post-injury" factors like the way in which they perceive the nature and implications of the injury. This model does not take account of possible gender differences in athletes' reactions to injury, however (see Box 9.4).

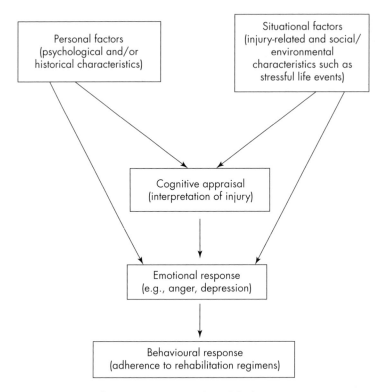

Figure 9.2 Diagram of cognitive appraisal model of injury reaction

Box 9.4 Thinking critically about . . . the role of gender in athletes' reactions to injury

Are there gender differences in the way in which athletes react to injuries? In an effort to answer this question, Granito (2002) interviewed thirty-one intercollegiate athletes (fifteen males and sixteen females) about their experiences of sports injuries. Results revealed differences between the male and female athletes in three key areas. First, the female athletes tended to be less satisfied than their male counterparts with regard to their post-injury relationship with their coaches. For example, many of the female performers felt ignored by their coaches after the injury had occurred. Also, they reported feeling unhappy about an apparent lack of sympathy from their coaches. Second, by contrast with the men interviewed, few of the female athletes in the study felt that they had received sufficient emotional support from their partners, friends and/or from family members. Finally, the female athletes in this study were more likely than the males to express concern over how their injuries might affect their future health.

Critical thinking questions

Are you satisfied that gender differences are the only possible explanation for these findings? If not, what other variables (e.g., the gender of the coach, the nature of the sport) might have affected the results of this study? Given the reliance of this study on retrospective recall by the athletes interviewed, what potential biases could have affected the findings? Also, Granito (2002) acknowledged that the time between injury onset and athletes' interviews was not standardised. How could this factor have affected the results? How could you test the theory that coaches communicate differently with male and female athletes after these performers have incurred injuries?

At the heart of Figure 9.2 is the assumption that injury is a form of stress for athletes. How valid is this assumption? Intuitively, it could be argued that a vulnerability to stress may render athletes susceptible to injury because muscle tension increases the possibility of sprains and other musculoskeletal damage (Gould, Petlichkoff, Prentice and Tedeschi, 2000). Unfortunately, this theory has not been tested adequately so far. Indeed, few researchers have sought to identify the precise theoretical mechanisms by which psychological factors like stress influence athletes' vulnerability to injury. Nevertheless, as we learned earlier in this chapter, there is evidence that certain kinds of life stress are associated with athletic injury. For example, J. M. Williams (2001) observed that athletes who had experienced a relatively high degree of stressful life events were between two and five times more likely to be injured than were athletes who had experienced relatively low levels of such stress. Let us now evaluate the cognitive appraisal model of injury reaction in more detail.

Critical evaluation of the cognitive appraisal model of injury reaction

From a cursory inspection of relevant research literature, it seems that the cognitive appraisal approach to injury reaction has generated more research than its predecessor, the grief stages model. This research may be classified into two categories (Brewer *et al.*, 2002): studies of the aetiology of injuries and research on the role of psychological factors in people's recovery from injuries. These two strands of research converge on a number of conclusions.

First, as predicted by the generic model, stressful life events are associated with increased vulnerability to injury. For example, Bramwell, Masuda, Wagner and Holmes (1975) discovered that the risk of injury to American football players grew in direct proportion to the amount of stressful life events that they had experienced. Similar findings were reported by Cryan and Alles (1983). The results of these studies should be interpreted cautiously, however, because they used retrospective data collection procedures which are vulnerable to memory biases and other cognitive distortions. Second, there is evidence that the way in which athletes think about, or try to make sense of, their injuries is related to their reactions to the trauma (see also Chapter 2 for a discussion of attributional processes in athletes). Specifically, athletes who attribute their injuries to internal factors (e.g., "it was entirely my fault") which have global consequences (e.g., "this injury has ruined my life") tend to experience more distress than do athletes with more optimistic explanatory styles. By contrast, athletes' adherence to physical rehabilitation programmes is associated with attributions to stable and personally controllable factors (e.g., "if I work hard on my exercises every day, I can get back to full fitness soon"). Third, research on the relationship between athletes' coping strategies for stress and the speed and/or success of their physical rehabilitation have produced mixed results. Thus Udry (1997) explored the relationship between injured athletes' coping skills, the social support which they received from others, and their adherence to post-surgery rehabilitation programmes. The injury studied in this research was a cruciate ligament rupture. Results showed that although "instrumental" coping strategies (e.g., attempting to locate as much information as possible about the injury) were related to adherence, social support was not associated with any rehabilitation outcome measures.

Despite receiving reasonable empirical support, cognitive appraisal models of injury reaction have at least two notable limitations. First, these models may be more appropriate in describing athletes' reactions to acute than to chronic injuries (J. M. Williams, 2001). To explain, whereas the former injuries are usually caused by sudden and potentially stressful incidents, the latter have unknown causes and are probably not mediated by stress-related mechanisms. In addition, the profusion of variables included in cognitive appraisal models (see Figure 9.2) makes it difficult to test causal relationships. In short, these models appear to be too all-embracing to serve as heuristic devices for hypothesis testing.

Conclusions about theories of injury reaction

Until the 1990s, psychological understanding of the way in which athletes react to injuries was based largely on intuition and clinical case studies (Udry and Andersen, 2002). Subsequently, this picture changed with the advent of two important theories in this field – namely, the grief stages and the cognitive appraisal models. Having explained these approaches separately in the previous sections, let us consider how they compare?

At first glance, there are certain similarities between these two models. For example, both of them claim that athletes' psychological reactions to injuries vary over time. On closer inspection, however, these models differ from each other in at least three ways. First, whereas grief stages models tend to neglect individual differences between athletes in reactions to injury, cognitive appraisal approaches begin with the assumption that athletes differ considerably in how they perceive and interpret their injuries. Second, whereas grief stages approaches dwell primarily on emotional factors, appraisal models claim that injuries affect athletes also at the cognitive and behavioural levels. Finally, the two approaches differ with regard to postulated theoretical mechanisms. In particular, whereas grief stages models appeal to the mediating influence of constructs such as emotional loss, cognitive appraisal models propose that stress mediates athletes' reactions to injury.

Unfortunately, as both loss and stress are rather nebulous constructs, little explanatory value has been achieved using either of these theoretical models. Despite these criticisms, the grief stages and cognitive appraisal models of injury reaction have been helpful to sport science researchers. Thus Udry and Andersen (2002) concluded that the former approach has been useful in illuminating not only "what" athletes experience after injury but also "when" they do so. By contrast, the cognitive approach may offer investigators some ideas about the reasons why athletes differ from each other in their emotional reactions to injuries.

At this stage, having reviewed available theoretical approaches, we need to consider an important practical question. Specifically, what psychological techniques are useful in facilitating the rehabilitation of injured athletes? In accordance with the theme of this book, we believe that the best techniques are those which combine theoretical rigour with practical utility.

Rehabilitation of injured athletes: from psychological theory to practice

The principal objective of any injury rehabilitation programme is to help the afflicted athlete to return to full fitness and active involvement in his or her chosen sport as quickly and as safely as possible. In order to achieve this objective, a number of theoretically based injury management principles and practical techniques may be identified as follows.

First, the appraisal model of injury reaction emphasises the importance of taking into account cognitive and perceptual factors such as the way in which the afflicted person makes sense of what has happened to him or her. Clearly, a practical implication of this theoretical approach is that athletes' beliefs about the causes and likely course of the injuries from which they are suffering should be addressed explicitly by the treatment specialist. Therefore, as early as possible, incorrect assumptions or naïve theories about the injury should be elicited and challenged. Influenced by this approach, A. M. Smith *et al.* (2001) stressed the need for therapists to convey to their patients an accurate understanding of the nature and prognosis of the injury in question. It is also important for treatment specialists to assess the degree to which injured athletes believe that they can exert control over the pace of the rehabilitation process. The theory here is that the more control that athletes perceive they have over the injury, the more likely they are to take personal responsibility for adhering to the prescribed treatment regime. Conversely, athletes who fail to understand the nature of their injury, and/or who believe that they are helpless to overcome it, will probably take longer to recover from it than will counterparts who have more accurate knowledge about it. In summary, the first principle of injury management is the idea that accurate knowledge and perceived control will help to reduce the stress generated by physical injuries.

Second, based on the grief stages model, it seems likely that afflicted athletes will tend to experience a characteristic sequence of emotional reactions as they work their way through the rehabilitation programme. Therefore, treatment is likely to be more effective if it is matched to the athlete's current position in this emotional sequence. Thus advice such as "cheer up, it could be worse" is ineffective and insensitive if the injured athlete is not ready to accept such comments (e.g., due to the fact that s/he is in the denial stage). The third injury management principle is concerned with the behavioural level of the injury experience. To explain, perhaps the biggest danger for recovering athletes is to make a premature return to their sport. As Robert Pires, the Arsenal and French international soccer star admitted after his long layoff through cruciate knee damage, "you need to be patient, not precipitate your return. You want to come back, that's natural, but it has to be all in good time" (cited in Fotheringham, 2002b, p. 2). Clearly, any unrealistic expectations of an early return to action must be dealt with sensitively during the rehabilitation programme. Therefore, the therapist should try to help athletes to discuss any fears which they may have about their impending return to sport. Interestingly, there is evidence that athletes who are passive and/or unco-operative tend to recover more slowly and less successfully than do athletes who take a more active role in the process. For example, Fisher, Damm and Wuest (1988) studied the differences between athletes who adherered to their rehabilitation programme and those who did not. Not surprisingly, results showed that the "adherers" scored higher on self-motivation and also worked harder to recover from their injuries than did the "non-adherers". A final treatment principle stems from research findings on the importance of helping athletes to develop constructive interpretations of their injuries in order to minimise the stress experienced. The key objective here is to encourage injured athletes to restructure depressive thinking ("this is the end of my career") in more optimistic terms (e.g., "this injury gives me the opportunity to work on my weaknesses").

Turning to practical psychological techniques used in injury rehabilitation, mental practice (see Chapter 5) is an obvious candidate. Thus many applied sport psychologists recommend that injured athletes should be encouraged to "see" and "feel" themselves performing their sport skills fluently and effortlessly. This type of healing-oriented imagery is common in applied sport medicine (Cupal, 1998). For example, in 2002 Jarrod Cunningham, the former London Irish rugby player, was diagnosed with amyotrophic lateral sclerosis (ALS) – a version of motor-neurone disease. One of the methods he used to tackle this condition was imagery. In particular, he claimed that he tried to "visualise sluggish electrons in the brain and spinal cord and to use mental imagery to inject energy and power into them" (quoted in Gallagher, 2002, p. S5). Apart from mental practice, physical relaxation techniques may also be useful in helping athletes to counteract muscular tension experienced in the site of the injury.

In Box 9.5, a number of psychological techniques used in psychological interventions with injured athletes are presented.

Box 9.5 Psychological techniques used in injury rehabilitation programmes

Goal-setting
Working backwards from the long-term goal of recovery from the injury and participation in sport, a number of intermediate stepping-stones to full fitness

should be agreed with the athlete in question. In general, positively phrased short-term goals are recommended to ensure optimal motivation for the daily rehabilitation schedule.

Constructive thinking
Injured athletes should be trained to acknowledge that although their injury is unfortunate and frustrating, it can provide them with an opportunity to take "time out" from their sport in order to rest, clarify their goals and "re-group" mentally.

Positive self-talk
Injured athletes can benefit from talking to themselves encouragingly using such phrases as "I can work out a plan to deal with this problem" or "I've been through situations like this before – this time is no different".

Mental imagery
Injured athletes should be trained to "see" and "feel" their injured limbs performing the skilled actions that they wish to regain.

Relaxation
Training injured athletes to breathe properly and to practise progressive muscular relaxation can be useful in counteracting the stress of injury.

Social support
Injury rehabilitation can be a rather lonely enterprise. Therefore, it is important to help athletes to identify people (e.g., friends, team-mates and family) who can provide support and encouragement during the recovery process. For example, a fit team-mate could attend the rehabilitation session of an injured colleague in order to provide him or her with some advice or encouragement. In general, social support serves as a buffer against the emotional distress typically caused by injuries. A good example here is the support given to each other by two injured French international athletes – the soccer star Robert Pires (Arsenal), who had been out of action for seven months between April and October 2002 due to a cruciate knee injury, and Thomas Castaignède (Saracens), the rugby player who was out for two years due to a ruptured Achilles tendon, before resuming in autumn 2002. Pires visited Castaignède in hospital in Paris and Castaignède visited Pires in London during their long spells of rehabilitation: "When you're injured, there's a certain level where there's not much you can say, it's just a question of being there" (cited in Fotheringham, 2002b, p. 2).

How effective are these psychological techniques when applied to the rehabilitation of injured athletes? Although research evidence on this issue is sparse, some evaluative data are available. To explain, Ievleva and Orlick (1991) studied thirty-two athletes who had attended a sports medicine clinic for rehabilitation treatment for knee and ankle injuries. Results showed that the techniques which were most strongly associated with fast healing were positive self-talk (see also Chapter 4), goal-setting and certain kinds of mental imagery. In a similar study, Davis (1991) evaluated the effects of using relaxation and imagery exercises with collegiate swimmers and football players. Results indicated that there was a 52 per cent reduction in injuries to the swimmers and a 33 per cent reduction in injuries to the football players. More recently, Evans, Hardy and Fleming (2000) used a longitudinal case study approach with three injured rugby players who were each receiving treatment for serious injuries. Results showed that the perceived efficacy of the psychological techniques used depended on the stage at which they were applied. For example, whereas emotional support was perceived as being important to the athletes in the initial stages of rehabilitation, task support was seen as being more useful in the middle to late stages of this process. An interesting feature of this study was that the researchers tackled the neglected question of re-entry for injured athletes. Briefly, they found that two key determinants of successful re-entry were gaining confidence in the injured body part and gaining confidence in overall fitness. Unfortunately, despite the apparent efficacy of many psychological techniques in injury rehabilitation settings, few researchers have explored the possible theoretical mechanisms that underlie these effects. However, one possible mechanism in this regard is self-efficacy. Put simply, these techniques may work simply because they strengthen athletes' sense of personal control over their physical condition. As yet, however, this proposition has not been tested systematically. Even in the absence of theoretical clarity, it is evident from the preceding evidence that effective injury rehabilitation is a collaborative enterprise involving the treatment specialist, the athlete, other health-related professionals (e.g., a physiotherapist, a psychologist), the coach and other significant members of the athlete's life and family. Indeed, research suggests that the importance of these team-members may vary with the stage of athletic rehabilitation in question. For example, Gilbourne and Taylor (1998) suggested that early in the treatment phase, the medical staff and the physiotherapist play a significant role. Later in the recovery process, however, the coach of the injured athlete may assume a special significance as the performer begins to contemplate the possibility of participation in the sport once again.

To summarise, Petitpas (2002) recommended that the following steps are necessary when working psychologically with injured athletes. First, the therapist must attempt to build up a rapport with the athlete in question. To do so, s/he must listen carefully to the athlete in order to find out what the injury means to him or her. The second step involves providing accurate and up-to-date information to the injured athlete on the nature of the injury, the medical and rehabilitation procedures required, and the goals of the rehabilitation programme. The third step of effective counselling for injured athletes involves identifying the nature and types of coping resources available to the athlete. Finally, the therapist and athlete must collaborate in working out specific, relevant and achievable "goal ladders" for the rehabilitation programme (see also Chapter 2 for advice about goal-setting techniques).

Before we conclude this section of the chapter, it might be helpful to read about an actual case study using a psychological approach to injury rehabilitation. This case study is based on the work of R. Cox (2002) and is presented in Box 9.6.

Box 9.6 Thinking critically about . . . a case study of injury rehabilitation in rugby

Recently, R. Cox (2002) reported a case study of the use of psychological techniques to facilitate the rehabilitation of a 21-year-old rugby player who had received a "severe spinal shock" injury during a match. Although this injury did not cause paralysis, it was severe enough to prevent the player from walking unaided for three months after the incident. He had sought psychological help because he had felt cut off from the club and the rest of the team. His goal was to return to pre-season training.

Using a behavioural approach to the problem, R. Cox (2002) developed a programme of activities based on the principle of "successive approximation" whereby the client is required to master a series of graded stages of actions. Initially, he explained to the player that there were at least three different fronts on which progress would have to be made simultaneously: physical (fitness), motor (skill) and psychological. For example, the physical aspect of the programme involved building up fitness in successive stages by adhering to a circuit-training programme involving six exercises (e.g., press-ups, sit-ups) twice a week as well as participating in his regular weekly five-a-side football match. Interestingly, although the programme was successful in helping the player to return to the first team at his club, it took a long time – three years!

Critical thinking questions
Are you surprised at the length of time it took for the rehabilitation programme to be completed successfully? Using a combination of the grief stages model and cognitive appraisal theory, can you think of any other practical strategies that could have been employed in working with this injured athlete?

New directions for research on "mental side" of injuries

At least five new directions can be identified for research on psychological aspects of injuries in sport.

To begin with, given the dearth of prospective studies in this field, Kirkby (1995) and J. M. Williams (2001) suggested that future researchers should use longitudinal designs in order to explore the physical and psychological consequences of rehabilitation programmes for athletes over the course of a competitive season. Of course, these studies would have to ensure that the athletes involved had been matched for age and type of injury beforehand. Unfortunately, most research on the psychological consequences of injury has been hampered by a significant methodological problem – namely, the failure to specify the pre-injury psychological characteristics of the athletes concerned (Quinn and Fallon, 1999). Second, little is known at present about either the nature or efficacy of the coping strategies used by athletes during the course of injury rehabilitation. Therefore, future studies should attempt to establish which strategies are most useful at which stages of physical rehabilitation regimes. Third, in an effort to counteract naïve expectations about the relationship between stress and injury, J.M. Williams (2001) urged future researchers to take into account such potentially important variables as type of sport, competitive level and gender. Fourth, research is required to explore expert–novice differences in injured athletes' "mental models" (i.e., their cognitive representation or understanding) of their problems. This type of research could address several important questions. For example, do elite athletes have a richer or more accurate understanding of their injuries than do less successful counterparts? Also, is there any relationship between the accuracy of athletes' understanding of their injuries and the success of their physical rehabilitation? Qualitative methods (such as "in-depth" interviews and "focus groups") could help researchers to address these questions. Finally, research is needed to establish the degree to which injured athletes can derive any significant benefits from their period of enforced absence from their chosen sports.

Ideas for research projects on injuries in sport

Here are three ideas for possible research projects on the psychology of injury in athletes.

1   Based on a suggestion by Granito (2002), it would be interesting to explore the relationship between gender and the cognitive and emotional reactions of athletes to different types (e.g., acute and chronic) of injuries.
2   Based on the research of Hemmings and Povey (2002), it would be interesting to find out if experienced chartered physiotherapists differ from relatively inexperienced colleagues in their views about the psychological content of their work.
3   Can you think of a way of establishing whether or not there is a relationship between the accuracy of athletes' understanding of their injury and their subsequent compliance with prescribed rehabilitation exercises?

Summary

Injury is an inevitable consequence of regular participation in sport and exercise – especially if vigorous physical contact occurs between athletes. Unfortunately, until relatively recently, little was known about the ways in which sports performers tend to perceive and/or react to the injuries which they experience. Therefore, the purpose of this chapter was to explore the mental side of sports injuries.

*   The chapter began with an attempt to trace the shift from a "physical" to a "mental" perspective on injuries in sport.
*   After that, a brief analysis was provided of the nature, prevalence and causes of athletic injuries. In this section, a number of conceptual and methodological issues were addressed. For example, no clear consensus exists about how to either define or measure the severity of a sports injury. Despite this problem,

two main theories have been postulated to describe how athletes react psychologically to injuries. These theories are the grief stages model and the cognitive appraisal approach.

- After a review of the strengths and limitations of these theories of injury reaction in athletes, I explained some practical psychological strategies used in the rehabilitation of injured athletes.
- After that, several potentially fruitful new directions for research on psychological aspects of injury were outlined.
- Finally, three suggestions were provided for possible research projects in this field.

Glossary

Achievement goal theory (see also "ego orientation" and "task orientation") A theory that postulates two types of motivational orientations in athletes – namely, task orientation and ego orientation – depending on how they interpret the meaning of achievement or success.

Achievement motivation The tendency to strive for success or to expend effort and display persistence in attempting to attain a desirable goal.

Aerobic exercise Physical activities that elevate heart rate and increase the ability of the cardiovascular system to take up and use oxygen.

Anaerobic exercise Physical activities that are relatively high in intensity and short in duration.

Anecdotal evidence Subjective evidence derived from examples or personal experience.

Anxiety An emotional state characterised by worry, feelings of apprehension and/or bodily tension that tends to occur in the absence of real or obvious danger.

Arousal A diffuse pattern of alertness and physiological activation that prepares the body for action.

Attention (see also "selective" and "divided" attention) The concentration of mental effort on sensory or mental events.

Attribution The process of drawing inferences from, or seeking explanations for, events, experiences and behaviour.

Attribution theory The study of people's explanations for the causes of events or behaviour in their lives.

Attributional style The characteristic manner in which people make sense of, or offer similar explanations for, different events in their lives.

Autonomic nervous system (ANS) Part of the peripheral nervous system that regulates the body's involuntary muscles (e.g., the heart) and internal organs.

Biofeedback A technique that allows people to monitor and gain control over certain bodily functions through the use of specialised equipment.

Bio-informational theory of imagery A theory that mental images are not "pictures in the head" but consist of stimulus, response and meaning propositions.

Brainstorming The generation of ideas or suggestions by members of a group in an effort to solve a problem.

Burnout A state of withdrawal from a valued activity that is usually caused by chronic stress and accompanied by feelings of physical and mental exhaustion.

Case study A research method that involves "in-depth" description or detailed examination of a single person or instance of a situation.

Catastrophe theory A theory which postulates that high levels of cognitive and somatic anxiety will produce a sudden and dramatic (hence "catastrophic") deterioration in performance.

Choking under pressure The sudden deterioration of normally expert athletic performance as a result of anxiety.

Chunk A well-learned, cognitive unit of information in memory that may contain several smaller components.

Chunking The process of combining individual items into larger, more meaningful units as an aid to remembering them.

Cognitive anxiety Worry – or having negative expectations about some current or impending task or situation.

Cognitive appraisal (see also "primary appraisal" and "secondary appraisal") The process of interpreting or making judgements about a given event or situation.

Cognitive evaluation theory A theory of motivation which postulates that rewards which are perceived as controlling tend to impair intrinsic motivation whereas those which are perceived as informative tend to strengthen it.

Cognitive processes Mental activities, such as thinking, by which people acquire, store and use their knowledge.

Cognitive restructuring A psychological technique that helps people to change the way in which they think so that they can learn to perceive feared situations as controllable challenges.

Cognitive sport psychology A branch of sport psychology that is concerned with understanding how the mind works in athletic situations.

Cohesion (see also "task cohesion" and "social cohesion") The extent to which a group of people is united by a common purpose and bonds together to achieve that objective.

Concentration (see also "focus") The ability to focus effectively on the task at hand, or on what is most important in any situation, while ignoring distractions.

Confidence (see also "self-efficacy") A belief in one's ability to perform a certain skill or to achieve a specific goal regardless of prevailing circumstances.

Conscious processing hypothesis A theory which proposes that performance may deteriorate when people try to exert conscious control over skills that had previously been automatic.

Construct An abstract or theoretical idea in psychology representing something that cannot be observed directly.

Construct validity The extent to which a psychological test actually measures what it purports to measure.

Controllability The ease with which mental images can be manipulated by the person who experiences them.

Correlational research A research method that measures the relationship or degree of association between two or more variables.

Declarative knowledge Knowledge of facts and rules that can be consciously retrieved and declared explicitly.

Deliberate practice A highly structured, purposeful and individualised form of practice in which the learner tries to improve a specific skill under the guidance of a specialist instructor.

Direction of anxiety The extent to which a person perceives anxiety to be either facilitative or debilitative of his or her performance.

Dispositional attributions Explanations of behaviour that invoke personality characteristics as the causes of a given outcome.

Divided attention The ability to perform two or more tasks equally well as a result of extensive practice.

Drive theory A theory of motivation which suggests that behaviour is fuelled from within by drives stemming from basic biological needs.

Dual-task approach A research method for studying divided attention in which participants are required to perform two tasks at once.

Effect size Statistical estimation of the effect of one variable on anther variable.

Ego orientation A type of motivation in which an athlete perceives success as performing better than others on a given task or skill.

Electroencephalograph (EEG) A neuroscientific technique for recording electrical activity in the brain using special electrodes placed on the scalp.

Electromyographic (EMG) activity A recording of the electrical activity of the muscles.

Endorphin A naturally occurring, opiate-like peptide substance in the brain that serves to reduce pain and increase pleasure.

Endorphin hypothesis The theory that the mood-enhancing effects of exercise are attributable to the effects of endorphins which are released during physical activity.

Event-related potential (ERP) A neuroscientific technique for measuring transient electrical changes in the brain evoked by certain information processing events.

Exercise Planned, structured and repetitive bodily movements that people engage in to improve or maintain physical fitness and/or health.

Exercise dependence (also known as "exercise addiction") A desire for leisure-time physical activity that may result in uncontrollable bouts of excessive exercise.

Experimental research A research method in which investigators examine the effects of manipulating one or more independent variables, under controlled conditions, on a designated dependent variable.

Expertise (see also "deliberate practice") Exceptional skills and/or knowledge in a specific area as a result of at least 10 years of deliberate practice in it.

Extrinsic motivation The impetus to engage in an activity for external rewards rather than for the satisfaction or enjoyment yielded by the activity itself.

Eye-tracking technology The use of special computerised equipment to record and analyse the location, duration and order of people's visual fixations when asked to inspect a given scene.

Fitness See "physical fitness".

Flow states See "peak performance experiences".

Focus See "concentration".

Focus group (see also "qualitative research") A qualitative data collection technique which involves a group discussion led by a trained facilitator and which attempts to understand participants' attitudes, experiences and perceptions of designated ideas or topics.

Functional equivalence theory The theory that mental imagery and perception share similar neural mechanisms and pathways in the brain.

Functional magnetic resonance imaging (FMRI) A neuroscientific imaging technique that detects changes in the activity of the brain by measuring the amount of oxygen brought to a particular location in it.

Goal-setting The process by which people establish targets or objectives to attain.

Grief stages model of injury reaction The theory that athletes react to injury as a form of loss and hence go through a predictable sequence of emotions during their physical rehabilitation process.

Grounded theory A qualitative research method that uses a systematic set of procedures to generate a theory from the data collected.

Group (see also "team") Two or more people who interact with, and exert mutual influence on, each other.

Group dynamics Psychological processes that generate change in groups.

Hardy personality A set of psychological characteristics that appear to protect people against stress by increasing their commitment to, and perceived control over, pressure situations.

Health psychology A field of psychology that is concerned with the promotion and maintenance of health as well as the prevention and treatment of physical illness.

Ideo-motor principle The theory that all thoughts have muscular concomitants.

Idiographic An approach in psychology that emphasises the uniqueness or individuality of behaviour rather than its general principles.

Imagery The cognitive ability to simulate in the mind information that is not currently being perceived by the sense organs.

Individual zone of optimal functioning (IZOF) A theory which suggests that optimal performance in sport occurs within a unique and individualised zone of arousal for the athlete concerned.

Internal consistency coefficient (see also "reliability coefficient") A type of reliability coefficient which assesses the degree to which the items of a test correlate with each other and hence measure the same construct.

Intrinsic motivation The impetus to engage in an activity for internal rewards such as enjoyment or satisfaction.

Inverted-U hypothesis A theory that postulates that the relationship between arousal and performance is curvilinear and takes the form of an inverted U shape.

Ironic theory of mental control A theory which proposes that under certain circumstances, the attempt to consciously suppress a specific thought or action can result in an ironic rebound effect whereby that thought or action becomes even more accessible than before.

Kinaesthetic imagery (also known as "motor imagery") "Feeling-oriented" imagery or the mental simulation of sensations associated with limb positions and bodily movements.

Likert scale A numerical rating scale used in tests or questionnaires in which respondents are required to choose a value that represents their attitude or belief concerning a specific topic.

Mental imagery See "imagery".

Mental practice (see also "imagery") The systematic use of mental imagery to rehearse an action in the mind's eye without engaging in the actual physical movements involved.

Mental toughness Informal term used loosely to describe athletes' resilience, ability to cope with pressure and determination to persist in the face of adversity.

Meta-analysis A technique which enables researchers to analyse and combine the results of a number of separate studies on the same topic in order to determine the overall size of a statistical effect.

Meta-attention People's knowledge about, and control over, their own attentional processes.

Metacognition People's knowledge about, and control over, their own cognitive processes.

Meta-imagery People's knowledge about, and control over, their own mental imagery processes.

Motivation Factors that initiate, guide and/or sustain behaviour.

Motivational climate The type of learning environment which a coach establishes for an athlete – namely, either ego-oriented or mastery-oriented.

Naturalistic observation A research method in which the investigator observes behaviour in its natural setting and attempts to avoid influencing the participants or behaviour being observed.

Neuromuscular theory of mental practice The theory that imagination of any physical action elicits a faint pattern of activity in the muscles used to perform that action.

Neuropsychology The study of the relationship between brain function, behaviour and experience.

Neuroscientific imaging Brain-scanning techniques that produce pictures of the structure and/or functioning of specific parts of the brain.

Neurotransmitter A chemical substance that carries signals across synapses from one neuron to another.

Norepinephrine A type of neurotransmitter in the brain.

Occipital lobe A region of the cerebral cortex at the back of the head that is concerned with visual information processing.

Overtraining Any abnormal extension of the training process that leads to feelings of staleness and fatigue in athletes or exercisers.

Paradigm The detailed framework of principles, theories, methods and assumptions that is shared by a group of researchers in a given field.

Paratelic dominance A state of mind in which the person's behaviour is adventurous, playful and fun-loving.

Parietal lobe A brain region at the top and rear centre of the head which is believed to be involved in regulating spatial attention and motor control.

Pattern recognition tasks An experimental technique used by researchers to investigate expert–novice differences in people's ability to remember briefly presented patterns of information in a particular field.

Peak performance experiences (also known as "flow states") Coveted but elusive experience in sport where an athlete performs to the best of his or her ability mainly as a result of being totally focused on the task at hand.

Performance goals Behavioural outcomes or targets (such as serving accurately in tennis) that are largely under the control of the performer.

Physical activity Bodily movements that are produced by the skeletal muscles and result in the expenditure of energy.

Physical fitness The capacity to respond successfully to the physical challenges of life.

Plasticity A property of the brain that allows it to be moulded by experience and enables it to adapt to and/or compensate for loss of function due to damage.

Positron emission tomography (PET) A neuroscientific imaging technique that measures the metabolic activity of the brain by tracking radioactive substances injected into the bloodstream.

Pre-performance routines Preferred sequences of preparatory thoughts and actions that athletes use in an effort to concentrate effectively before the execution of key skills.

Primary appraisal One's initial perception of a situation as benign, neutral or threatening.

Procedural knowledge Implicit knowledge of how to perform actions and cognitive and/or motor skills.

Protocol analysis A research method which involved recording what people say as they "think aloud" while solving a problem.

Psychometric data Information that is yielded by psychological tests and measures.

Psychometric testing The use of standardised psychological tests to measure people's abilities, beliefs, attitudes, preferences or activities.

Psychophysiology A field of psychology that explores the physiological processes underlying behaviour and experience.

Qualitative research A broad range of data collection techniques used by researchers in an attempt to understand and represent the quality, meaning or richness of people's lived experiences.

Quantitative research A range of research methods which are concerned with measuring and drawing statistical inferences from the data rather than with attempting to understand the subjective meaning or experience of this information.

Reliability coefficient A statistic that is used in psychological measurement to indicate the consistency of a test or the degree to which it can be expected to yield the same results on different occasions.

Response set A tendency to respond to a survey, questionnaire or test in a particular way regardless of the person's actual attitudes or beliefs.

Result goals Behavioural outcomes or targets that can be defined objectively (such as winning a race or defeating an opponent) but which are not directly under one's own control.

Reversal theory (see also "telic dominance" and "paratelic dominance") A theory of personality which suggests that people alternate or "reverse" between paired metamotivational states such as "telic" and "paratelic" dominance.

Saccadic eye movements A series of high-speed, involuntary jumps of the eye which shift people's gaze from one fixation location to another.

Secondary appraisal One's perception of the adequacy of one's personal resources in dealing with a source of stress.

Selective attention The ability to focus on task-relevant information while ignoring distractions.

Self-efficacy People's expectations about their ability to perform a given task.

Self-serving attributional bias A tendency for people to attribute their successes to internal causes and their failures to external causes.

Self-talk The internal or covert dialogue which people engage in when they "talk" to themselves inside their heads.

Sensation seeking A variable which refers to people's need for, and willingness to take risks in pursuing, various novel, complex or adventurous experiences.

Serotonin A type of neurotransmitter in the brain.

Short-term memory See "working memory".

Simulation training The theory that athletes can learn to concentrate more effectively in real-life pressure situations if they have practised under simulated versions of these conditions.

Situational attributions Explanations of behaviour that invoke environmental factors as the causes of a given outcome.

Snooker A game played on a billiard table in which people use a cue to hit a white ball to send 21 coloured balls in a set order into the pockets around the table.

Social cohesion (see also "team spirit") The desire by team members to form and maintain interpersonal bonds.

Social desirability A bias that occurs when people who are answering questions try to make themselves "look good" rather than responding truthfully.

Social facilitation The improvement in people's performance that can occur when they are either part of a group or are being observed by other people.

Social loafing The tendency of people to work less hard on a task when they are part of a group than as individuals due to a diffusion of responsibility.

Sociogram A technique that is used to measure social cohesion by asking group members confidentially to indicate their like or dislike of other members.

Somatic anxiety An unpleasant state of bodily tension that is usually accompanied by increased heart rate, rapid breathing and "butterflies" in the stomach.

Sport and exercise psychology An academic discipline and profession in which the principles, methods and findings of psychology are applied to sport and exercise settings.

Sports injury Any physical or medical condition that prevents an athlete from participating in a training session or competitive encounter.

State anxiety Transient, situation-specific feelings of fear, worry and physiological arousal.

Strategic knowledge The ability to recognise and respond to various patterns of play in a given sport.

Survey research A research method in which questionnaires or interviews are used to obtain information from a sample of people about specific beliefs, attitudes, preferences or activities.

Task cohesion The desire by group members to complete a common task.

Task orientation A type of motivation in which an athlete perceives success as mastering a given skill or task to a self-defined standard of excellence.

Team (see also "group") A task-related group which is characterised by a collective sense of identity and a set of distinctive roles.

Team-building The attempt to improve team performance by developing communication and cohesion among team members.

Team spirit A term that is used loosely to indicate the degree of social cohesion that is apparent.

Telic dominance A state of mind in which a person's behaviour is serious and goal-directed.

Temporal occlusion paradigm A research method in which people are asked to guess what happens next when viewing information presented in slides, film or video.

Ten-year rule The theory that it takes approximately ten years of sustained practice to become an expert in any field.

Thought sampling A research method in which people are equipped with electronic beepers and cued to reveal their thoughts and feelings at specific moments.

Trait anxiety A consistent and pervasive tendency to perceive certain situations as threatening.

Transcranial magnetic stimulation (TMS) A neuroscientific technique in which a high-intensity magnetic coil is placed over a person's skull in an effort to stimulate neural activity in the brain.

Transtheoretical model (TTM) of behaviour change A theory of long-term behaviour change which proposes that people go through certain stages and use certain psychological processes when they attempt to implement relevant intentions.

Trigger words Instructional cues used by athletes and coaches to help them to concentrate on what is most important when executing a skill.

Validity See "construct validity".

Visualisation See "imagery".

Visual search task An experimental technique used by researchers to determine people's speed and accuracy in detecting target stimuli presented in complex arrays containing distractors.

Vividness The apparent clarity, realism or richness of a mental image.

Working memory (see also "short-term memory") Part of the conscious memory system that stores, retrieves and manipulates transient formation for current use – formerly known as "short-term memory".

References

Abernethy, B. (2001). Attention. In R.N. Singer, H. A. Hausenblas, and C. M. Janelle (Eds.), *Handbook of sport psychology* (2nd ed., pp. 53–85). New York: John Wiley.

Abernethy, B., Neal, R. J., and Koning, P. (1994). Visual-perceptual and cognitive differences between expert, intermediate, and novice snooker players. *Applied Cognitive Psychology, 8,* 185–2121.

Abernethy, B., and Russell, D. G. (1987). The relationship between expertise and visual search strategy in a racquet sport. *Human Movement Science, 6,* 283–319.

Abernethy, B., Summers, J. J., and Ford, S. (1998). Issues in the measurement of attention. In J. L. Duda (Ed.), *Advances in sport and exercise psychology measurement* (pp. 173–193). Morgantown, WV: Fitness Information Technology.

Abma, C. L., Fry, M. D., Li, Y., and Relyea, G. (2002). Differences in imagery content and imagery ability between high and low confident track and field athletes. *Journal of Applied Sport Psychology, 14,* 67–75.

Aidman, E. V., and Woollard, S. (2003). The influence of self-reported exercise addiction on acute emotional and physiological responses to brief exercise deprivation. *Psychology of Sport and Exercise, 4,* 225–236.

Ajzen, I. (1988). *Attitudes, personality and behaviour.* Chicago: Dorsey Press.

Ajzen, I., and Fishbein, M. (1974). Factors influencing intentions and the intention–behaviour relation. *Human Relations, 27,* 1–15.

Allen, R. (2000). *The new Penguin English dictionary.* London: Penguin Books.

Ames, C. (1992). Achievement goals, motivational climate, and motivational processes. In G. Roberts (Ed.), *Motivation in sport and exercise* (pp. 161–176). Champaign, IL: Human Kinetics.

Andersen, J. L., Schjerling, P., and Saltin, B. (2000). Muscle, genes and athletic performance. *Scientific American,* September, pp. 48–55.

REFERENCES

Anderson, A. (2002). The Assessment of Consultant Effectiveness instrument. *Newsletter – Sport and Exercise Psychology Section* (The British Psychological Society), *17*, 4–7.

Anshel, M. (1995). Anxiety. In T. Morris and J. Summers (Eds.), *Sport psychology* (pp. 29–62). Brisbane: John Wiley.

Aronoff, S. R., and Spilka, B. (1984–1985). Patterning of facial expressions among terminal cancer patients. *Omega, 15*, 101–108.

Aronson, E., Wilson, T. D., and Akert, R. M. (2002). *Social psychology* (4th ed.). Upper Saddle River, NJ: Prentice-Hall.

Austin, M. (1998). "Geller to bend the World Cup England's way". *The Sunday Times*, 5 April, p. 15.

Azar, B. (1996). Researchers explore why some athletes "choke". *American Psychological Association Monitor on Psychology, 27*, July, p. 21.

Bakeman, R., and Helmreich, R. (1975). Cohesiveness and performance: Covariation and causality in an undersea environment. *Journal of Experimental Social Psychology, 11*, 478–489.

Bakker, F. C., Boschker, M. S. J., and Chung, T. (1996). Changes in muscular activity while imagining weight lifting using stimulus or response propositions. *Journal of Sport and Exercise Psychology, 18*, 313–324.

Bandura, A. (1997). *Self-efficacy: The exercise of control*. New York: W. H. Freeman.

Baron, R. A., and Kalsher, M. J. (2002). *Essentials of psychology* (3rd ed.). Boston, MA: Allyn & Bacon.

Baumeister, R. F. (1984). Choking under pressure: Self-consciousness and the paradoxical effects of incentives on skilled performance. *Journal of Personality and Social Psychology, 46*, 610–620.

Baumeister, R.F., and Showers, C.J. (1986). A review of paradoxical performance effect: Choking under pressure in sports and mental tests. *European Journal of Social Psychology, 16*, 361–383.

Beauchamp, M. R., Bray, S. R., and Albinson, J. G. (2002). Pre-competition imagery, self-efficacy and performance in collegiate golfers. *Journal of Sports Sciences, 20*, 697–705.

Bedon, B. G., and Howard, D. E. (1992). Memory for the frequency of occurrence of karate techniques: A comparison of experts and novices. *Bulletin of the Psychonomic Society, 30*, 117–119.

Begley, S. (2000). "Mind games". *Newsweek*, 25 September, pp. 60–61.

Behrmann, M. (2000). The mind's eye mapped onto the brain's matter. *Current Directions in Psychological Science, 9*, 50–54.

Beilock, S. L., and Carr, T. H. (2001). On the fragility of skilled performance: What governs choking under pressure? *Journal of Experimental Psychology: General, 130*, 701–725.

Beilock, S. L., Carr, T. H., MacMahon, C., and Starkes, J. (2002). When paying attention becomes counterproductive: Impact of divided versus skill-focused attention on novice and experienced performance of sensorimotor skills. *Journal of Experimental Psychology: Applied, 8*, 6–16.

Bent, I., McIlroy, R., Mousley, K., and Walsh, K. (2000). *Football confidential*. London: BBC.

Berger, B. G., and Motl, R. W. (2000). Exercise and mood: A selective review and synthesis of research employing the Profile of Mood States. *Journal of Applied Sport Psychology, 12*, 69–92.

Berger, B. G., and Motl, R. W. (2001). Physical activity and quality of life. In R. N. Singer, H. A. Hausenblas, and C. M. Janelle (Eds.), *Handbook of sport psychology* (2nd ed., pp. 636–671). New York: John Wiley.

Bernthal, P. R., and Insko, C. A. (1993). Cohesiveness without groupthink. *Group and Organisation Management, 18*, 66–87.

Bettenhausen, K. L. (1991). Five years of group research: What we have learned and what needs to be addressed. *Journal of Management, 17*, 345–381.

Biddle, S. J., and Hanrahan, S. (1998). Attributions and attributional style. In J. L. Duda (Ed.), *Advances in sport and exercise psychology measurement* (pp. 3–19). Morgantown, WV: Fitness Information Technology.

Biddle, S. J. H., and Nigg, C. R. (2000). Theories of exercise behaviour. *International Journal of Sport Psychology, 31*, 290–304.

Biddle, S. J., and Mutrie, N. (2001). *Psychology of physical activity: Determinants, well-being and interventions.* London: Routledge.

Biddle, S.J. , Hanrahan, S. J., and Sellars, C. N. (2001). Attributions: Past, present and future. In R. N. Singer, H. A. Hausenblas, and C. M. Janelle (Eds.), *Handbook of sport psychology* (2nd ed., pp. 444–471). New York: John Wiley.

Blair, S. N., Kohl, H. W., Gordon, N. F., and Paffenbarger, R. S. (1992). How much physical activity is good for health? *Annual Review of Public Health, 13*, 99–126.

Blau, E. (1998). "Nervous issues". *The Guardian*, 2 October, pp. 16–17 (Review).

Bloom, B. S. (1985). Generalizations about talent development. In B. S. Bloom (Ed.), *Developing talent in young people* (pp. 507–549). New York: Ballantine Books.

Blumenthal, J. A., O'Toole, L. C., and Chang, J. L. (1984). Is running an analogue of anorexia nervosa? An empirical study of obligatory running and anorexia nervosa. *Journal of the American Medical Association, 14*, 145–154.

Bodin, M., and Hartig, T. (2003). Does the outdoor environment matter for psychological restoration gained through running? *Psychology of Sport and Exercise, 4*, 141–153.

Bond, J. W. (2002). Applied sport psychology: Philosophy, reflections, and experience. *International Journal of Sport Psychology, 33*, 19–37.

Bond, J., and Sargent, G. (1995). Concentration skills in sport: An applied perspective. In T. Morris and J. Summers (Eds.). *Sport Psychology: Theory, applications and issues* (pp. 386–419). Chichester: John Wiley.

Boutcher, S. H. (2000). Cognitive performance, fitness, and ageing. In S. J. H. Biddle, K. R. Fox, and S. H. Boutcher (Eds.), *Physical activity and mental well-being* (pp. 118–129). London: Routledge.

Boutcher, S. H. (2002). Attentional processes and sport performance. In T. Horn (Ed.), *Advances in sport psychology* (2nd ed., pp. 441–457). Morgantown, WV: Fitness Information Technology.

Bozoian, S., Rejeski, W. J., and McAuley, E. (1994). Self-efficacy influences feeling states associated with acute exercise. *Journal of Sport and Exercise Psychology, 16*, 326–333.

Bramwell, S. T., Masuda, M., Wagner, N. N., and Holmes, T. H. (1975). Psychosocial factors in athletic injuries: Development and application of the Social and Athletic Readjustment Rating Scale (SARRS). *Journal of Human Stress, 1*, 6–20.

Brawley, L. R., Carron, A. V., and Widmeyer, W. N. (1987). Assessing the cohesion of teams: Validity of the Group Environment Questionnaire. *Journal of Sport Psychology, 9*, 275–294.

Brawley, L. R., and Paskevich, D. M. (1997). Conducting team building research in the context of sport and exercise. *Journal of Applied Sport Psychology, 9*, 11–40.

Brewer, B. W. (1994). Review and critique of models of psychological adjustment to athletic injury. *Journal of Applied Sport Psychology, 6*, 87–100.

Brewer, B. W. (1998). Introduction to the special issue: Theoretical, empirical and applied issues in the psychology of sport injury. *Journal of Applied Sport Psychology, 10*, 1–4.

Brewer, B. W. (1999). Causal attribution dimensions and adjustment to sport injury. *Journal of Personal and Interpersonal Loss, 4*, 215–224.

Brewer, B. W. (2001a). Emotional adjustment to sport injury. In J. Crossman (Ed.), *Coping with sports injuries: Psychological strategies for rehabilitation* (pp. 1–19). Oxford: Oxford University Press.

Brewer, B. W. (2001b). Psychology of sport injury rehabilitation. In R. N. Singer, H. A. Hausenblas, and C. M. Janelle (Eds.), *Handbook of sport psychology* (2nd ed., pp. 787–809). New York: Macmillan.

Brewer, B. W., Andersen, M. B., and Van Raalte, J. L. (2002). Psychological aspects of sport rehabilitation: Toward a biopsychosocial approach. In D. L. Mostofsky and L. D. Zaichkowsky (Eds.), *Medical and psychological aspects of sport and exercise* (pp. 41–54). Morgantown, WV: Fitness Information Technology.

Brewer, B. W., and Van Raalte, J. L. (2002). Introduction to sport and exercise psychology. In J. L. Van Raalte and B. W. Brewer (Eds.), *Exploring sport and exercise psychology* (2nd ed., pp. 3–9). Washington, DC: American Psychological Association.

Brewer, B. W., Van Raalte, J. L., Linder, D.E., and Van Ralte, N. S. (1991). Peak performance and the perils of retrospective introspection. *Journal of Sport and Exercise Psychology, 8*, 227–238.

Brodkin, J. (2001). "Pumped up for the mind games". *The Guardian*, 14 September, p. 34 (Sport).

Browne, P. J. (2000). "Best of the rest". *The Sunday Tribune*, 21 December, p. 6 (Sport).

Buckworth, J., and Dishman, R. K. (2002). *Exercise psychology*. Champaign, IL: Human Kinetics.

Budney, A. J., Murphy, S. M., and Woolfolk, R. L. (1994). Imagery and motor performance: What do we really know? In A. A. Sheikh and E. R. Korn (Eds.), *Imagery in sports and physical performance* (pp. 97–120). Amityville, NY: Baywood.

Bull, S. J., Albinson, J. G., and Shambrook, C. J. (1996). *The mental game plan*. Eastbourne, East Sussex: Sports Dynamics.

Burton, D. (1989). Winning isn't everything: Examining the impact of performance goals on collegiate swimmers' cognitions and performance. *The Sport Psychologist, 32*, 105–132.

Burton, D. (1998). Measuring competitive state anxiety. In J. L. Duda (Ed.), *Advances in sport and exercise psychology measurement* (pp. 129–148). Morgantown, WV: Fitness Information Technology.

Burton, D., and Naylor, S. (2002). The Jekyll/Hide nature of goals: Revisiting and updating goal-setting in sport. In T. Horn (Ed.), *Advances in sport psychology* (2nd ed., pp. 459–499). Champaign, IL: Human Kinetics.

Burton, D., Naylor, S., and Holliday, B. (2001). Goal setting in sport. In R. N. Singer, H. A Hausenblas, and C. M. Janelle (Eds.), *Handbook of sport psychology* (2nd ed., pp. 497–528). New York: John Wiley.

Burton, D., Weinberg, R. S., Yukelson, D., and Weigand, D. (1998). The goal-effectiveness paradox in sport: Examining the goal practices of collegiate athletes. *The Sport Psychologist, 12*, 404–418.

Butt, J., Weinberg, R., and Horn, T. (2003). The intensity and directional interpretation of anxiety: Fluctuations throughout competition and relationship to performance. *The Sport Psychologist, 17*, 35–54.

Callaghan, P., Eves, F. F., Norman, P., Chang, A. M., and Yuk Lung, C. (2002). Applying the transtheoretical model of change to exercise in young Chinese people. *British Journal of Health Psychology, 7*, 267–282.

Callow, N., Hardy. L., and Hall, C. (1998). The effect of a motivational-mastery imagery intervention on the sport confidence of three elite badminton players. *Journal of Applied Sport Psychology, 10*, 135S.

Camic, P. M., Rhodes, J. E., and Yardley, L. (Eds.) (2003). *Qualitative research in psychology: Expanding perspectives in methodology and design*. Washington, DC: American Psychological Association.

Capostagno, A. (2002). "Wegerle pitches up in a whole new ball game". *The Guardian*, 17 January, p. 31.

Carpenter, W. B. (1894). *Principles of mental physiology*. New York: Appleton-Century-Crofts.

Carr, A. (2004). *Positive psychology*. Hove: Brunner-Routledge.

Carron, A. V. (1982). Cohesiveness in sport groups: Interpretations and considerations. *Journal of Sport Psychology, 4*, 123–128.

Carron, A. V., and Ball, J. R. (1977). Cause-effect characteristics of cohesiveness and participation motivation in intercollegiate hockey. *International Review of Sport Sociology, 12*, 49–60.

Carron, A. V., Brawley, L. R., and Widmeyer, W. N. (1998). The measurement of cohesiveness in sport groups. In J. L. Duda (Ed.), *Advances in sport and exercise psychology measurement* (pp. 213–226). Morgantown, WV: Fitness Information Technology.

Carron, A. V., Bray, S. R., and Eys, M. A. (2002a). Team cohesion and team success in sport. *Journal of Sports Sciences, 20*, 119–126.

Carron, A. V., and Chelladurai, P. (1981). Cohesion as a factor in sport performance. *International Review of Sport Sociology, 16*, 2–41.

Carron, A. V., Colman, M. M., Wheeler, J., and Stevens, D. (2002b). Cohesion and performance in sport: A meta analysis. *Journal of Sport and Exercise Psychology, 24*, 168–188.

Carron, A. V., and Hausenblas, H. (1998). *Group dynamics in sport* (2nd ed.). Morgantown, WV: Fitness Information Technology.

Carron, A. V., Hausenblas, H. A., and Estabrooks, P. A. (2003). *The psychology of physical activity*. Boston, MA: McGraw-Hill.

Carron, A. V., and Spink, K. S. (1993). Team building in an exercise setting. *The Sport Psychologist, 7*, 8–18.

Carron, A. V., Spink, K. S., and Prapavessis, H. (1997). Team building and cohesiveness in the sport and exercise setting: Use of indirect interventions. *Journal of Applied Sport Psychology, 9*, 61–72.

Carron, A. V., Widmeyer, W. N., and Brawley, L. R. (1985). The development of an instrument to assess cohesion in sport teams: The Group Environment Questionnaire. *Journal of Sport Psychology, 7*, 244–266.

Casby, A., and Moran, A. (1998). Exploring mental imagery in swimmers: A single-case study design. *The Irish Journal of Psychology, 19*, 525–531.

Cashmore, E. (1998). "What drove Glenn Hoddle to seek the help of a faith-healer?" *The Sunday Tribune*, 26 April, p. 9 (Sportsweek).

Cashmore, E. (2002). *Sport psychology: The key concepts*. London: Routledge.

Caspersen, C. J. (1985). Physical activity, exercise, and physical fitness: Definitions and distinctions for health-related research. *The Physician and Sportsmedicine, 13*, 162.

Caspersen, C. J., and Merritt, R. K. (1995). Physical activity trends among 26 states, 1986–1990. *Medicine and Science in Sports and Exercise, 27*, 713–720.

Chan, C. S., and Grossman, H. Y. (1988). Psychological effects of running loss on consistent runners. *Perceptual and Motor Skills, 66*, 875–883.

Chase, W. G., and Ericsson, K. A. (1981). Skilled memory. In J. R. Anderson (Ed.), *Cognitive skills and their acquisition* (pp. 141–189). Hillsdale, NJ: Lawrence Erlbaum Associates, Inc.

Chase, W. G., and Simon, H. A. (1973). Perception in chess. *Cognitive Psychology, 4*, 55–81.

Chauloff, F. (1997). The serotonin hypothesis. In W. P. Morgan (Ed.), *Physical activity and mental health* (pp. 179–198). Washington, DC: Taylor & Francis.

Cleary, T. J., and Zimmerman, B. J. (2001). Self-regulation differences during athletic practice by experts, non-experts and novices. *Journal of Applied Sport Psychology, 13*, 185–206.

Clews, G. J., and Gross, J. B. (1995). Individual and social motivation in Australian sport. In T. Morris and J. Summers (Eds.), *Sport psychology: Theory, applications and issues* (pp. 90–121). Brisbane: John Wiley.

Clough, P., Earle, K., and Sewell, D. (2002). Mental toughness: The concept and its measurement. In I. Cockerill (Ed.), *Solutions in sport psychology* (pp. 32–45). London: Thomson.

Coaching Excellence (1996). Mental toughness questions answered: Tim Henman and Greg Rusedski. *Coaching Excellence, 13*, p. 3.

Cockerill, I. (2002). Becoming a sport psychologist. *The Psychologist, 15*, 421–422.

Cohen, J. (1992). A power primer. *Psychological Bulletin, 112*, 155–159.

Coop, R., and Morrice, P. (2002). "Why you choke and what to do about it". *Golf Magazine, 44*, 110–118.

Cooper, T. (2003). "Join the human race". *The Daily Telegraph*, 12 April, p. 15 (Weekend).

Cottell, C. (2003). "Don't stretch". *The Times*, 18 April, p. 9 (T2).

Couture, R. T., Jerome, W., and Tihanyi, J. (1999). Can associative and dissociative strategies affect the swimming performance of recreational swimmers? *The Sport Psychologist, 13*, 334–343.

Cox, R. (2002). The psychological rehabilitation of a severely injured rugby player. In I. Cockerill (Ed.), *Solutions in sport psychology* (pp. 159–172). London: Thomson.

Cox, R. H. (2002). *Sport psychology: Concepts and applications* (5th ed.). Boston, MA: McGraw-Hill.

Crace, R. K., and Hardy, C. J. (1997). Individual values and the team building process. *Journal of Applied Sport Psychology, 9*, 41–60.

Craft, L. C., Magyar, T. M., Becker, B. J., and Feltz, D. L. (2003). The relationship between the Competitive State Anxiety Inventory-2 and sport performance: A meta-analysis. *Journal of Sport and Exercise Psychology, 25*, 44–65.

Cratty, B.J. (1983). *Psychology in contemporary sport*. Englewood Cliffs, NJ: Prentice-Hall.

Cremades, J. G. (2002). The effects of imagery perspective as a function of skill level on alpha activity. *International Journal of Psychophysiology, 43*, 261–271.

Crews, D. J., and Boutcher, S. H. (1986). Effects of structured preshot behaviours on beginning golf performance. *Perceptual and Motor Skills, 62*, 291–294.

Cryan, P., and Alles, W. (1983). The relationship between stress and college football injuries. *Journal of Sports Medicine and Physical Fitness, 23*, 52–58.

Csikszentmihalyi, M. (1975). *Beyond boredom and anxiety*. San Francisco: Jossey-Bass.

Csikszentmihalyi, M. (1990). *Flow: The psychology of optimal experience*. New York: Harper & Row.

Culos-Reed, S. N., Gyurcsik, N. C., and Brawley, L. R. (2001). Using theories of motivated behaviour to understand physical activity. In R. N. Singer, H. A. Hausenblas, and C. M. Janelle (Eds.), *Handbook of sport psychology* (2nd ed., pp. 695–717). New York: John Wiley.

Culver, D. M., Gilbert, W. D., and Trudel, P. (2003). A decade of qualitative research in sport psychology journals: 1990–1999. *The Sport Psychologist, 17*, 1–15.

Cumming, J., and Ste-Marie, D. M. (2001). The cognitive and motivational effects of imagery training: A matter of perspective. *The Sport Psychologist, 15*, 276–288.

Cumming, J., and Hall, C. (2002a). Athletes' use of imagery in the off-season. *The Sport Psychologist, 16*, 160–172.

Cumming, J., and Hall, C. (2002b). Deliberate imagery practice: The development of imagery skills in competitive athletes. *Journal of Sports Sciences, 20*, 137–145.

Cupal, D. D. (1998). Psychological interventions in sport injury prevention and rehabilitation. *Journal of Applied Sport Psychology, 10*, 103–123.

Curtis, R. (2000). Sydney 2000. *The Mirror*, 2 October, p. 29.

Davies, D. (2001). "Relaxed Woods identifies the major pressure points". *The Guardian*, 6 April, p. 26.

Davies, D. (2002). "Els has sights set on Tiger". *The Irish Times*, 2 February, p. 7 (Sport).

Davies, D. (2003). "Psychology forms a closer Love". *The Guardian*, 1 April, p. 30.

Davies, J. (1998). "Time we turned the pitch into a mind field". *The Independent on Sunday*, 25 October 1998, p. 12 (Supplement).

Davis, J. O. (1991). Sports injuries and stress management: An opportunity for research. *The Sport Psychologist, 5*, 175–182.

de Groot, A. D. (1965). *Thought and choice in chess*. The Hague, Netherlands: Mouton.

De Weerd, P. (2002). Attention, neural basis of. In L. Nadel (Ed.), *Encyclopaedia of cognitive science* (Vol. 1, pp. 238–246). London: Nature Publishing Group.

DeAngelis, T. (1996). "Seligman: Optimism can be a vaccination". *American Psychological Association Monitor on Psychology*, *27*, October, p. 33.

DeAngelis, T. (2002). "If you do just one thing, make it exercise". *American Psychological Association Monitor on Psychology*, *33*, July/August, pp. 49–51.

Decety, J., and Ingvar, D. H. (1990). Brain structures participating in mental simulation of motor behaviour: A neuropsychological interpretation. *Acta Psychologica*, *73*, 13–34.

Decety, J., Jeannerod, M., Durozard, M., and Baverel, G. (1993). Central activation of autonomic effectors during mental simulation of motor actions. *Journal of Physiology*, *461*, 549–563.

Decety, J., Jeannerod, M., and Prablanc, C. (1989). The timing of mentally represented actions. *Behavioural and Brain Research*, *34*, 35–42.

Decety, J., and Michel, F. (1989). Comparative analysis of actual and mental movement times in two graphic tasks. *Brain and Cognition*, *11*, 87–97.

Deci, E. L. (1971). Effects of externally mediated rewards on intrinsic motivation. *Journal of Personality and Social Psychology*, *18*, 105–115.

Deci, E. L., and Ryan, R. M. (1991). A motivational approach to self: Integration in personality. In R. Dienstiber (Ed.), *Nebraska symposium on motivation: Perspectives on motivation* (Vol. 38, pp. 37–288). Lincoln, NE: University of Nebraska Press.

Delingpole, J. (2001). "Anything to escape the tyranny of comfort". *The Sunday Times*, 5 August, p. 8 (News Review).

Denis, M. (1985). Visual imagery and the use of mental practice in the development of motor skills. *Canadian Journal of Applied Sport Sciences*, *10*, 4s–16s.

Desharnis, R., Jobin, J., Côte, C., Lévesque, L. and Godin, G. (1993). Aerobic exercise and the placebo effect: A controlled study. *Psychosomatic Medicine*, *55*, 149–154.

Dion, K. L. (2000). Group cohesion: From "field of forces" to multidimensional construct. *Group Dynamics*, *4*, 7–26.

Dishman, R. K. (1983). Identity crises in North American sport psychology: Academics in professional issues. *Journal of Sport Psychology*, *5*, 123–134.

Dishman, R. K. (2001). The problem of exercise adherence: Fighting sloth in nations with market economies. *Quest*, *53*, 279–294.

Dixon, L. (2002). "Wenger's formula based on science". *The Daily Telegraph*, 24 December, p. S2 (Sport).

Dobson, R. (1998). "In the grip of the yips". *The Guardian*, 31 March, p. 16 (Sport).

Doka, K. J. (1995). Coping with life-threatening illness: A task model. *Omega: Journal of Death and Dying*, *32*, 111–122.

Drawer, S., and Fuller, C. W. (2002). Evaluating the level of injury in English professional football using a risk based assessment process. *British Journal of Sports Medicine*, *36*, 446–451.

Dreyfus, H. (1997). Intuitive, deliberative, and calculative models of expert performance. In C. E. Zsambok and G. Klein (Eds.), *Naturalistic decision making* (pp. 17–28). Mahwah, NJ: Lawrence Erlbaum Associates, Inc.

Driskell, J. E., Copper, C., and Moran, A. (1994). Does mental practice enhance performance? *Journal of Applied Psychology*, *79*, 481–492.

Duda, J. (Ed.) (1998). *Advances in sport and exercise psychology measurement*. Morgantown, WV: Fitness Information Technology.

Duda, J. (2001). Goal perspectives research in sport: Pushing the boundaries and clarifying some misunderstandings. In G. C. Roberts (Ed.), *Advances in motivation in sport and exercise* (pp. 129–182). Champaign, IL: Human Kinetics.

Duda, J. L., and Hall, H. (2001). Achievement goal theory in sport. In R. N. Singer, H. A. Hausenblas, and C. M. Janelle (Eds.), *Handbook of sport psychology* (pp. 417–443). New York: John Wiley.

Duda, J., and Nicholls, J. G. (1992). Dimensions of achievement motivation in schoolwork and sport. *Journal of Educational Psychology, 84*, 290–299.

Duda, J., and Pensgaard, M. (2002). Enhancing the quantity and quality of motivation: The promotion of task involvement in a junior football team. In I. Cockerill (Ed.), *Solutions in sport psychology* (pp. 49–57). London: Thomson.

Duda, J., and Whitehead, J. (1998). Measurement of goal perspectives in the physical domain. In J. L. Duda (Ed.), *Advances in sport and exercise psychology measurement* (pp. 21–48). Morgantown, WV: Fitness Information Technology.

Dugdale, J. R., and Eklund, R. C. (2002). Do not pay any attention to the umpires: Thought suppression and task-relevant focusing strategies. *Journal of Sport and Exercise Psychology, 24*, 306–319.

Duggan, K. (2002). "Plunging to the depths of sport". *The Irish Times*, 26 October, p. 8 (Sport).

Dunn, J. G. H. (1999). A theoretical framework for structuring the content of competitive worry in ice hockey. *Journal of Sport and Exercise Psychology, 21*, 259–279.

Dunn, J. G. H., Causgrove Dunn, J., Wilson, P., and Syrotuik, D. G. (2000). Re-examining the factorial composition and factor structure of the Sport Anxiety Scale. *Journal of Sport and Exercise Psychology, 22*, 183–193.

Dunn, J. G. H., and Syrotuik, D. G. (2003). An investigation of multidimensional worry dispositions in a high contact sport. *Psychology of Sport and Exercise, 4*, 265–282.

Durand-Bush, N., and Salmela, J. (2002). The development and maintenance of expert athletic performance: Perceptions of world and Olympic champions. *Journal of Applied Sport Psychology, 14*, 154–171.

Durand-Bush, N., Salmela, J., and Green-Demers, I. (2001). The Ottawa Mental Skills Assessment Tool (OMSAT-3*). *The Sport Psychologist, 15*, 1–19.

Dyce, J. A., and Cornell, J. (1996). Factorial validity of the Group Environment Questionnaire among musicians. *Journal of Social Psychology, 136*, 263–264.

Eccles, D. W., Walsh, S. E., and Ingledew, D. K. (2002). A grounded theory of expert cognition in orienteering. *Journal of Sport and Exercise Psychology, 24*, 68–88.

Economist, The (1999). "Freaks under pressure". *The Economist*, 18 December, pp. 90–92.

Edwards, T., Kingston, K., Hardy, L., and Gould, D. (2002). A qualitative analysis of catastrophic performances and the associated thoughts, feelings, and emotions. *The Sport Psychologist, 16*, 1–19.

Edworthy, S. (2002). "Brazil buoyant in World Cup final rehearsal". *The Daily Telegraph*, 28 June, p. S4 (Sport).

Ericsson, K. A. (Ed.) (1996). *The road to excellence: The acquisition of expert performance in the arts and sciences, sports and games*. Mahwah, NJ: Lawrence Erlbaum Associates, Inc.

Ericsson, K. A. (2001a). Attaining excellence through deliberate practice: Insights from the study of expert performance. In M. Ferrari (Ed.), *The pursuit of excellence in education* (pp. 21–55). Hillsdale, NJ: Lawrence Erlbaum Associates, Inc.

Ericsson, K. A. (2001b). The path to expert golf performance: Insights from the masters on how to improve performance by deliberate practice. In P. R. Thomas (Ed.), *Optimising performance* (pp. 1–57). Brisbane: Australian Academic Press.

Ericsson, K. A, and Charness, N. (1994). Expert performance: Its structure and acquisition. *American Psychologist, 49*, 725–747.

Ericsson, K. A., and Charness, N. (1997). Cognitive and developmental factors in expert performance. In P. J. Feltovich, K. M. Ford, and R. R. Hoffman (Eds.), *Expertise in context* (pp. 3–41). Cambridge, MA: MIT Press.

Ericsson, K. A., Krampe, R. T., and Tesch-Romer, C. (1993). The role of deliberate practice in the acquisition of expert performance. *Psychological Review, 100*, 363–406.

Ericsson, K. A., and Lehmann, A. C. (1996). Expert and exceptional performance: Evidence on maximal adaptations on task constraints. *Annual Review of Psychology, 47*, 273–305.

Eriksson, S-G. (with Willi Railo) (2002). *On management*. London: Carlton Books.

Estabrooks, P., and Carron, A. V. (1999). The influence of the group with elderly exercisers. *Small Group Research, 30*, 438–452.

Estabrooks, P., and Dennis, P. W. (2003). The principles of team building and their application to sport teams. In R. Lidor and K. P. Henschen (Eds.), *The psychology of team sports* (pp. 99–113). Morgantown, WV: Fitness Information Technology.

Etnier, J. L., Salazar, W., Landers, D. M., Petruzzello, S. J., Han, M. W., and Nowell, P. (1997). The influence of physical activity, fitness, and exercise upon cognitive functioning: A meta-analysis. *Journal of Sport and Exercise Psychology, 19*, 249–277.

Eton, D. T., Gilner, F. H., and Munz, D. C. (1998). The measurement of imagery vividness: A test of the reliability and validity of the Vividness of Visual Imagery and the Vividness of Movement Imagery Questionnaire. *Journal of Mental Imagery, 22*,125–136.

Evans, L., and Hardy, L. (1995). Sport injury and grief responses: A review. *Journal of Sport and Exercise Psychology, 17*, 227–245.

Evans, L., Hardy, L., and Fleming, S. (2000). Intervention strategies with injured athletes: An action research study. *The Sport Psychologist, 14*, 186–206.

Evans, R. (2002). "Breaking point". *The Sunday Times*, 19 May, p. 24 (Sport).

Evening Herald (2001). "One Tiger that will never crouch". *Evening Herald*, 9 April, p. 61.

Everton, C. (1998). Six-time champion Davis nervous as ever. *The Guardian*, 21 April, p. 24 (Sport).

Everton, C. (2002). "Ebdon's regime pays off". *The Irish Times*, 8 May, p. 25.

Everton, C. (2003). "Williams' bareknuckle victory". *The Guardian*, 7 May, p. 31.

Every, D. (2002). UEFA pro licence mid season master class. *Insight: The FA Coaches Association Journal, 2*, 1–4.

Eysenck, M.W. (1992). *Anxiety: The cognitive perspective*. Hove, East Sussex: Lawrence Erlbaum Associates Ltd.

Eysenck, M. W., and Calvo, M. (1992). Anxiety and performance: The processing efficiency theory. *Cognition and Emotion, 6*, 409–434.

Fanning, D. (2002). "Coping with a stress factor". *Sunday Independent*, 6 October, p. 6 (Sport).

Feltz, D. L., and Chase, M. A. (1998). The measurement of self-efficacy and confidence in sport. In J. L. Duda (Ed.), *Advances in sport and exercise psychology measurement* (pp. 65–80). Morgantown, WV: Fitness Information Technology.

Feltz, D. L., and Kontos, A. P. (2002). The nature of sport psychology. In T. Horn (Ed.), *Advances in sport psychology* (2nd ed., pp. 3–37). Champaign, IL: Human Kinetics.

Feltz, D., and Landers, D. M. (1983). The effects of mental practice on motor skill learning and performance: A meta-analysis. *Journal of Sport Psychology, 5*, 25–57.

Feltz, D. L., and Lirgg, C. D. (2001). Self-efficacy beliefs of athletes, teams, and coaches. In R. N. Singer, H. A. Hausenblas, and C. M. Janelle (Eds.), *Handbook of sport psychology* (2nd ed., pp. 340–361). New York: John Wiley.

Fenz, W. D., and Epstein, S. (1967). Gradients of physiological arousal in parachutists as a function of an approaching jump. *Psychosomatic Medicine, 29*, 33–51.

Fernandez-Duque, D., and Johnson, M. L. (1999). Attention metaphors: How metaphors guide the cognitive psychology of attention. *Cognitive Science, 23*, 83–116.

Festinger, L., Schacter, S., and Back, K. (1950). *Social pressures in informal groups*. Stanford, CA: Stanford University Press.

Fisher, A. C., Damm, M. A., and Wuest, D. A. (1988). Adherence sports-injury rehabilitation programs. *The Physician and Sportsmedicine, 16*, 47–51.

REFERENCES

Fitness fundamentals (2003, 9 August). *Guidelines for personal exercise programs.* http://www.fitness.gov/fitness.html

Fitzmaurice, A. (2002). "O'Neill ready to answer Ireland's World Cup call". *Evening Herald*, 19 February, pp. 84–85.

Fleming, M. (2003). "Monty, Hugh and Sandra, too". *Daily Express*, 31 January, pp. 72–73.

Flint, F. (1998). Integrating sport psychology and sports medicine in research: The dilemmas. *Journal of Applied Sport Psychology, 10*, 83–102.

Folkins C., and Sime, W. (1981). Physical fitness training and mental health. *American Psychologist, 36*, 373–389.

Ford, I., and Gordon, S. (1999). Coping with sport injury: Resource loss and the role of social support. *Journal of Personal and Interpersonal Loss, 4*, 243–256.

Fosterling, F. (1988). *Attribution theory in clinical psychology.* Chichester, England: Wiley.

Fotheringham, W. (2002a). "Rushed return gives Pires the taste for more". *The Guardian*, 26 October, p. 3 (Sport).

Fotheringham, W. (2002b). "Shared pain that sealed a French connection". *The Guardian*, 26 October, pp. 2–3 (Sport).

Fox, K. R. (2000). The influence of exercise on self-perceptions and self-esteem. In S. J. H. Biddle, K. R. Fox, and S. H. Boutcher (Eds.), *Physical activity and mental well-being* (pp. 78–111). London: Routledge.

Fox, K. R. (2001). Exercise psychology and the world of health services research, policy, and practice. In B. Cripps, S. Drew, and S. Woolfson (Eds.), *Activity for life: Theoretical and practical issues for exercise psychologists* (pp. 35–42). Leicester: The British Psychological Society.

Fox, K. R. (2002). Self-perceptions and sport behaviour. In T. Horn (Ed.), *Advances in sport psychology* (2nd ed., pp. 83–99). Champaign, IL: Human Kinetics.

Francis, S. R., Andersen, M. B., and Maley, P. (2000). Physiotherapists' and male professional athletes' views on psychological skills for rehabilitation. *Journal of Science and Medicine in Sport, 3*, 17–29.

Frost, R. O., and Henderson, K. J. (1991). Perfectionism and reaction to athletic competition. *Journal of Sport and Exercise Psychology, 13*, 323–335.

Funday Times (2002). "Sachin Tendulkar". *The Funday Times* (Supplement to *The Sunday Times*), 678, 8 September, p. 12.

Gallagher, B. (2002). "Cunningham imagines the comeback of his life". *The Daily Telegraph*, 27 November, p. S5 (Sport).

Galton, F. (1883). *Inquiries into human faculty.* London: Dent.

Gammage, K. L., Hall, C. R., and Rodgers, W. M. (2000). More about exercise imagery. *The Sport Psychologist, 14*, 348–359.

Gauron, E. (1984). *Mental training for peak performance.* Lansing, NY: Sport Science Associates.

Gauvin, L., and Rejeski, W. J. (1993). The Exercise-Induced Feeling Inventory: Development and initial validation. *Journal of Sport and Exercise Psychology, 15*, 403–423.

Gauvin, L., and Spence, J. C. (1995). Psychological research on exercise and fitness: Current research trends and future challenges. *The Sport Psychologist, 9*, 434–448.

Gauvin, L., and Spence, J. C. (1998). Measurement of exercise-induced changes in feeling states: Affect, mood, and emotions. In J. L. Duda (Ed.), *Advances in sport and exercise psychology* (pp. 325–350). Morgantown, WV: Fitness Information Technology.

Gazzaniga, M. S., Ivry, R. B., and Mangun, G. R. (2002). *Cognitive neuroscience: The biology of the mind* (2nd ed.). New York: W. W. Norton.

Gilbourne, D., and Taylor, A. H. (1998). From theory to practice: The integration of goal perspective theory and life development approaches within an injury-specific goal-setting program. *Journal of Applied Sport Psychology, 10*, 124–139.

Gill, D. (1980). *Quest: The life of Elizabeth Kübler-Ross*. New York: Harper & Row.

Gill, D. L. (1987). Journal of Sport and Exercise Psychology. *Journal of Sport Psychology, 9,* 1–2.

Gill, D. L. (2000). *Psychological dynamics of sport and exercise* (2nd ed.). Champaign, IL: Human Kinetics.

Gilleece, D. (1996). "Breathe deeply and be happy with second". *The Irish Times, 27* September, p. 7.

Gilleece, D. (1999). "So near and yet so far". *The Irish Times*, 6 July, p. 23.

Gilleece, D. (2002). "When finishing first is all in the mind". *Sunday Independent*, 15 December, pp. 6–7 (Sport).

Glasser, W. (1976). *Positive addiction*. New York: Harper & Row.

Goldenberg, S. (2003). "Footballers who paid the penalty for failure". *The Guardian*, 19 April, p. 6.

Gordin, R. D. (1998). Composure: Arousal and anxiety dynamics. In M. A. Thompson, R. A. Vernacchia, and W. E. Moore (Eds.), *Case studies in applied sport psychology: An educational approach* (pp. 37–62). Dubuque, IA: Kendall/Hunt.

Gordin, R. D. (2003). Ethical issues in team sports. In R. Lidor and K. P. Henschen (Eds.), *The psychology of team sports* (pp. 57–68). Morgantown, WV: Fitness Information Technology.

Gordon, D. (2001). "The dominator". *Newsweek*, 18 June, pp. 60–65.

Gould, D. (1998). Goal setting for peak performance. In J. M. Williams (Ed.), *Applied sport psychology: Personal growth to peak performance* (3rd ed., pp. 182–196). Mountain View, CA: Mayfield.

Gould, D., Damarjian, N., and Greenleaf, C. (2002). Imagery training for peak performance. In J. L. Van Raalte and B. W. Brewer (Eds.), *Exploring sport and exercise psychology* (2nd ed., pp. 49–74). Washington, DC: American Psychological Association.

Gould, D., Dieffenbach, K., and Moffett, A. (2002). Psychological characteristics and their development in Olympic champions. *Journal of Applied Sport Psychology, 14,* 172–204.

Gould, D., Greenleaf, C., and Krane, V. (2002). Arousal-anxiety and sport. In T. Horn (Ed.), *Advances in sport psychology* (2nd ed., pp. 207–241). Champaign, IL: Human Kinetics.

Gould, D., Petlichkoff, L. M., Prentice, B., and Tedeschi, F. (2000). Psychology of sports injuries. *Sports Science Exchange Roundtable, 11,* Number 2.

Granito, V. J., Jr. (2002). Psychological responses to injury: Gender differences. *Journal of Sport Behaviour, 25,* 243–259.

Grant, T. (Ed.) (2000). *Physical activity and mental health: National consensus statements and guidelines for practice*. London: Health Education Authority.

Graydon, J. (2002). Stress and anxiety in sport. *The Psychologist, 15,* 408–410.

Green, C. D. (2003). Psychology strikes out: Coleman R. Griffith and the Chicago Cubs. *History of Psychology, 6,* 267–283.

Greenlees, I., and Moran, A. (Eds.) (2003). *Concentration skills training in sport*. Leicester: The British Psychological Society (Sport and Exercise Psychology Section).

Grimmer, K. A., Jones, D., and Williams, J. (2000). Prevalence of adolescent injury from recreational exercise: An Australian perspective. *Journal of Adolescent Health, 27,* 266–272.

Grouios, G. (1992). Mental practice: A review. *Journal of Sport Behaviour, 15,* 42–59.

Grove, J. R., and Prapavessis, H. (1992). Preliminary evidence for the reliability and validity of an abbreviated profile of mood states. *International Journal of Sport Psychology, 23,* 93–109.

Gruber, J. J., and Gray, G. R. (1982). Responses to forces influencing cohesion as a function of player status and level of male varsity basketball competition. *Research Quarterly for Exercise and Sport, 53,* 27–36.

Gully, S. M., Devine, D. J., and Whitney, D. J. (1995). A meta-analysis of cohesion and performance: Effects of level of analysis and task interdependence. *Small Group Research*, *26*, 497–520.

Guscott, J. (with Nick Cain) (1997). *The Lions' diary*. London: Michael Joseph.

Hagger, M. S., Chatzisarantis, N. L. D., and Biddle, S. J. H. (2002). A meta-analytic review of the theories of reasoned action and planned behaviour in physical activity: Predictive validity and the contributions of additional variables. *Journal of Sport and Exercise Psychology*, *24*, 3–32.

Hall, C.R. (1998). Measuring imagery abilities and imagery use. In J.L. Duda (Ed.), *Advances in sport and exercise psychology measurement* (pp. 165–172). Morgantown, WV: Fitness Information Technology.

Hall, C. R. (2001). Imagery in sport and behaviour. In R. N. Singer, H. A Hausenblas., and C. M. Janelle (Eds.), *Handbook of sport psychology* (2nd ed., pp. 529–549). New York: John Wiley.

Hall, C., Mack, D., Paivio, A., and Hausenblas, H. A. (1998). Imagery use by athletes: Development of the Sport Imagery Questionnaire. *International Journal of Sport Psychology*, *29*, 73–89.

Hall, C. R., and Martin, K. A. (1997). Measuring movement imagery abilities: A revision of the Movement Imagery Questionnaire. *Journal of Mental Imagery*, *21*, 143–154.

Hall, H. K., and Kerr, A. W. (2001). Goal setting in sport and physical activity: Tracing empirical developments and establishing conceptual direction. In G. C. Roberts (Ed.), *Advances in motivation in sport and exercise* (pp. 183–233). Champaign, IL: Human Kinetics.

Hanin, Y. (1997). Emotions and athletic performance: Individual zones of optimal functioning hypothesis. *European Yearbook of Sport Psychology*, *1*, 29–72.

Hanin, Y. (Ed.) (2000). *Emotions in sport*. Champaign, IL: Human Kinetics.

Hannigan, D. (2001a). "Goosen's guru on hot streak". *The Sunday Tribune*, 24 June, p. 4 (Sport).

Hannigan, M. (2001b). "Planet football". *The Irish Times*, 20 August, p. 8 (Sport).

Hanrahan, C., and Vergeer, I. (2000–2001). Multiple uses of mental imagery by professional modern dancers. *Imagination, Cognition and Personality*, *20*, 231–255.

Hanrahan, S. J., and Grove, J. R. (1990). A short form of the Sport Attributional Style Scale. *Australian Journal of Science and Medicine in Sport*, *22*, 97–101.

Hanrahan, S. J., Grove, J. R., and Hattie, J. A. (1989). Development of a questionnaire measure of sport-related attributional style. *International Journal of Sport Psychology*, *20*, 114–134.

Hansen, A. (1998). "Will Shearer be the same?" *The Evening Herald*, 19 January, p. 76.

Hansen, A. (with Jason Thomas) (1999). *A matter of opinion*. London: Bantam Books.

Hanton, S., and Jones, G. (1999). The acquisition and development of cognitive skills and strategies: I. Making the butterflies fly in formation. *The Sport Psychologist*, *13*, 1–21.

Harada, T., Okagawa, S., and Kubota, K. (2001). *Habitual jogging improves performance of prefrontal tests*. Society for Neuroscience Abstracts, program number 311.17, 12 November, 31st Annual Meeting, San Diego, CA.

Hardy, C. J., and Crace, R. K. (1997). Foundations of team building: Introduction to the team building primer. *Journal of Applied Sport Psychology*, *9*, 1–10.

Hardy, L. (1990). A catastrophe model of anxiety and performance. In G. Jones and L. Hardy (Eds.), *Stress and performance in sport* (pp. 81–106). Chichester: John Wiley.

Hardy, L. (1996). Testing the predictions of the cusp catastrophe model of anxiety and performance. *The Sport Psychologist*, *10*, 140–156.

Hardy, L. (1997). The Coleman Roberts Griffith address: Three myths about applied consultancy work. *Journal of Applied Sport Psychology*, *9*, 277–294.

Hardy, L., and Callow, N. (1999). Efficacy of external and internal visual imagery perspectives for the enhancement of performance on tasks in which form is important. *Journal of Sport and Exercise Psychology*, *21*, 95–112.

Hardy, L., and Fazey, J. (1990). *Concentration training: A guide for sports performers.* Headingley, Leeds: The National Coaching Foundation.

Hardy, L., Gammage, K., and Hall, C. (2001). A descriptive study of athletes' self-talk. *The Sport Psychologist, 15*, 306–318.

Hardy, L., Jones, G., and Gould, D. (1996). *Understanding psychological preparation for sport: Theory and practice of elite performers.* Chichester: John Wiley.

Hardy, L., and Parfitt, C. G. (1991). A catastrophe model of anxiety and performance. *British Journal of Psychology, 82*, 163–178.

Harle, S. K., and Vickers, J. N. (2001). Training quiet eye improves accuracy in the basketball free throw. *The Sport Psychologist, 15*, 289–305.

Harlow, J. (1999). "Fear drives actors from the stage". *The Sunday Times*, 14 February, p. 13.

Harwood, C. (2002). Assessing achievement goals in sport: Caveats for consultants and a case for contextualisation. *Journal of Applied Sport Psychology, 14*, 106–119.

Harwood, C., and Biddle, S, (2002). The application of achievement goal theory in youth sport. In I. Cockerill (Ed.), *Solutions in sport psychology* (pp. 58–73). London: Thomson.

Hatfield, B. M., and Hillman, C. H. (2001). The psychophysiology of sport. In R. N. Singer, H. A. Hausenblas, and C. M. Janelle (Eds.), *Handbook of sport psychology* (2nd ed., pp. 362–386). New York: John Wiley.

Hatzigeorgiadis, A. (2002). Thoughts of escape during competition: Relationships with goal orientation and self-consciousness. *Psychology of Sport and Exercise, 3*, 195–207.

Hatzigeorgiadis, A., and Biddle, S. J. H. (2000). Assessing cognitive interference in sport: Development of the Thought Occurrence Questionnaire for Sport. *Anxiety, Stress, and Coping, 13*, 65–86.

Hausenblas, H. A., Carron, A. V., and Mack, D. E. (1997). Application of the theories of reasoned action and planned behaviour to exercise behaviour: A meta-analysis. *Journal of Sport and Exercise Psychology, 19*, 36–51.

Hausenblas, H. A., and Downs, D. S. (2002). Exercise dependence: A systematic review. *Psychology of Sport and Exercise, 3*, 89–123.

Hausenblas, H. A., Hall, C. R., Rodgers, W. M., and Munroe, K. J. (1999). Exercise imagery: Its nature and measurement. *Journal of Applied Sport Psychology, 11*, 171–180.

Hayes, J. (1985). Three problems in teaching general skills. In J. Segal, S. Chipman, and R. Glaser (Eds.), *Thinking and learning skills, Vol. 2: Research and open questions* (pp. 391–406). Hillsdale, NJ: Lawrence Erlbaum Associates, Inc.

Hecker, J. E., and Kaczor, L. M. (1988). Application of imagery theory to sport psychology: Some preliminary findings. *Journal of Sport and Exercise Psychology, 10*, 363–373.

Heider, F. (1958). *The psychology of interpersonal relations.* New York: John Wiley.

Heil, J. (1993). *Psychology of sport injury.* Champaign, IL: Human Kinetics.

Helsen, W. E., and Starkes, J. L. (1999). A multidimensional approach to skilled perception and performance in sport. *Applied Cognitive Psychology, 13*, 1–27.

Helsen, W., Starkes, J., and Hodges, N. J. (1998). Team sports and the theory of deliberate practice. *Journal of Sport and Exercise Psychology, 20*, 12–34.

Hemmings, B., and Povey, L. (2002). Views of chartered physiotherapists on the psychological content of their practice: A preliminary study in the United Kingdom. *British Journal of Sports Medicine, 36*, 61–64.

Henderlong, J., and Lepper, M. R. (2002). The effects of praise on children's intrinsic motivation: A review and synthesis. *Psychological Bulletin, 128*, 774–795.

Herbert, R. D., Dean, C., and Gandevia, S. C. (1998). Effects of real and imagined training on voluntary muscle activation during maximal isometric contractions. *Acta Physiologica Scandinavica, 163*, 361–368.

Herbert, R. D., and Gabriel, M. (2002). Effects of stretching before and after exercising on muscle soreness and risk of injury: Systematic review. *British Medical Journal, 325*, 468–470.

Heuzé, J-P., and Fontayne, P. (2002). Questionnaire sur l'Ambiance du Groupe: A French-language instrument for measuring group cohesion. *Journal of Sport and Exercise Psychology, 24*, 42–67.

Highfield, R. (2002). "Scientists discover what puts you in the mood for dancing". *The Daily Telegraph*, 19 September, p. 4.

Hoberman, J. D. (1992). *Mortal engines: The science of performance and the dehumanization of sport*. New York: The Free Press.

Hodge, K. (1995). Team dynamics. In T. Morris and J. Summers (Eds.), *Sport psychology: Theory, application and issues* (pp. 190–212). Brisbane: John Wiley.

Hodge, K., and McKenzie, A. (1999). *Thinking rugby: Training your mind for peak performance*. Auckland, New Zealand: Reed.

Hodges, N., and Starkes J. L. (1996). Wrestling with the nature of expertise: A sport specific test of Ericsson, Krampe and Tesch-Romer's theory of deliberate practice. *International Journal of Sport Psychology, 27*, 1–25.

Hodgkinson, M. (2002). "The top 10 worst sporting excuses". *The Sunday Times*, 6 October, p. 24 (Sport).

Hoey, K. (2002). "UK is still way behind when it comes to sports medicine". *The Daily Telegraph*, 18 November, p. S7 (Sport).

Hoffmann, P. (1997). The endorphin hypothesis. In W. P. Morgan (Ed.), *Physical activity and mental health* (pp. 163–177). Washington, DC: Taylor & Francis.

Holmes, P., and Collins, D. (2002). Functional equivalence solutions for problems with motor imagery. In I. Cockerill (Ed.), *Solutions in sport psychology* (pp. 120–140). London: Thomson.

Holmes, T.H., and Rahe, R. H. (1967). The Social and Readjustment Rating Scale. *Journal of Psychosomatic Research, 11*, 213–218.

Holt, N. L., and Sparkes, A. C. (2001). An ethnographic study of cohesiveness in a college soccer team over a season. *The Sport Psychologist, 15*, 237–259.

Hooper, S. L., Traeger Mackinnon, L., Gordon, R. D., and Bachmann, A. W. (1993). Hormonal responses of elite swimmers to overtraining. *Medicine and Science in Sports and Exercise, 25*, 741–747.

Hopps, D. (2002). "It's official: England's injuries are the worst in the world". *The Guardian*, 3 September, p. 22.

Horwood, J. (2002). "Sick of work? Bingo!" *The Psychologist, 15*, p. 544.

Hudson, J., and Walker, N. C. (2002). Metamotivational state reversals during matchplay golf: An idiographic approach. *The Sport Psychologist, 16*, 200–217.

Hughes. S. (2002). "Darts feels the power of Taylor's tungsten". *The Daily Telegraph*, 7 January, p. S7 (Sports).

Hull, C. L. (1943). *Principles of behaviour*. New York: Appleton-Century-Crofts.

Hunt, M. (1997). *How science takes stock: The story of meta-analysis*. New York: Russell Sage Foundation.

Hurley, O. (2003). *Psychological understanding of, and responses to, sporting injuries in elite athletes*. Unpublished Ph.D thesis, Department of Psychology, University College, Dublin.

Hyllegard, R. (1991). The role of baseball seam pattern in pitch recognition. *Journal of Sport and Exercise Psychology, 13*, 80–84.

Ievleva, L., and Orlick, T. (1991). Mental links to enhanced healing: An exploratory study. *The Sport Psychologist, 5*, 25–40.

Isaac, A. (1992). Mental practice: Does it work in the field? *The Sport Psychologist, 6*, 192–198.

Isaac, A., Marks, D., and Russell, E. (1986). An instrument for assessing imagery of movement:

The Vividness of Movement Imagery Questionnaire (VMIQ). *Journal of Mental Imagery, 10,* 23–30.

Jackson, R. C., and Baker, J. S. (2001). Routines, rituals, and rugby: Case study of a world class goal kicker. *The Sport Psychologist, 15,* 48–65.

Jackson, S. A. (1995). Factors influencing the occurrence of flow state in elite athletes. *Journal of Applied Sport Psychology, 7,* 138–166.

Jackson, S. A. (1996). Toward a conceptual understanding of the flow experience in elite athletes. *Research Quarterly for Exercise and Sport, 67,* 76–90.

Jackson, S. A., and Eklund, R. C. (2002). Assessing flow in physical activity: The Flow State Scale-2 and Dispositional Flow Scale-2. *Journal of Sport and Exercise Psychology, 24,* 133–150.

Jackson, S. A., and Roberts, G. C. (1992). Positive performance states of athletes: Toward a conceptual understanding of peak performance. *The Sport Psychologist, 6,* 156–171.

Jackson, S. A., Thomas, P. R., Marsh, H. W., and Smethurst, C. J. (2001). Relationships between flow, self-concept, psychological skills, and performance. *Journal of Applied Sport Psychology, 13,* 129–153.

Jacob, G. (2003). "The game". *The Times,* 19 May, p. 5.

Jacobson, E. (1932). Electrophysiology of mental activities. *American Journal of Psychology, 44,* 677–694.

Jago, R. (2002). "Interview: Jelena Dokic". *The Guardian* (Sport), 17 June, pp. 18–19.

James, D. (2003). "I am ready and able to handle the real thing". *The Times,* 22 March, p. 36 (Sport).

James, W. (1890). *Principles of psychology.* New York: Holt, Rinehart & Winston.

James, W. (1899). *Talks to teachers on psychology: And to students on some of life's ideals.* New York: H. Holt.

Janelle, C. M. (1999). Ironic mental processes in sport: Implications for sport psychologists. *The Sport Psychologist, 13,* 201–220.

Janelle, C. M. (2002). Anxiety, arousal and visual attention: A mechanistic account of performance variability. *Journal of Sports Sciences, 20,* 237–251.

Janelle, C. M., Singer, R. N., and Williams, A. M. (1999). External distractions and attentional narrowing: Visual search evidence. *Journal of Sport and Exercise Psychology, 21,* 70–91.

Johnston, L., and Carroll, D. (2000). The psychological impact of injury: Effects of prior sport and exercise involvement. *British Journal of Sports Medicine, 34,* 436–439.

Jones, G. (1995). More than just a game: Research developments and issues in competitive anxiety in sport. *British Journal of Psychology, 86,* 449–478.

Jones, G., and Hanton, S. (2001). Pre-competitive feeling states and directional anxiety interpretations. *Journal of Sports Sciences, 19,* 385–395.

Jones, G., Hanton, S., and Swain, A. B. J. (1994). Intensity and interpretation of anxiety symptoms in elite and non-elite sports performers. *Personality and Individual Differences, 17,* 756–663.

Jones, G., Hanton, S., and Connaughton, D. (2002). What is this thing called mental toughness? An investigation of elite sport performers. *Journal of Applied Sport Psychology, 14,* 205–218.

Jones, G., and Swain, A. B. J. (1992). Intensity and direction as dimensions of competitive state anxiety and relationships with competitiveness. *Perceptual and Motor Skills, 74,* 467–472.

Jones, G., and Swain, A. B. J. (1995). Predispositions to experience debilitative and facilitative anxiety in elite and non-elite performers. *The Sport Psychologist, 9,* 201–211.

Jones, M. V., and Uphill, M. (2003, in press). Responses to the Competitive State Anxiety Inventory-2(d) by athletes in anxious and excited scenarios. *Psychology of Sport and Exercise.*

Jones, R. T. (2002). "Golden moment as Lynch storms to glory". *Irish Independent*, 23 September, p. 15 (Sport).

Jones, S. (1995). "Inside the mind of perfection". *The Independent*, 11 December 1995, p. 10.

Jones, S. (1997). "Seigne's only song: Je ne regrette rien". *The Sunday Times*, 5 October, p. 14 (Sport Section).

Junge, A., and Dvorak, J. (2000). Influence of definition and data collection on the incidence of injuries in football. *American Journal of Sports Medicine, 28*, 540–546.

Kahneman, D. (1973). *Attention and effort*. New York: Prentice-Hall.

Keane, R. (with Eamon Dunphy) (2002). *Keane: The autobiography*. London: Michael Joseph.

Keefe, R. (2003). *On the sweet spot: Stalking the effortless present*. New York: Simon & Schuster.

Kelly, L. (2002). "Professional injuries on the increase as stars' fitness regimes get tougher". *The Irish Independent*, 21 January, p. 11 (Sport).

Kerr, G. A., and Miller, P. S. (2001). Coping strategies. In J. Crossman (Ed.), *Coping with sports injuries: Psychological strategies for rehabilitation* (pp. 83–102). Oxford: Oxford University Press.

Kerr, J. H. (1997). *Motivation and emotion in sport: Reversal theory*. Hove, East Sussex: Psychology Press.

Kervin, A. (2001). "The power and the glory". *The Times* (Sport), 7 August, p. S6.

Kimiecik, J. C., and Jackson, S. A. (2002). Optimal experience in sport: A flow perspective. In T. S. Horn (Ed.), *Advances in sport psychology* (2nd ed., pp. 501–527). Champaign, IL: Human Kinetics.

Kimmage, P. (1998). "I could almost tell the ball where to go". *Sunday Independent*, 24 May, p. 29L.

Kingston, K. M., and Hardy, L. (1997). Effects of different types of goals on processes that support performance. *The Sport Psychologist, 11*, 277–293.

Kirkby, R. (1995). Psychological factors in sport injuries. In T. Morris and J. Summers (Eds.), *Sport psychology: Theory, applications and issues* (pp. 456–473). Brisbane: Wiley.

Kirkendall, D. T., and Garrett, W. E. (2001). Heading in soccer: Integral skill or grounds for cognitive dysfunction? *Journal of Athletic Training. Special issue: Concussion in athletes, 36*, 328–333.

Kirkendall, D. T., Jordan, S. E., and Garrett, W. E. (2001). Heading and head injuries in soccer. *Sports Medicine, 31*, 369–386.

Kishi, Y., Robinson, R. G., and Forrester, A. W. (1994). Prospective longitudinal study of depression following spinal cord injury. *Journal of Neuropsychiatry and Clinical Neuroscience, 6*, 237–244.

Klavora, P. (1978). An attempt to derive inverted-U curves based on the relationship between anxiety and athletic performance. In D. M. Landers and R. W. Christina (Eds.), *Psychology of motor behaviour and sport* (Vols. 1 and 11, pp. 369–377). Champaign, IL: Human Kinetics.

Klein, M., and Christiansen, G. (1969). Group composition, group structure and group effectiveness of basketball teams. In J. W. Loy and G. S. Kenyon (Eds.), *Sport, culture, and society* (pp. 397–408). London: Macmillan.

Knowles, E. (Ed.) (1999). *The Oxford dictionary of quotations* (5th ed.). Oxford: Oxford University Press.

Kobasa, S. C. (1979). Stressful life events, personality, and health: An inquiry into hardiness. *Journal of Personality and Social Psychology, 37*, 1–11.

Kohl, R. M., and Roenker, D. L. (1980). Bilateral transfer as a function of mental imagery. *Journal of Motor Behaviour, 12*, 197–206.

Kohl, R. M., and Roenker, D. L. (1983). Mechanism involvement during skill imagery. *Journal of Motor Behaviour, 15*, 179–190.

Kolb, B., and Whishaw, I. Q. (2003). *Fundamentals of human neuropsychology* (5th ed.). New York: Worth Publishers.

Kosslyn, S. M. (1994). *Image and brain: The resolution of the imagery debate*. Cambridge, MA: MIT Press.

Kosslyn, S. M., Ganis, G., and Thompson, W. L. (2001). Neural foundations of imagery. *Nature Reviews: Neuroscience, 2*, 635–642.

Kosslyn, S. M., Ganis, G., and Thompson, W. L. (2003). Mental imagery: Against the nihilistic hypothesis. *Trends in Cognitive Sciences, 7*, 109–111.

Kosslyn, S. M., Seger, C., Pani, J. R., and Hillger, L. A. (1990). When is imagery used in everyday life? A diary study. *Journal of Mental Imagery, 14*, 131–152.

Kowler, E. (1999). Eye movements and visual attention. In R. A. Wilson and F. C Keil (Eds.), *The MIT encyclopaedia of the cognitive sciences* (pp. 306–309). Cambridge, MA: MIT Books.

Krane, V. (1994). The Mental Readiness Form as a measure of competitive state anxiety. *The Sport Psychologist, 8*, 189–202.

Krane, V., Greenleaf, C. A., and Snow, J. (1997). Reaching for gold and the price of glory: A motivational case study of an elite gymnast. *The Sport Psychologist, 11*, 53–71.

Kremer, J., and Busby, G. (1998). Modelling participant motivation in sport and exercise: An integrative approach. *The Irish Journal of Psychology, 19*, 447–463.

Kremer, J., and Scully, D. (1994). *Psychology in sport*. London: Taylor & Francis.

Kremer, J., and Scully, D. (1998). What applied sport psychologists often don't do: On empowerment and independence. In H. Steinberg, I. Cockerill and A. Dewey (Eds.), *What sport psychologists do* (pp. 21–27). Leicester: The British Psychological Society (Sport and Exercise Psychology Section).

Kremer, J., and Scully, D. (2002). "The team just hasn't gelled". In I. Cockerill (Ed.), *Solutions in sport psychology* (pp. 3–15). London: Thomson.

Kremer, J., Sheehy, N., Reilly, J., Trew, K., and Muldoon, O. (2003). *Applying social psychology*. Basingstoke, Hampshire: Palgrave Macmillan.

Kübler-Ross, E. (1969). *On death and dying*. New York: Macmillan.

Kujala, U. M. (2002). Injury prevention. In D. L. Mostofsky and L. D. Zaichowsky (Eds.), *Medical and psychological aspects of sport and exercise* (pp. 33–40). Morgantown, WV: Fitness Information Technology.

Kyllo, L. B., and Landers, D. M. (1995). Goal-setting in sport and exercise: A research synthesis to resolve the controversy. *Journal of Sport and Exercise Psychology, 17*, 117–137.

Lacey, D. (1998). "Owen gets England nod ahead of Fowler". *The Guardian*, 3 February, p. 24.

Land, M. F., and McLeod, P. (2000). From eye movements to actions: How batsmen hit the ball. *Nature Neuroscience, 3*, 1340–1345.

Landers, D. M., and Arent, S. M. (2001). Physical activity and mental health. In R. N. Singer, H. A. Hausenblas, and C. M. Janelle (Eds.), *Handbook of sport psychology* (2nd ed., pp. 740–765). New York: John Wiley.

Landers, D. M., and Boutcher, S. H. (1998). Arousal-performance relationships. In J. M. Williams (Ed.), *Applied sport psychology: Personal growth to peak performance*. (3rd ed., pp. 197–218). Mountain View, CA: Mayfield.

Landers, D. M., and Luschen, G. (1974). Team performance outcome and cohesiveness of competitive coacting groups. *International Review of Sport Sociology, 9*, 57–71.

Landers, D.M., Qi, W.M., and Courtet, P. (1985). Peripheral narrowing among experienced and inexperienced rifle-shooters under low- and high-stress conditions. *Research Quarterly for Exercise and Sport, 56*, 122–130.

Landin, D., and Herbert, E. P. (1999). The influence of self-talk on the performance of skilled female tennis players. *Journal of Applied Sport Psychology, 11*, 263–282.

Lang, P. J. (1977). Imagery in therapy: An information-processing analysis of fear. *Behaviour Therapy, 8*, 862–886.

Lang, P. J. (1979). A bio-informational theory of emotional imagery. *Psychophysiology, 17*, 495–512.

Lang., P., Greenwald, M. K., Bradley, M. M., and Hamm, O. (1993). Looking at pictures: Affective, facial, visceral and behavioural reactions. *Psychophysiology, 30*, 261–273.

Lang, P., Kozak, M., Miller, G. A., Levin, D. N., and McLean, A. (1980). Emotional imagery: Conceptual structure and pattern of somato-visceral response. *Psychophysiology, 17*, 179–192.

Larson, G. A., Starkey, C., and Zaichkowsky, L. D. (1996). Psychological aspects of athletic injuries as perceived by athletic trainers. *The Sport Psychologist, 10*, 37–47.

Lashley, K. (1915). The acquisition of skill in archery. *Carnegie Institutions Publications, 7*, 107–128.

Lau, R. R., and Russell, D. (1980). Attributions in the sports pages: A field test of some current hypotheses about attribution research. *Journal of Personality and Social Psychology, 39*, 29–38.

Laurence, J. (1998). "A saunter for champs". *Irish Independent*, 1 July, p. 23.

Lavallee, D., and Cockerill, I. (Eds.) (2002). *Counselling in sport and exercise contexts.* Leicester: The British Psychological Society (Sport and Exercise Psychology Section).

Lavallee, D., Grove, J. R., Gordon S., and Ford, I. W. (1998). The experience of loss in sport. In J. H. Harvey (Ed.), *Perspectives on loss: A sourcebook* (pp. 241–252). Philadelphia: Brunner/Mazel.

Lavallee, D., Kremer, J., Moran, A., and Williams, M. (2004). *Sport psychology: Contemporary themes.* Basingstoke, Hampshire: Palgrave Macmillan.

Lawlor, D. A., and Hopker, S. W. (2001). The effectiveness of exercise as an intervention in the management of depression: Systematic review and meta-regression analysis of randomised controlled trials. *British Medical Journal, 322*, 1–8.

Lazarus, R. S. (1993). From psychological stress to the emotions: A history of changing outlooks. *Annual Review of Psychology, 44*, 1–21.

Lazarus, R. S., and Folkman, S. (1984). *Stress, appraisal, and coping.* New York: Springer.

Leddy, M. H., Lambert, M. J., and Ogles, B. M. (1994). Psychological consequences of athletic injury among high-level competitors. *Research Quarterly for Exercise and Sport, 65*, 347–354.

Lee, A. J., Garraway, W. M., Hepburn, W., and Laidlaw, R. (2001). Influence of rugby injuries on players' subsequent health and lifestyle: Beginning a long term follow up. *British Journal of Sports Medicine, 35*, 38–42.

Lehmann, A. C., and Ericsson, K. A. (2002). Expertise. In L. Nadel (Ed.), *Encyclopaedia of cognitive science* (Vol. 2, pp. 79–85). London: Nature Publishing Group.

Lejeune, M., Decker, C., and Sanchez, X. (1994). Mental rehearsal in table tennis performance. *Perceptual and Motor Skills, 79*, 627–641.

Lemyre, P-N., Roberts, G. C., and Ommundsen, Y. (2002). Achievement goal orientations, perceived ability, and sportspersonship in youth soccer. *Journal of Applied Sport Psychology, 14*, 120–136.

Lenk, H. (1969). Top performance despite internal conflict: An antithesis to a functionalist proposition. In J. W. Loy and G. S. Kenyon (Eds.), *Sport, culture, and society: A reader on the sociology of sport* (pp. 393–396). Toronto: Collier Macmillan.

Lenk, H. (1977). *Team dynamics.* Champaign, IL: Stipes.

LeUnes, A., and Nation, J. R. (2002). *Sport psychology* (3rd ed.). Pacific Grove, CA: Wadsworth.

Lewin, K. (1935). *A dynamic theory of personality.* New York: McGraw-Hill.

Li, F., and Harmer, P. (1996). Confirmatory factor analysis of the Group Environment Questionnaire with an intercollegiate sample. *Journal of Sport and Exercise Psychology, 18*, 49–63.

Liao, C-M., and Masters, R. S. W. (2002). Self-focused attention and performance failure under psychological stress. *Journal of Sport and Exercise Psychology, 24*, 289–305.

Lidor, R., and Singer, R. N. (2003). Preperformance routines in self-paced tasks: Developmental and educational considerations. In R. Lidor and K. P. Henschen (Eds.), *The psychology of team sports* (pp. 69–98). Morgantown, WV: Fitness Information Technology.

Lippke, S., Knäuper, B., and Fuchs, B. (2003). Subjective theories of exercise course instructors: Causal attributions for dropouts in health and leisure exercise programmes. *Psychology of Sport and Exercise, 4*, 155–173.

Locke, E. A. (1991). Problems with goal-setting research in sports – and their solution. *Journal of Sport and Exercise Psychology, 8*, 311–316.

Locke, E. A., and Latham, G. P. (1985). The application of goal setting to sports. *Journal of Sport Psychology, 7*, 205–222.

Locke, E. A., and Latham, G. P. (1990). *A theory of goal setting and task performance.* Englewood Cliffs, NJ: Prentice-Hall.

Locke, E. A., and Latham, G. P. (2002). Building a practically useful theory of goal setting and task motivation. *American Psychologist, 57*, 705–717.

Locke, E. A., Shaw, K. N., Saari, L. M., and Latham, G. P. (1981). Goal setting and task performance: 1969–1980. *Psychological Bulletin, 90*, 125–152.

Logie, R. H. (1999). Working memory. *The Psychologist, 12*, 174–178.

Long, B. C., and van Stavel, R. (1995). Effects of exercise training on anxiety: A meta-analysis. *Journal of Applied Sport Psychology, 7*, 167–189.

Lutz, R. S. (2003). Covert muscle excitation is outflow from the central generation of motor imagery. *Behavioural Brain Research, 140*, 149–163.

MacGinty, K. (2002). "Blind fear of Ryder rookies", *Irish Independent*, 26 September, p. 19.

MacIntyre, T. (1996). *Imagery validation: How do we know that athletes are imaging during mental practice?* Unpublished MA thesis, Department of Psychology, University College, Dublin.

MacMahon, K. M. A., and Masters, R. S. W. (2002). The effects of secondary tasks on implicit motor skill performance. *International Journal of Sport Psychology, 33*, 307–324.

MacRury, D. (1997). *Golfers on golf.* London: Virgin Books.

McAuley, E., and Blissmer, B. (2002). Self-efficacy and attributional processes in physical activity. In T. Horn (Ed.), *Advances in sport psychology* (2nd ed., pp. 185–205). Champaign, IL: Human Kinetics.

McClelland, D. C., Atkinson, J. W., Clark, R. W., and Lowell, E. J. (1953). *The achievement motive.* New York: Appleton-Century-Crofts.

McCullagh, P. (1995). Sport psychology: A historical perspective. *The Sport Psychologist, 9*, 363–365.

McDermott, K. (2000). "Doherty butt of 'black' comedy", *The Irish Independent*, 2 March, p. 20.

McErlane, M. (2002). "Acting up". *The Sunday Times*, p. 3 (Style Section).

McGinley, M., Kremer, J., Trew, K., and Ogle, S. (1998). Socio-cultural identity and attitudes to sport in Northern Ireland. *The Irish Journal of Psychology, 19*, 464–471.

McGrory, D. (2002). "Heading football killed Jess Astle, coroner says". *The Times*, 12 November, p. 3.

McIlveen, R. (1992). An investigation of attributional bias in a real-world setting. In R. McIlveen, L. Higgins, and A. Wadeley (Eds.), *BPS manual of psychology practicals* (pp. 78–92). Leicester: The British Psychological Society.

McIntosh, M. (2002). "Hate drives Lennon out". *The Guardian*, 22 August, p. 34.

McKenzie, A. D., and Howe, B. L. (1991). The effect of imagery on tackling performance in rugby. *Journal of Human Movement Studies, 20*, 163–176.

McLean, N. (1995). Building and maintaining an effective team. In T. Morris and J. Summers (Eds.), *Sport psychology: Theory, applications and issues* (pp. 420–434). Brisbane: John Wiley.

McNair, D. M., Lorr, M., and Droppleman, L. F. (1992). *Revised manual for the Profile of Mood States*. San Diego, CA: Educational & Industrial Testing Services.

McPherson, S. L. (2000). Expert-novice differences in planning strategies during collegiate singles tennis competition. *Journal of Sport and Exercise Psychology, 22*, 39–62.

Maehr, M. L., and Nicholls, J. G. (1980). Culture and achievement motivation: A second look. In N. Warren (Ed.), *Studies in cross-cultural psychology* (pp. 221–267). New York: Academic Press.

Mahoney, M. J., and Avener, M. (1977). Psychology of the elite athlete: An exploratory study. *Cognitive Therapy and Research, 1*, 135–141.

Mair, L. (2002). "A photo at the finish fails to spoil Woods' day". *The Daily Telegraph*, 23 September, p. S9.

Mallett, C. J., and Hanrahan, S. J. (1997). Race modelling: An effective cognitive strategy for the 100 m sprinter? *The Sport Psychologist, 11*, 72–85.

Mallett, C. J., and Hanrahan, S. J. (2003, in press). Elite athletes: why does the "fire" burn so brightly? *Psychology of Sport and Exercise.*

Marcotti, G. (2001). "Made, not born". *The Sunday Tribune*, 7 October, p. 9 (Sport).

Marcus, B. H., Bock, B. C., Pinto, B. M., Napolitano, M. A., and Clark, M. M. (2002). Exercise initiation, adoption, and maintenance in adults: Theoretical models and empirical support. In J. Van Raalte and B. W. Brewer (Eds.), *Exploring sport and exercise psychology* (2nd ed., pp. 185–208). Washington, DC: American Psychological Association.

Marcus, B. H., and Forsyth, L. H. (2003). *Motivating people to be physically active*. Champaign, IL: Human Kinetics.

Marcus, B. H., and Simkin, L. R. (1993). The stages of exercise behaviour. *Journal of Sports Medicine and Physical Fitness, 33*, 83–88.

Martens, M. P., and Webber S. N. (2002). Psychometric properties of the Sport Motivation Scale: An evaluation with college varsity athletes from the US. *Journal of Sport and Exercise Psychology, 24*, 254–270.

Martens, R. (1977). *Sport competition anxiety test*. Champaign, IL: Human Kinetics.

Martens, R., Burton, D., Vealey, R. S., Bump, L. A., and Smith, D. E. (1990). Development and validation of the Competitive State Anxiety Inventory-2 (CSAI-2). In R. Martens, R. S. Vealey, and D. Burton (Eds.), *Competitive anxiety in sport*. (pp. 117–190). Champaign, IL: Human Kinetics.

Martens, R., Landers, R. M., and Loy, J. W. (1972). *Sport cohesiveness questionnaire*. Unpublished manuscript, University of Illinois. Champaign, IL.

Martin, J. J., and Gill, D. L. (1991). The relationships among competitive orientation, sport-confidence, self-efficacy, anxiety and performance. *Journal of Sport and Exercise Psychology, 13*, 149–159.

Martin, K. A., Moritz, S. E., and Hall, C. (1999). Imagery use in sport: A literature review and applied model. *The Sport Psychologist, 13*, 245–268.

Martin, K. B., Kellmann, M., Lavallee, D., and Page, S. J. (2002). Development and psychometric evaluation of the Sport Psychology Attitude – Revised Form: A multiple group investigation. *The Sport Psychologist, 16*, 272–290.

Martinsen, E. W. and Morgan, W. P. (1997). Antidepressant effects of physical activity. In W. P. Morgan (Ed.), *Physical activity and mental health* (pp. 93–106). Washington, DC: Taylor & Francis.

Masters, K. S., and Ogles, B. M. (1998). Associative and dissociative cognitive strategies in exercise and running: 20 years later, what do we know? *The Sport Psychologist, 12*, 253–270.

Masters, R. S. W. (1992). Knowledge, "knerves" and know-how: The role of explicit versus implicit knowledge in the breakdown of a complex motor skill under pressure. *British Journal of Psychology, 83*, 343–358.

Matheson, H., Mathes, S., and Murray, M. (1995). Group cohesion of female intercollegiate coacting and interacting teams across a competitive season. *International Journal of Sport Psychology, 27,* 37–49.

Matlin, M. W. (2002). *Cognition* (5th ed.). Fort Worth: Harcourt Brace.

Maynard, I. (1998). *Improving concentration.* Headingley, Leeds: The National Coaching Foundation.

Mears, P., and Voehl, F. (1994). *Team building: A structured learning approach.* Delray Beach, FL: St Lucie Press.

Mellet, E., Petit, L., Mazoyer, B., Denis, M., and Tzourio, N. (1998). Reopening the mental imagery debate: Lessons from functional anatomy. *Neuoimage, 8,* 129–139.

Melnick, M. J., and Chemers, M. M. (1974). Effects of group structure on the success of basketball teams. *Research Quarterly for Exercise and Sport, 45,* 1–8.

Meyers, A. W. (1997). Sport psychology services to the United States Olympic Festival: An experiential account. *The Sport Psychologist, 11,* 454–468.

Middleton, C. (1996). "Losing out as the mind muscles in". *The Sunday Telegraph,* 30 June, p. 15 (Sport).

Miller, B. (1997). *Gold minds: The psychology of winning in sport.* Marlborough, Wiltshire: The Crowood Press.

Miller, P. S., and Kerr, G. A. (2002). Conceptualizing excellence: Past, present and future. *Journal of Applied Sport Psychology, 14,* 140–153.

Miracle, A. W., and Rees, C. R. (1994). *Lessons of the locker-room: The myth of school sports.* Amherst, NJ: Prometheus.

Moore, G. (2000). "Sympathy but little satisfaction for Robson". *The Independent,* 4 December, p. 3.

Moran, A. P. (1993). Conceptual and methodological issues in the measurement of mental imagery skills in athletes. *Journal of Sport Behaviour, 16,* 156–170.

Moran, A. P. (1996). *The psychology of concentration in sport performers: A cognitive analysis.* Hove, East Sussex: Psychology Press.

Moran, A. P. (1998). *The pressure putt: Doing your best when it matters most in golf* (audiotape). Aldergrove, Co. Antrim, N. Ireland: Tutorial Services (UK) Ltd.

Moran, A. P. (2000a). Improving sporting abilities: Training concentration skills. In J. Hartley and A. Branthwaite (Eds.), *The applied psychologist* (2nd ed., pp. 92–110). Buckingham: Open University Press.

Moran, A. P. (2000b). *Managing your own learning at university: A practical guide* (Rev. ed., first published 1997). Dublin: UCD Press.

Moran, A. P. (2001). What makes a winner? The psychology of expertise in sport. *Studies, 90,* 266–275.

Moran, A. P. (2002a). In the mind's eye. *The Psychologist, 15,* 414–415.

Moran, A. P. (2002b). "Shrinking" or expanding? The role of sport psychology in professional football. *Insight – The FA Coaches Journal, 6,* 41–43.

Moran, A. P. (2003a). Improving concentration skills in team-sport performers: Focusing techniques for soccer players. In R. Lidor and K. P. Henschen (Eds.), *The psychology of team sports* (pp. 161–190). Morgantown, WV: Fitness Information Technology.

Moran, A. P. (2003b). The state of concentration skills training in applied sport psychology. In I. Greenlees and A. P. Moran (Eds.) (2003), *Concentration skills training in sport* (pp. 7–19). Leicester: The British Psychological Society (Division of Sport and Exercise Psychology).

Moran, A. P., Byrne, A., and McGlade, N. (2002). The effects of anxiety and strategic planning on visual search behaviour. *Journal of Sports Sciences, 20,* 225–236.

Moran, A. P., and MacIntyre, T. (1998). "There's more to an image than meets the eye": A qualitative study of kinaesthetic imagery among elite canoe-slalomists. *The Irish Journal of Psychology, 19,* 406–423.

Moran, S. (2001). The Gaelic Athletic Association and professionalism in Irish sport. *Studies, 90*, 276–282.

Morgan, W. P. (1977). Involvement in vigorous physical activity with special reference to adherence. In L. I. Gedvilas and M. W. Kneer (Eds.), *Proceedings of the National College Physical Education Association* (pp. 235–246). Chicago: University of Illinois–Chicago Publication Service.

Morgan, W. P. (1979). Negative addiction in runners. *The Physician and Sportsmedicine, 7*, 57–70.

Morgan, W. P. (1985). Affective beneficience of vigorous physical activity. *Medicine and Science in Sports and Exercise. 17*, 94–100.

Morgan, W. P. (1997). Mind games: The psychology of sport. In D. R. Lamb and R. Murray (Eds.), *Perspectives in exercise science and sports medicine: Optimizing sport performance* (Vol. 10, pp. 1–62). Carmel, IN: Cooper Publishing Company.

Morgan, W. P. (2000). Psychological factors associated with distance running and the marathon. In D. T. Pedloe (Ed.), *Marathon medicine* (pp. 293–310). London: The Royal Society of Medicine Press.

Morgan, W. P. (2001). Prescription of physical activity: A paradigm shift. *Quest, 53*, 366–382.

Morgan, W. P., Brown, D. R., Raglin, J. S., O'Connor, P. J., and Ellickson, K. A. (1987). Psychological monitoring of overtraining and staleness. *British Journal of Sports Medicine, 21*, 107–114.

Morgan, W. P., and Dishman, R. K. (2001). Adherence to exercise and physical activity: Preface. *Quest, 53*, 277–278.

Morris, L., Davis, D., and Hutchings, C. (1981). Cognitive and emotional components of anxiety: Literary review and revised worry-emotionality scale. *Journal of Educational Psychology, 73*, 541–555.

Morris, P. E., Tweedy, M., and Gruneberg, M. M. (1985). Interest, knowledge and the memorizing of soccer scores. *British Journal of Psychology, 76*, 415–425.

Mudrack, P. E. (1989a). Defining group cohesiveness: A legacy of confusion? *Small Group Behaviour, 20*, 37–49.

Mudrack, P. E. (1989b). Group cohesiveness and productivity: A closer look. *Human Relations, 42*, 771–785.

Muir, D. E. (1991). Club tennis: A case study in taking leisure very seriously. *Sociology of Sport Journal, 8*, 70–78.

Mullen, B., and Copper, C. (1994). The relation between group cohesiveness and performance: An integration. *Psychological Bulletin, 115*, 210–227.

Munroe, K. J., Giaccobi, Jr., P. R., Hall, C. R., and Weinberg, R. (2000). The four w's of imagery use: Where, when, why, and what. *The Sport Psychologist, 14*, 119–137.

Murphy, S. (1999). The cheers and the tears: A healthy alternative to the dark side of youth sports today. San Francisco: Jossey-Bass.

Murphy, S. (2001). "Back to nature". *The Guardian*, 22 September, p. 69 (Weekend Section).

Murphy, S. M. (1994). Imagery interventions in sport. *Medicine and Science in Sports and Exercise, 26*, 486–494.

Murphy, S. M., and Jowdy, D. P. (1992). Imagery and mental practice. In T. Horn (Ed.), *Advances in sport psychology* (pp. 221–250). Champaign, IL: Human Kinetics.

Murphy, S. M., and Martin, K. A. (2002). The use of imagery in sport. In T. Horn (Ed.), *Advances in sport psychology* (2nd. ed., pp. 405–439). Champaign, IL: Human Kinetics.

Mutrie, N. (2001). The transtheoretical model of behaviour change: An examination of its applicability to exercise behaviour change. In B. Cripps, S. Drew, and S. Woolfson (Eds.), *Activity for life: Theoretical and practical issues for exercise psychologists* (pp. 27–34). Leicester: The British Psychological Society.

Mutrie, N. (2002). Healthy body, healthy mind? *The Psychologist, 15*, 412–413.

Mutrie, N., Carney, C., Blamey, A., Crawford, C., Aitchison, T., and Whitelaw, A. (2002). "Walk in to work out": A randomised controlled trial of a self help intervention to promote active commuting. *Journal of Epidemiological Community Health, 56*, 407–412.

Nadel, L., and Piattelli-Palmarini, M. (2002). What is cognitive science? In L. Nadel (Ed.), *Encyclopaedia of cognitive science* (Vol. 1, pp. xiii–xli). London: Nature Publishing Group.

Nakamura, J., and Csikszentmihalyi, M. (2002). The concept of flow. In C. R. Snyder and S. J. Lopez (Eds.), *Handbook of positive psychology* (pp. 89–105). New York: Oxford University Press.

National Coaching Foundation (1996). *Motivation and mental toughness*. Headingley, Leeds; National Coaching Foundation.

Navon, D., and Gopher, D. (1979). On the economy of the human information-processing system. *Psychological Review, 86*, 214–255.

Neiss, R. (1988). Reconceptualizing arousal: Psychobiological states in motor performance. *Psychological Bulletin, 103*, 345–366.

Newman, B. (1984). Expediency as benefactor: How team building saves time and gets the job done. *Training and Development Journal, 38*, 26–30.

Nicholas, M. (2002). "Control freak Faldo gives pointer to Hussain's men". *The Daily Telegraph*, 9 December, p. S6 (Sport).

Nichols, P. (2000). "Ice-man Faulds keeps his cool". *The Guardian*, 21 September, p. 7 (Sport).

Nicholls, J. G. (1992). The general and the specific in the development and expression of achievement motivation. In G. Roberts (Ed.), *Motivation in sport and exercise* (pp. 31–56). Champaign, IL: Human Kinetics.

Nideffer, R. (1976). Test of Attentional and Interpersonal Style. *Journal of Personality and Social Psychology, 34*, 394–404.

Nideffer, R. M., Sagal, M-S., Lowry, M., and Bond, J. (2001). Identifying and developing world-class performers. In G. Tenenbaum (Ed.), *The practice of sport psychology* (pp. 129–144). Morgantown, WV: Fitness Information Technology.

Nisbett, R. E., and Wilson, T. D. (1977). Telling more than we can know: Verbal reports on mental processes. *Psychological Review, 84*, 231–259.

Noyes, F. R., Lindenfeld, T. N., and Marshall, M. T. (1988). What determines an athletic injury (definition)? Who determines an injury (occurrence)? *American Journal of Sports Medicine, 21*, 78–91.

Ntoumanis, N., Biddle, S., and Haddock, G. (1999). The mediating role of coping strategies on the relationship between achievement motivation and affect in sport. *Anxiety, Stress and Coping, 12*, 299–327.

O'Brien Cousins, S. (2003). Grounding theory in self-referent thinking: Conceptualizing motivation for older adult physical activity. *Psychology of Sport and Exercise, 4*, 81–100.

O'Connor, P. J., Raglin, J. S., and Martinsen, E. W. (2000). Physical activity, anxiety and anxiety disorders. *International Journal of Sport Psychology, 31*, 136–155.

Ogden, J. (2000). *Health psychology*. Buckingham: Open University Press.

Ogden, J., Veale, D., and Summers, Z. (1997). The development and validation of the Exercise Dependence Questionnaire. *Addiction Research, 5*, 343–356.

Ogles, B. M., and Masters, K. S. (2003). A typology of marathon runners based on cluster analysis of motivations. *Journal of Sport Behaviour, 26*, 69–85.

Onions, C. T. (Ed.) (1996). *The Oxford dictionary of English etymology*. Oxford: Clarendon Press.

Orbach, I., Singer, R., and Price, S. (1999). An attribution training programme and achievement in sport. *The Sport Psychologist, 13*, 69–82.

Orchard, J., and Seward, H. (2002). Epidemiology of injuries in the Australian Football League, seasons 1997–2000. *British Journal of Sports Medicine, 36*, 39–45.

Orliaguet, J. P., and Coello, Y. (1998). Differences between actual and imagined putting movements in golf: A chronometric analysis. *International Journal of Sport Psychology*, *29*, 157–169.

Orlick, T. (1986). *Psyching for sport: Mental training for athletes*. Champaign, IL: Human Kinetics.

Orlick, T. (1990). *In pursuit of excellence*. Champaign, IL: Leisure Press.

O'Sullivan, J. (2002a). "Captain steers a steady ship". *The Irish Times*, 26 September, p. 19.

O'Sullivan, J. (2002b). "Clark shows his strength as he leads from the front". *The Irish Times*, 30 September, p. 4 (Sport).

Otway, G. (1999). "Clarke enjoys special K day". *The Sunday Times*, 1 August 1999. p. 13 (Sport).

Oxendine, J. B. (1984). *Psychology of motor learning*. Englewood Cliffs, NJ: Prentice-Hall.

Paivio, A. (1985). Cognitive and motivational functions of imagery in human performance. *Canadian Journal of Applied Sport Science*, *10*, 22–28.

Palmeri, T. J. (2002). Automaticity. In L. Nadel (Ed.), *Encyclopaedia of cognitive science* (Vol. 1, pp. 290–301). London: Nature Publishing Group.

Papaxanthis, C., Pozzo, T., Kasprinski, R., and Berthoz, A. (2003). Comparison of actual and imagined execution of whole-body movements after a long exposure to microgravity. *Neuroscience Letters*, *339*, 41–44.

Passer, M. W., and Smith, R. E. (2001). *Psychology: Frontiers and applications*. Boston, MA: McGraw-Hill.

Pedersen, D. M. (1997). Perceptions of high risk sports. *Perceptual and Motor Skills*, *85*, 756–758.

Pedersen, P. (1986). The grief response and injury: A special challenge for athletes and athletic trainers. *Athletic Training*, *21*, 1–10.

Pensgaard, A. M., and Roberts, G. C. (2003). Achievement goal orientations and the use of coping strategies among Winter Olympians. *Psychology of Sport and Exercise*, *4*, 101–116.

Perry, C., and Morris, T. (1995). Mental imagery in sport. In T. Morris and J. Summers (Eds.), *Sport psychology: Theory, applications and issues* (pp. 339–385). Brisbane, Australia: John Wiley.

Perry, H. M. (1939). The relative efficiency of actual and imaginary practice in five selected tasks. *Archives of Psychology*, *34*, 5–75.

Peterson, C., Buchanan, G. M., and Seligman, M. E. P. (1995). Explanatory style: History and evolution of the field. In G. M. Buchanan and M. E. P. Seligman (Eds.), *Explanatory style* (pp. 1–20). Hillsdale, NJ: Lawrence Erlbaum Associates, Inc.

Peterson, C., Semmel, A., Von Baeyer, C., Abramson, Y. L., Metalsky, G. I., and Seligman, M. E. P. (1982). The Attributional Style Questionnaire. *Cognitive Therapy and Research*, *6*, 287–299.

Peterson, T. R., and Aldana, S. G. (1999). Improving exercise behaviour; An application of the stages of change model in a worksite setting. *American Journal of Health Promotion*, *13*, 229–232.

Petitpas, A. J. (2002). Counselling interventions in applied sport psychology. In J. L. Van Raalte and B. W. Brewer (Eds.), *Exploring sport and exercise psychology* (2nd ed., pp. 253–268). Washington, DC: American Psychological Association.

Petrie, T. A., and Falkstein, D. L. (1998). Methodological, measurement, and statistical issues in research on sport injury prediction. *Journal of Applied Sport Psychology*, *10*, 26–45.

Pitt, N. (1998a). "Golden days beckon for Henman". *The Sunday Times*, 29 September, p. 13 (Sport).

Pitt, N. (1998b). "Out of the Woods". *The Sunday Times*, 19 July, p. 5 (Sport).

Prapavessis, H., Carron, A. V., and Spink, K. S. (1996). Team building in sport. *International Journal of Sport Psychology*, *27*, 269–285.

President's Council on Physical Fitness and Sports (2002). Cost and consequences of sedentary living: New battleground for an old enemy. *Research Digest*, *3*, 1–8.

Prochaska, J. O., and DiClemente, C. C. (1983). Stages and processes of self-change in smoking. Towards an integrative model of change. *Journal of Consulting and Clinical Psychology, 51,* 390–395.

Prochaska, J. O., and DiClemente, C. C. (1984). Toward a comprehensive model of change. In W. E. Miller and N. Heather (Eds.), *Treating addictive behaviours* (pp. 3–27). London: Plenum Press.

Psychologist, The (2003). "Not bowled over by sport psychology". *The Psychologist, 16,* p. 117.

Pylyshyn, Z. (1973). What the mind's eye tells the mind's brain. *Psychological Bulletin, 80,* 1–24.

Pylyshyn, Z. (2003). Explaining mental imagery: Now you see it, now you don't. *Trends in Cognitive Sciences, 7,* 111–112.

Quinn, A. M., and Fallon, B. J. (1999). The changes in psychological characteristics and reactions of elite athletes from injury onset until full recovery. *Journal of Applied Sport Psychology, 11,* 210–229.

Radford, T. (2000). "Physics gets hit for six". *The Guardian,* 24 February, p. S2.

Radlo, S. J., Steinberg, G. M., Singer, R. N., Barba, D. A., and Melnikov, A. (2002). The influence of an attentional focus strategy on alpha brain wave activity, heart rate, and dart-throwing performance. *International Journal of Sport Psychology, 33,* 205–217.

Rahnama, N., Reilly, T., and Lees, A. (2002). Injury risk associated with playing actions during competitive soccer. *British Journal of Sports Medicine, 36,* 354–359.

Ravizza, K. H. (2002). A philosophical construct: A framework for performance enhancement. *International Journal of Sport Psychology, 33,* 4–18.

Reed, C. L. (2002). Chronometric comparisons of imagery to action: Visualizing versus physically performing springboard dives. *Memory and Cognition, 30,* 1169–1178.

Reid, A. (2002). "Subtle captaincy gave Europe edge". *The Sunday Times,* 6 October, p. 22 (Sport).

Rejeski, W. J., and Thompson, A. (1993). Historical and conceptual roots of exercise psychology. In P. Seragananian (Ed.), *Exercise psychology: The influence of physical exercise on psychological processes* (pp. 3–38). New York: John Wiley.

Rettew, D., and Reivich, K. (1995). Sports and explanatory style. In G. M. Buchanan and M. E. P. Seligman (Eds.), *Explanatory style* (pp. 73–185). Hillsdale, NJ: Lawrence Erlbaum Associates, Inc.

Richardson, A. (1967a). Mental practice: A review and discussion, Part 1. *Research Quarterly, 38,* 95–107.

Richardson, A. (1967b). Mental practice: A review and discussion, Part II. *Research Quarterly, 38,* 263–273.

Richardson, A. (1995). *Individual differences in imaging: Their measurement, origins and consequences.* Amityville, NY: Baywood.

Richardson, J. T. E. (1999). *Imagery.* Hove, East Sussex: Psychology Press.

Ripoll, H., Kerlirzin, Y., Stein, J. F., and Reine, B. (1993). Decision making and visual strategies of boxers in a simulated problem solving situation. In G. d'Ydewalle and J. Van Rensbergen (Eds.), *Perception and cognition: Advances in eye movement research (Studies in visual information processing,* Vol. 4, pp. 141–147). Amsterdam: North-Holland/Elsevier.

Roberts, G. (2001). Understanding the dynamics of motivation in physical activity: The influence of achievement goals on motivational processes. In G. C. Roberts (Ed.), *Advances in motivation in sport and exercise* (pp. 1–50). Champaign, IL: Human Kinetics.

Roberts, G. C., Spink, K. S., and Pemberton, C. L. (1999). *Learning experiences in sport psychology* (2nd ed.). Champaign, IL: Human Kinetics.

Roberts, G. C., Treasure, D. C., and Balague, G. (1998). Achievement goals in sport: The development and validation of the Perceptions of Success Questionnaire. *Journal of Sports Sciences, 16,* 337–347.

Robertson, I. (2002). *The mind's eye: An essential guide to boosting your mental power.* London: Bantam Press.

Robson, C., Cripps, B., and Steinberg, H. (Eds.) (1996). *Quality and quantity: Research methods in sport and exercise psychology.* Leicester: The British Psychological Society (Sport and Exercise Psychology Section).

Rotella, B. (1985). The psychological care of the injured athlete. In L. K. Bunker, R. J. Rotella, and A. S. Reilly (Eds.), *Sport psychology: Psychological considerations in maximizing sort performance* (pp. 273–287). Ann Arbor, MI: Mouvement.

Rousseau, J-J. (1953, originally published in 1781). *The confessions.* Harmondsworth, Middlesex: Penguin.

Rozelle, R. M., and Campbell, D. T. (1969). More plausible rival hypotheses in the cross-lagged panel correlation technique. *Psychological Bulletin, 71,* 74–80.

Sachs, M. L. (1981). Running therapy for the depressed client. *Topics in Clinical Nursing, 3,* 770–786.

Sachs, M. L., Burke, K., and Schrader, D. C. (Eds.) (2001). *Directory of graduate programs in applied sport psychology* (6th ed.). Morgantown, WV: Fitness Information Technology.

Sackett, R. S. (1934). The influence of symbolic rehearsal upon the retention of a maze habit. *Journal of General Psychology, 10,* 376–395.

Sarkar, P. (2002). "Olympic champion falls to earth and retires". *The Guardian,* 23 November, p. 16 (Sport).

Schmid, A., and Peper, E. (1998). Strategies for training concentration. In J. M. Williams (Ed.), *Applied sport psychology: Personal growth to peak performance* (3rd ed., pp. 316–328). Mountain View, CA: Mayfield.

Schmidt, R. A., and Lee, T. D. (1999). *Motor control and learning: A behavioural emphasis* (3rd ed.). Champaign, IL: Human Kinetics.

Schrader, M. P., and Wann, D. L. (1999). High-risk recreation: The relationship between participant characteristics and degree of involvement. *Journal of Sport Behaviour, 22,* 426–441.

Schutz, R. W., Eom, H. J., Smoll, F. L., and Smith, R. E. (1994). Examination of the factorial validity of the Group Environment Questionnaire. *Research Quarterly for Exercise and Sport, 65,* 226–236.

Scott, S. (1999). Out of the Woods. *SportsWrite,* July, pp. 44–48.

Scully, D., and Hume, A. (1995). Sport psychology: Status, knowledge and use among elite level coaches and performers in Ireland. *The Irish Journal of Psychology, 16,* 52–66.

Seligman, M. E. P. (1998). *Learned optimism: How to change your mind and your life* (2nd ed.). New York: Pocket Books.

Seligman, M. E. P., Nolen-Hoeksema, S., Thornton, N., and Thornton, K. M. (1990). Explanatory style as a mechanism of disappointing athletic performance. *Psychological Science, 1,* 143–146.

Sellars, C. (1996). *Mental skills: An introduction for sport coaches.* Headingley, Leeds: The National Coaching Foundation.

Selvey, M. (1998). "Getting up for the Ashes". *The Guardian,* 20 November, p. 2 (Sport).

Seppa, N. (1996). Psychologists making it to the big leagues. *American Psychological Association Monitor on Psychology, 27,* July, p. 28.

Shaw, D. (2002). Confidence and the pre-shot routine in golf: A case-study. In I. Cockerill (Ed.), *Solutions in sport psychology* (pp. 108–119). London: Thomson.

Shaw, W. A. (1938). The distribution of muscular action potentials during imaging. *Psychological Record, 2,* 195–216.

Shields, D. L., and Bredemeier, B. L. (2001). *Moral development and behaviour in sport.* In R. N. Singer, H. A. Hausenblas, and C. M. Janelle (Eds.), *Handbook of sport psychology* (2nd ed., pp. 585–603). New York: John Wiley.

Shontz, L. (1999). *Area cyclists line up to share a ride with Spain's Indurain.* Available

HTTP: <http:www.post-gazette.com/sports_headlines/19990602cycle6.asp> (retrieved 29 April 2003).

Short, S. E., Bruggerman, S. G., Engel, S. G., Marback, T. L., Wang, L. J., Willadsen, A., and Short, M. W. (2002). The effect of imagery function and imagery direction on self-efficacy and performance on a golf-putting task. *The Sport Psychologist, 16*, 48–67.

Siebold, G. L. (1999). The evolution of measurement of cohesion. *Military Psychology, 11*, 5–26.

Sime, W. (2002). Guidelines for clinical application of exercise therapy for mental health case studies. In J. Van Raalte and B. W. Brewer (Eds.), *Exploring sport and exercise psychology* (2nd ed., pp. 225–251). Washington, DC: American Psychological Association.

Simon, H. A., and Gilmartin, K. (1973). A simulation of memory for chess positions. *Cognitive Psychology, 5*, 29–46.

Simons, J. (1999). Concentration. In M. A. Thompson, R.A. Vernacchia, and W. E. More (Eds.), *Case studies in applied sport psychology: An educational approach* (pp. 89–114). Dubuque, IA: Kendall/Hunt.

Singer, R. N. (2000). Performance and human factors: Considerations about cognition and attention for self-paced and externally-paced events. *Ergonomics, 43*, 1661–1680.

Singer, R. N. (2002). Preperformance state, routines, and automaticity: What does it take to realize expertise in self-paced tasks? *Journal of Sport and Exercise Psychology, 24*, 359–375.

Singer, R. N., and Burke, K. L. (2002). Sport and exercise psychology: A positive force in the new millennium. In J. Van Raalte and B. W. Brewer (Eds.), *Exploring sport and exercise psychology* (2nd ed., pp. 525–529). Washington, DC: American Psychological Association.

Singer, R. N., Cauragh, J. H., Chen, D., Steinberg, G. M., and Frehlich, S. G. (1996). Visual search, anticipation, and reactive comparisons between highly-skilled and beginning tennis players. *Journal of Applied Sport Psychology, 8*, 9–26.

Sinnott, K., and Biddle, S. (1998). Changes in attributions, perceptions of success and intrinsic motivation after attributions in children's sport. *International Journal of Adolescence and Youth, 7*, 137–144.

Slade, J. M., Landers, D. M., and Martin, P. E. (2002). Muscular activity during real and imagined movements: A test of inflow explanations. *Journal of Sport and Exercise Psychology, 24*, 151–167.

Smith, A. M., Adler, C. H., Crews, D., Wharen, R. E., Laskowski, E. E., Barnes, K., Bell, C. V., Pelz, D., *et al.* (2003). The "yips" in golf: A continuum between a focal dystonia and choking. *Sports Medicine, 33*, 13–31.

Smith, A. M., Hartman, A. D., and Detling, N. J. (2001). Assessment of the injured athlete. In J. Crossman (Ed.), *Coping with sports injuries: Psychological strategies for rehabilitation* (pp. 20–50). Oxford: Oxford University Press.

Smith, C. (1998). "Clarke's finest hour as rivals are blown away by birdie blitz". *Irish Independent*, 18 May, p. 1 (Sport).

Smith, E. E., Adams, N. E., and Schorr, D. (1978). Fact retrieval and the paradox of intelligence. *Cognitive Psychology, 10*, 438–464.

Smith, M. (2002a). "Football Diary". *The Daily Telegraph*, 8 February, p. S3 (Sport).

Smith, M. (2002b). "Practice makes perfect". *The Daily Telegraph*, 15 February, p. S3 (Sport).

Smith, M. (2003). "Keepers focus on the spot". *The Daily Telegraph*, 13 March, p. S3 (Sport).

Smith, R. E., and Smoll, F. L. (1996). *Way to go, coach*. Portola Valley, CA: Warde Publishers.

Smith, R. E., and Smoll, F. L. (2002). Youth sport interventions. In J. Van Raalte and B. Brewer (Eds.), *Exploring sport and exercise psychology* (2nd ed., pp. 341–371). Washington, DC: American Psychological Association.

Smith, R. E., Smoll, F. L., and Schutz, R. W. (1990). Measurement and correlates of sport-specific cognitive and somatic trait anxiety: The Sport Anxiety Scale. *Anxiety Research, 2*, 263–280.

Smith, R. E., Smoll, F. L., and Wiechman, S. A. (1998). Measurement of trait anxiety in sport. In J. L. Duda (Ed.), *Advances in sport and exercise psychology measurement* (pp. 105–127). Morgantown, WV: Fitness Information Technology.

Snooker: The World Championship (2003). Coverage of the 2003 World Championship, Sheffield. Presented by Hazel Irvine with Steve Dabikd and John Parrott. BBC2, 5 May.

Solnit, R. (2001). *Wanderlust: A history of walking.* London: Verso.

Solso, R. (1998). *Cognitive Psychology* (5th ed.). Boston, MA: Allyn and Bacon.

Spence, J. C., and Lee, R. E. (2003). Toward a comprehensive model of physical activity. *Psychology of Sport and Exercise, 4,* 7–24.

Spielberger, C. S. (1966). Theory and research on anxiety. In C. S. Spielberger (Ed.), *Anxiety and behaviour* (pp. 3–20). New York: Academic Press.

Spink, K. S. (1990). Collective efficacy in the sport setting. *International Journal of Sport Psychology, 21,* 380–395.

Spitz, H. H. (1997). *Non-conscious movements: From mystical messages to facilitated communication.* Mahwah, NJ: Lawrence Erlbaum Associates, Inc.

Starkes, J. (2001). The road to expertise: Can we shorten the journey and lengthen the stay? In A. Papaionnaou, M. Goudas and Y. Theodorakis (Eds.), *Proceedings of International Society of Sport Psychology's 10th World Congress of Sport Psychology* (Vol. 3, pp. 198–205). Thessaloniki, Greece: Christodoulidi Publications.

Starkes, J., and Ericsson, K. A. (Eds.) (2003). *Expert performance in sports: Advances in research on sport expertise.* Champaign, IL: Human Kinetics.

Starkes, J. L., Deakin, J. M., Allard, F. M., Hodges, N. J., and Hayes, A. (1996). Deliberate practice in sports: What is it anyway? In K. A. Ericsson (Ed.), *The road to excellence: The acquisition of expert performance in the arts and sciences, sports and games* (pp. 81–106). Mahwah, NJ: Lawrence Erlbaum Associates, Inc.

Starkes, J. L., Helsen, W., and Jack, R. (2001). Expert performance in sport and dance. In R. N. Singer, H. A. Hausenblas, and C. M. Janelle (Eds.), *Handbook of sport psychology* (2nd. ed., pp. 174–201). New York: John Wiley.

Starmer-Smith, C. (2002). "Stories behind the headlines". *The Daily Telegraph,* 8 March, p. S5 (Sport).

Steinberg, H., Cockerill, I., and Dewey, A. (Eds.) (1998). *What sport psychologists do.* Leicester: The British Psychological Society (Sport and Exercise Psychology Section).

Sternberg, R. J. (1999). *Cognitive Psychology* (2nd ed.). Fort Worth, TX: Harcourt Brace.

St John, L. (1997). "Positive Nicholas locates major key". *The Sunday Times,* 3 August, p. 9, (Sport).

Strauss, B. (2002). Social facilitation in motor tasks: A review of research and theory. *Psychology of Sport and Exercise, 3,* 237–256.

Suinn, R. M. (1994). Visualization in sports. In A. A. Sheikh and E. R. Korn (Eds.), *Imagery in sports and physical performance* (pp. 23–42). Amityville, NY: Baywood.

Summers, J. J. (1999). Skill acquisition: Current perspectives and future directions. In R. Lidor and M. Bar-Eli (Eds.), *Sport psychology: Linking theory and practice* (pp. 83–107). Morgantown, WV: Fitness Information Technology.

Summers, J.J., and Ford, S.K. (1990). The Test of Attentional and Interpersonal Style: An evaluation. *International Journal of Sport Psychology, 21,* 102–111.

Sunday Times, The (2001). "Talking head: Al Pacino". *The Sunday Times,* 23 June, p. 12.

Sutcliffe, P. (1997). "Out of tune with the rest of us". *The Sunday Times,* 8 June, p. 6 (Supplement: Stress Manager, Part 4: Raising Your Game).

Swain, A. B. J., and Jones, G. (1995). Effects of goal setting interventions on selected basketball skills: A single-subject design. *Research Quarterly for Exercise and Sport, 66,* 51–63.

Swain, A. B. J., and Jones, G. (1996). Explaining performance variance: The relative contributions of intensity and direction dimensions of competitive state anxiety. *Anxiety, Stress and Coping, 9,* 1–18.

316

Swift, E. J. (1910). Relearning a skilful act: An experimental study of neuromuscular memory. *Psychological Bulletin*, *7*, 17–19.

Syer, J. (1986). *Team spirit*. London: Sportspages.

Tackle, D. (1998). "Let's go mental toughness". *The Guardian*, 27 November, p. 16 (Sport).

Taylor, D. (2003). "Warnock's walks on the wild side keep Blades on edge". *The Guardian*, 12 April, p. 2 (Sport).

Taylor, F. W. (1967). *The principles of scientific management*. New York: Norton (originally published in 1911).

Taylor, G. (2002). "There is still a reluctance to recognise the part that psychology can play". *The Daily Telegraph*, 1 June, p. S3 (Sport).

Teigen, K. H. (1994). Yerkes-Dodson: A law for all seasons. *Theory and Psychology*, *4*, 525–547.

Tenenbaum, G., Jones, C. M., Kitsantas, A., Sacks, D. N., and Berwick, J. P. (2003). Failure adaptation: An investigation of the stress response process in sport. *International Journal of Sport Psychology*, *34*, 27–62.

Tenenbaum, G., Sar-El, T., and Bar-Eli, M. (2000). Anticipation of ball location in low- and high-skill performers: A developmental perspective. *Psychology of Sport and Exercise*, *1*, 117–128.

Terry, P., Hardy, L., Jones, G., and Rodgers, S. (1997). Psychological support. *British Journal of Sports Medicine*, *31*, 79.

Thomas, O., Hanton, S., and Jones, G. (2002). An alternative approach to short-form self-report assessment of competitive anxiety: A research note. *International Journal of Sport Psychology*, *33*, 325–336.

Thornley, G. (1993). "Graf profits as Novotna loses her nerve". *The Irish Times*, 5 July, p. 6.

Thornley, G. (1997). "Irish call in two psychologists". *The Irish Times*, 16 October, p. 20.

Thorp, M. (1998). "Ferdinand has the faith not to falter at the final hurdle". *The Guardian*, 22 May, p. 5 (Sport).

Thorp, M. (1999). "Sheringham praises Ferguson's pep talk". *The Guardian*, 28 May, p. 34.

Times, The (2002). "The Premiership today: Bergkamp faces FA probe, Royle lines up raid on Maine Road and Taylor calls in the shrinks", *The Times*, 30 October, p. 43.

Title, The (1998). "Daly is still fighting off the shakes". *The Title*, 29 November, p. 8.

Tolman, E. E. (1932). *Purposive behaviour in animals and men*. New York: Appleton-Century-Crofts.

Triplett, N. (1898). The dynamogenic factors in pacemaking and competition. *American Journal of Psychology*, *9*, 507–533.

Trost, S. G., Pate, R. R., Sallis, J. F., Freedson, P. S., Taylor, W. C., Dowda, M., and Sirad, J. (2002). Age and gender differences in objectively measured physical activity in youth. *Medicine and Science in Sports and Exercise*, *34*, 350–355.

Tuckman, B. W. (1965). Developmental sequence in small groups. *Psychological Bulletin*, *63*, 384–399.

Turman, P. D. (2003). Coaches and cohesion: The impact of coaching techniques on team cohesion in the small group sport setting. *Journal of Sport Behaviour*, *26*, 86–104.

Turner, E. E., Rejeski, W. J., and Brawley, L. R. (1997). Psychological benefits of physical activity are influenced by the social environment. *Journal of Sport and Exercise Psychology*, *19*, 119–130.

Tyldesley, C. (2003). "Blame it on the boogie". *The Daily Telegraph*, 9 May, p. S3 (Sport).

Udry, E. (1997). Coping and social support among injured athletes following surgery. *Journal of Sport and Exercise Psychology*, *19*, 71–90.

Udry, E. (1999). The paradox of injuries: Unexpected positive consequences. In D. Pargman (Ed.), *Psychological bases of sport injuries* (2nd ed., pp. 79–88). Morgantown, WV: Fitness Information Technology.

Udry, E., and Andersen, M. B. (2002). Athletic injury and sport behaviour. In T. S. Horn (Ed.), *Advances in sport psychology* (2nd ed., pp. 529–553). Champaign, IL: Human Kinetics.

Uhlig, R. (2001). "Thinking about exercise 'can beef up biceps'". *The Daily Telegraph*, 22 November, p. 3.

Uitenbroek, D. G. (1996). Sports, exercise, and other causes of injuries: Results of a population survey. *Research Quarterly for Exercise and Sport, 67*, 380–385.

Ungerleider, R. S., and Golding, J. M. (1991). Mental practice among Olympic athletes. *Perceptual and Motor Skills, 72*, 1007–1017.

United States Department of Health and Human Services (1996). *Physical activity and health: A report of the Surgeon General*. Atlanta, GA: US Department of Health and Human Services, Centres for Disease Control and Prevention, National Centre for Chronic Disease Prevention and Health Promotion.

Vallerand, R. J., Brière, N. M., Blanchard, C., and Provencher, P. (1997). Development and validation of the Multidimensional Sportspersonship Orientations Scale. *Journal of Sport and Exercise Psychology, 19*, 197–206.

Vallerand, R. J., and Fortier, M. S. (1998). Measures of intrinsic and extrinsic motivation in sport and physical activity: A review and critique. In J. L. Duda (Ed.), *Advances in sport and exercise psychology measurement* (pp. 81–101). Morgantown, WV: Fitness Information Technology.

Vallerand, R. J., and Rousseau, F. L. (2001). Intrinsic and extrinsic motivation in sport and exercise. In R. N. Singer, H. A. Hausenblas, and C. M. Janelle (Eds.), *Handbook of sport psychology* (2nd ed., pp. 389–416). New York: John Wiley.

Vandenberg, S., and Kuse, A. R. (1978). Mental rotations: A group test of three-dimensional spatial visualization. *Perceptual and Motor Skills, 47*, 599–604.

Vealey, R. S., and Greenleaf, C. A. (1998). Seeing is believing: Understanding and using imagery in sport. In J. M. Williams (Ed.), *Applied Sport Psychology* (3rd ed., pp. 237–269). Mountain View, CA: Mayfield.

Vealey, R. S., and Walter, S. M. (1994). On target with mental skills: An interview with Darrell Pace. *The Sport Psychologist, 8*, 428–441.

Vickers, J. N. (1992). Gaze control in putting. *Perception, 21*, 117–132.

Vickers, J. N. (1996). Control of visual attention during the basketball free throw. *American Journal of Sports Medicine, 24*, S93–S97.

Vidal, J. (2001). "Call of the wild". *The Guardian*, 9 June, p. 2 (G2).

Vyse, S. (1997). *Believing in magic: The psychology of superstition*. New York: Oxford University Press.

Walling, M. D., Duda, J. L., and Chi, L. (1993). The perceived motivational climate in sport questionnaire: Construct and predictive validity. *Journal of Sport and Exercise Psychology, 15*, 172–183.

Walsh, D. (2000). "The gene machine". *The Sunday Times*, 19 November 2000, p. 23 (Sport).

Walter, D. D., Sutton, J. R., McIntosh, J. M., and Connolly, C. (1985). The aetiology of sports injuries: A review of methodologies. *Sports Medicine, 2*, 47–58.

Wann, D. L. (1997). *Sport psychology*. Upper Saddle River, NJ: Prentice-Hall.

Ward, P., and Williams, A. M. (2003). Perceptual and cognitive skill development in soccer: The multidimensional nature of expert performance. *Journal of Sport and Exercise Psychology, 25*, 93–111.

Washburn, M. F. (1916). *Movement and mental imagery*. Boston, MA: Houghton Mifflin.

Watson, J. B. (1913). Psychology as the behaviourist views it. *Psychological Review, 20*, 158–177.

Watterson, J. (1997). "Doherty still late but better than ever". *The Irish Times*, 8 November, p. 8.

Webster, R. (1984). *Winning ways*. Sydney: Fontana.

Wegner, D. M. (1994). Ironic processes of mental control. *Psychological Review, 101*, 34–52.

Wegner, D. M. (2002). Thought suppression and mental control. In L. Nadel (Ed.), *Encyclopaedia of cognitive science* (Vol. 4, pp. 395–397). London: Nature Publishing Group.

Weinberg, R. S. (1988). *The mental ADvantage: Developing your mental skills in tennis.* Champaign, IL: Human Kinetics.

Weinberg, R. S. (2002). Goal setting in sport and exercise: Research to practice. In J. Van Raalte and B. Brewer (Eds.), *Exploring sport and exercise psychology* (2nd ed., pp. 25–48). Washington, DC: American Psychological Association.

Weinberg, R. S., Bruya, L. D., Garland, H., and Jackson, A. (1990). Effect of goal difficulty and positive reinforcement on endurance performance. *Journal of Sport and Exercise Psychology, 12*, 144–156.

Weinberg, R. S., Bruya, L. D., and Jackson, A. (1985). The effects of goal proximity and goal specificity on endurance performance. *Journal of Sport Psychology, 7*, 296–305.

Weinberg, R. S., and Gould, D. (1999). *Foundations of sport and exercise psychology* (2nd ed.). Champaign, IL: Human Kinetics.

Weinberg, R. S., Stitcher, T., and Richardson, P. (1994). Effects of seasonal goal setting on lacrosse performance. *The Sport Psychologist, 8*, 166–175.

Weinberg, R. S., and Weigand, D. A. (1996). Let the discussions continue: A reaction to Locke's comments on Weinberg and Weigand. *Journal of Sport and Exercise Psychology, 18*, 89–93.

Weiss, M. R., and Ferrer-Caja, E. (2002). Motivational orientations and sport behaviour. In T. Horn (Ed.), *Advances in sport psychology* (2nd ed., pp. 101–183). Champaign, IL: Human Kinetics.

Westerterp, K. R. (2001). Pattern and intensity of physical activity. *Nature, 410*, 539.

Weston, P. (2002). "How to use exercise to aid diabetes". *The Irish Times*, 21 November, p. 15.

Whelan, J. P., Epkins, C., and Meyers, A. W. (1990). Arousal interventions for athletic performance: Influence of mental preparation and competitive experience. *Anxiety Research, 2*, 293–307.

Whelan, J. P., Meyers, A. W., and Elkins, T. D. (2002). Ethics in sport and exercise psychology. In J. L. Van Raalte and B. W. Brewer (Eds.), *Exploring sport and exercise psychology* (2nd ed., pp. 503–523). Washington, DC: American Psychological Association.

Whitaker, D. (1999). *The spirit of teams.* Marlborough, Wiltshire: The Crowood Press.

White, J. (1999). "Ferguson assumes full control in title campaign". *The Guardian*, 17 February, p. 26.

White, J. (2001). "Interview: Stephen Hendry". *The Guardian*, 15 October, pp. 18–19 (Sport).

White, J. (2002a). "Interview: Garry Sobers". *The Guardian*, 10 June, pp. 20–21 (Sport).

White, J. (2002b). "Interview: Ian Woosnam". *The Guardian*, 15 July, pp. 22–23 (Sport).

White, J. (2002c). "A potter's tale: any colour but the blues". *The Guardian*, 20 April 2002, pp. 10–11 (Sport).

White, J. (2003). "Interview: Peter Ebdon". *The Guardian*, pp. 20–21 (Sport).

Widmeyer, W. N., Brawley, L. R., and Carron, A. V. (2002). Group dynamics in sport. In T. Horn (Ed.), *Advances in sport psychology* (2nd ed., pp. 285–308). Champaign, IL: Human Kinetics.

Widmeyer, W. N., Carron, A. V., and Brawley, L. R. (1993). Group cohesion in sport and exercise. In R. N. Singer, M. Murphey, and L. K. Tennant (Eds.), *Handbook of research on sport psychology* (pp. 672–694). New York: Macmillan.

Wiese-Bjornstal, D. M., Smith, A. M., Shaffer, S. M., and Morrey, M. A. (1998). An integrated model of response to sport injury: Psychological and sociological dynamics. *Journal of Applied Sport Psychology, 10*, 46–69.

Wilde, S. (1998). "Freudian slips get new meaning with mind games catching on". *The Times*, May 18, p. 33 (Times Sport).

Williams, A. M. (2002a). Visual search behaviour in sport. *Journal of Sports Sciences, 20*, 169–170.

Williams, A. M. (2002b). Perceptual and cognitive expertise in sport. *The Psychologist, 15*, 416–417.

Williams, A. M. (2003). Developing selective attention skill in fast ball sports. In I. Greenlees and A. P. Moran (Eds.), *Concentration skills training in sport* (pp. 20–32). Leicester: The British Psychological Society (Division of Sport and Exercise Psychology).

Williams, A. M., and Burwitz, L. (1993). Advance cue utilization in soccer. In T. Reilly, J. Clarys, and A. Stibbe (Eds.), *Science and football II* (pp. 239–243). London: E. & F. N. Spon.

Williams, A. M., and Davids, K. (1998). Perceptual expertise in sport: Research, theory and practice. In H. Steinberg, I. Cockerill, and A. Dewey (Eds.), *What sport psychologists do* (pp. 48–57). Leicester: The British Psychological Society.

Williams, A. M., Davids, K., and Williams, J. G. (1999). *Visual perception and action in sport*. London: E. & F. N. Spon.

Williams, J. M. (2001). Psychology of injury risk and prevention. In R. N. Singer, H. A. Hausenblas, and C. M. Janelle (Eds.), *Handbook of sport psychology* (2nd ed., pp. 766–786). New York: Macmillan.

Williams, J. M., and Hacker, C. M. (1982). Causal relationships among cohesion, satisfaction, and performance in women's intercollegiate field hockey teams. *Journal of Sport and Exercise Psychology*, 4, 324–337.

Williams, J. M., and Harris, D. V. (1998). Relaxation and energizing techniques for regulation of arousal. In J. M. Williams (Ed.), *Applied sport psychology: Personal growth to peak performance* (3rd ed., pp. 219–236). Mountain View, CA: Mayfield.

Williams, J. M., and Krane, V. (2001). Psychological characteristics of peak performance. In J. M. Williams (Ed.), *Applied Sport Psychology: Personal growth to peak performance* (4th ed., pp. 137–147). Mountain View, CA: Mayfield.

Williams, J. M., and Leffingwell, T. R. (2002). Cognitive strategies in sport and exercise psychology. In J. Van Raalte and B. W. Brewer (Eds.), *Exploring sport and exercise psychology* (2nd ed., pp. 75–98). Washington, DC: American Psychological Association.

Williams, J. M., and Roepke, N. (1993). Psychology of injury and injury rehabilitation. In R. N. Singer, M. Murphey and L. K. Tennant (Eds.), *Handbook of research on sport psychology* (pp. 815–839). New York: Macmillan.

Williams, J. M., Rotella, R. J., and Heyman, S. R. (1998). Stress, injury, and the psychological rehabilitation of athletes. In J. M. Williams (Ed.), *Applied Sport Psychology* (3rd ed., pp. 409–428). Mountain View, CA: Mayfield.

Williams, R. (2002a). "Captains split on the million dollar question". *The Guardian*, 24 September, p. 28.

Williams, R. (2002b). "Sublime Serena celebrates the crucial difference". *The Guardian*, 8 July, p. 6 (Sport).

Williams, R. (2002c). "Torrance masters the fine art of creating an unbreakable bond". *The Guardian*, 2 October, p. 30.

Wilson, V., Ainsworth, M., and Bird, E. (1985). Assessment of attentional abilities in male volleyball players. *International Journal of Sport Psychology*, 16, 296–306.

Winter, H. (2002a). "Coaches try to win mind games". *The Daily Telegraph*, 8 November, p. S3 (Sport).

Winter, H. (2002b). "Henry puts success down to work ethic". *Irish Independent*, 30 November, p. 21.

Winter, G., and Martin, C. (1991). *Sport "psych" for tennis*. Adelaide, South Australia: South Australian Sports Institute.

Witol, A. D., and Webbe, F. M. (2003). Soccer heading frequency predicts neuropsychological deficits. *Archives of Clinical Neuropsychology*, 18, 397–417.

Woll, S. (2002). *Everyday thinking: Memory, reasoning and judgment in the real world*. Hillsdale, NJ: Lawrence Erlbaum Associates, Inc.

Wood, B. (2002). "Morariu on mettle". *The Daily Telegraph*, 28 August, p. S5 (Sport).

Woodman, T., and Hardy, L. (2001). Stress and anxiety. In R. N. Singer, H. A. Hausenblas, and C. M. Janelle (Eds.), *Handbook of sport psychology* (2nd ed., pp. 290–318). New York: John Wiley.

Woods, C., Hawkins, R., Hulse, M., and Hodson, A. (2002). The Football Association Medical Research Programme: An audit of injuries in professional football – analysis of preseason injuries. *British Journal of Sports Medicine, 36*, 436–44.

Woods, C. B., Mutrie, N., and Scott, M. (2002). A transtheoretical model based intervention designed to help sedentary young adults become active. *Health Education Research, 17*, 451–460.

Woolfson, S. (2002). The professional game. *The Psychologist, 15*, 4.

Wraga, M., and Kosslyn, S. (2002). Imagery. In L. Nadel (Ed.), *Encyclopaedia of cognitive science* (Vol. 2, pp. 466–470). London: Nature Group.

Yerkes, R. M., and Dodson, J. D. (1908). The relationship of strength of stimulus to rapidity of habit formation. *Journal of Comparative Neurology and Psychology, 18*, 459–482.

Young, B. W., and Salmela, J. H. (2002). Perceptions of training and deliberate practice of middle distance runners. *International Journal of Sport Psychology, 33*, 167–181.

Yue, G., and Cole, K. J. (1992). Strength increases from the motor program – comparison of training with maximal voluntary and imagined muscle contractions. *Journal of Neurophysiology, 67*, 1114–1123.

Yukelson, D. (1997). Principles of effective team building interventions in sport: A direct services approach at Penn State University. *Journal of Applied Sport Psychology, 9*, 73–96.

Yukelson, D., Weinberg, R., and Jackson, A. (1984). A multidimensional group cohesion instrument for intercollegiate basketball teams. *Journal of Sport Psychology, 6*, 103–117.

Zaichkowsky, L. D., and Baltzell, A. (2001). Arousal and performance. In R. N. Singer, H. A. Hausenblas, and C. M. Janelle (Eds.), *Handbook of sport psychology* (2nd ed., pp. 319–339). New York: John Wiley.

Zizzi, S., Zaichkowsky, L., and Perna, F. M. (2002). Certification in sport and exercise psychology. In J. L. Van Raalte and B. W. Brewer (Eds.), *Exploring sport and exercise psychology* (2nd ed., pp. 459–477). Washington, DC: American Psychological Association.

Zorpette, G. (1999). Extreme sports, sensation seeking and the brain. *Scientific American, 10*, 57–59 ("Work, Home and Play" section).

Zuckerman, M. V. (1979). *Sensation seeking: Beyond optimal levels of arousal.* Hillsdale, NJ: Lawrence Erlbaum Associates, Inc.

Zuckerman, M. V. (1984). Experience and desire: A new format for sensation seeking scales. *Journal of Behavioural Assessment, 6*, 101–114.

Zuckerman, M. V. (1994). *Behavioural expressions and biosocial bases of sensation seeking.* Cambridge: Cambridge University Press.

Author index

Subject index

GRIMSBY INSTITUTE OF FURTHER & HIGHER EDUCATION
LIBRARIES